Workbook to Accompany

Understanding

Health Insurance

D1398306

A Guide to Billing and Reimbursement

Eleventh Edition

Workbook to Accompany
Understanding
Health
Insurance
A Guide to Billing and Reimbursement

Eleventh Edition

Michelle A. Green, MPS, RHIA, FAHIMA, CPC

SUNY Distinguished Teaching Professor
Health Information Technology
Alfred State College, Alfred NY

Linda Hernandez

Instructor, Medical Billing and Coding
Franklin Career College, Ontario CA

DELMAR
CENGAGE Learning·

Australia · Brazil · Japan · Korea · Mexico · Singapore · Spain · United Kingdom · United States

DELMAR
CENGAGE Learning·

Workbook to Accompany Understanding Health Insurance: A Guide to Billing and Reimbursement, Eleventh Edition

Michelle A. Green
Linda Hernandez

Vice President, Health Care Business Unit: Dave Garza

Director of Learning Solutions: Matthew Kane

Managing Editor: Marah Bellegarde

Senior Acquisitions Editor: Rhonda Dearborn

Product Manager: Amy Wetsel

Editorial Assistant: Lauren Whalen

Marketing Director: Jennifer Baker

Executive Marketing Manager: Wendy Mapstone

Senior Marketing Manager: Nancy Bradshaw

Marketing Coordinator: Piper Huntington

Technology Director: Tom Smith

Technology Product Manager: Mary Colleen Liburdi

Technology Project Manager: Erin Zeggert

Production Manager: Andrew Crouth

Senior Content Project Manager: Andrea Majot

Senior Art Director: Jack Pendleton

For product information and technology assistance, contact us at
Cengage Learning Customer & Sales Support, 1-800-354-9706

For permission to use material from this text or product,
submit all requests online at **www.cengage.com/permissions**
Further permissions questions can be emailed to
permissionrequest@cengage.com

ISBN-13: 978-1-133-28375-1

ISBN-10: 1-133-28375-6

Delmar
Executive Woods
5 Maxwell Drive
Clifton Park, NY 12065-2919
USA

Cengage Learning is a leading provider of customized learning solutions with office locations around the globe, including Singapore, the United Kingdom, Australia, Mexico, Brazil, and Japan. Locate your local office at **www.cengage.com/global**

Cengage Learning products are represented in Canada by Nelson Education, Ltd.

To learn more about Delmar, visit **www.cengage.com/delmar**

Purchase any of our products at your local bookstore or at our preferred online store **www.cengagebrain.com**

Printed in the United States of America
1 2 3 4 5 6 7 12

CONTENTS

INTRODUCTION

INTRODUCTION

The Workbook is designed to help learners apply the concepts presented in the textbook. This is accomplished through application-based assignments that are directly related to the content of the textbook. This edition of the Workbook is updated and redesigned for maximum effectiveness.

This Workbook can be used by college and vocational school programs to train health insurance specialists, medical assistants, medical office administrators, and health information technicians. It can also be used as an in-service training tool for new medical office personnel and independent billing services, or independently by insurance specialists who wish to increase their skills and scope of knowledge.

OBJECTIVES

After completing the assignments in each chapter, the learner will be able to:

1. Contact and interview a health insurance specialist (or similar professional) and explore career opportunities.
2. Create a professional cover letter and résumé.
3. Conduct an effective job search utilizing the Internet and local resources.
4. Access networking sites for professionals, such as listservs.
5. Interpret health insurance statistics.
6. Explain the effects of managed care on a physician's office.
7. Interpret remittance advice and explanation of benefits documents, and appeal denied claims.
8. Differentiate between fraud and abuse and HIPAA's privacy and security rules.
9. Accurately assign ICD and CPT/HCPCS codes, and differentiate among reimbursement methodologies according to healthcare setting.
10. Accurately enter required information on CMS-1500 claims according to individual payer requirements.

NEW TO THE ELEVENTH EDITION WORKBOOK

- In Chapter 1, Assignment 1.2 was revised to require students to complete a job search log.
- In Chapter 4, a new assignment was added to provide students with practice writing appeal letters.
- In Chapter 5, a new assignment entitled Hospital Inpatient Quality Reporting Program was added.
- Chapter 6 was split into Chapter 6A (ICD-9-CM Coding) and Chapter 6B (ICD-10-CM Coding) to facilitate student learning of each classification system.
- All CMS-1500 answer keys in the instructor's manual were edited to match claims completion instructions in textbook chapters.
- New case studies were added to provide additional CMS-1500 claims completion practice.
- In Chapter 17, a new workers' compensation intake form assignment was added.
- The Appendix A mock exam for CMRS certification from American Medical Billing Association (AMBA) was updated, and ICD-10-CM coding questions were added.
- The Appendix B mock exam for CPC-P certification from American Academy of Professional Coders (AAPC) was updated, and ICD-10-CM coding questions were added.
- Appendix C features case studies for use with the free CD-ROM of Medical Office Simulation Software (MOSS) 2.0 packaged in the back of this workbook; the instructions for using MOSS 2.0 were revised and new screen shots were added.

CHAPTER 1
Health Insurance Specialist Career

INTRODUCTION

This chapter familiarizes students with interviewing a professional, creating a résumé and cover letter, interpreting (and understanding) information from professional journal articles, networking with other professionals via professional discussion forums, and interpreting professional codes of ethics. This chapter is placed in the front of the workbook to allow students time to create or revise their résumé, build networking skills, and prepare for job interviews. Often it takes several weeks for a job search to be conducted and interviews to be scheduled. Practicing in these areas is important before you complete this course or graduate from a program of study in this field.

> **ASSIGNMENT 1.1**   Interview of a Professional

OBJECTIVES

At the conclusion of this assignment, the student should be able to:
1. State the responsibilities of a professional employed in this field of study.
2. Explain whether this position would be one the student would be interested in obtaining.

OVERVIEW

Health insurance specialists often have similar educational backgrounds; however, their job responsibilities and roles vary greatly depending upon the organization by which they are employed. This assignment will familiarize the student with specific job responsibilities of a professional employed in this field.

INSTRUCTIONS

1. Prepare 10 questions that you would like to ask of a professional employed in your field of study.

   > **NOTE:** Your instructor might devote classroom time to brainstorming such questions (or use a discussion board forum if you are an Internet-based student). This will allow you to share questions with other students in your course and obtain additional questions to ask of the professional.

2. Identify a credentialed professional in your field of study (e.g., CCS, CPC, and so on), and contact the professional to schedule an onsite interview. When you contact the professional, conduct yourself in a professional manner, and explain that you are a student completing a required assignment.

   > **NOTE:** If it is not possible to schedule an onsite interview, check with your instructor to determine whether a telephone or e-mail interview would be acceptable.

3. Prepare for the interview by reviewing and organizing the questions you will ask of the professional.

4. Dress appropriately (as if for a job interview), and arrive 10 minutes early for the interview.

5. Adopt a professional and respectful manner when asking interview questions, and be prepared to answer questions asked of you. Be sure to take notes as the professional responds to the interview questions. If you choose to tape-record the interview, be sure to ask the professional for permission to do so.

6. After the interview, thank the professional for his or her time. Request a business card and e-mail address. Be sure to follow up the interview within 10 days by mailing a handwritten thank-you note.

7. Prepare a three-page, double-spaced, word-processed document summarizing the interview, as follows:

   a. Identify the professional's name, position, and facility.

   b. Writing in the third person, summarize the professional's responses to your interview questions. Be sure to organize the interview content in logical paragraphs. (A paragraph consists of at least three sentences.) Do **not** prepare this paper in a question/answer format. If you have questions about how to write this paper, ask your instructor for clarification.

   c. In the last paragraph of the paper, summarize your reaction to the interview and state whether you would be interested in having this professional's position (along with why or why not). Also, predict your future by writing about where you will be in 10 years (in terms of employment, family, etc.).

   d. Check and double-check spelling, grammar, and punctuation. Have at least one other person review your document (e.g., college writing lab, English teacher, family member or friend who has excellent writing skills, and so on).

ASSIGNMENT 1.2   Ready, Set, Get a Job!

OBJECTIVES

At the conclusion of this assignment, the student should be able to:

1. Conduct a job search using local resources and the Internet.
2. Create a professional career résumé and cover letter.
3. Research organizations in preparation for a job interview.
4. Determine personal worth to an organization, to facilitate salary negotiation.
5. Anticipate questions that could be asked during a job interview.
6. Describe appropriate follow-up to be performed after a job interview.

OVERVIEW

Begin your successful job search by creating a professional career résumé and cover letter. Prepare for a job interview by practicing for the interview, researching the organization, and determining your worth. Follow up after the interview by mailing a handwritten thank-you note to the interviewer.

> **NOTE:** Some facilities require students to submit a cover letter and résumé for consideration by the clinical supervisor prior to placement for professional practice. This assignment will assist in that process.

Searching for a Job

To conduct a successful job search, you must assess your skills, establish goals, plan your job search, and understand the job market (Figure 1-1). Because it can take six to nine months to complete a successful job search, be sure to contact your school's career services department at least three months before graduation. Be prepared to complete the job search approximately six months after graduation. (Some job searches can take longer!) Consider following the steps on page 5 to conduct your job search:

CLASSIFIED ADS. The "Help Wanted" ads in newspapers list numerous jobs. You should realize, however, that many other job openings are not listed, and that the classified ads sometimes do not give all of the important information. They may offer little or no description of the job, working conditions, or pay. Some ads do not identify the employer. They may simply give a post office box to mail your résumé to, making follow-up inquiries very difficult. Some ads offer out-of-town jobs; others advertise employment agencies rather than actual employment opportunities. When using classified ads, keep the following in mind:

- Do not rely solely on the classifieds to find a job; follow other leads as well.

- Answer ads promptly because openings may be filled quickly, even before the ad stops appearing in the paper.

- Read the ads every day, particularly the Sunday edition, which usually includes the most listings.

- Beware of "no experience necessary" ads, which may signal low wages, poor working conditions, or commission work.

- Keep a record of all ads to which you have responded, including the specific skills, educational background, and personal qualifications required for the position.

COMMUNITY AGENCIES. Many nonprofit organizations, including religious institutions and vocational rehabilitation agencies, offer counseling, career development, and job placement services, generally targeted to a particular group, such as women, youth, minorities, ex-offenders, or older workers.

EMPLOYERS. Through your library (e.g., local yellow page listings for physicians and clinics) and Internet research, develop a list of potential employers in your desired career field. Employer websites often contain lists of job openings. Websites and business directories can provide you with information on how to apply for a position or whom to contact. Even if no open positions are posted, do not hesitate to contact the employer and the relevant department. Set up an interview with someone working in the same area you wish to work. Ask them how they got started, what they enjoy or dislike about the work, what type of qualifications are necessary for the job, and what type of personality succeeds in that position. Even if they don't have a position available, they may be able to put you in contact with other people who might hire you and they can keep you in mind if a position opens up. Make sure to send them your résumé and a cover letter. If you are able to obtain an interview, be sure to send a thank-you note. Directly contacting employers is one of the most successful means of job hunting.

FEDERAL GOVERNMENT. Information on federal government jobs is available from the Office of Personnel Management through the Internet at **www.usajobs.opm.gov**.

INTERNET NETWORKS AND RESOURCES. The Internet provides a variety of information, including job listings and job search resources and techniques. However, no single network or resource will contain all of the information available on employment or career opportunities, so be prepared to search for what you need.

© Cengage Learning 2013

FIGURE 1-1 Job search methods (Reprinted according to Bureau of Labor Statistics reuse policy.)   (continues)

FIGURE 1-1   (continued)

Remember that job listings may be posted by field or discipline, so begin your search using keywords. When searching employment databases on the Internet, it is sometimes possible to send your résumé to an employer by e-mail or to post it on-line. Some sources allow you to send e-mail free of charge, but be careful that you are not going to incur any additional charges for postings or updates.

LABOR UNIONS. Labor unions provide various employment services to members, including apprenticeship programs that teach a specific trade or skill. Contact the appropriate labor union or State apprenticeship council for more information.

PERSONAL CONTACTS. Your family, friends, and acquaintances may offer one of the most effective ways to find a job. They may help you directly or put you in touch with someone else who can. Such networking can lead to information about specific job openings, many of which may not be publicly posted.

PRIVATE EMPLOYMENT AGENCIES AND CAREER CONSULTANTS. These agencies can be helpful, but they are in business to make money. Most operate on a commission basis, with the fee dependent upon a percentage of the salary paid to a successful applicant. You or the hiring company will pay a fee. Find out the exact cost and who is responsible for paying associated fees before using the service. Although employment agencies can help you save time and contact employers who otherwise might be difficult to locate, the costs may outweigh the benefits if you are responsible for the fee. Contacting employers directly often will generate the same type of leads that a private employment agency will provide. Consider any guarantees the agency offers when determining if the service is worth the cost.

PROFESSIONAL ASSOCIATIONS. Many professions have associations that offer employment information, including career planning, educational programs, job listings, and job placement. To use these services, associations usually require that you be a member of their association; information can be obtained directly from an association through the Internet, by telephone, or by mail.

SCHOOL CAREER PLANNING AND PLACEMENT OFFICES. High school and college placement offices help their students and alumni find jobs. They set up appointments and allow recruiters to use their facilities for interviews. Placement offices usually have a list of part-time, temporary, and summer jobs offered on campus. They also may have lists of jobs for regional, nonprofit, and government organizations. Students can receive career counseling and testing and job search advice. At career resource libraries they may attend workshops on such topics as job search strategy, résumé writing, letter writing, and effective interviewing; critique drafts of résumés and watch videotapes of mock interviews; explore files of résumés and references; and attend job fairs conducted by the placement office.

STATE EMPLOYMENT SERVICE OFFICES. The State employment service, sometimes called Job Service, operates in coordination with the U.S. Department of Labor's Employment and Training Administration. Local offices, found nationwide, help job seekers find jobs and help employers find qualified workers at no cost to either. To find the office nearest you, look in the State government telephone listings under "Job Service" or "Employment."

(continues)

FIGURE 1-1 (continued)

- *JOB MATCHING AND REFERRAL.* At the State employment service office, an interviewer will determine if you are "job ready" or if you need help from counseling and testing services to assess your occupational aptitudes and interests and to help you choose and prepare for a career.

  After you are "job ready," you may examine available job listings and select openings that interest you. A staff member can then describe the job openings in detail and arrange for interviews with prospective employers.

- *AMERICA'S JOB BANK*, sponsored by the U.S. Department of Labor, is an Internet site that allows you to search through a database of over one million jobs nationwide, create and post your résumé online, and set up an automated job search. The database contains a wide range of mostly full-time private sector jobs that are available all over the country. Job seekers can access America's Job Bank at **www.JobBankInfo.org**. Computers with access to the Internet are available to the public in any local public employment service office, school, library, and military installation. *Tips for Finding the Right Job*, a U.S. Department of Labor pamphlet, offers advice on determining your job skills, organizing your job search, writing a résumé, and making the most of an interview.

- *JOB SEARCH GUIDE: STRATEGIES FOR PROFESSIONALS*, another U.S. Department of Labor publication, discusses specific steps that job seekers can follow to identify employment opportunities. This publication includes sections on handling job loss, managing personal resources, assessing personal skills and interests, researching the job market, conducting the job search, and networking. Check with your State employment service office, or order a copy of these and other publications from the U.S. Government Printing Offices Superintendent of Documents by telephone at (202) 512-1800 or via the Internet at **www.gpo.gov** or **www.doleta.gov**.

- *SERVICES FOR SPECIAL GROUPS.* By law, veterans are entitled to priority for job placement at State employment service centers. If you are a veteran, an employment representative can inform you of available assistance and help you deal with problems. States have One-Stop Service Centers that provide various special groups and the general public with employment, training, and related services available under the Workforce Investment Act of 1998.

© Cengage Learning 2013

1. Perform a self-assessment by identifying your accomplishments, experience, goals, interests, skills, and values. (You have to figure out what you want from a job before you can determine what you have to offer prospective employers.)
2. Research career options and employers. Completing an internship or obtaining part-time or summer employment in your field of study will allow you to network with professionals in that field, leading to job opportunities. Researching prospective employers helps you decide which ones to contact for possible employment.
3. Plan your job search by establishing a target date for obtaining a position, remembering that it can take several months to find a job. Decide how much time you can devote to your job search, get organized, and spend time each week working on your search. Consider using multiple strategies (Figure 1-1) to seek employment; the more contacts you make, the more interviews you will get.

4. Document your job search by keeping a record of résumés mailed, interviews scheduled, and thank-you notes sent. This process allows a job seeker to easily follow up with contacts and increases credibility with prospective employers.

5. Searching for a job is very hard work, and you must be persistent because it can be discouraging. Treating the search like a job will help you produce results. (After your successful job search, establish an action plan for career progression that includes continuing education and professional networking.)

> **NOTE:** It is acceptable to submit your résumé to a prospective employer more than once. Some employers maintain résumés for only 30 days, so if your job search takes months, it is possible that you will need to submit your résumé more than once. Such persistence also demonstrates your enthusiasm and interest in that employer.

INSTRUCTIONS

1. Go to **www.Keirsey.com** and click on Keirsey Temperament Sorter II, at the pull-down menu, click on "take KTS II"; you must first register to take this test by entering your e-mail address and name. The KTS II is a type of assessment that helps individuals discover their "innate tendencies, preferences, and motivations that make up their personality."

2. Go to **www.monster.com**, and click on the **Advice** link to begin your research process about résumé writing, interviewing, salary and benefits, and more.

3. Go to the *Occupational Outlook Handbook* at **www.bls.gov/oco.** This "is a nationally recognized source of career information, designed to provide valuable assistance to individuals making decisions about their future work lives. Revised every two years, the *Handbook* describes what workers do on the job, working conditions, the training and education needed, earnings, and expected job prospects in a wide range of occupations."

4. Go to **www.hoovers.com** to access its database of 12 million companies and research information on prospective employers.

5. Select one or more of the following general Web sites to research available positions:

Career Builder	**www.careerbuilder.com**
Federal Jobs	**www.usajobs.gov**
Juju Job Search Engine	**www.job-search-engine.com**
Monster	**www.monster.com**
Nation Job	**www.nationjob.com**
Riley Guide	**www.rileyguide.com**

> **NOTE:** Develop a list of prospective job titles before conducting a search for available positions. Titles can include: admitting representative, biller, cash poster, certified coder, clerical support, commercial biller, commercial collector, front office receptionist, hospital account representative, medical biller, registration coordinator, and so on.

6. Select one or more of the following healthcare Web sites to research available positions:

Advance for Health Information Professionals	**health-information.advanceweb.com**
Allied Health Careers	**www.alliedhealthcareers.com**
American Academy of Professional Coders	**www.aapc.com**
American Association of Medical Assistants	**www.aama-ntl.org**
American Health Information Management Association	**www.ahima.org**
For the Record	**www.fortherecordmag.com**
Health Information Job Search	**www.hipjobs.net**
H.I.M. Recruiters	**www.himjobs.com**
On Assignment	**www.insights-search.com**

MedHunters.com   **www.medhunters.com**

Medical Workers.com   **www.medicalworkers.com**

Professional Association   **www.pahcom.com**
of Health Care Office
Management

Creating a Résumé and Cover Letter

A résumé won't get you a job; however, it can eliminate you from the pool of candidates if unprofessionally prepared. Employers often identify interview candidates by reviewing résumés to eliminate those unqualified. Résumés or cover letters that contain typographical errors or evidence of poor communication skills are discarded because employers are unwilling to spend valuable time interviewing such candidates.

Carol Woughter
Placement & Transfer Expert

Your cover letter (Figure 1-2) is actually a marketing tool because it focuses on your qualifications as a prospective employee. It should be well written so that the employer will review your résumé. When creating your cover letter, be sure to consider the following:

1. Research the prospective employer's organization to personalize the letter. Your knowledge of the organization demonstrates your interest in the employer.
2. Briefly explain several special abilities or significant accomplishments so the employer will be interested in you. Be sure you do not misrepresent your experience or skills. If you do not meet every job qualification, emphasize your strengths.
3. Group similar information within the same paragraph, and organize paragraphs logically so the cover letter is easy to read. Use action verbs to make the cover letter interesting and display energy.
4. Write in a formal style. Be clear, objective, and persuasive (as opposed to just describing your education and experience background).
5. Do not include any information that might cause the employer to question your ability to do the job. (Everyone has weaknesses, but there is no sense pointing them out to a prospective employer in your cover letter! Save this information for the interview, where it will allow you to appear modest about your professional skills.)
6. Check and double-check spelling and grammar. Consider having at least one other person review your cover letter (e.g., school career services professional, English teacher, and so on).

If you are a recent graduate, your career résumé (Figure 1-3) should probably be limited to one page; however, if you have extensive work experience in a health-related field, a two-page résumé is acceptable. Because the purpose of your résumé is to get an interview, the résumé should contain information appropriate to the position you wish to obtain so that it convinces a prospective employer that you have the skills necessary for the available position. In addition, when preparing your résumé, be sure to focus on the prospective employer's needs. This may mean revising your résumé each time you apply for a position (e.g., rewrite the job objective in the résumé).

EXAMPLE: You see an advertisement for a position that seems perfect for you, and along with plenty of others you send the employer a cover letter with your résumé. By the application deadline, human resources personnel are ready to review hundreds of résumés. (A job notice routinely pulls in between 100 and 1,000 résumés.)

The cover letters and résumés are reviewed quickly, with those containing any errors immediately discarded to narrow the applicant pool. Your résumé, however, is not only perfectly written but also well organized and pertinent to the available position. Thus, it is carefully reviewed and placed on the small stack of résumés that will be used to schedule interviews.

Street Address
City, State Zip
Current date

> Call the human resources department at the prospective employer to find out to whom the cover letter should be addressed.

Name
Title
Company
Street Address
City, State Zip

Dear Mr./Ms.:

Paragraph 1—Explain why you are writing, and identify the position and your source of information. Summarize your strongest qualifications for the position using a series of phrases (e.g., I am applying for the Coding & Reimbursement Specialist position as advertised in *The Alfred Sun*, October 9, YYYY. My coding/insurance processing skills and attention to detail are my strongest qualifications for this position.).

Paragraph 2—Detail your strongest qualifications and relate them to the position requirements. Provide evidence of related education and employment experiences. Refer to your enclosed résumé (e.g., I will graduate in May YYYY with a Certificate in Insurance and Reimbursement Specialist from Alfred State College, where I completed extensive coursework in coding and insurance processing. My 240-hour professional practice experience allowed me to perform coding and insurance duties at Alfred State Medical Center. The completed evaluation of this experience documents my attention to detail, excellent work ethic, and superior coding and insurance processing skills. My education also included general education courses, which has provided me with an excellent background in computer applications and human sciences. I plan to take the C.C.A. certification examination in June YYYY, after I graduate. Please refer to the enclosed résumé for additional information.).

Paragraph 3—Request an interview and indicate how and when you can be contacted. Suggest that you will place a follow-up call to discuss interview possibilities. Thank the employer for his or her consideration (e.g., Please contact me at (607) 555-1234 after 4 p.m., Monday through Friday, to schedule an interview at a mutually convenient time. I will contact you next week to ensure that you received my cover letter and résumé. Thank you for your consideration.).

Sincerely,

[*handwritten signature*]

Your typed name

Enclosure

FIGURE 1-2   Sample cover letter

SALLY S. STUDENT

| 5 Main Street | Alfred, NY 14802 | (607) 555-1111 |

JOB OBJECTIVE An entry-level insurance and coding specialist position.

EDUCATION STATE UNIVERSITY OF NEW YORK, COLLEGE OF TECHNOLOGY AT ALFRED, Alfred, N.Y. Candidate for Associate in Applied Science, Coding & Reimbursement Specialist, May YYYY.

HONORS & AWARDS: Dean's List, Fall YYYY, Spring YYYY, and Fall YYYY.

Recipient, Outstanding Coding & Reimbursement Specialist Student Award, May YYYY.

CERTIFICATION C.C.A. eligible, June YYYY.

PROFESSIONAL AFFILIATIONS Student Member, American Health Information Management Association. Member, Alfred State College Health Information Management Club.

WORK EXPERIENCE Coding and Insurance Professional Practice, Alfred State Medical Center, Alfred, N.Y. Assigned ICD-9-CM, CPT, and HCPCS level II codes to inpatient, outpatient, and emergency department records. Abstracted inpatient cases using MediSoft abstracting software. Generated CMS-1500 and UB-04 claims. Processed denials by correcting claims and resubmitted for payment. Summer YYYY.

Cashier, Burger King, Hornell, N.Y. Assisted customers, operated cash register, and opened/closed store. August YYYY – Present.

AVAILABILITY May YYYY.

REFERENCES Available upon request.

FIGURE 1-3 Sample career résumé

The Interview Process

An interview gives you the opportunity to demonstrate your qualifications to an employer, so it pays to be well prepared.

Bureau of Labor Statistics

During a job interview, you are evaluated on how well suited you are for the available position. Therefore, when preparing for a job interview, be sure that you have a good understanding of the organization, job responsibilities and duties, corresponding skills required, and how your experience relates to the position.

Job Interview Tips. (Permission to reprint in accordance with Bureau of Labor Statistics reuse policy.)

Preparation

- Learn about the organization.
- Have a specific job or jobs in mind.
- Review your qualifications for the job.
- Prepare answers to broad questions about yourself.
- Review your résumé.
- Schedule a mock interview with your school's career services office.
- Arrive before the scheduled time of your interview.

Personal Appearance

- Be well groomed.
- Dress appropriately (e.g., professionally).
- Do not chew gum or smoke.

> **NOTE:** Avoid smoking prior to the interview, because the smell of tobacco can be obvious and offensive to a nonsmoking interviewer.

The Interview

- Relax, and answer each question concisely.

> **NOTE:** It is acceptable to ask that a question be repeated. You can also bring a pen and paper to the interview to record questions and take notes.

- Respond promptly.
- Maintain eye contact and good posture.
- Use good manners.
- Do not interrupt the interviewer.
- Highlight ways in which you can be an asset to the organization based on your experience, education, skills, and knowledge.

> **NOTE:** Be absolutely truthful. Do not misrepresent any information about yourself.

- Learn the name of your interviewer and shake hands as you meet.
- Use proper English; avoid slang.
- Be cooperative and enthusiastic.
- Ask questions about the position and the organization (e.g., salary range, working hours, clarification of job functions, working environment, and when the interview results will be available).
- Do not speak negatively about a previous place of employment.
- Thank the interviewer verbally when you leave and, as a follow-up, in writing.

Testing. Some organizations require applicants to complete an exam onsite to demonstrate proficiency (e.g., coding, medical terminology, and so on).

- Listen closely to instructions.
- Read each question carefully.
- Write legibly and clearly.
- Budget your time wisely and do not dwell on one question.

Information to Take to an Interview

- Social security card
- Government-issued identification (e.g., driver's license)
- Evidence of certification if professional certification is required for the job (e.g., coding credential)
- Résumé

> **NOTE:** Although an employer may not require applicants to bring a résumé to the job interview, you should be able to furnish the interviewer with information about your education, training, and previous employment. Because you may become nervous during the interview, it is helpful to have your résumé available to prompt you for this information.

- References

> **NOTE:** Employers typically require three professional references. Be sure to obtain permission before using anyone as a reference, and make sure the person will give you a good reference. Avoid using relatives and friends.

INTERNET LINKS

The following Web sites contain more information about preparing for an interview:

College View	**www.collegeview.com**
Job-Interview	**www.job-interview.net**
Resume Magic	**www.resume-magic.com**

Following Up After the Interview. Be sure to send the interviewer a handwritten thank-you letter (Figure 1-4) after an interview. The letter indicates that you are considerate and polite, and it also allows you to reemphasize your positive attributes to the interviewer. The thank-you letter should be written the same day of the interview and mailed that night. Be sure to thank the interviewer for his or her time and mention something that happened or was discussed to remind the interviewer of who you are.

Evaluating a Job Offer. (Permission to reprint in accordance with Bureau of Labor Statistics reuse policy.)

Once you receive a job offer, you are faced with a difficult decision and must evaluate the offer carefully. Fortunately, most organizations will not expect you to accept or reject an offer immediately. There are many issues to consider when assessing a job offer. Will the organization be a good place to work? Will the job be interesting? Are there opportunities for advancement? Is the salary fair? Does the employer offer good benefits? If you have not already figured out exactly what you want, the following discussion may help you develop a set of criteria for judging job offers, whether you are starting a career, reentering the labor force after a long absence, or planning a career change.

Dear [name of interviewer]:

Thank you for interviewing me for the [name of position] position at [name of organization]. After meeting with you, I am convinced that my background and skills will meet your needs.

I appreciate that you took the time to familiarize me with the organization. I believe I could learn a great deal from you and would certainly enjoy working with you.

In addition to my qualifications and experience, I will bring excellent work habits and judgment to this position. With the countless demands on your time, I am sure that you require people who can be trusted to carry out their responsibilities with minimal supervision.

I look forward to hearing from you concerning your hiring decision. Again, thank you for your time and consideration.

Sincerely,

[your signature]

© Cengage Learning 2013

FIGURE 1-4   Sample thank-you letter

The Organization

Background information on an organization can help you decide whether it would be a good place for you to work (Figure 1-5). Factors to consider include the organization's business or activity, financial condition, age, size, and location. You can generally get background information on an organization, particularly a large organization, by telephoning its public relations office. A public company's annual report to the stockholders tells about its corporate philosophy, history, products or services, goals, and financial status. Most government agencies can furnish reports that describe their programs and missions. Press releases, company newsletters or magazines, and recruitment brochures also can be useful. Ask the organization for any other items that might interest a prospective employee. If possible, speak to current or former employees of the organization.

Background information on the organization may be available at your public or school library. If you cannot get an annual report, check the library for reference directories that may provide basic facts about the company, such as earnings, products and services, and number of employees. Some directories widely available in libraries include:

- *Dun & Bradstreet's Million Dollar Directory*
- *Moody's Industrial Manual*
- *Standard and Poor's Register of Corporations*
- *Thomas' Register of American Manufacturers*
- *Ward's Business Directory*

Stories about an organization in magazines and newspapers can tell a great deal about its successes, failures, and plans for the future. You can identify articles on a company by looking under its name in periodical or computerized indexes in libraries. However, it probably will not be useful to look back more than two or three years.

The library also may have government publications that present projections of growth for the industry in which the organization is classified. Long-term projections of employment and output for more than 200 industries, covering the entire economy, are developed by the Bureau of

Does the organization's business or activity match your own interests and beliefs?
It is easier to apply yourself to the work if you are enthusiastic about what the
organization does.

How will the size of the organization affect you? Large firms generally offer a
greater variety of training programs and career paths, more managerial levels for
advancement, and better employee benefits than small firms. Large employers
may also have more advanced technologies. However, jobs in large firms may
tend to be highly specialized. Jobs in small firms may offer broader authority and
responsibility, a closer working relationship with top management, and a chance to
clearly see your contribution to the success of the organization.

Should you work for a relatively new organization or one that is well-established?
New businesses have a high failure rate, but for many people, the excitement of
helping create a company and the potential for sharing in its success more than
offsets the risk of job loss. However, it may be just as exciting and rewarding to
work for a young firm that already has a foothold on success.

Does it make a difference if the company is private or public? An individual or a
family may control a privately owned company, and key jobs may be reserved for
relatives and friends. A board of directors responsible to the stockholders controls
a publicly owned company and key jobs are usually open to anyone.

Is the organization in an industry with favorable long-term prospects? The most
successful firms tend to be in industries that are growing rapidly.

Permission to reprint in accordance with Bureau of Labor Statistics reuse policy.

FIGURE 1-5 Questions to ask before you accept the position

Labor Statistics and revised every two years—see the *Monthly Labor Review* for the most recent
projections. The *U.S. Industry and Trade Outlook,* published annually by the U.S. Department
of Commerce, presents detailed analyses of U.S. industries. Trade magazines also may include
articles on the trends for specific industries.

Career centers at colleges and universities often have information on employers that is
not available in libraries. Ask a career center representative how to find out about a particular
organization.

Nature of the Job. Even if everything else about the job is attractive, you will be unhappy if you
dislike the day-to-day work. Determining in advance whether you will like the work may be difficult (Figure 1-6). However, the more you find out about the job before accepting or rejecting an
offer, the more likely you are to make the right choice. Actually working in the industry and, if possible, for the company, would provide considerable insight. You can gain work experience through
part-time, temporary, or summer jobs, or through internship or work-study programs while in
school. All of these can also lead to permanent job offers.

Opportunities Offered by Employers. A good job offers you opportunities to learn new skills,
increase your earnings, and rise to positions of greater authority, responsibility, and prestige. A
lack of opportunities can dampen your interest in the work and result in frustration and boredom.
The company should have a training plan for you. Be sure to ask the following questions:

- What valuable new skills does the company plan to teach you?
- What promotion possibilities are available within the organization?
- What is the next step on the career ladder?

Where is the job located? If the job is in another section of the country, you need to consider the cost of living, the availability of housing and transportation, and the quality of educational and recreational facilities in that section of the country. Even if the job location is in your area, you should consider the time and expense of commuting.

Does the work match your interests and make good use of your skills? The duties and responsibilities of the job should be explained in enough detail to answer this question.

How important is the job in this company? An explanation of where you fit in the organization and how you are supposed to contribute to its overall objectives should give you an idea of the job's importance.

Are you comfortable with the hours? Most jobs involve regular hours—for example, 40 hours a week, during the day, Monday through Friday. Other jobs require night, weekend, or holiday work. In addition, some jobs routinely require overtime to meet deadlines or sales or production goals, or to better serve customers. Consider the effect the work hours will have on your personal life.

How long do most people who enter this job stay with the company? High turnover can mean dissatisfaction with the nature of the work or something else about the job.

FIGURE 1-6 Questions to ask before you accept the position

- If you have to wait for a job to become vacant before you can be promoted, how long does this usually take?
- When opportunities for advancement do arise, will you compete with applicants from outside the company?
- Can you apply for jobs for which you qualify elsewhere within the organization, or is mobility within the firm limited?

Salaries and Benefits. Wait for the employer to introduce the subjects of salaries and benefits. Some companies will not talk about pay until they have decided to hire you. To know if an offer is reasonable, you need a rough estimate of what the job should pay. You may have to go to several sources for this information. Try to find family, friends, or acquaintances recently hired in similar jobs. Ask your teachers and the staff in placement offices about starting pay for graduates with your qualifications. Help-wanted ads in newspapers sometimes give salary ranges for similar positions. Check the library or your school's career center for salary surveys, such as those conducted by the National Association of Colleges and Employers or various professional associations.

If you are considering the salary and benefits for a job in another geographic area, make allowances for differences in the cost of living, which may be significantly higher in a large metropolitan area than in a smaller city, town, or rural area.

You also should learn the organization's policy regarding overtime. Depending on the job, you may or may not be exempt from laws requiring the employer to compensate you for overtime. Find out how many hours you will be expected to work each week and whether you receive overtime pay or compensatory time off for working more than the specified number of hours in a week.

Also take into account that a starting salary is just that—the start. Your salary should be reviewed on a regular basis; many organizations do it every year. How much can you expect to earn after one, two, or three or more years? An employer cannot be specific about the amount of pay if it includes commissions and bonuses. Benefits can also add a lot to your base pay, but they vary widely. Find out exactly what the benefit package includes and how much of the cost you must bear (e.g., health insurance).

If You Do Not Get the Job. If you do not get the job, consider contacting the organization to find out why. Ask the following questions:

- What was your general impression of me during the interview?
- In what ways could I improve the way I interview?
- What were my weaknesses, and how can I strengthen them?
- What things did impress you, and why?
- What suggestions do you have for improving my cover letter or résumé?
- Is there anything else you would advise me to work on?
- What were the characteristics of the successful candidate?
- Do you have any other positions available for which I might be suitable?
- Finally, is there anything else I should ask you?

Remember that there will be additional opportunities for job interviews. Try not to get so discouraged that you discontinue your job search. Although it is hard to be turned down, it is part of the search process. Keep looking, and you will find the right job with the right employer.

INSTRUCTIONS

7. Write a cover letter and create a résumé, referring to the samples in Figure 1-2 and 1-3.

8. Write a thank-you letter, referring to the sample in Figure 1-4.

9. Contact five prospective employers that currently have available positions and complete a job search log. (Submit the log to your instructor for review.)

JOB SEARCH #1

Title of job posted: _____
Date prospective employer contacted: _____
Name and address of organization: _____
Phone number of organization: _____
Fax number of organization: _____
Email address of organization: _____
Name of person contacted at organization: _____
Application method: ❑ Fax ❑ In person ❑ Online ❑ ____

JOB SEARCH #2

Title of job posted: _____
Date prospective employer contacted: _____
Name and address of organization: _____
Phone number of organization: _____
Fax number of organization: _____
Email address of organization: _____
Name of person contacted at organization: _____
Application method: ❑ Fax ❑ In person ❑ Online ❑ ____

JOB SEARCH #3

Title of job posted: _____

Date prospective employer contacted: _____

Name and address of organization: _____

Phone number of organization: _____

Fax number of organization: _____

Email address of organization: _____

Name of person contacted at organization: _____

Application method: ❑ Fax ❑ In person ❑ Online ❑ _____

JOB SEARCH #4

Title of job posted: _____

Date prospective employer contacted: _____

Name and address of organization: _____

Phone number of organization: _____

Fax number of organization: _____

Email address of organization: _____

Name of person contacted at organization: _____

Application method: ❑ Fax ❑ In person ❑ Online ❑ _____

JOB SEARCH #5

Title of job posted: _____

Date prospective employer contacted: _____

Name and address of organization: _____

Phone number of organization: _____

Fax number of organization: _____

Email address of organization: _____

Name of person contacted at organization: _____

Application method: ❑ Fax ❑ In person ❑ Online ❑ _____

INTERNET LINKS

The U.S. Industry and Trade Outlook is available at **www.ita.doc.gov.**

The Monthly Labor Review is available as a link from **www.bls.gov.**

National, state, and metropolitan area data from the National Compensation Survey, which integrates data from three existing Bureau of Labor Statistics programs—the Employment Cost Index, the Occupational Compensation Survey, and the Employee Benefits Survey—are available at **www.bls.gov/ncs.**

Data on earnings by detailed occupation from the Occupational Employment Statistics Survey are available at **www.bls.gov/oes.**

ASSIGNMENT 1.3 Journal Abstract

OBJECTIVES

At the conclusion of this assignment, the student should be able to:

1. Identify the name of the professional association's journal.
2. Write a journal abstract of an article from a professional association's journal.

OVERVIEW

Professional association journals communicate information about healthcare advances, new technology, changing regulations, and much more. This assignment familiarizes students with the contents of professional journals in their fields and requires students to prepare an abstract (summary) of a selected article.

INSTRUCTIONS

1. Locate the name of your professional association's journal in Table 1-1.
2. Locate a journal by:
   a. going to its Web site (many journals are posted online).
   b. borrowing a journal through interlibrary loan (e.g., college library, local library).
   c. contacting a professional in your field of study or your instructor to borrow a journal.

   > **NOTE:** Borrowing a journal from a professional in your field of study is an excellent way to start the networking process that will lead to employment. If you borrow a journal, be sure to return it promptly, and include a thank-you note. (Student members of professional associations do receive their profession's journal. Because it can take eight weeks to receive your first journal after joining your professional association, your best option is to go to the library or borrow a journal.)

3. Select and read an article from a recent edition (e.g., within the past year) of your professional association's journal.
4. Prepare a one-page, double-spaced, word-processed document that summarizes the journal article. Be sure to include the following information:
   a. Name of article
   b. Name of author
   c. Name of journal
   d. Date of journal
   e. Summary of journal article

   > **NOTE:** Do *not* include your opinion about the article's content.

5. Check and double-check spelling, grammar, and punctuation. Have at least one other person review your document (e.g., college writing lab, English teacher, family member or friend who has excellent writing skills, and so on).

TABLE 1-1 Professional Journals

PROFESSION	PROFESSIONAL JOURNAL	PROFESSIONAL ASSOCIATION	WEB SITE
Coding & Reimbursement Specialist	**CodeWrite**	Society for Clinical Coding (of the American Health Information Management Association)	**www.ahima.org**
	Coding Edge	American Academy of Professional Coders	**www.aapc.com**

ASSIGNMENT 1.4　Professional Discussion Forums (Listservs)

OBJECTIVES

At the conclusion of this assignment, the student should be able to:

1. Explain the value of joining professional discussion forums.
2. Join a professional discussion forum.
3. Review discussion forum contents to identify topics relevant to a particular field of study.
4. Participate in a professional discussion forum.

OVERVIEW

Networking, or sharing information among professionals, is a valuable professional activity. The Internet has made it much easier to network with other professionals by using Web-based professional forums. This assignment familiarizes the student with the value of Internet professional discussion forums.

INSTRUCTIONS

1. Go to **list.nih.gov,** and click on "What Is LISTERV?" to learn all about online discussion forums (listservs). To access the listserv forums, register for an account and login.
2. Select a professional discussion forum from Table 1-2, and follow its membership instructions.

> **NOTE:** Joining professional discussion forums is usually free!

3. Access archived forum discussions and observe current discussions for the period designated by your instructor (e.g., one to three weeks), noting topics that are relevant to your field of study.
4. Post a discussion comment or question on the forum and observe responses from subscribers.
5. At the end of the period of observation and participation, determine whether the forum would be helpful to you on the job.

TABLE 1-2　Discussion Forums and Internet Sites for Professionals

PROFESSIONAL	NAME OF FORUM	INTERNET SITE
AHIMA members	Communities of Practice	**cop.ahima.org**
Coders	Bulletin Boards	**community.advanceweb.com** Click on "HIM Insider: Forums," and click on any of the "coding" discussions.
Medicare Part B claims specialists	Part B News® (Medicare Part B-L)	**www.partbnews.com** Click on "Join Part B-L Listserv" and register for a 21-day free trial
Reimbursement specialists (Medicare)	Medicare Prospective Payment Communication	**list.nih.gov** Click "Browse," scroll down and click on the "PPS-L."

ASSIGNMENT 1.5   Learning About Professional Credentials

OBJECTIVES

At the conclusion of this assignment, the student should be able to:

1. Access professional association Web sites to locate information about insurance and coding credentials.
2. List available credentials and describe eligibility requirements for each.
3. Determine annual continuing education requirements for maintaining professional credentials.

OVERVIEW

Credentialing examinations are offered by the American Academy of Professional Coders (AAPC), American Association of Medical Assistants (AAMA), American Health Information Management Association (AHIMA), American Medical Billing Association (AMBA), Medical Association of Billers (MAB). Educational requirements, examination fees, and required or recommended experience vary for each credential, depending on association requirements. Becoming credentialed is an important achievement. This assignment will allow you to compare credentials offered by professional associations, so you can determine which is best for you!

INSTRUCTIONS

1. Go to the appropriate professional association Web site indicated in Table 1-3.
2. Locate information about professional credentials offered by each professional association. (Be sure to review the professional association's examination application booklet to obtain all of the information needed to complete Table 1-3. This will require the use of Adobe Reader software, which is available as a free download from **www.adobe.com.**)
3. Complete the table.

> **NOTE:** Navigate each Web site to locate information needed to complete the table. This will help you learn how to locate information at professional association Web sites, which often requires using tool bars and pull-down menus.

TABLE 1-3   Professional Association Credentials

American Academy of Professional Coders (AAPC) (continued)
www.aapc.com

CREDENTIAL ABBREVIATION	MEANING OF CREDENTIAL	EDUCATION	EXPERIENCE	EXAM FEE	CONTINUING EDUCATION UNITS (CEU) REQUIREMENTS
CPC					
CPC-H					
CPC-P					

(continues)

TABLE 1-3 (continued)

American Association of Medical Assistants (AAMA) www.aama-ntl.org					
CREDENTIAL ABBREVIATION	MEANING OF CREDENTIAL	EDUCATION	EXPERIENCE	EXAM FEE	CEU REQUIREMENTS
CMA					

American Health Information Management Association www.ahima.org					
CREDENTIAL ABBREVIATION	MEANING OF CREDENTIAL	EDUCATION	EXPERIENCE	EXAM FEE	CEU REQUIREMENTS
CCA					
CCS					
CCS-P					

American Medical Billers Association www.ambanet.net					
CREDENTIAL ABBREVIATION	MEANING OF CREDENTIAL	EDUCATION	EXPERIENCE	EXAM FEE	CEU REQUIREMENTS
CMRS					

Medical Association of Billers (MAB) www.physicianswebsites.com					
CREDENTIAL ABBREVIATION	MEANING OF CREDENTIAL	EDUCATION	EXPERIENCE	EXAM FEE	CEU REQUIREMENTS
CMBS					

ASSIGNMENT 1.6   Professionalism

OBJECTIVES

At the completion of this assignment, the student should be able to:

1. Explain the importance of professionalism.

2. Discuss qualities and skills that characterize a professional person.

INTRODUCTION

The *Merriam-Webster Dictionary* defines professionalism as the "conduct or qualities that characterize a professional person." Healthcare facility managers establish rules of behavior so employees know how to behave professionally. Employees are expected to develop certain skills to demonstrate workplace professionalism, which results in personal growth and success.

INSTRUCTIONS

Match the definition in column A with its corresponding skill in column B, entering the appropriate letter on the blank line for each.

	Column A	Column B
_____	1. Ability to differentiate between technical descriptions of similar procedures.	a. Attitude
_____	2. Ability to be friendly, helpful and positive while performing their job duties.	b. Conflict Management
_____	3. Having the ability to be confident, have better relationships, self-respect, and a successful career.	c. Critical Thinking
_____	4. Ability to provide excellent service when addressing questions and concerns to patients and colleagues.	d. Customer Service
_____	5. Someone who motivates team members to reach their goals.	e. Leadership
_____	6. A person who is motivated to increase their knowledge by participating in continuing education and certification.	f. Managing Change
_____	7. Ability to work alone, or pitch in and help coworkers when needed.	g. Productivity
_____	8. Ability to be flexible and try new ideas.	h. Professional Ethics
_____	9. Ability to resolve issues with positive outcomes.	i. Self-Esteem
_____	10. Ability to know the difference between right and wrong.	j. Team Building

ASSIGNMENT 1.7 Telephone Messages

OBJECTIVES

At the completion of this assignment, the student should be able to:

1. Explain the importance of documenting complete telephone messages.
2. Determine the information to be obtained from callers.
3. Accurately prepare telephone messages.

INTRODUCTION

The telephone can be an effective means of patient access to the healthcare system because a healthcare team member serves as an immediate contact for the patient. Participating in telephone skills training and following established protocols (policies) allow healthcare team members to respond appropriately to patients. When processes for handling all telephone calls are developed and followed by healthcare team members, the result is greater office efficiency and less frustration for healthcare team members and patients. It is essential that healthcare team members accurately and completely document information from a caller, promptly deliver messages to the appropriate team member, and maintain confidentiality about the content of all messages.

INSTRUCTIONS

1. Review voice message case scenarios, which were recorded as voicemail on Dr. Al A. Sickmann, M.D.'s office telephone during lunch.

2. Enter key elements on each telephone message form, including:

    a. Name of person for whom the message was left.

    b. Caller's name (obtain correct spelling), company or department, and return telephone number.

    c. Date and time of the call.

    d. Message for the healthcare team member.

    e. Action to be taken (e.g., please call ..., will call back, urgent, and so on).

3. After reviewing voice message data, complete a blank message form to communicate each telephone messages to Dr. *Al A. Sickmann, M.D.*

    a. Case 1

    Mrs. Faye Slift, an established patient called at 12:15 p.m. on 9/8/YYYY to let us know that she needs a refill on her high blood pressure medication. Her phone number is (123) 934-6857. She would like us to call her pharmacy to have the prescription refilled. She states that we have her pharmacy number on file. She would also like us to call her to verify that we got her message. She states she only has enough medication for the rest of this week.

```
DATE  _____   TIME _____
TO    _____

              WHILE YOU WHERE OUT

MR./MRS.  _____
FROM    ( _____ ) _____
PHONE   _____

TELEPHONED        _____   PLEASE CALL BACK   _____
CALLED TO SEE YOU _____   WILL CALL AGAIN    _____
RETURNED YOUR CALL _____  URGENT             _____
MESSAGE: _____
_____
_____
_____
_____

              TAKEN BY  _____
```

© Cengage Learning 2013

Case 2

Ed Overeels, a new patient called at 12:40 p.m. on 9/11/YYYY to let us know that he was new to the area and was looking for a local doctor close to his home to treat his chronic lower back pain that he has had for a couple years. He works evenings so he is available anytime in the morning for an appointment, and would like to get in as soon as possible because he is currently experiencing a flare up due to the recent move from Ohio. His number is (123) 212-6588.

```
DATE  _____   TIME _____
TO    _____

              WHILE YOU WHERE OUT

MR./MRS.  _____
FROM    ( _____ ) _____
PHONE   _____

TELEPHONED        _____   PLEASE CALL BACK   _____
CALLED TO SEE YOU _____   WILL CALL AGAIN    _____
RETURNED YOUR CALL _____  URGENT             _____
MESSAGE: _____
_____
_____
_____
_____

              TAKEN BY  _____
```

© Cengage Learning 2013

b. Case 3

Tristan N. Shout, a returning patient called at 1:00 p.m. on 9/20/YYYY to let us know that he has recently changed jobs and his insurance has changed. He can now return to our office since Dr. Sickmann is a participating provider in his insurance network. His wife keeps reminding him that needs to schedule an annual exam before the year is up. He would like to make an appointment for the latest appointment that we have available on a Friday. If we could please call him at his number (123) 319-6531 as soon as we get his message he would appreciate it.

DATE _____	TIME _____
TO _____	
WHILE YOU WHERE OUT	
MR./MRS. _____	
FROM ( ) _____	
PHONE _____	

TELEPHONED	_____	PLEASE CALL BACK	_____
CALLED TO SEE YOU	_____	WILL CALL AGAIN	_____
RETURNED YOUR CALL	_____	URGENT	_____

MESSAGE: _____

_____

_____

_____

_____

TAKEN BY _____

ASSIGNMENT 1.8   Multiple Choice Review

1. The concept that every procedure or service reported to a third-party payer must be linked to a condition that justifies that procedure or service is called medical
   a. condition.
   b. necessity.
   c. procedure.
   d. requirement.

2. The administrative agency responsible for establishing rules for Medicare claims processing is called the
   a. Centers for Medicare and Medicaid Services (CMS).
   b. Department of Education and Welfare (DEW).
   c. Department of Health and Human Services (DHHS).
   d. Office of Inspector General (OIG).

3. When answering the telephone at a providers office, you must
   a. place patient on hold without asking.
   b. say the name of your office clearly.
   c. take a message on scratch paper.
   d. use healthcare jargon.

4. Which organization is responsible for administering the Certified Medical Reimbursement Specialist certification exam?
   a. AAPC
   b. AMBA
   c. AHIMA
   d. CMS

5. Which clause is implemented if the requirements associated with preauthorization of a claim prior to payment are not met?
   a. eligibility
   b. hold harmless
   c. no fault
   d. nonparticipation

6. The ability to motivate team members to complete a common organizational goal display is called _____.
   a. autonomy
   b. collegiality
   c. leadership
   d. management

7. Patients with health insurance may require _____ (prior approval) for treatment by specialists and documentation of post-treatment reports.
   a. billing.
   b. coding.
   c. electronic data interchange.
   d. preauthorization.

8. Which protects business contents (e.g., buildings and equipment) against fire, theft, and other risks?
   a. bonding insurance
   b. business liability insurance
   c. property insurance
   d. workers' compensation insurance

9. Which is another title for the health insurance specialist?
   a. coder
   b. health information manager
   c. medical assistant
   d. reimbursement specialist

10. If a patient is seen by a provider who orders a chest x-ray, which diagnosis should be linked with the procedure to prove medical necessity?
    a. abdominal distress
    b. heartburn
    c. shortness of breath
    d. sinus pain

11. **The principles of right or good conduct are known as**
    a. bylaws.
    b. ethics.
    c. rights.
    d. standards.

12. **The notice sent by the insurance company to the provider, which contains payment information about a claim, is the**
    a. claim form that was submitted.
    b. electronic data interchange.
    c. explanation of benefits.
    d. remittance advice.

13. **When an individual chooses to perform services for another under an express or implied agreement and is not subject to the other's control, the individual is defined as a(n)**
    a. casual employee.
    b. dependent contractor.
    c. independent contractor.
    d. statutory employee.

14. **Employers are generally considered liable for the actions and omissions of employees as performed and committed within the scope of their employment. This is known as**
    a. the chain of command.
    b. errors and omissions.
    c. *respondeat superior.*
    d. the scope of practice.

15. **Third-party payer _____ review CMS-1500 claims to determine whether the charges are reasonable for payment.**
    a. claims examiners
    b. coders
    c. providers
    d. remitters

16. **Which type of insurance should be purchased by health insurance specialist independent contractors?**
    a. bonding
    b. errors and omissions
    c. medical malpractice
    d. workers' compensation

17. **ICD-9-CM (or ICD-10-CM) codes are assigned to _____ on inpatient and outpatient claims**
    a. diagnoses
    b. procedures
    c. services
    d. treatments

18. **Some health insurance companies require _____ for treatment provided by specialists and documentation of post-treatment reports.**
    a. authentication
    b. cost-reduction campaigns
    c. preauthorization
    d. retrospective review

19. **High blood pressure is an example of a**
    a. code.
    b. diagnosis.
    c. procedure.
    d. service.

20. **According to the *Occupational Outlook Handbook,* which setting offers the fastest employment growth and majority of new jobs for health information technicians (including those who perform insurance specialist functions)?**
    a. health insurance companies
    b. hospitals
    c. physician offices
    d. schools/colleges

CHAPTER 2
Introduction to Health Insurance

INTRODUCTION

This chapter familiarizes students with health insurance coverage statistics and major developments in health insurance. Students will interpret health insurance coverage statistics and create an Excel chart to display health insurance data. Students will also perform a literature search to evaluate resources appropriate for preparing a research paper that explains major developments in health insurance and their impact on healthcare access, delivery, quality, reimbursement, and technology.

ASSIGNMENT 2.1   Health Insurance Coverage Statistics

OBJECTIVES

At the conclusion of this assignment, the student should be able to:
1. Interpret U.S. health insurance coverage statistics.
2. Compare U.S. health insurance coverage from one year to another.
3. Create a pie chart to display U.S. health insurance coverage statistics using Microsoft Excel.

OVERVIEW

The ability to properly interpret health insurance statistics and effectively communicate findings is a valuable skill for the health insurance specialist. This assignment requires students to interpret statistical data and display it by creating a pie chart using Microsoft Excel.

INSTRUCTIONS

1. Review the information about U.S. health insurance statistics in Chapter 2 of your textbook.

2. Refer to Figure 2-1 to answer the following questions:
   a. Which type of health insurance coverage decreased for the U.S. population?
   b. What was the percentage change in Medicaid coverage from Year 1 to Year 2?
   c. Which type of health insurance coverage remained statistically the same?
   d. Which two factors could explain the decrease in the number of individuals covered by private health insurance? (Use critical thinking to answer this question.)
   e. Which three concerns would face individuals who do not have health insurance coverage? (Use critical thinking to answer this question.)

3. Refer to Figure 2-2 to answer the following questions:
   a. What does Figure 2-2 illustrate?
   b. Compare the percentage of men and women with healthcare coverage between Year 1 and Year 4. What conclusion can you draw from comparing these two populations?
   c. Which population group had the smallest percentage of individuals with continuous health insurance coverage?
   d. What trend applies to every population group identified in Figure 2-2?

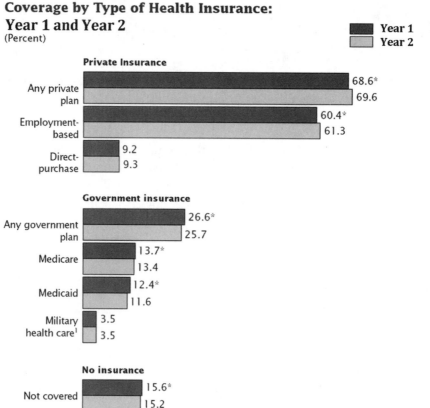

Coverage by Type of Health Insurance: Year 1 and Year 2
(Percent)

Legend: Year 1 / Year 2

Private Insurance

- Any private plan: 68.6* (Year 1), 69.6 (Year 2)
- Employment-based: 60.4* (Year 1), 61.3 (Year 2)
- Direct-purchase: 9.2 (Year 1), 9.3 (Year 2)

Government insurance

- Any government plan: 26.6* (Year 1), 25.7 (Year 2)
- Medicare: 13.7* (Year 1), 13.4 (Year 2)
- Medicaid: 12.4* (Year 1), 11.6 (Year 2)
- Military health care[1]: 3.5 (Year 1), 3.5 (Year 2)

No insurance

- Not covered: 15.6* (Year 1), 15.2 (Year 2)

* Statistically different at the 90-percent confidence level.
[1] Military health care includes: Tricare and CHAMPVA

Note: The estimates by type of coverage are not mutually exclusive; people can be covered by more than one type of health insurance during the year.
Source: U.S. Census Bureau

U.S. Census Bureau; generated by Michelle A. Green; using American FactFinder; http://factfinder.uscensus.gov; (20 September 2011).

FIGURE 2-1   Coverage by type of health insurance: Year 1 and Year 2

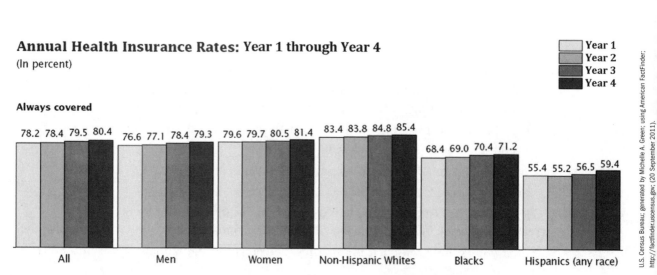

Annual Health Insurance Rates: Year 1 through Year 4
(In percent)

Legend: Year 1 / Year 2 / Year 3 / Year 4

Always covered

- All: 78.2, 78.4, 79.5, 80.4
- Men: 76.6, 77.1, 78.4, 79.3
- Women: 79.6, 79.7, 80.5, 81.4
- Non-Hispanic Whites: 83.4, 83.8, 84.8, 85.4
- Blacks: 68.4, 69.0, 70.4, 71.2
- Hispanics (any race): 55.4, 55.2, 56.5, 59.4

U.S. Census Bureau; generated by Michelle A. Green; using American FactFinder; http://factfinder.uscensus.gov; (20 September 2011).

FIGURE 2-2   Annual health insurance rates: Year 1 through Year 4 (always covered)

4. **Case Study:** Dr. Jason Brook is an orthopedist in a small, rural town in New York State. His practice consists of a high percentage of patients who have either Medicaid or Medicare with Medicaid as a secondary payer. Dr. Brook will meet with colleagues and representatives of the state government to discuss the impact a proposed cut in Medicaid funding will have on providers who practice in rural areas of New York, including the impact on patient access to health care. Dr. Brook has asked you, his health insurance specialist, to assist him by preparing a document that illustrates his patient population. Use the data in Table 2-1 to create a pie chart in Microsoft Excel (Table 2-2), illustrating the breakdown of health insurance coverage in the practice. (Dr. Brook has also instructed you to use vibrant colors and to create a three-dimensional effect.)

TABLE 2-1 Dr. Brook's Patient Population According to Health Insurance Coverage

TYPE OF HEALTH INSURANCE COVERAGE	PERCENTAGE OF PATIENTS COVERED
HMO	45%
Medicaid	18%
Medicare	23%
Military	4%
Self-pay	10%

TABLE 2-2 Instructions for Creating a Pie Chart Using Microsoft Excel

1.	Open Microsoft Excel.
2.	If a blank worksheet does not automatically display, left click on the Office Button (located in the upper left corner of Excel) to open a blank document.
3.	Key "Type of Health Insurance Coverage" in cell A1. Press the Enter key on your keyboard.
4.	Key "Percentage of Patients Covered" in cell B1. Press the Enter key on your keyboard.
5.	Key the types of health insurance coverage plans from column one in Table 2-1 in cells A2 through A6, respectively. Press the Enter key on your keyboard as you enter each type of plan.
6.	Key the data from column two in Table 2-1 in cells B2 through B6, respectively. Press the Enter key on your keyboard as you enter the data for each type of plan.
	a. Highlight cells B2 through B6, and left click on the Center icon in the Alignment toolbar.
	b. Highlight cells B2 through B6 (again), right click, left click on Format Cells . . . , and left click on Percentage.
	c. Increase the column width to properly display data. Place your cursor between columns A and B until the double arrow icon displays, and double click to increase the width of column A. Repeat to increase the width of column B by placing your cursor between columns B and C.

	A	B
1	Type of Health Insurance Coverage	Percentage of Patients Covered
2	HMO	45%
3	Medicaid	18%
4	Medicare	23%
5	Military	4%
6	Self-pay	10%

7.	Highlight cells A1 through B6, click Insert (located toolbar), left click on Pie, and left click on the exploded pie in 3-D. (The pie chart will appear on the spreadsheet, below the data entered in columns A and B.)
8.	Save your document, using the naming convention of Lastname_Firstname_PieChart.xls (e.g., Green_Michelle_PieChart.xls).
9.	Depending on your instructor's preference, print the spreadsheet and submit to your instructor or e-mail the *.xls file as an attachment to your instructor.

> **ASSIGNMENT 2.2** Major Developments in Health Insurance (Research Paper)

OBJECTIVES

At the end of this assignment, the student should be able to:

1. Use information literacy skills to research topics.
2. Perform a literature search to evaluate resources appropriate for a research paper.
3. Prepare an annotated bibliography.
4. Cite literature sources to avoid plagiarism.
5. Write a research paper that explains major developments in health insurance for a specific period of time.
6. Demonstrate relationships between major developments in health insurance and their impact on healthcare access, delivery, quality, reimbursement, and technology.

OVERVIEW

Performing a literature search to select and evaluate information resources is the first step in writing a research paper. An annotated bibliography (Figure 2-3) is a great opportunity for students to learn how to conduct literature searches. It contains citations (reference sources, such as books or journal articles) and a brief description of each cited item that summarizes the accuracy, quality, and relevance of the source. Writing a research paper is an excellent way for students to demonstrate their understanding of concepts that require interpretation and critical thinking skills (e.g., impact of health insurance regarding current healthcare issues).

This informative, practical article by the project director of the Payment Error Prevention Support Peer Review Organization (PEPSPRO) in Texas discusses the issue of diagnosis related group (DRG) billing as a major contributor to inaccurate Medicare payments and describes the negative consequences of undercoding and upcoding for the hospital. Recommendations are made and tools provided for completing a comprehensive assessment of records, staff qualifications, training, and use of coding resources; coding policies; and safeguards against upcoding. The author also discusses the various aspects of following up on a completed assessment, including implementing new policies, providing appropriate training, and monitoring compliance.

Fletcher, Robin. "The Importance of Addressing Inaccurate Diagnosis Related Group Assignment as a Risk Area." Journal of Health Care Compliance 4.5 (Sept./Oct. 2002): 40–46.

The author reports on the trend of hospitals using Internet-based automated compliance checking in place of more traditional billing methods to fulfill the requirements of the Medicare Correct Coding Initiative (CCI). Using Holy Cross Hospital in Ft. Lauderdale, Florida, as a case example, the author fully details the many benefits of using the automated system, including the reduction of billing errors, ease of use, evaluation of coding risk areas, and preventing noncompliance and the resulting penalty fees.

Moynihan, James J. "Automated Compliance Checker Helps Ensure Billing Accuracy." Healthcare Financial Management 54.7 (July 2000): 78.

© Cengage Learning 2013

FIGURE 2-3 Sample annotated bibliography with two works cited

Plagiarism is the act of stealing someone else's words or phrases and presenting them as your own. This means that when content is cut and pasted from an article into a research paper, the literature source must be cited. Your college may require you to review and sign a plagiarism policy; a sample policy is shown in Figure 2-4.

AVOIDING PLAGIARISM

Plagiarism is the act of stealing someone else's words or phrases and presenting them as your own. This is most commonly done when students "cut and paste" from an article directly into their report without citing the literature reference. There are two basic types of plagiarism:

Accidental plagiarism—you did a "cut and paste" of some key points into a working draft copy of your report but failed to remove them from the final version.

Deliberate plagiarism—you knew what you were doing when you did it, and you just hoped that you wouldn't get caught.

So, how do you avoid either type of plagiarism?

CITE THE SOURCE! If you are using a phrase and think that it is perfect, then you insert it something like this:

> According to Edna Huffman, the old adage "in God we trust, all else must document" is as true today as it was in the 1940s when Ms. Huffman first used the phrase (Huffman 1940).

On the reference page, you then list this source:

> Huffman, E. 1940. <u>Health Information Management,</u> 10th ed. Physicians' Record Company.

PARAPHRASE! Even if you don't use the exact words, but rely heavily on another author's work, you should still give credit. It might read like this:

> These days, everyone has a grudge about documentation standards, but those standards exist for a reason. The country may trust in God, but the court systems trust only in the record.

Huffman put you on the right track—so, give her credit in the reference page; besides, your paper will be stronger for showing more references.

TAKE NOTES, AND THEN TAKE A BREAK! A good strategy is to read several pages and take notes in your own hand. Then go away and come back to write the report just from your notes—don't look at the reference materials. In this way, you are forced to choose your own words and make your own logical conclusions.

Have enough confidence in yourself and what you know. Draw your own conclusions—even when your opinion is different than what you read in the published literature.

I have read the plagiarism policy above, and I understand the policy.

_____   _____

Student's Name   Date

FIGURE 2-4   Sample plagiarism policy to be signed by students

Annotated Bibliography

1. Select a healthcare topic that interests you (e.g., health insurance programs for children in poverty).

2. Go to your academic library to locate citations (e.g., journal articles) about your topic. (Refer to Table 1-1, in Chapter 1 of this workbook, for a list of professional journals.)

3. Review the citations to determine whether they contain useful information and ideas about your topic, and select two to read thoroughly.

4. Prepare the annotated bibliography in the American Psychological Association (APA) style or the Modern Language Association (MLA) style, depending on your instructor's preference (refer to Figure 2-3).

NOTE: The APA has established a style that is used in all its published books and journals, and many authorities in social and behavioral sciences have adopted this style as their standard. The MLA style is recommended for the preparation of scholarly manuscripts and student research papers. Be sure to ask your instructor which style you should use.

INTERNET LINK

Go to **www.thewritesource.com,** and click on the APA link (below Research) or the MLA link to view examples of reference citations.

5. Summarize the article, incorporating at least four of the items below:
   - Description of the content or focus of the article
   - Consideration of whether the article content is useful
   - Limitations of the article (e.g., outdated)
   - Audience for which the article is intended
   - Evaluation of any research methods used in the article
   - Author's background
   - Any conclusions the author(s) made about the topic
   - Your reaction to the article

6. Check and double-check spelling, grammar, and punctuation. Have at least one other person review your paper (e.g., college writing lab, English teacher, family member or friend who has excellent writing skills, and so on).

Plagiarism Policy

1. Review the plagiarism policy in Figure 2-4.
2. Sign and date the policy.
3. Remove the policy from the workbook and submit to your instructor.

Research Paper

Instructions

1. Select a period of time (e.g., 1995–2010) during which to conduct research on the major developments in health insurance, along with their impact on healthcare quality, access, technology, reimbursement, and so on.

2. Select a minimum of five references (other than the *UHI* textbook) to include in your paper:
   - Two references should be articles (consider using the two sources cited in your annotated bibliography).
   - Two references should be books.

- One reference can be an Internet Web site.
- A sixth reference can be the *UHI* textbook.

NOTE: You will need to conduct a literature search of at least 15 to 20 references before selecting just five to use as references in your paper.

3. Write an introductory paragraph that indicates the period of time selected and lists major developments in health insurance for that period. The last sentence of this paragraph should include a list of healthcare issues affected by those developments.
4. For each subsequent paragraph, explain how major developments in health insurance affected each healthcare issue (e.g., access, delivery, and so on). Write a separate paragraph for each issue.
5. Write a concluding paragraph that summarizes all of the points made in your paper, and indicate which healthcare issue was affected most significantly by developments in health insurance and why.
6. Write a bibliography in APA (or MLA) style. (Check with your instructor to see if footnotes are required.)
7. Check and double-check spelling, grammar, and punctuation. Be sure to double-space your paper and follow the format required by your instructor. Have at least one other person review your reference paper (e.g., college writing lab, English teacher, family member or friend who has excellent writing skills, and so on).

ASSIGNMENT 2.3 Calculating Reimbursement

OBJECTIVES

At the conclusion of this assignment, the student should be able to:
1. Determine the amount for a physician's fee, patient's copayment, and/or patient's coinsurance.
2. Calculate the amount a patient reimburses a provider, payer reimburses a provider, and provider "writes off" a patient's account.

OVERVIEW

A *copayment (copay)* is a provision in an insurance policy that requires the policyholder or patient to pay a specified dollar amount to a healthcare provider (e.g., physician) for each visit or medical service received. Coinsurance is the percentage of costs a patient shares with the health plan (e.g., plan pays 80 percent of costs and patient pays 20 percent). The reimbursement amount due to the provider for provision of services includes the amount reimbursed by the payer after the copayment or coinsurance amount is paid by the patient. Any amount remaining is "written off" by the provider. For this activity, the physician is a participating provider (PAR), which means the provider has contracted with the third-party payer and will provide a discount to the patient.

INSTRUCTIONS

Calculate the amounts paid by the payer and the patient and the amount the provider must "write off."
1. The patient is seen by his family physician for follow-up treatment of recently diagnosed asthmatic bronchitis. The physician's fee is $75. The patient's copayment is $20. The payer reimburses the physician $28.

   a. Enter the amount the patient pays the provider: _____
   b. Enter the amount the payer reimburses the provider: _____
   c. Enter the amount the provider "writes off" the account: _____

2. The patient undergoes chemical ablation of one facial lesion in her physician's office. The physician's fee is $240. The patient's copayment is $18. The payer reimburses the physician $105.

    a. Enter the amount the patient pays the provider: _____

    b. Enter the amount the payer reimburses the provider: _____

    c. Enter the amount the provider "writes off" the account: _____

3. The patient undergoes arthroscopic surgery at an ambulatory surgical center. The surgeon's fee is $890. The patient's coinsurance is 20% of the $700 fee schedule. The payer reimburses the surgeon 80% of the $700 fee schedule.

    a. Enter the amount the patient pays the provider: _____

    b. Enter the amount the payer reimburses the provider: _____

    c. Enter the amount the provider "writes off" the account: _____

4. The patient was referred to an orthopedic specialist for evaluation of chronic ankle pain. The physician's fee is $150. The patient's coinsurance is 30%. The payer reimburses the physician 70% of the $100 fee schedule for this service.

    a. Enter the amount the patient pays the provider: _____

    b. Enter the amount the payer reimburses the provider: _____

    c. Enter the amount the provider "writes off" the account: _____

5. The patient received preventive medicine services. The physician's fee is $150. The patient's copayment is $10 (of the $75 fee schedule). The payer reimburses the physician 80% of the $75 fee schedule.

    a. Enter the amount the patient pays the provider: _____

    b. Enter the amount the payer reimburses the provider: _____

    c. Enter the amount the provider "writes off" the account: _____

ASSIGNMENT 2.4   Multiple Choice Review

1. **Evidence of the first health insurance policy to provide private healthcare coverage for injuries that did not result in death appeared in which year?**

    a. 1842   c. 1915

    b. 1850   d. 1920

2. **Which has as its goal access to health coverage for every individual, regardless of the system implemented to achieve that goal?**

    a. government health programs   c. socialized medicine

    b. single-payer plan   d. universal health insurance

3. **The terms electronic health record (EHR) and electronic medical record (EMR) are often used interchangeably, but the _____ is a more global concept that includes the collection of patient information documented by a number of providers at different facilities regarding one patient.**

    a. computer-based patient record   c. electronic medical record

    b. electronic health record   d. personal health record

4. *Current Procedural Terminology (CPT)* **was developed by which organization in 1966?**

    a. American Hospital Association   c. Social Security Administration

    b. American Medical Association   d. World Health Organization

5. **Total practice management software (TPMS) is used to generate the EMR, automating which of the following medical practice functions:**
   a. medical necessity
   b. patient registration
   c. personal health record
   d. healthcare clearinghouse

6. **If a veteran is rated as 100 percent permanently and totally disabled as a result of a service-connected condition, which program will provide benefits to the veteran's dependents?**
   a. CHAMPUS
   b. CHAMPVA
   c. COBRA
   d. TRICARE

7. **Which coding system was created in 1984?**
   a. CPT
   b. DSM
   c. HCPCS
   d. ICD-9-CM

8. **A new fee schedule for Medicare services was implemented as part of OBRA 1989 and 1990, replacing the regional "usual and reasonable" payment basis with a fixed fee schedule called**
   a. DRGs.
   b. RBRVS.
   c. RUGs.
   d. SNFPPS.

9. **Quality standards for all laboratory testing to ensure the accuracy, reliability, and timeliness of patient test results regardless of where the tests are performed were established specifically by _____ legislation.**
   a. CLIA
   b. COBRA
   c. DRG
   d. TEFRA

10. **CMS developed the National Correct Coding Initiative (NCCI) to**
    a. decrease the amount of money paid out by the Medicare program.
    b. eliminate improper coding and promote national correct coding methodologies.
    c. encourage coders to further their education to qualify for advancement.
    d. reduce the number of codes in the CPT and HCPCS coding systems.

11. **The skilled nursing facility prospective payment system (SNFPPS) generates _____ payments for each skilled nursing facility admission.**
    a. capitation
    b. cost-based
    c. fee-for-service
    d. *per diem*

12. **In 2000, which type of health plan was introduced as a way to encourage individuals to locate the best health care at the lowest price possible, with the goal of holding down healthcare costs?**
    a. consumer-driven
    b. major medical
    c. private
    d. retrospective

13. **By whom is the employer identification number (EIN) assigned?**
    a. Centers for Medicare and Medicaid Services
    b. Department of Health and Human Services
    c. Internal Revenue Service
    d. Social Security Administration

14. **The systematic method of documentation that consists of four components (database, problem list, initial plan, and progress notes) is called the _____.**
    a. integrated record
    b. problem oriented record
    c. SOAP notes
    d. source oriented record

15. **The primary purpose of the record is to provide for _____, which involves documenting patient care services so that others who treat the patient have a source of information to assist with additional care and treatment.**
    a. continuity of care
    b. personal health recordkeeping
    c. record linkage
    d. surveillance and reporting

16. Which would be considered a Medicare *meaningful EHR user* if it can demonstrate that certified EHR technology is connected in a manner that provides for the electronic exchange of health information to improve the quality of health care?

    a. clinic

    b. hospital

    c. physician

    d. nursing facility

17. Physicians receive decreased Medicare Part B payments beginning in _____ if they were eligible to be *meaningful EHR users* by 2015 but did not implement an electronic health record (EHR).

    a. 2015

    b. 2016

    c. 2017

    d. 2018

18. In a teaching hospital, general documentation guidelines allow _____ to document physician services in the patient's medical record.

    a. both residents and teaching physicians

    b. neither residents nor teaching physicians

    c. residents only

    d. teaching physicians only

19. The Patient Protection and Affordable Care Act (PPCA) amended the time period for filing Medicare fee-for-service claims to _____ the maximum time period for submission of all Medicare FFS claims to one calendar year after the date of service.

    a. decrease

    b. increase

20. The Health Care and Education Reconciliation Act (HCERA) amended PACA to implement health care reform initiatives, which _____ tax credits for individuals so they could purchase healthcare insurance.

    a. decreased

    b. denied

    c. increased

    d. reduced

CHAPTER 3
Managed Health Care

INTRODUCTION

This chapter familiarizes students with types of managed care plans, legislation that has affected the managed care industry, and ways in which consumers and professionals can obtain information about the quality of health insurance plans.

ASSIGNMENT 3.1 National Committee for Quality Assurance (NCQA) Health Plan Report Card

---

OBJECTIVES

At the conclusion of this assignment, the student should be able to:

1. State the purpose of the NCQA health plan report card.
2. Generate and interpret an NCQA health plan report card.

OVERVIEW

The NCQA health plan report card is an interactive tool that helps consumers and professionals evaluate health plans. Report card results are based on an assessment of health plan processes and systems, clinical quality, and member satisfaction.

INSTRUCTIONS

1. Create a customized report card about health plans in your state by going to **reportcard .ncqa.org** and entering the required information.
2. Prepare a one-page, double-spaced, word-processed document that summarizes the results of the report card generated. Be sure to include the following information in the summary:
   a. Comparison of accreditation outcomes for the plans
   b. Number of health plans that earned an "excellent" rating
   c. Significance of an "excellent" rating
3. Check and double-check spelling, grammar, and punctuation. Have at least one other person review your document (e.g., college writing lab, English teacher, family member or friend who has excellent writing skills, and so on).

ASSIGNMENT 3.2 Managed Health Care Federal Legislation

OBJECTIVES

At the conclusion of this assignment, the student should be able to:

1. List managed health care federal legislation and year of implementation.
2. Identify legislation that most significantly influenced the growth of managed care, and state why this legislation was significant.

INSTRUCTIONS

1. Review Table 3-2, "Timeline for managed care federal legislation," in Chapter 3 of the textbook, and select legislation that most significantly influenced the growth of managed care. (You can select more than one piece of legislation for this purpose.)

> **NOTE:** Base your selection of significant legislation on classroom discussion as well as the textbook description of each piece of legislation. You are welcome to select more than one piece of legislation.

2. Conduct a literature search to locate at least 10 articles about the legislation you selected. Print (or make a copy of) each article.

> **NOTE:** If you selected more than one piece of legislation, be sure you conduct literature searches on each. You will probably locate more than 10 articles.

3. Carefully review each article to identify reasons the legislation you selected most significantly influenced the growth of managed care. (Using a highlighter pen to mark pertinent material in the articles may be helpful. Be sure you mark up a *copy* of the article, not the original article.)
4. Prepare a two- to three-page, double-spaced, word-processed document that summarizes your findings. Be sure to organize the document as follows:
   a. First paragraph—legislation you selected as most significantly influencing the growth of managed care
   b. Second and subsequent paragraphs—reasons that support your choice of that legislation as being the most influential regarding the growth of managed care (based on content in articles)
   c. Last paragraph—conclusion about the growth of managed care as the result of the legislation you selected as being most influential
   d. Bibliography (of 10 articles located as the result of performing the literature search)
5. Check and double-check spelling, grammar, and punctuation. Have at least one other person review your paper (e.g., college writing lab, English teacher, family member or friend who has excellent writing skills, and so on).

ASSIGNMENT 3.3 The Joint Commission

OBJECTIVES

At the conclusion of this assignment, the student should be able to:
1. State the types of facilities accredited by The Joint Commission.
2. List the types of certifications granted by The Joint Commission.
3. Define and discuss a sentinel event.
4. Discuss The Joint Commission's performance measurement initiatives.

OVERVIEW

The Joint Commission is an independent, not-for-profit organization that provides accreditation to a variety of healthcare facilities. Given the variety of healthcare facilities and the ability of all of these facilities to utilize the expertise of a medical coding or medical billing expert, it is important that you are aware of The Joint Commission's role in the U.S. healthcare system.

INSTRUCTIONS

1. Go to the Web site for The Joint Commission at **www.jointcommission.org** and explore the site to find out information about this organization.

2. Prepare a one- to two-page, double-spaced, word-processed document summarizing information on The Joint Commission that was accessed from the Web site. Be sure to include the following information in your summary:

   a. Identify types of healthcare facilities that The Joint Commission accredits.

   b. Identify types of certifications that The Joint Commission awards.

   c. Define and discuss a sentinel event.

   d. Discuss The Joint Commission's performance measurement initiatives.

3. Check and double-check spelling, grammar, and punctuation. Have at least one person review your document (e.g., college writing lab, English teacher, family member or friend who has excellent writing skills, and so on).

> **NOTE:** Navigate The Joint Commission Web site to research information needed for your summary. This will help you learn how to locate information using the Internet as a research tool and how to use Web sites, which often require using tool bars and pull-down menus.

ASSIGNMENT 3.4   HealthEast Care System

OBJECTIVES

At the conclusion of this assignment, the student should be able to:

1. Discuss privacy policy related to payment for HealthEast Care System.
2. Discuss other aspects of this integrated delivery system (wellness, disease programs, etc.).

OVERVIEW

HealthEast Care System is an integrated delivery system (IDS) that provides a variety of medical services to a diverse population of patients. The IDS also has many wellness and health programs focused on disease prevention.

INSTRUCTIONS

1. Go to the Web site for HealthEast Care System at **www.healtheast.org** and explore the site to find out information about this organization.

2. Prepare a one- to two-page, double-spaced, word-processed document that summarizes information on HealthEast that was accessed from the Web site. Be sure to include the following information in your summary:

   a. Discuss HealthEast's privacy policy for payment purposes.

   b. Identify types of disease-focused programs offered by this IDS.

   c. Explain HealthEast's patient safety focus.

   d. Discuss HealthEast's wellness program.

3. Check and double-check spelling, grammar, and punctuation. Have at least one person review your document (e.g., college writing lab, English teacher, family member or friend who has excellent writing skills, and so on).

> **NOTE:** Navigate the HealthEast Care System Web site to research information needed for your summary. This will help you learn how to locate information using the Internet as a research tool and how to use Web sites, which often require using tool bars and pull-down menus.

ASSIGNMENT 3.5 Multiple Choice Review

1. **Employees and dependents who join a managed care plan are called**
   a. case managers.
   b. enrollees.
   c. providers.
   d. health plans.

2. **Which act of legislation permitted large employers to self-insure employee healthcare benefits?**
   a. ERISA
   b. HEDIS
   c. OBRA
   d. TEFRA

3. **If a physician provides services that cost less than the managed care capitation amount, the physician will**
   a. lose money.
   b. lose his or her managed care contract.
   c. make a profit.
   d. reduce the patient load.

4. **The primary care provider is responsible for**
   a. ensuring that enrollees pay their premiums.
   b. providing care according to the enrollee's preferences.
   c. supervising and coordinating healthcare services for enrollees.
   d. the quality of care provided by consultants.

5. **Which is the method of controlling healthcare costs and quality of care by reviewing the appropriateness and necessity of care provided to patients?**
   a. administrative oversight
   b. case management
   c. quality assurance
   d. utilization management

6. **Accreditation is a _____ process that a healthcare facility can undergo to show that standards are being met.**
   a. required
   b. licensure
   c. voluntary
   d. mandatory

7. **Which type of health plan funds healthcare expenses by insurance coverage and allows the individual to select one of each type of provider to create a customized network?**
   a. capitated plan
   b. customized sub-capitation plan
   c. healthcare reimbursement account
   d. health savings security account

8. **Which type of consumer-directed health plan carries the stipulation that any funds unused will be lost?**
   a. managed care organization
   b. healthcare reimbursement account
   c. health reimbursement arrangement
   d. health savings security account

9. **Which is assessed by the National Committee for Quality Assurance?**
   a. ambulatory care facilities
   b. hospitals
   c. long-term care facilities
   d. managed care plans

10. **A case manager is responsible for**
    a. educating enrollees about their health plan benefits.
    b. developing patient care plans for health services provided to enrollees.
    c. providing healthcare services to enrollees.
    d. submitting claims on behalf of enrollees.

11. Currently, more than 60 _____ Americans are enrolled in some type of managed care program in response to regulatory initiatives affecting healthcare cost and quality.
    a. thousand
    b. million
    c. billion
    d. trillion

12. Accreditation organizations develop _____ that are reviewed during a survey process that is conducted both offsite and onsite.
    a. laws
    b. legislation
    c. regulations
    d. standards

13. Which was created to provide standards to assess managed care systems in terms of indicators such as membership, utilization of services, quality, and access?
    a. ERISA
    b. HEDIS
    c. HIPAA
    d. TEFRA

14. Which act of legislation provided states with the flexibility to establish HMOs for Medicare and Medicaid programs?
    a. BBA
    b. COBRA
    c. OBRA
    d. TEFRA

15. Which would likely be subject to a managed care plan quality review?
    a. amount of money spent on construction upgrades
    b. cost of new equipment for a member facility
    c. number of patient payments made by credit card
    d. results of patient satisfaction surveys

16. The Quality Improvement System for Managed Care (QISMC) was established by
    a. The Joint Commission.
    b. Medicaid.
    c. Medicare.
    d. National Committee for Quality Assurance.

17. Arranging for a patient's transfer to a rehabilitation facility is an example of
    a. concurrent review.
    b. discharge planning.
    c. preadmission review.
    d. preauthorization.

18. Administrative services performed on behalf of a self-insured managed care company can be outsourced to a(n)
    a. accrediting agency.
    b. external quality review organization.
    c. third-party administrator.
    d. utilization management company.

19. Before a patient schedules elective surgery, many managed care plans require a
    a. payment applied to the cost of the surgery.
    b. physician incentive plan disclosure.
    c. quality assurance review.
    d. second surgical opinion.

20. A *health delivery network* is another name for a(n)
    a. exclusive provider organization (EPO).
    b. integrated delivery system (IDS).
    c. preferred provider organization (PPO).
    d. triple option plan (TOP).

CHAPTER 4
Processing an Insurance Claim

INTRODUCTION

This chapter familiarizes students with the encounter form, remittance advice (RA), and explanation of benefits (EOB) form used in the payment of health insurance claims. Students will learn the contents of an encounter form, as well as how to interpret data contained on a remittance advice and an explanation of benefits.

ASSIGNMENT 4.1   Completing Insurance Verification Forms

OBJECTIVES

At the conclusion of this assignment, the student should be able to:
1. Explain the purpose of an insurance verification form.
2. Accurately complete insurance verification forms.

OVERVIEW

Accounts receivable management assists providers in the collection of appropriate reimbursement for services rendered, and includes the function entitled *insurance verification and eligibility*, which involves confirming patient insurance plan and eligibility information with the third-party payer to determine the patient's financial responsibility for services rendered.

EXAMPLE:

DOCTORS GROUP · MAIN STREET · ALFRED NY 12345 NPI: 8529637410		PATIENT REGISTRATION FORM
PATIENT INFORMATION		
Last Name Rogers	First Name Melissa	Middle Name Ann
Street 5 High Street	City Alfred	State / Zip Code NY 14802
Patient's Date of Birth 05/05/1968	Social Security Number 123-45-6789	Home Phone Number (101) 555-1234
Student Status ☐ Full-time ☐ Part-time	Employment Status ☒ Full-time ☐ Part-time ☐ Unemployed	Marital Status ☒ Single ☐ Married ☐ Separated ☐ Divorced ☐ Widowed
Gender ☐ Male ☒ Female	Visit is related to on-the-job injury ☒ No ☐ Yes Date: _____	Prior treatment received for injury ☒ No ☐ Yes Doctor: _____ WC No. _____
Employer Phone Number (101) 555-8521	Referred by:	
Emergency Contact Cindy Reynolds	Address 235 Church Street, Elmira NY 14901	Telephone Number (101) 732-1234
Name/Address of Employer Bon Ton Department Store, PO Box 183, Rochester NY 14201	Occupation Director of Human Resources	
Visit is related to automobile accident ☒ No ☐ Yes Date: _____	Name and Credentials of Treating Provider Beth Watkins, MD	NPI 7419638520

© Cengage Learning 2013

GUARANTOR'S BILLING INFORMATION

Last Name	First Name	Middle Name
Rogers	Melissa	Ann

Street	City	State / Zip Code
5 High Street	Alfred	NY 14802

Relationship to Patient	Social Security Number	Home Phone Number
Self	123-45-6789	(101) 555-1234

Name of Employer	Address of Employer	Employer Phone Number
Bon Ton Department Store	PO Box 183, Rochester NY 14201	(101) 555-8521

INSURANCE INFORMATION

PRIMARY INSURED INFORMATION

Last Name	First Name / Middle Initial
Rogers	Melissa A.

Address	City / State / Zip Code
5 High Street	Alfred NY 14802

Relationship to Insured	Gender
☒ Self ☐ Spouse ☐ Child ☐ Other	☐ Male ☒ Female

Insured's Date of Birth	Home Phone Number
05/05/1968	(101) 555-1234

Name and Address of Insurance Company
Bell Atlantic, 100 Provider Row, Anywhere NY 12345-9597

Insurance Identification Number	Group Number	Effective Date
987654321-01		04-29-1989

Name of Employer Sponsoring Plan
Bon Ton Department Store

SECONDARY INSURED INFORMATION

Last Name	First Name / Middle Initial

Address	City / State / Zip Code

Relationship to Insured	Gender
☐ Self ☐ Spouse ☐ Child ☐ Other	☐ Male ☐ Female

Insured's Date of Birth	Home Phone Number

Name and Address of Insurance Company

Insurance Identification Number	Group Number	Effective Date

Name of Employer Sponsoring Plan

Bell Atlantic HMO
(800) 333-5555

Medical ▪ Dental ▪ Vision ▪ Prescriptions
EFFECTIVE DATE OF COVERAGE: 04-29-1989

POLICYHOLDER:	ROGERS, MELISSA, A
IDENTIFICATION NUMBER:	987654321-01
OFFICE COPAYMENT:	$10
RX BIN:	61410

FOR REFERRAL TO SPECIALISTS, CALL (800) 333-5555.

ONLINE INSURANCE ELIGIBILITY VERIFICATION

Rogers, Melissa, A	05-05-68	☒ Female ☐ Male
Patient's Last Name, First Name, Middle Initial	Patient's DOB	Gender
Mary Smith, CMA	06-20-YY	Beth Watkins, M.D.
Insurance Specialist or Office Manager's Name	Date Verified	Provider's Name
Bell Atlantic HMO	n/a	987654321-01
Health Insurance Plan Name	Group No.	Health Insurance Policy Number
04-29-1989	Eligible	n/a
Health Insurance Plan Effective Date	Status	Health Insurance Plan Termination Date

Plan Type (circle one): PPO (HMO) POS Group MC Capitated WC

$ NONE	$ NONE	$10	☐ Yes ☒ No
Deducible Amount	Amount not Satisfied	Copayment Amount	Pre-existing Clause

Percentage of Reimbursement: NONE %
Coinsurance

What is plan coverage? Medical, Dental, Vision, Prescriptions

What are the plan requirements? Referral required for specialist services (1-800-333-5555)

INSTRUCTIONS

1. Review content in the patient registration form below, and complete the insurance verification form.

DOCTORS GROUP · MAIN STREET · ALFRED NY 12345
NPI: 8529637410   **PATIENT REGISTRATION FORM**

PATIENT INFORMATION

Last Name	First Name	Middle Name
Zapp	Dawn	Laura

Street	City	State / Zip Code
663 Hilltop Drive	Anywhere	NY 12345

Patient's Date of Birth	Social Security Number	Home Phone Number
02/12/1967	444-55-6666	(101) 333-4445

Student Status	Employment Status	Marital Status
❑ Full-time ❑ Part-time	☒ Full-time ❑ Part-time ❑ Unemployed	☒ Single ❑ Married ❑ Separated ❑ Divorced ❑ Widowed

Gender	Visit is related to on-the-job injury	Prior treatment received for injury
❑ Male ☒ Female	☒ No ❑ Yes Date: _____	☒ No ❑ Yes Doctor:_____ WC No. _____

Employer Phone Number	Referred by:
(101) 313-9854	

Emergency Contact	Address	Telephone Number
Bill Miller	3301 Sunny Drive, NY 12346	(101) 937-0070

Name/Address of Employer	Occupation
Superfresh Foods, PO Box 111, Main NY 12458	Cashier

Visit is related to automobile accident	Name and Credentials of Treating Provider	NPI
☒ No ❑ Yes Date: _____	Donald Givings, MD	1234567890

GUARANTOR'S BILLING INFORMATION

Last Name	First Name	Middle Name
Zapp	Dawn	Laura

Street	City	State / Zip Code
663 Hilltop Drive	Anywhere	NY 12345

Relationship to Patient	Social Security Number	Home Phone Number
Self	444-55-6666	(101) 333-4445

Name of Employer	Address of Employer	Employer Phone Number
Superfresh Foods	PO Box 111, Main NY 12458	(101) 313-9854

INSURANCE INFORMATION

PRIMARY INSURED INFORMATION		SECONDARY INSURED INFORMATION	
Last Name	First Name / Middle Initial	Last Name	First Name / Middle Initial
Zapp	Dawn L.		
Address	City / State / Zip Code	Address	City / State / Zip Code
663 Hilltop Drive	Anywhere NY 12345		
Relationship to Insured	Gender	Relationship to Insured	Gender
☒ Self ❑ Spouse ❑ Child ❑ Other	❑ Male ☒ Female	❑ Self ❑ Spouse ❑ Child ❑ Other	❑ Male ❑ Female
Insured's Date of Birth	Home Phone Number	Insured's Date of Birth	Home Phone Number
02/12/1967	(101) 333-4445		
Name and Address of Insurance Company		Name and Address of Insurance Company	
NorthWest Health, 500 Carr Street, Anywhere NY 12345-9597			

Insurance Identification Number	Group Number	Effective Date	Insurance Identification Number	Group Number	Effective Date
444556666-01	430	10/20/2004			

Name of Employer Sponsoring Plan	Name of Employer Sponsoring Plan
Superfresh Foods	

NORTHWEST HEALTH PPO
(877) 555-6598

Medical ▪ Prescriptions

EFFECTIVE DATE OF COVERAGE: 10-20-2004

POLICYHOLDER:	ZAPP, DAWN, L
IDENTIFICATION NUMBER:	444556666-01
OFFICE COPAYMENT:	$25
COINSURANCE:	80/20
DEDUCTIBLE:	$200
RX BIN: A304/RX GRP:	430
PRESCRIPTION COPAYMENT:	**BRAND:** $25 **GENERIC:** $10

© Cengage Learning 2013

INSURANCE ELIGIBILITY VERIFICATION

❏ Female   ❏ Male
Gender

_____
Patient's Last Name, First Name, Middle Initial

_____
Patient's DOB

_____
Insurance Specialist or Office Manager's Name

_____
Date Verified

_____
Provider Name

_____
Health Insurance Plan Name

_____
Group No.

_____
Health Insurance Policy Number

_____
Health Insurance Plan Effective Date

_____
Status

_____
Health Insurance Plan Termination Date

Plan Type (circle one):   PPO   HMO   POS   Group   MC   Capitated   WC

$ _____
Deducible Amount

$ _____
Amount not Satisfied

$ _____
Copayment Amount

❏ Yes   ❏ No
Pre-existing Clause

Percentage of Reimbursement: _____ %
Coinsurance

What is plan coverage?   _____

What are the plan requirements?   _____

© Cengage Learning 2013

2. Review content in the patient registration form below, and complete the insurance verification form.

DOCTORS GROUP · MAIN STREET · ALFRED NY 12345
NPI: 8529637410

PATIENT REGISTRATION FORM

PATIENT INFORMATION

Last Name	First Name	Middle Name
Branch	James	

Street	City	State / Zip Code
401 Cartvalley Court	Anywhere	NY 12345

Patient's Date of Birth	Social Security Number	Home Phone Number
05/03/1986	345-67-9910	(101) 333-5555

Student Status	Employment Status	Marital Status
☐ Full-time ☐ Part-time	☒ Full-time ☐ Part-time ☐ Unemployed	☐ Single ☒ Married ☐ Separated ☐ Divorced ☐ Widowed

Gender	Visit is related to on-the-job injury	Prior treatment received for injury
☒ Male ☐ Female	☒ No ☐ Yes Date: _____	☒ No ☐ Yes Doctor:_____ WC No. _____

Employer Phone Number	Referred by:
(101) 499-7117	

Emergency Contact	Address	Telephone Number
Bethany Branch	401 Cartvalley Court, Anywhere NY 12345	(101) 333-5555

Name/Address of Employer	Occupation
Gateway US, 2021 Blue Ave, Nowhere NY 12354	Sales

Visit is related to automobile accident	Name and Credentials of Treating Provider	NPI
☒ No ☐ Yes Date: _____	Lisa M. Mason, M.D.	4567897890

GUARANTOR'S BILLING INFORMATION

Last Name	First Name	Middle Name
Branch	James	

Street	City	State / Zip Code
2021 Blue Ave	Nowhere	NY 12354

Relationship to Patient	Social Security Number	Home Phone Number
Self	345-67-9910	(101) 333-5555

Name of Employer	Address of Employer	Employer Phone Number
Gateway US	2021 Blue Ave, Nowhere NY 12354	(101) 499-7117

INSURANCE INFORMATION

PRIMARY INSURED INFORMATION		SECONDARY INSURED INFORMATION	
Last Name	First Name / Middle Initial	Last Name	First Name / Middle Initial
Branch	James		
Address	City / State / Zip Code	Address	City / State / Zip Code
2021 Blue Ave	Nowhere NY 12354		
Relationship to Insured	Gender	Relationship to Insured	Gender
☒ Self ☐ Spouse ☐ Child ☐ Other	☒ Male ☐ Female	☐ Self ☐ Spouse ☐ Child ☐ Other	☐ Male ☐ Female
Insured's Date of Birth	Home Phone Number	Insured's Date of Birth	Home Phone Number
05/03/1986	(111) 333-5555		
Name and Address of Insurance Company		Name and Address of Insurance Company	
Metropolitan, PO Box 232, Nowhere NY 12354			
Insurance Identification Number / Group Number / Effective Date		Insurance Identification Number / Group Number / Effective Date	
2122245-01 / M411 / 09/08/2010			
Name of Employer Sponsoring Plan		Name of Employer Sponsoring Plan	
Gateway US			

METROPOLITAN
(800) 319-6531

HMO PLAN
Medical · Dental · Rx

INSURED: BRANCH, JAMES   **ISSUE DATE:** 09/08/2010
ID Number: 2122245-01   **Group No.** M411
OFFICE COPAYMENT: $20   **EMG:** $250
RX COPAYMENT: **BRAND:** $25   **GENERIC:** $15
NURSE ADVISOR AVAILABLE 24 HOURS

INSURANCE ELIGIBILITY VERIFICATION

❏ Female ❏ Male

_____   _____   _____
Patient's Last Name, First Name, Middle Initial   Patient's DOB   Gender

_____   _____   _____
Insurance Specialist or Office Manager's Name   Date Verified   Provider Name

_____   _____   _____
Health Insurance Plan Name   Group No.   Health Insurance Policy Number

_____   _____   _____
Health Insurance Plan Effective Date   Status   Health Insurance Plan Termination Date

Plan Type (circle one):   PPO   HMO   POS   Group   MC   Capitated   WC

$ _____ $ _____ $ _____   ❏ Yes ❏ No
Deducible Amount   Amount not Satisfied   Copayment Amount   Pre-existing Clause

Percentage of Reimbursement: _____ %
                                        Coinsurance

What is plan coverage?   _____

What are the plan requirements?   _____

ASSIGNMENT 4.2   Payment of Claims: Encounter Form

OBJECTIVES

At the conclusion of this assignment, the student should be able to:
1. Explain the purpose of an encounter form.
2. Interpret the information contained on an encounter form.

OVERVIEW

An *encounter form* is the source document used to generate the insurance claim. In addition to patient identification information and the date of service, it contains abbreviated diagnosis and brief procedure/service descriptions and corresponding codes (e.g., ICD, CPT, HCPCS). The provider circles the appropriate codes on the encounter form, and the insurance specialist enters the office charge, amount paid by the patient, and total due.

INSTRUCTIONS

Review the encounter form in Figure 4-1 to familiarize yourself with its organization and contents. Use the encounter form to answer the following questions:
1. Which CPT codes listed on the encounter form are reported for new patient office visits? (Refer to your CPT coding manual to answer this question.)
2. The provider conducted a consultation on a new patient. What is the title of the section of the encounter form that the provider would reference to select a service code?
3. The provider performed an EKG with interpretation during the office visit. Identify the CPT code located on the encounter form that would be reported for this service.
4. During processing of the encounter form (to generate the claim), the insurance specialist notices that the provider entered a check mark in front of the procedure, "Blood, occult (feces)," and a check mark in front of the diagnosis, "Hypertension." Because *medical necessity* requires the diagnosis selected to justify the procedure performed, what should the insurance specialist do next?
5. The patient paid his $20 copayment during registration for today's encounter. What is the title of the section of the encounter from where the amount received is entered?

ENCOUNTER FORM

Tel: (101) 555-1111
Fax: (101) 555-2222

Kim Donaldson, M.D.
INTERNAL MEDICINE
101 Main Street, Suite A
Alfred NY 14802

EIN: 11-9876543
NPI: 1234567890

OFFICE VISITS	NEW	EST	OFFICE PROCEDURES		INJECTIONS	
☐ Level I	99201	99211	☐ EKG with interpretation	93000	☐ Influenza virus vaccine	90656
☐ Level II	99202	99212	☐ Oximetry with interpretation	94760	☐ Admin of Influenza vaccine	G0008
☐ Level III	99203	99213	**LABORATORY TESTS**		☐ Pneumococcal vaccine	90732
☐ Level IV	99204	99214	☐ Blood, occult (feces)	82270	☐ Admin of pneumococcal vaccine	G0009
☐ Level V	99205	99215	☐ Skin test, Tb, intradermal (PPD)	86580	☐ Hepatitis B vaccine, adult	90746
OFFICE CONSULTS (NEW or EST)			☐		☐ Admin of Hepatitis B vaccine	G0010
☐ Level I	99241		☐		☐ Tetanus toxoid vaccine	90703
☐ Level II	99242		☐		☐ Immunization administration	90471
☐ Level III	99243		☐		☐	
☐ Level IV	99244		☐		☐	
☐ Level V	99245		☐		☐	

DIAGNOSIS					
☐ Abnormal heart sounds	785.3	☐ Chronic ischemic heart disease	414.9	☐ Hypertension	401.9
☐ Abnormal pain	789.0__	☐ Chronic obstructive lung disease	496	☐ Hormone replacement	V07.4
☐ Abnormal feces	787.7	☐ Congestive heart failure	428.0	☐ Hyperlipidemia	272.4
☐ Allergic rhinitis	477.9	☐ Cough	786.2	☐ Hyperthyroidism	242.9__
☐ Anemia, pernicious	281.0	☐ Depressive disorder	311	☐ Influenza	487.1
☐ Anxiety	300.0__	☐ Diabetes mellitus	250.____	☐ Loss of weight	783.21
☐ Asthma	493.9__	☐ Diarrhea	787.91	☐ Nausea	787.02
☐ Atrophy, cerebral	331.0	☐ Dizziness	780.4	☐ Nausea with vomiting	787.01
☐ B-12 deficiency	281.1	☐ Emphysema	492.8	☐ Pneumonia	486
☐ Back pain	724.5	☐ Fatigue and malaise	780.79	☐ Sore throat	462
☐ Bronchitis	490	☐ Fever	780.60	☐ Vaccine, hepatitis B	V05.3
☐ Cardiovascular disease	429.2	☐ Gastritis, atrophic	535.1__	☐ Vaccine, influenza	V04.81
☐ Cervicalgia	723.1	☐ Heartburn	787.1	☐ Vaccine, pneumococcus	V03.82
☐ Chest pain	786.5__	☐ Hematuria	599.70	☐ Vaccine, tetanus toxoid	V03.7
☐	_____	☐	_____	☐	_____

PATIENT IDENTIFICATION

PATIENT NAME:	
PATIENT NUMBER:	
DATE OF BIRTH:	

ENCOUNTER DATE

DATE OF SERVICE:	/ /

RETURN VISIT DATE

DATE OF RETURN VISIT:	/ /

FINANCIAL TRANSACTION DATA

INVOICE NO.	
ACCOUNT NO.	
TOTAL FOR SERVICE:	$
AMOUNT RECEIVED:	$
PAID BY:	☐ Cash ☐ Check ☐ Credit Card
CASHIER'S INITIALS:	

FIGURE 4-1 Encounter form

ASSIGNMENT 4.3   Payment of Claims: Remittance Advice

OBJECTIVES

At the conclusion of this assignment, the student should be able to:
1. Explain the purpose of a remittance advice.
2. Interpret data contained in a remittance advice.

OVERVIEW

Once the claims adjudication process has been finalized, the claim is either denied or approved for payment. The provider receives a remittance advice (RA), which contains information used to process payments and adjustments to patient accounts. Payers often include multiple patients on the same remittance advice, which means that the insurance specialist must carefully review the document to properly process payments and adjustments. The remittance advice is also reviewed to make sure that there are no processing errors, which would result in the office resubmitting a corrected claim (e.g., coding errors).

INSTRUCTIONS

Review the remittance advice forms in Figures 4-2 through Figure 4-7 to familiarize yourself with the organization and legend (explanation of abbreviated terms).

> **NOTE:** Use the remittance advice in Figure 4-2 to answer questions 1 through 5.

1. What is the check number and amount paid to the provider as recorded on the remittance advice? (HINT: This information is recorded in two different places on the remittance advice.)
2. What was patient John Cofee's coinsurance amount for his visit on 0406YYYY?
3. Patient James Eicher was not charged a coinsurance amount for his 0415YYYY visit. What is a possible explanation for this?
4. What is patient Jenny Baker's account number?
5. What is the allowed amount for procedure code 99213?

> **NOTE:** Use the remittance advice in Figure 4-3 to answer questions 6 through 10.

6. What is patient John Humphrey's health insurance claim number?
7. How many patients in Figure 4-3 authorized assignment of benefits to Dr. Wilkins?
8. What is patient Grayson Kihlberg's coinsurance amount for CPT code 99204?
9. What was Craig Zane's coinsurance amount for code 73600?
10. What was the amount billed for patient Angel Brennan's visit?

> **NOTE:** Use the remittance advice in Figure 4-4 to answer questions 11 through 15.

11. What was the date of service for patient Christopher Hesse?
12. What procedure code is listed for patient Mary Schwartz?
13. How much did the provider bill the insurance company for the care of patient Andrew Gagner?
14. Identify the place-of-service code for each patient.
15. According to the remittance advice, how much was Dr. Kelley paid?

```
ABC INSURANCE COMPANY
100 MAIN STREET
ALFRED, NY 14802
1-800-555-1234                                                          REMITTANCE ADVICE

DAVID MILLER, M.D.                                                      PROVIDER #:   123456
101 NORTH STREET                        PAGE #: 1 OF 1                  DATE:         05/05/YY
ALFRED, NY 14802                                                        CHECK#:       235698
```

	SERV DATES	POS	PROC	BILLED	ALLOWED		COINS		REIM
BAKER, JENNY	HICN 235962541		ACNT BAKE1234567-01					ASG Y	MOA MA01
236592ABC	0405 0405YY	11	99213	75.00	60.00		15.00		45.00
PT RESP: 15.00		CLAIM TOTAL: 75.00							
									NET: 45.00
COFEE, JOHN	HICN 569856217		ACNT COFE2326254-01					ASG Y	MOA MA01
326526ABC	0406 0406YY	11	99214	100.00	80.00		20.00		60.00
PT RESP: 20.00		CLAIM TOTAL: 100.00							
									NET: 60.00
DAVIS, JEANNE	HICN 562659452		ACNT DAVI2369214-01					ASG Y	MOA MA01
123652ABC	0410 0410YY	11	99212	50.00	40.00		10.00		30.00
PT RESP: 10.00		CLAIM TOTAL: 50.00							
									NET: 30.00
EICHER, JAMES	HICN 626594594		ACNT EICH2365214-01					ASG Y	MOA MA01
126954ABC	0415 0415YY	11	99385	125.00	125.00		0.00		125.00
PT RESP: 0.00		CLAIM TOTAL: 125.00							
$0 COPAY FOR PREVENTIVE SERVICES									NET: 125.00
FEINSTEIN, ED	HICN 365956214		ACNT FEIN1236521-01					ASG Y	MOA MA01
695214ABC	0420 0420YY	11	17000	750.00	650.00		50.00		600.00
PT RESP: 50.00		CLAIM TOTAL: 750.00							
									NET: 600.00

```
TOTALS:
# BILLED                    BILLED         ALLOWED      COINSURANCE     NET          CHECK
CLAIMS                      AMOUNT         AMOUNT       AMOUNT          AMOUNT       AMOUNT

5                           1100.00        955.00       95.00           860.00       860.00
```

LEGEND
HICN (health insurance claim number)
SERV DATES (dates of service)
POS (place-of-service code)
PROC (CPT procedure/service code)
BILLED (amount provider billed payer)
ALLOWED (amount authorized by payer)
COINS (amount patient paid)
PROVIDER PAID (amount provider was reimbursed by payer)
NET (amount payer paid to provider)
PT RESP (amount patient paid)
ACNT (account number)
ASG Y (patient has authorized provider to accept assignment)
MOA MA01 (indicator that if denied, claim can be appealed)

FIGURE 4-2   Remittance advice (multiple claims)

XYZ INSURANCE COMPANY
500 SOUTH STREET
CHICAGO, ILLINOIS 60186
1-800-555-4321

REMITTANCE ADVICE

CYNTHIA WILKINS M.D.
100 STATE STREET
DENVER, COLORADO 80200

PROVIDER #: 654321
DATE: 05/31/YY
CHECK #:   871267

	SERV DATES		POS	PROC	BILLED	ALLOWED		COINS	REIMB
ALDRIDGE, MORTON	HICN 370553029		ACNT ALDR4557516-01			ASG	Y		
112233XYZ	05/05	05/05/YY	11	10120	120.00	100.00		20.00	80.00
PT RESP: 20.00			CLAIM TOTAL: 120.00						NET: 80.00
BRENNAN, ANGEL	HICN 703459203		ACNT BREN5761282-01			ASG	Y		
757557XYZ	05/05	05/05/YY	11	99213	80.00	65.00		15.00	50.00
PT RESP: 15.00			CLAIM TOTAL: 80.00						NET: 50.00
HUMPHREY, JOHN	HICN 454545544		ACNT HUMP6721357-01			ASG	Y		
673112XYZ	05/10	05/10/YY	11	29130	50.00	35.00		15.00	20.00
PT RESP: 15.00			CLAIM TOTAL: 50.00						NET: 20.00
KIHLBERG, GRAYSON	HICN 716372688		ACNT KIHL1242495-02			ASG	Y		
876543XYZ	05/12	05/12/YY	11	99204	135.00	125.00		27.00	98.00
PT RESP: 27.00			CLAIM TOTAL: 125.00						NET: 98.00
ZANE, CRAIG	HICN 737682574		ACNT ZANE4963518-01			ASG	Y		
302353XYZ	05/17	05/17/YY	11	99213	80.00	65.00		15.00	50.00
				73600	55.00	45.00		0.00	45.00
PT RESP: 15.00			CLAIM TOTAL: 110.00						NET: 95.00

TOTALS:

# BILLED CLAIMS:	BILLED AMOUNT:	ALLOWED AMOUNT:	COINSURANCE AMOUNT:	NET AMOUNT:
5	520.00	435.00	92.00	343.00

LEGEND
HICN (health insurance claim number)
SERV DATES (dates of service)
POS (place-of-service code)
PROC (CPT procedure/service code)
BILLED (amount provider billed payer)
ALLOWED (amount authorized by payer)
COINS (amount patient paid)
PROVIDER PAID (amount provider was reimbursed by payer)
NET (amount payer paid to provider)
PT RESP (amount patient paid)
ACNT (account number)
ASG Y (patient has authorized provider to accept assignment)
MOA MA01 (indicator that if denied, claim can be appealed)

© Cengage Learning 2013

FIGURE 4-3   Remittance advice (multiple claims)

ACME INSURANCE COMPANY
911 RED LIGHT DRIVE
DALLAS, TEXAS 52222
1-800-555-5555

REMITTANCE ADVICE

ROSS KELLEY, M.D.
100 STATE STREET
BUFFALO, NEW YORK 14202

PROVIDER #: 5872
DATE: 05/31/YY
CHECK #:   37767

	SERV DATES		POS	PROC	BILLED	ALLOWED	COINS	REIMB
GAGNER, ANDREW	HICN 621884549	ACNT GAGN032974-01				ASG Y		
745221	05/07	05/07/YY	11	99204	150.00	135.00	15.00	120.00
				74247	320.00	285.00	57.00	228.00
PT RESP: 72.00		CLAIM TOTAL: 470.00						NET: 348.00
HESS, CHRISTOPHER	HICN 258369147	ACNT HESS3129657-01				ASG Y		
246810	05/08	05/08/YY	11	99213	80.00	65.00	20.00	45.00
PT RESP: 20.00		CLAIM TOTAL: 80.00						NET: 45.00
SCHWARTZ, MARY	HICN 147953128	ACNT SCHW4963813-01				ASG Y		
999924	05/10	05/10/YY	11	46600	212.00	185.00	37.00	148.00
PT RESP: 37.00		CLAIM TOTAL: 212.00						NET: 148.00
STAVE, GABRIELLA	HICN 752319567	ACNT STAV462978-04				ASG Y		
225932	05/12	05/12/YY	11	99212	90.00	80.00	10.00	70.00
PT RESP: 10.00		CLAIM TOTAL: 90.00						NET: 70.00
THOMAS, MICHAEL	HICN 121770222	ACNT THOM699224-02				ASG Y		
930512	05/17	05/17/YY	11	83013	110.00	95.00	30.00	65.00
PT RESP: 30.00		CLAIM TOTAL: 110.00						NET: 65.00

TOTALS:				
# BILLED		BILLED	ALLOWED	COINS	NET
CLAIMS:		AMOUNT:	AMOUNT:	AMOUNT:	AMOUNT:
5		962.00	845.00	169.00	676.00

LEGEND
HICN (health insurance claim number)
SERV DATES (dates of service)
POS (place-of-service code)
PROC (CPT procedure/service code)
BILLED (amount provider billed payer)
ALLOWED (amount authorized by payer)
COINS (amount patient paid)
PROVIDER PAID (amount provider was reimbursed by payer)
NET (amount payer paid to provider)
PT RESP (amount patient paid)
ACNT (account number)
ASG Y (patient has authorized provider to accept assignment)
MOA MA01 (indicator that if denied, claim can be appealed)

© Cengage Learning 2013

FIGURE 4-4   Remittance advice (multiple claims)

> **NOTE:** Use the remittance advice in Figure 4-5 to answer questions 16 through 20.

16. What does the abbreviation "NET" represent, according to the legend at the bottom of the remittance advice?
17. How much was the allowed amount for code 11442?
18. What was the total coinsurance amount paid on the Figure 4-5 remittance advice?
19. How much is patient Paulette Melfi's coinsurance amount for her visit on 05/01/YY?
20. What is patient Susan Brisbane's account number?

> **NOTE:** Use the remittance advice in Figure 4-6 to answer questions 21 through 25.

21. How much was Dr. Horne paid by the insurance company for patient Jason Brook's visit?
22. What is Dr. Horne's provider number?
23. What is the telephone number for White Health Care Systems?
24. How much did the provider bill the insurance company for the care of patient Jason Brook?
25. What does "POS" represent, according to the legend at the bottom of the remittance advice?

> **NOTE:** Use the remittance advice in Figure 4-7 to answer questions 26 through 30.

26. What is Dr. Brown's title?
27. What was the date of service for Kathleen Smith's visit?
28. On what date was the remittance advice generated?
29. How many patient visits were listed for 05/22/YY?
30. How much was the allowed amount for code 30300?

ASSIGNMENT 4.4   Payment of Claims: Explanation of Benefits

OBJECTIVES

At the conclusion of this assignment, the student should be able to:

1. Explain the purpose of an explanation of benefits.
2. Interpret data contained in an explanation of benefits.

OVERVIEW

Once the claims adjudication process has been finalized, the claim is either denied or approved for payment. The patient receives an explanation of benefits (EOB), which contains information about the claim with regard to what was paid by the insurance company and what amount (if any) is the patient's responsibility for payment. The patient should review the explanation of benefits to make sure that there are no errors. If the patient detects an error, the patient may contact the provider's office and speak with a health insurance specialist for assistance and resubmission of a corrected claim as necessary.

> **NOTE:** If the physician is a nonparticipating provider (nonPAR), the office will not receive a remittance advice from Medicare. To assist patients in obtaining Medicare reimbursement so that they can pay the bills mailed to them by the physician's office, the insurance specialist will need to review the EOB that the patient received from Medicare. This exercise provides students with practice interpreting an EOB.

UPAY INSURANCE COMPANY
1000 MAIN STREET
BOSTON, MASSACHUSETTS 02100
1-800-555-5432

REMITTANCE ADVICE

GEORGE WILLIAMS, M.D.
25 SOUTH STREET
NORFOLK, VIRGINIA 23500

PROVIDER #:   21137
DATE: 05/31/YY
CHECK #:   665821

	SERV DATES		PROC	Code(s)	BILLED	ALLOWED		COINS	REIMB
BRISBANE, SUSAN	HICN 125692479		ACNT BRIS396715-01			ASG	Y		
456212UPAY	05/01	05/01/YY	11	11402	105.00	100.00		20.00	80.00
PT RESP: 20.00		CLAIM TOTAL: 105.00							NET: 80.00
MELFI, PAULETTE	HICN 746931251		ACNT MELF551374-02			ASG	Y		
221123UPAY	05/01	05/01/YY	11	99211	40.00	25.00		0.00	25.00
PT RESP: 0.00		CLAIM TOTAL: 40.00							NET: 25.00
SWANSON, LYNN	HICN 446285791		ACNT SWAN333333-01			ASG	Y		
821547UPAY	05/06	05/06/YY	11	11442	220.00	190.00		38.00	152.00
PT RESP: 38.00		CLAIM TOTAL: 220.00							NET: 152.00
WILSON, STACEY	HICN 020868543		ACNT WILS211232-01			ASG	Y		
323215UPAY	05/08	05/08/YY	11	99203	140.00	125.00		15.00	110.00
PT RESP: 15.00		CLAIM TOTAL: 140.00							NET: 110.00
ZIGLER, PEGGY	HICN 702515313		ACNT ZIGL945625-03			ASG	Y		
565981UPAY	05/10	05/10/YY	11	11720	75.00	70.00		10.00	60.00
PT RESP: 10.00		CLAIM TOTAL: 75.00							NET: 60.00

TOTALS:

# BILLED CLAIMS:	BILLED AMOUNT:	ALLOWED AMOUNT:	COINS AMOUNT:	NET AMOUNT:
5	580.00	510.00	83.00	427.00

LEGEND
HICN (health insurance claim number)
SERV DATES (dates of service)
POS (place-of-service code)
PROC (CPT procedure/service code)
BILLED (amount provider billed payer)
ALLOWED (amount authorized by payer)
COINS (amount patient paid)
PROVIDER PAID (amount provider was reimbursed by payer)
NET (amount payer paid to provider)
PT RESP (amount patient paid)
ACNT (account number)
ASG Y (patient has authorized provider to accept assignment)
MOA MA01 (indicator that if denied, claim can be appealed)

© Cengage Learning 2013

FIGURE 4-5 Remittance advice (multiple claims)

```
WHITE HEALTH CARE SYSTEMS
500 SEASIDE LANE
SAN FRANCISCO, CALIFORNIA 94100
1-800-555-2468                                                  REMITTANCE ADVICE

DAVID HORNE, M.D.                                               PROVIDER #:   31055
1 EYEBALL LANE                                                  DATE :        05/31/YY
ORLANDO, FLORIDA 31000                                         CHECK #:      26854
```

	SERV DATES		POS	PROC	BILLED		ALLOWED	COINS	REIMB
BROOK, JASON	HICN 123456789	ACNT BROO444444-01			ASG	Y			
WHCS242678	05/15	05/15/YY	11	99203	112.00		95.00	20.00	75.00
PT RESP: 20.00		CLAIM TOTAL: 112.00							NET: 75.00
CAPTAIN, TERESA	HICN 875123466	ACNT CAPT5881125			ASG	Y			
WHCS082543	05/16	05/16/YY	11	65205	80.00		72.00	15.00	57.00
PT RESP: 15.00		CLAIM TOTAL: 80.00							NET: 57.00

TOTALS:

# BILLED CLAIMS:	BILLED AMOUNT:	ALLOWED AMOUNT:	COINS AMOUNT:	NET AMOUNT:
2	192.00	167.00	35.00	132.00

LEGEND

HICN (health insurance claim number)
SERV DATES (dates of service)
POS (place-of-service code)
PROC (CPT procedure/service code)
BILLED (amount provider billed payer)
ALLOWED (amount authorized by payer)
COINS (amount patient paid)
PROVIDER PAID (amount provider was reimbursed by payer)
NET (amount payer paid to provider)
PT RESP (amount patient paid)
ACNT (account number)
ASG Y (patient has authorized provider to accept assignment)
MOA MA01 (indicator that if denied, claim can be appealed)

FIGURE 4-6   Remittance advice (multiple claims)

INSTRUCTIONS

Review the EOB forms in Figures 4-8 through 4-12 to familiarize yourself with the organization and the comments.

> **NOTE:** Use the EOB in Figure 4-8 to answer questions 1 through 5.

1. How much was The Keystone Plan charged for Mary S. Patient's visit of 04/05/YYYY?
2. How much has Mary S. Patient paid out of pocket year to date?
3. What is Mary S. Patient's identification number?
4. What was the allowed amount charged by Dr. Miller for Mary S. Patient's visit of 04/05/YY?
5. What is Mary S. Patient's annual medical/surgical deductible, according to the explanation of benefits?

SOUTHWEST ADMINISTRATORS
24 HOUR STREET
MIAMI, FLORIDA 33010
1-800-555-6789

MARK BROWN, D.O.
1500 ANGLER BOULEVARD
NORFOLK, VIRGINIA 23500

REMITTANCE ADVICE

PROVIDER # : 21137
DATE: 05/31/YY
CHECK #:   665821

	SERV DATES	POS	PROC	BILLED	ALLOWED	COINS	REIMB
BRISTER, SUZETTE	HICN 121113659	ACNT BRIS061667-04			ASG Y	MOA	MA01
SA4452814	05/20 05/20/YY	11	99214	135.00	120.00	0.00	120.00
PT RESP: 0.00	CLAIM TOTAL: 135.00						NET: 120.00
SMITH, KATHLEEN	HICN 112167258	ACNT SMIT081159-05			ASG Y	MOA	MA01
SA216552	05/22 05/22/YY	11	99212	90.00	75.00	5.00	70.00
PT RESP: 5.00	CLAIM TOTAL: 90.00						NET: 70.00
WHITE, AMOS	HICN 020347181	ACNT WHIT020347-03			ASG Y	MOA	MA01
SA12300405	05/22 05/22/YY	11	30300	75.00	65.00	15.00	50.00
PT RESP: 15.00	CLAIM TOTAL: 75.00						NET: 50.00

TOTALS:

# BILLED CLAIMS:	BILLED AMOUNT:	ALLOWED AMOUNT:	COINS AMOUNT:	NET AMOUNT:
3	300.00	260.00	20.00	240.00

LEGEND
HICN (health insurance claim number)
SERV DATES (dates of service)
POS (place-of-service code)
PROC (CPT procedure/service code)
BILLED (amount provider billed payer)
ALLOWED (amount authorized by payer)
COINS (amount patient paid)
PROVIDER PAID (amount provider was reimbursed by payer)
NET (amount payer paid to provider)
PT RESP (amount patient paid)
ACNT (account number)
ASG Y (patient has authorized provider to accept assignment)
MOA MA01 (indicator that if denied, claim can be appealed)

© Cengage Learning 2013

FIGURE 4-7   Remittance advice (multiple claims)

> **NOTE:** Use the EOB in Figure 4-9 to answer questions 6 through 10.

6. What was the copayment for this encounter?
7. What is the payer's health insurance contract number (HICN)?
8. What amount did Dr. Smith charge for this encounter?
9. What amount did the plan benefit allow for this encounter?
10. What amount did Dr. Smith "write off" for this encounter?

THE KEYSTONE PLAN

P.O. BOX 900
ALFRED NY 14802-0900
(800) 555-9000

DATE:	04/05/YYYY
ID #:	BLS123456789
ENROLLEE:	MARY S. PATIENT
HICN:	300500
BENEFIT PLAN:	STATE OF NEW YORK

MARY S. PATIENT
100 MAIN ST
ALFRED NY 14802

EXPLANATION
OF BENEFITS

SERVICE DETAIL

PATIENT/RELAT CLAIM NUMBER	PROVIDER/ SERVICE	DATE OF SERVICE	AMOUNT CHARGED	NOT COVERED	AMOUNT ALLOWED	COPAY/ DEDUCTIBLE	%	PLAN BENEFITS	REMARK CODE
ENROLLEE 5629587	D MILLER OFFICE VISITS	04/05/YY	60.25		40.25	8.00	100	32.25*	D1

PLAN PAYS	32.25

*THIS IS A COPY OF INFORMATION SENT TO THE PROVIDER. THANK YOU FOR USING THE PARTICIPATING PROVIDER PROGRAM.

REMARK CODE(S) LISTED BELOW ARE REFERENCED IN THE *SERVICE DETAIL* SECTION UNDER THE HEADING *REMARK CODE*

(D1)   THANK YOU FOR USING A NETWORK PROVIDER. WE HAVE APPLIED THE NETWORK CONTRACTED FEE. THE MEMBER IS NOT
RESPONSIBLE FOR THE DIFFERENCE BETWEEN THE AMOUNT CHARGED AND THE AMOUNT ALLOWED BY THE CONTRACT.

BENEFIT PLAN PAYMENT SUMMARY INFORMATION	
D MILLER	$32.25

PATIENT NAME	MEDICAL/SURGICAL DEDUCTIBLE		MEDICAL/SURGICAL OUT OF POCKET		PHYSICAL MEDICINE DEDUCTIBLE	
	ANNUAL DEDUCT	YYYY YEAR TO-DATE	ANNUAL MAXIMUM	YYYY YEAR TO-DATE	ANNUAL DEDUCT	YYYY YEAR TO-DATE
ENROLLEE	$249.00	$0.00	$1804.00	$121.64	$250.00	$0.00

THIS CLAIM WAS PROCESSED IN ACCORDANCE WITH THE TERMS OF YOUR EMPLOYEE BENEFITS PLAN. IN THE EVENT THIS CLAIM HAS BEEN DENIED, IN WHOLE OR IN PART, A REQUEST
FOR REVIEW MAY BE DIRECTED TO THE KEYSTONE PLAN AT THE ALFRED ADDRESS OR PHONE NUMBER SHOWN ABOVE. THE REQUEST FOR REVIEW MUST BE SUBMITTED WITHIN 60 DAYS
AFTER THE CLAIM PAYMENT DATE, OR THE DATE OF THE NOTIFICATION OF DENIAL OF BENEFITS. WHEN REQUESTING A REVIEW, PLEASE STATE WHY YOU BELIEVE THE CLAIM
DETERMINATION OR PRE-CERTIFICATION IMPROPERLY REDUCED OR DENIED YOUR BENEFITS. ALSO, SUBMIT ANY DATA OR COMMENTS TO SUPPORT THE APPEAL.

THIS IS NOT A BILL.

© Cengage Learning 2013

FIGURE 4-8   Sample explanation of benefits (EOB) form

> **NOTE:** Use the EOB in Figure 4-10 to answer questions 11 through 15.

11. What was the date of service for this encounter?
12. What type is the benefit plan on this EOB?
13. What amount did Dr. Smith charge for this encounter?
14. What amount did the patient pay at the time of the encounter?
15. What amount did the payer reimburse Dr. Smith for this encounter?

United HealthCare

P.O. BOX 100
ALFRED NY 14802-0100
(800) 555-1000

JOHN PATIENT
100 MAIN ST
ALFRED NY 14802

DATE:	10/01/YYYY
ID #:	BLS123456789
ENROLLEE:	JOHN PATIENT
HICN:	895632
BENEFIT PLAN:	ALSTOM

EXPLANATION OF BENEFITS

SERVICE DETAIL

PATIENT/RELAT CLAIM NUMBER	PROVIDER/ SERVICE	DATE OF SERVICE	AMOUNT CHARGED	NOT COVERED	AMOUNT ALLOWED	COPAY/ DEDUCTIBLE	%	PLAN BENEFITS	REMARK CODE
ENROLLEE 6759235	D MILLER OFFICE VISIT	06/10/YY	75.00		40.00	18.00	100	22.00	D1

PLAN PAYS	22.00

THIS IS A COPY OF INFORMATION SENT TO THE PROVIDER. THANK YOU FOR USING THE PARTICIPATING PROVIDER PROGRAM.

REMARK CODE(S) LISTED BELOW ARE REFERENCED IN THE *SERVICE DETAIL* SECTION UNDER THE HEADING *REMARK CODE*
(D1)   THANK YOU FOR USING A NETWORK PROVIDER. WE HAVE APPLIED THE NETWORK CONTRACTED FEE. THE MEMBER IS NOT RESPONSIBLE FOR THE DIFFERENCE BETWEEN THE AMOUNT CHARGED AND THE AMOUNT ALLOWED BY THE CONTRACT.

BENEFIT PLAN PAYMENT SUMMARY INFORMATION	
D MILLER	$22.00

PATIENT NAME	MEDICAL/SURGICAL DEDUCTIBLE		MEDICAL/SURGICAL OUT OF POCKET		PHYSICAL MEDICINE DEDUCTIBLE	
	ANNUAL DEDUCT	YYYY YEAR TO-DATE	ANNUAL MAXIMUM	YYYY YEAR TO-DATE	ANNUAL DEDUCT	YYYY YEAR TO-DATE
ENROLLEE	$850.00	$0.00	$2500.00	$1699.50	$1250.00	$0.00

THIS CLAIM WAS PROCESSED IN ACCORDANCE WITH THE TERMS OF YOUR EMPLOYEE BENEFITS PLAN. IN THE EVENT THIS CLAIM HAS BEEN DENIED, IN WHOLE OR IN PART, A REQUEST FOR REVIEW MAY BE DIRECTED TO THE KEYSTONE PLAN AT THE ALFRED ADDRESS OR PHONE NUMBER SHOWN ABOVE. THE REQUEST FOR REVIEW MUST BE SUBMITTED WITHIN 60 DAYS AFTER THE CLAIM PAYMENT DATE, OR THE DATE OF THE NOTIFICATION OF DENIAL OF BENEFITS. WHEN REQUESTING A REVIEW, PLEASE STATE WHY YOU BELIEVE THE CLAIM DETERMINATION OR PRE-CERTIFICATION IMPROPERLY REDUCED OR DENIED YOUR BENEFITS. ALSO, SUBMIT ANY DATA OR COMMENTS TO SUPPORT THE APPEAL.

THIS IS NOT A BILL.

FIGURE 4-9   Explanation of benefits (EOB)

NOTE: Use the EOB in Figure 4-11 to answer questions 16 through 20.

16. What is Ima Gayle's identification number?
17. What was the allowed amount charged by Dr. Raja for Ima Gayle's visit of 03/05/YY?
18. What is Ima Gayle's annual medical/surgical deductible, according to the EOB?
19. What was the date of service for this encounter?
20. How much has Ima Gayle paid year to date for her medical/surgical out of pocket?

Aetna

P.O. BOX 500
ALFRED NY 14802-0500
(800) 555-5000

DATE:	10/01/YYYY
ID #:	BLS123456789
ENROLLEE:	CINDY MATTESON
HICN:	123XYZ
BENEFIT PLAN:	COMMERCIAL

CINDY MATTESON
5 GREENE ST
ALFRED NY 14802

EXPLANATION OF BENEFITS

SERVICE DETAIL

PATIENT/RELAT CLAIM NUMBER	PROVIDER/ SERVICE	DATE OF SERVICE	AMOUNT CHARGED	NOT COVERED	AMOUNT ALLOWED	COPAY/ DEDUCTIBLE	%	PLAN BENEFITS	REMARK CODE
ENROLLEE 5629587	A SMITH OFFICE VISIT	09/01/YY	875.00		367.00	18.00	100	349.00	D1
						PLAN PAYS		349.00	

*THIS IS A COPY OF INFORMATION SENT TO THE PROVIDER. THANK YOU FOR USING THE PARTICIPATING PROVIDER PROGRAM.

REMARK CODE(S) LISTED BELOW ARE REFERENCED IN THE *SERVICE DETAIL* SECTION UNDER THE HEADING *REMARK CODE*
(D1)   THANK YOU FOR USING A NETWORK PROVIDER. WE HAVE APPLIED THE NETWORK CONTRACTED FEE. THE MEMBER IS NOT RESPONSIBLE FOR THE DIFFERENCE BETWEEN THE AMOUNT CHARGED AND THE AMOUNT ALLOWED BY THE CONTRACT.

BENEFIT PLAN PAYMENT SUMMARY INFORMATION	
A SMITH	$349.00

PATIENT NAME	MEDICAL/SURGICAL DEDUCTIBLE		MEDICAL/SURGICAL OUT OF POCKET		PHYSICAL MEDICINE DEDUCTIBLE	
	ANNUAL DEDUCT	YYYY YEAR TO-DATE	ANNUAL MAXIMUM	YYYY YEAR TO-DATE	ANNUAL DEDUCT	YYYY YEAR TO-DATE
ENROLLEE	$850.00	$875.00	$2500.00	$1699.50	$1250.00	$0.00

THIS CLAIM WAS PROCESSED IN ACCORDANCE WITH THE TERMS OF YOUR EMPLOYEE BENEFITS PLAN. IN THE EVENT THIS CLAIM HAS BEEN DENIED, IN WHOLE OR IN PART, A REQUEST FOR REVIEW MAY BE DIRECTED TO THE KEYSTONE PLAN AT THE ALFRED ADDRESS OR PHONE NUMBER SHOWN ABOVE. THE REQUEST FOR REVIEW MUST BE SUBMITTED WITHIN 60 DAYS AFTER THE CLAIM PAYMENT DATE, OR THE DATE OF THE NOTIFICATION OF DENIAL OF BENEFITS. WHEN REQUESTING A REVIEW, PLEASE STATE WHY YOU BELIEVE THE CLAIM DETERMINATION OR PRE-CERTIFICATION IMPROPERLY REDUCED OR DENIED YOUR BENEFITS. ALSO, SUBMIT ANY DATA OR COMMENTS TO SUPPORT THE APPEAL.

THIS IS NOT A BILL.

© Cengage Learning 2013

FIGURE 4-10   Explanation of benefits (EOB)

> **NOTE:** Use the EOB in Figure 4-12 to answer questions 21 through 25.

21. What is Jose Raul's annual medical/surgical deductible, according to the EOB?

22. How much was Bell Atlantic charged for Jose X. Raul's visit of 06/25/YY?

23. What amount did the patient pay at the time of the encounter for visit 06/20/YY?

24. What amount did Dr. Cardiac "write off" for this encounter?

25. What is the telephone number for Bell Atlantic?

CONN GENERAL

P.O. BOX 800
ALFRED NY 14802-0900
(800) 555-8000

IMA GAYLE
101 HAPPY DRIVE
ANYWHERE NY 12345-1234

DATE: 04/01/YY
ID #: 2100010121
ENROLLEE: IMA GAYLE
HICN: 300400
BENEFIT PLAN: STATE OF NEW YORK

EXPLANATION OF BENEFITS

SERVICE DETAIL

PATIENT/RELAT CLAIM NUMBER	PROVIDER/ SERVICE	DATE OF SERVICE	AMOUNT CHARGED	NOT COVERED	AMOUNT ALLOWED	COPAY/ DEDUCTIBLE	%	PLAN BENEFITS	REMARK CODE
ENROLLEE 0930194	S RAJA OFFICE VISIT	03/05/YY	85.00		60.00	12.00	100	48.00	D1
						PLAN PAYS		48.00	

THIS IS A COPY OF INFORMATION SENT TO THE PROVIDER. THANK YOU FOR USING THE PARTICIPATING PROVIDER PROGRAM.

REMARK CODE(S) LISTED BELOW ARE REFERENCED IN THE *SERVICE DETAIL* SECTION UNDER THE HEADING *REMARK CODE*

(D1)   THANK YOU FOR USING A NETWORK PROVIDER. WE HAVE APPLIED THE NETEWORK CONTRACTED FEE. THE MEMBER IS NOT RESPONSIBLE FOR THE DIFFERENCE BETWEEN THE AMOUNT CHARGED AND THE AMOUNT ALLOWED BY THE CONTRACT.

BENEFIT PLAN PAYMENT SUMMARY INFORMATION
S RAJA $48.00

PATIENT NAME	MEDICAL/SURGICAL DEDUCTIBLE		MEDICAL/SURGICAL OUT OF POCKET		PHYSICAL MEDICINE DEDUCTIBLE	
	ANNUAL DEDUCT	YYYY YEAR TO-DATE	ANNUAL MAXIMUM	YYYY YEAR TO-DATE	ANNUAL DEDUCT	YYYY YEAR TO-DATE
ENROLLEE	$100.00	$0.00	$1500.00	$80.00	$250.00	$0.00

THIS CLAIM WAS PROCESSED IN ACCORDANCE WITH THE TERMS OF YOUR EMPLOYEE BENEFITS PLAN. IN THE EVEN THIS CLAIM HAS BEEN DENIED, IN WHOLE OR IN PART, A REQUEST FOR REVIEW MAY BE DIRECTED TO THE KEYSTONE PLAN AT THE ALFRED ADDRESS OR PHONE NUMBER SHOWN ABOVE. THE REQUEST FOR REVIEW MUST BE SUBMITTED WITHIN 60 DAYS AFTER THE CLAIM PAYMENT DATE, OR THE DATE OF THE NOTIFICATION OF DENIAL OF BENEFITS. WHEN REQUESTING A REVIEW, PLEASE STATE WHY YOU BELIEVE THE CLAIM DETERMINATION OR PRE-CERTIFICATION IMPROPERLY REDUCED OR DENIED YOUR BENEFITS. ALSO, SUBMIT ANY DATA OR COMMENTS TO SUPPORT THE APPEAL.

THIS IS NOT A BILL.

FIGURE 4-11   Explanation of benefits (EOB)

BELL ATLANTIC

P.O. BOX 600
ALFRED NY 14802-0900
(800) 555-6000

JOSE X RAUL
10 MAIN STREET
ANYWHERE NY 12345-1234

DATE: 07/19/YY
ID #: 222304040
ENROLLEE: JOSE X RAUL
HICN: J5987558
BENEFIT PLAN: STATE OF NEW YORK

EXPLANATION OF BENEFITS

SERVICE DETAIL

PATIENT CLAIM NUMBER	PROVIDER/ SERVICE	DATE OF SERVICE	AMOUNT CHARGED	NOT COVERED	AMOUNT ALLOWED	COPAY/ DEDUCTIBLE	%	PLAN BENEFITS	REMARK CODE
ENROLLEE 0101196	H CARDIAC OFFICE VISIT	06/20/YY	60.00		47.00	10.00	100	37.00	D1
	OFFICE VISIT	06/25/YY	60.00		47.00	10.00	100	37.00	D1
						PLAN PAYS		74.00	

THIS IS A COPY OF INFORMATION SENT TO THE PROVIDER. THANK YOU FOR USING THE PARTICIPATING PROVIDER PROGRAM.

REMARK CODE(S) LISTED BELOW ARE REFE RENCED IN THE *SERVICE DETAIL* SECTION UNDER THE HEADING *REMARK CODE*
(D1)   THANK YOU FOR USING A NETWORK PROVIDER. WE HAVE APPLIED THE NETEWORK CONTRACTED FEE. THE MEMBER IS NOT RESPONSIBLE FOR THE DIFFERENCE BETWEEN THE AMOUNT CHARGED AND THE AMOUNT ALLOWED BY THE CONTRACT.

BENEFIT PLAN PAYMENT SUMMARY INFORMATION

H CARDIAC	$74.00

PATIENT NAME	MEDICAL/SURGICAL DEDUCTIBLE		MEDICAL/SURGICAL OUT OF POCKET		PHYSICAL MEDICINE DEDUCTIBLE	
	ANNUAL DEDUCT	YYYY YEAR TO-DATE	ANNUAL MAXIMUM	YYYY YEAR TO-DATE	ANNUAL DEDUCT	YYYY YEAR TO-DATE
ENROLLEE	$150.00	$25.00	$1000.00	$0.00	$150.00	$0.00

THIS CLAIM WAS PROCESSED IN ACCORDANCE WITH THE TERMS OF YOUR EMPLOYEE BENEFITS PLAN. IN THE EVEN THIS CLAIM HAS BEEN DENIED, IN WHOLE OR IN PART, A REQUEST FOR REVIEW MAY BE DIRECTED TO THE KEYSTONE PLAN AT THE ALFRED ADDRESS OR PHONE NUMBER SHOWN ABOVE. THE REQUEST FOR REVIEW MUST BE SUBMITTED WITHIN 60 DAYS AFTER THE CLAIM PAYMENT DATE, OR THE DATE OF THE NOTIFICATION OF DENIAL OF BENEFITS. WHEN REQUESTING A REVIEW, PLEASE STATE WHY YOU BELIEVE THE CLAIM DETERMINATION OR PRE-CERTIFICATION IMPROPERLY REDUCED OR DENIED YOUR BENEFITS. ALSO, SUBMIT ANY DATA OR COMMENTS TO SUPPORT THE APPEAL.

THIS IS NOT A BILL.

© Cengage Learning 2013

FIGURE 4-12 Explanation of benefits (EOB)

ASSIGNMENT 4.5   Writing Appeal Letters

OBJECTIVES

At the conclusion of this assignment, the student should be able to:

1. Review a remittance advice to determine claims submission errors that resulted in payment denials.
2. Prepare appeal letters that explain why a resubmitted claim should be reconsidered for third-party payer payment.

OVERVIEW

An appeal is documented as a letter signed by the provider explaining why a claim should be reconsidered for payment. If appropriate, copies of medical record documentation are included with the appeal letter (for which the patient has signed a release-of-information authorization). A remittance advice (Figure 4-13) indicates payment denials for reasons other than processing errors, which may include (1) procedure or service not medically necessary, (2) pre-existing condition not covered, (3) non-covered benefit, (4) termination of coverage, (5) failure to obtain preauthorization, (6) out-of-network provider used, or (7) lower level of care could have been provided.

When starting the appeal process, review the provider's documentation in the medical record is accurate, clear and complete. A copy of pertinent portions of the medical record may need to be included with the appeal letter. When preparing appeal letters (Figure 4-14 and Figure 4-15), include the following information:

- Patient demographic information
- Third-party payer information
- Date of service or procedure
- Place of service or procedure
- Remittance advice denial code and reason
- Proof of medical necessity of the service or procedure

Sending the appeal letter via certified mail ensures that the office has a record of its receipt by the third-party payer.

INSTRUCTIONS

1. Review the remittance advice (Figure 4-13), and circle the *payment denial reason codes*.
2. Determine whether each *payment denial reason code* would result in writing a(n):

- Appeal letter to the third-party payer (Figure 4-14).
- Collection letter to the patient (Figure 4-15).

3. Refer to the sample letters in Figure 4-14 and Figure 4-15, and prepare appeal letter(s) and/or collection letter(s) for each *payment denial reason code*. (Do not prepare provider letters of medical necessity.)

US HEALTH
100 MAIN STREET
ALFRED NY 14802

Remittance Advice

DATE: 05/25/YYYY
(800) 555-1234
FAX: (800) 555-4321

ERIN A HELPER MD
101 MEDIC DRIVE
ANYWHERE NY 12345

PAGE#: 1 OF 1

PROVIDER#: 98979697
CHECK#: 1121314

PATIENT: DOVER, AILEEN   **ACCOUNT#:** DOVER123456-01
                                HICN: 1231199091

Service Date	POS	CPT	Billed	Allowed	Copay/Coins	ASG	Paid	Adjustment	Reason Code(s)
0416YYYY	11	99212	45.00	34.00	0.00	Y	34.00	11.00	001
Totals:			45.00	34.00	0.00		34.00	11.00	NET: 34.00

PATIENT: SHOWER, ANITA   **ACCOUNT#:** SHOWER778899-01
                                HICN: 1234587702

Service Date	POS	CPT	Billed	Allowed	Copay/Coins	ASG	Paid	Adjustment	Reason Code(s)
0409YYYY	11	99211	40.00	35.00	10.00	Y	25.00	5.00	001
0409YYYY	11	81003	12.00	0.00	0.00	Y	0.00	12.00	005
Totals:			52.00	35.00	10.00		25.00	17.00	NET: 25.00

PATIENT: LOTT, NOAH   **ACCOUNT#:** LOTT556633-01
                             HICN: 5758594631

Service Date	POS	CPT	Billed	Allowed	Copay/Coins	ASG	Paid	Adjustment	Reason Code(s)
0407YYYY	11	99213	60.00	0.00	0.00	Y	0.00	0.00	002, 003
Totals:			60.00	0.00	0.00		0.00	0.00	NET: 0.00

PATIENT: PAYNE, OPHELIA   **ACCOUNT#:** PAYNE223344-01
                                 HICN: 4263355970

Service Date	POS	CPT	Billed	Allowed	Copay/Coins	ASG	Paid	Adjustment	Reason Code(s)
0429YYYY	11	74270	118.00	0.00	0.00	Y	0.00	0.00	005
Totals:			118.00	0.00	0.00		0.00	0.00	NET: 0.00

LEGEND

ASG   Accept assignment
             Y = Provider accepts assignment
             N = Provider does not accept assignment
Copay/Coins Copayment or coinsurance amount paid by patient
CPT   Current Procedural Terminology (CPT code number)
POS   Place of Service
             11 = Provider's office

Reason Codes

001 Patient receives discount—care received from in-network provider
002 Denied—invalid HICN number
003 Denied—termination of coverage
004 Denied—procedure or service not covered
005 Denied—service not medically necessary
006 Covered service—no charge

FIGURE 4-13   Remittance advice

ERIN A. HELPER M.D.

101 MEDIC DRIVE, ANYWHERE NY 12345

(800) 555-1234 (OFFICE)   (800) 555-4321 (FAX)

May 5, YYYY

Name of Patient: **Mary Jane Shumway**
HICN: **987456321**

To Whom It May Concern:

Per our review of the remittance advice dated **May 1, YYYY**, please accept this letter as an appeal of the **Blue Cross Blue Shield** decision to deny payment for services provided on **April 18, YYYY** due to reason code **005 (service not medically necessary)**.

Attached for your review is the **provider's letter of medical necessity, which includes a description of services rendered and reasons for services**. **Also attached is a copy of the patient's record for services provided on April 18, YYYY**. Please review the attached information and reprocess the outstanding claim immediately.

If you have any questions, please contact me at (800) 555-1234. Thank you for your prompt attention to this matter.

Sincerely,

Sandy Schilling

Sandy Schilling, CPC-P
Medical Billing Specialist

FIGURE 4-14   Sample appeal letter to patient

ERIN A. HELPER M.D.
101 MEDIC DRIVE, ANYWHERE NY 12345
(800) 555-1234 (OFFICE)   (800) 555-4321 (FAX)

May 5, YYYY

Jane Samson
5 Main St
Somewhere NY 12367

Dear Ms. Samson,

The CMS-1500 insurance claim that our office submitted on your behalf to **Blue Cross Blue Shield** for services provided during your visit on **April 1, YYYY** was denied and returned due to an **invalid insurance ID number**, which means the insurance company will not send reimbursement to our office.

Please call our office to provide a **valid insurance ID number**. Should the ID number you provide match that which was submitted on the CMS-1500 insurance claim, **Blue Cross Blue Shield** will deny a resubmitted claim. Thus, per the advance beneficiary notice that you signed prior to our providing services to you on **April 15, YYYY**, you will receive an invoice in the amount of **$150.00** that must be paid promptly.

If you have any questions please to contact me at (800) 555-1234. Thank you for your prompt attention to this matter.

Sincerely,

Sandy Schilling

Sandy Schilling, CPC-P
Medical Billing Specialist

FIGURE 4-15   Sample collection letter to patient

ASSIGNMENT 4.6   Multiple Choice Review

1. **Which is an example of supporting documentation?**
   a. completed CMS-1500 claim form
   b. explanation of benefits
   c. operative report
   d. remittance advice

2. **Supporting documentation that is attached to the CMS-1500 is either copied from the patient's chart or developed (e.g., letter delineating unlisted service provided). The latter is referred to (in the CPT coding manual) as a(n) _____.**
   a. attachment
   b. detailed report
   c. enclosed note
   d. special report

3. **Which claim status is assigned by the payer to allow the provider to correct errors or omissions on the claim and resubmit for payment consideration?**
   a. clean
   b. denied
   c. pending
   d. voided

4. **A public or private entity that processes or facilitates the processing of nonstandard elements into standard data elements is called a**
   a. clearinghouse.
   b. covered entity.
   c. network.
   d. third-party administrator.

5. **The intent of mandating HIPAA's national standards for electronic transactions was to**
   a. decrease the costs associated with Medicare and Medicaid programs.
   b. improve the continuity and the quality of care provided to patients.
   c. improve the efficiency and effectiveness of the healthcare system.
   d. increase the number of individuals enrolled in government health plans.

6. **Electronic claims are**
   a. always submitted by health insurance professionals who are certified by the AAPC.
   b. checked for accuracy by billing software programs or a healthcare clearinghouse.
   c. not complicated by such requirements as claims attachments or other documents.
   d. submitted directly to payers for the processing of reimbursement to patients.

7. **Which CPT modifier will require supporting documentation for payment?**
   a. -22 (unusual procedural services)
   b. -26 (professional component)
   c. -50 (bilateral procedure)
   d. -57 (decision for surgery)

8. **Patients can be billed for**
   a. extended procedures.
   b. noncovered procedures.
   c. reduced services.
   d. unauthorized services.

9. **If the claim was denied because the service is not covered by the payer, the claim is _____.**
   a. appealed by the provider's office
   b. filed with a clearinghouse instead
   c. not paid by the third-party payer
   d. submitted to a third-party administrator

10. **The person in whose name the insurance policy is issued is the**
    a. patient.
    b. plan.
    c. policyholder.
    d. provider.

11. **The life cycle of an insurance claim is initiated when the**
    a. health insurance specialist completes the CMS-1500 claim.
    b. patient pays the balance due after the provider has been reimbursed.
    c. payer sends the provider an electronic remittance advice.
    d. provider sends supporting documentation for unusual services.

12. **Which form is considered the financial source document?**
    a. history and physical exam
    b. patient registration
    c. statement of charges
    d. superbill or encounter form

13. **Another name for the patient account record is the patient**
    a. day sheet.
    b. encounter form.
    c. explanation of benefits.
    d. ledger.

14. **A chronological summary of all transactions posted to individual patient accounts on a specific day is recorded on a(n)**
    a. day sheet.
    b. encounter form.
    c. patient ledger.
    d. remittance advice.

15. **What special handling is required if a patient requests a copy of the remittance advice (RA) that contains information about multiple patients?**
    a. Patients are not permitted to view or receive copies of the RA.
    b. Remove identifying information about all patients except the requesting patient.
    c. The patient must sign a confidentiality statement prior to receiving a copy of the RA.
    d. The provider must document the request for a copy of the RA in the patient's record.

16. **Which federal law protects consumers against harassing or threatening phone calls from collectors?**
    a. Fair Credit and Charge Card Disclosure Act
    b. Fair Credit Billing Act
    c. Fair Credit Reporting Act
    d. Fair Debt Collection Practices Act

17. **The time period between the point at which a claim is submitted and when the claim is paid is called the _____ period.**
    a. aging
    b. collection
    c. delinquent
    d. past-due

18. **The provision in group health insurance policies that specifies in what sequence coverage will be provided when more than one policy covers the claim is**
    a. accepting assignment.
    b. assignment of benefits.
    c. claims adjudication.
    d. coordination of benefits.

19. **A clearinghouse that coordinates with other entities to provide additional services during the processing of claims is a**
    a. claims processor.
    b. network commission.
    c. third-party administrator.
    d. value-added network.

20. **To determine if a patient is receiving concurrent care for the same condition by more than one provider, the payer will check the claim against the**
    a. common data file.
    b. electronic flat file.
    c. insurance claims registry.
    d. patient's billing history.

CHAPTER 5
Legal and Regulatory Issues

INTRODUCTION

This chapter emphasizes the importance of maintaining the confidentiality of protected health information (or patient information). In addition, students will review case studies to determine if healthcare fraud or abuse was present.

ASSIGNMENT 5.1   HIPAA: Student Confidentiality Statement

OBJECTIVES

At the conclusion of this assignment, the student should be able to:

1. Explain the importance of maintaining the confidentiality of patient information.
2. State the significance of signing a student confidentiality statement prior to beginning a professional practice experience (or internship).

OVERVIEW

Health insurance specialist students who complete professional practice experiences (or internships) as part of their course of study will have access to protected health information (PHI) at the provider's office. It is essential that students maintain the confidentiality of PHI at all times. This assignment allows the student to review and sign a student confidentiality statement.

INSTRUCTIONS

1. Carefully review the student confidentiality statement in Figure 5-1.
2. Sign and date the statement, and have a witness sign and date the form.
3. Submit the completed form to your instructor.

ASSIGNMENT 5.2   HIPAA: Preventing Healthcare Fraud and Abuse

---

OBJECTIVES

At the conclusion of this assignment, the student should be able to:

1. Define healthcare fraud and abuse.
2. Differentiate between forms of healthcare fraud and abuse.

OVERVIEW

The Health Insurance Portability and Accountability Act (HIPAA) defines *fraud* as "an intentional deception or misrepresentation that someone makes, knowing it is false, that could result in an unauthorized payment." *Abuse* "involves actions that are inconsistent with accepted, sound medical, business or fiscal practices."

PROTECTED HEALTH INFORMATION (PHI) CONFIDENTIALITY STATEMENT

In consideration of my status as a student at _____ and/or association with healthcare facilities and provider offices that offer internship opportunities, I agree that I will not at any time access or use protected health information, or reveal or disclose to any persons within or outside the healthcare facility or provider office, any protected health information except as may be required in the course of my duties and responsibilities and in accordance with applicable legislation, and corporate and departmental policies governing proper release of information.

I understand that my obligations outlined above will continue after my association with the school and/or facility ends. I further understand that my obligations concerning the protection of the confidentiality of health information relate to all protected health information whether I acquired the information through my association with the school and/or facility.

I also understand that unauthorized use or disclosure of such information will result in a disciplinary action up to and including involuntary expulsion from the school, the imposition of fines pursuant to relevant state and federal legislation, and a report to my professional regulatory body.

_____

Date Signed

_____

Date Signed

_____

Signature of Student

_____

Student's Printed Name

_____

Signature of Witness

FIGURE 5-1 Student confidentiality statement

INSTRUCTIONS

Review Chapter 5 content in your textbook to familiarize yourself with examples of fraud and abuse. Then determine whether each situation below is fraud (F) or abuse (A).

_____ 1. An insurance company did not follow applicable rules when setting rates it charged for healthcare benefits under its Federal Employees Health Benefits Program (FEHBP) contracts, and failed to give the healthcare program the same discounted rates it gave similarly situated commercial customers. It also failed to coordinate FEHBP benefits with those provided to Medicare eligible annuitants and submitted statements to the Office of Personnel Management (OPM) that failed to fully disclose rate adjustments due to FEHBP.

_____ 2. The state of California and the county of Los Angeles billed Medicaid for services provided to minors when these jurisdictions had no basis for concluding that these individuals financially qualified for Medicaid services. The services at issue in this matter were treatment for drug and alcohol abuse, pregnancy and pregnancy-related services, family planning, sexual assault treatment, sexually transmitted diseases treatment, and mental health services.

_____3. A physician documented the medical necessity of a number of medical supplies for a patient's care in the office. Upon review, Medicare denied reimbursement for the claim, stating that the number of medical supplies ordered was excessive.

_____4. An insurance company failed to process Medicare claims properly, and then submitted false information to CMS regarding the accuracy of and the timeliness with which it had handled those claims.

_____5. The provider ordered a number of the same laboratory tests on several different patients, carefully documenting the medical necessity of each. Upon review, Medicare determined that half of the patients did not need to have those tests performed, and reimbursement was denied.

_____6. An insurance company breached its Medicare contract by failing to report errors identified in the quality assurance process. It concealed its true error rate by deleting claims selected for review by CMS and replacing them with claim files that would not significantly affect the error rate (and thus preserve its standing within payer performance rankings).

_____7. A chiropractor performed ultrasonography to follow the progress of a patient treated for back pain. Medicare denied the payment because it determined that this was not a legitimate use for ultrasonography.

_____8. An ambulance company submitted false claims for reimbursement to Medicare.

_____9. A consulting firm submitted false hospital cost reports to the Medicare and Medicaid programs on behalf of its client hospitals. The consulting firm knowingly made claims that were false, exaggerated, or ineligible for payment, and it concealed errors from government auditors, thereby permitting the client hospitals to retain funds to which they were not entitled.

_____10. A spinal videofluoroscopy was performed to demonstrate the extent to which joint motion of a patient was restricted. Medicare determined that physical examination procedures (e.g., asking the patient to bend) provided enough information to guide treatment of the patient and denied reimbursement.

ASSIGNMENT 5.3   HIPAA: Privacy and Security Rules

OBJECTIVES

At the conclusion of this assignment, the student should be able to:
1. Explain the HIPAA privacy and security rules.
2. Differentiate between privacy and security provisions of HIPAA.

OVERVIEW

The _privacy rule_ establishes standards for how protected health information should be controlled, and it establishes the uses (e.g., continuity of care) and disclosures (e.g., third-party reimbursement) authorized or required, as well as the rights patients have with respect to their health information (e.g., patient access). The _security rule_ defines administrative, physical, and technical safeguards to protect the availability, confidentiality, and integrity of electronic PHI. HIPAA provisions require covered entities to implement basic safeguards to protect electronic PHI from unauthorized access, alteration, deletion, and transmission.

INSTRUCTIONS

Determine whether the statements below are associated with the HIPAA privacy rule (P) or the security rule (S).

_____1. Defines authorized users of patient information to control access.

_____2. Implements a tracking procedure to sign out records to authorized personnel.

_____ 3. Establishes fines and penalties for misuse of protected health information.

_____ 4. Limits record storage access to authorized users.

_____ 5. Gives patients greater access to their own medical records and more control over how their personal health information is used.

_____ 6. Creates national standards to protect individuals' medical records and other personal health information.

_____ 7. Requires that record storage areas be locked at all times.

_____ 8. Addresses obligations that physicians, hospitals, and other healthcare providers have to obtain a patient's written consent and an authorization before using or disclosing PHI to carry out treatment, payment, or healthcare operations (TPO).

_____ 9. Exempts psychotherapy notes from a patient's right to access his or her own records.

_____ 10. Requires the original medical record to remain in the facility at all times.

ASSIGNMENT 5.4   Covered Entities

OBJECTIVES

At the conclusion of this assignment, the student should be able to:

1. Discuss and define *covered entities*.
2. Discuss the Office for Civil Rights (OCR).

OVERVIEW

HIPAA has various components known as titles; one of these governs the privacy of protected health information (PHI). The Department of Health and Human Services provides consumers with information via the Internet on privacy rights and laws. This information is provided in the form of fact sheets and publications.

INSTRUCTIONS

Go to the Web site for HIPAA privacy information at **www.hhs.gov** to access information about the Office for Civil Rights and other information related to individual privacy rights. Click on the regulations link, and then click on the links located below Health Information Privacy (HIPAA) to locate answers to the following questions.

1. What three types of covered entities are specified in the HIPAA privacy rule? _____
_____

2. How many regions does the Office for Civil Rights divide the United States into to assign regional offices? _____

3. In what region are the states of Maryland and Virginia? _____
_____

4. In what city is the regional office of the OCR located for region VI? _____
_____

5. In addition to using the Web site, what other method can an individual use to find out more information about his or her privacy rights? _____

NOTE: Navigate the insurance information Web site to research information needed for your summary. This will help you learn how to locate information using the Internet as a research tool and using Web sites, which often requires using tool bars and pull-down menus.

ASSIGNMENT 5.5   Telephone Calls Requesting Release of Patient Information

---

OBJECTIVES

At the conclusion of this assignment, the student should be able to:
1. Explain the protocol for responding to telephone requests for release of patient information.
2. Appropriately respond to verbal requests for patient information.

OVERVIEW

Healthcare professionals receive numerous telephone requests for patient information. This assignment will familiarize students with the appropriate response to a verbal request for patient information.

Instructions

1. Carefully read the telephone simulations in Figure 5-2.
2. Respond to the following questions about each telephone simulation.

Simulation #1

1. How would you rate the RHIT's greeting?

_____

2. Did the RHIT respond appropriately to the patient's request?

_____

3. Do you agree with the RHIT's reason for not releasing records immediately to the new physician? Why or why not?

_____

4. What is the significance of the RHIT using the patient's name during the conversation?

_____

5. What would you have said differently from what was said in the scenario?

_____

Simulation #2

6. How would you rate the MA's phone response?

_____

7. Did the MA respond appropriately to the request?

_____

8. What would you have said differently from what was said in the scenario?

_____

Simulation #3

9. Critique Barbara's greeting.

_____

10. Determine how you would handle this situation if you were Barbara. What would you have done differently, if anything, from the onset?

_____

11. Given the situation, what would you do next?

_____

Simulation #4

12. What information can be released over the telephone?

_____

13. What information should Susie have requested from the caller?

_____

14. What release of information protocol did Susie violate?

_____

SIMULATION #1: The caller is a patient who requests that the health records from her recent hospitalization be forwarded to her new physician in Billings, Montana. The patient, Janice McDonald, has relocated to a suburb of Billings, Montana.

The telephone in the health information department rings three times and the registered health information technician (RHIT) answers the phone.

RHIT [professional tone of voice]: "Good afternoon (morning). Health Information Department. May I help you?"

JANICE [questioning tone of voice]: "Hi! Ummm, this is Janice McDonald. I've moved to Montana and want to get my latest inpatient records sent to my new doctor. Can you do that?"

RHIT [friendly tone of voice]: "Sure, Ms. McDonald. I'll just need to send you a release of information authorization form. You'll need to complete it, sign it, and date it. Then, return it in the envelope provided."

JANICE [confused tone of voice]: "Oh. I'm seeing the new doctor next week. Do you think that you can just send the records to him?"

RHIT [polite tone of voice]: "I'm sorry, Ms. McDonald. Your health records are confidential and we cannot release copies without your written authorization."

JANICE [resigned tone of voice]: "Oh, okay. I guess that will have to do."

RHIT [reassuring tone of voice]: "Ms. McDonald, the department is really just trying to maintain privacy of your records. If you like, I can fax the authorization form to you. Then, you could overnight express it to the department. We can't accept a fax of the completed form because we need your original signature. That's hospital policy."

JANICE [pleased tone of voice]: "Oh! That would be great. I'll call my new doctor and get his fax number and give you a call back with it. Okay?"

RHIT [friendly tone of voice]: "That would be just fine, Ms. McDonald."

The conversation is ended. The RHIT hangs up the phone.

FIGURE 5-2 Telephone simulations

(continues)

FIGURE 5-2   (continued)

SIMULATION #2: Joe Turner from the State Farm Insurance Company is an angry insurance agent who calls to inform the physician's office that the company mailed a proper authorization three weeks ago for release of records on a recently discharged patient.

The telephone rings six times before the medical assistant (MA) answers the phone.

MA [quick professional tone of voice]: "Good afternoon (morning). Doctor's office."

TURNER [brusque tone of voice]: "Hello. I'm calling to find out why the records I requested three weeks ago have not been sent to me yet. Oh. This is Joe Turner from State Farm Insurance Company."

MA [courteous tone of voice—recognizes an impatient person]: "Could you tell me the name of the patient, please?"

TURNER [brusque tone of voice]: "Mary Jones. Her birth date is 10/02/55. She was discharged on September 1 of this year. I need copies of the doctor's notes in order to get the claim paid. She has called me several times this past couple of weeks. I guess the office keeps sending bills for her to pay and she is as disgusted as I am about this situation!"

MA [courteous tone of voice]: "Mr. Turner, would you like to hold while I check this or could I call you back?"

TURNER [brusque tone of voice]: "No way am I going to let you off the hook. I'll hold!"

MA [courteous tone of voice—but showing signs of wear]: "No problem Mr. Turner. I'll be with you in a couple of minutes."

One minute passes and the MA takes Mr. Turner off hold.

MA [pleasant tone of voice]: "Mr. Turner, I checked our correspondence log and found that copies of Mary Jones's records were forwarded to your attention last week. You should have them."

TURNER [impatient tone of voice]: "Well, I don't! Oh . . . I guess they were placed on my desk while I wasn't looking. Here they are. Sorry about that. Goodbye."

Mr. Turner hangs up.

(continues)

FIGURE 5-2 (continued)

SIMULATION #3: Barbara Allen is a new health information technology graduate hired by the medical center's health information management department. This is her first day on the job.

The telephone rings twice and is answered by the department secretary. The call is forwarded to Barbara Allen, correspondence technician.

BARBARA: "Correspondence Section. May I help you?"

DOCTOR: "Hello, this is Dr. Ahbibe from Breyne's Clinic in Columbia, New Mexico. We have a patient here by the name of Garrick Tanner who was admitted for status epilepticus. We need a past history for this patient and all pertinent documents sent to us immediately. The seizure activity is progressing in frequency and the patient is unable to provide information about drug allergies."

BARBARA: "Would you hold while I pull the patient's record?"

DOCTOR: "Certainly."

Several minutes pass as Barbara searches by checking the Master Patient Index (MPI) and retrieving the record. Upon inspection of the record, she realizes that this is a "sealed file" because of a pending lawsuit. She also notes that Garrick Tanner has an extensive history of cocaine abuse that has been the main cause of his seizures. She closes the record, confused as to how she should handle this situation.

SIMULATION #4: Susie Sits is answering the telephone for the correspondence technician who is on break. Susie usually works in the discharge analysis section of the health information department.

The telephone rings twice, and Susie picks up.

SUSIE: "Good morning, Health Information Management Department. Susie Sits speaking."

DOCTOR: "This is Dr. Jones's office calling from Phoenix, Arizona. Could you please give me the final diagnosis for Alfred Peoples, who was recently discharged from your facility?"

SUSIE: "Well, just hold a minute and I will get everything you need."

The doctor is on hold for three minutes while Susie pulls the health record.

SUSIE: "Hello, I think I have everything you need. Mr. Peoples was a patient in our alcohol rehab unit last month."

ASSIGNMENT 5.6   Hospital Inpatient Quality Reporting Program

---

OBJECTIVES

1. Explain the purpose of the hospital inpatient quality reporting program.
2. State the intent of the *Hospital Compare* WebWeb site.
3. Use the *Hospital Compare* WebWeb site.

OVERVIEW

The *Hospital Inpatient Quality Reporting (Hospital IQR) program* was developed to equip consumers with quality of care information so they can make more informed decisions about healthcare options. The Hospital IQR program requires hospitals to submit specific quality measures data about health conditions common among Medicare beneficiaries and that typically result in hospitalization. (Eligible hospitals that do *not* participate in the Hospital IQR program receive an annual market basket update with a 2.0 percentage point reduction.)

The Centers for Medicare and Medicaid Services (CMS) and the Hospital Quality Alliance (HQA) created the *Hospital Compare* Web site in cooperation with the Hospital Quality Alliance (HQA). CMS is an agency of the Department of Health and Human Resources (DHHS), and the HQA is a public-private collaboration established to promote reporting on hospital quality of care. The HQA consists of organizations that represent consumers, hospitals, doctors and nurses, employers, accrediting organizations, and federal agencies.

Hospital Compare displays rates for the following:

- *Process of Care* measures, which indicate whether or not hospitals provide some of the care that is recommended for patients being treated for a heart attack, heart failure, pneumonia, asthma (children only), or patients having surgery. Hospitals submit data from patient records about treatments their patients receive for these conditions.

- *Outcome of Care* measures, which indicate what happened after patients with certain conditions received hospital care. Measures include death rate (whether patients died within 30 days of hospitalization) and readmission rate (whether patients were hospitalized again within 30 days).

- *Use of Medical Imaging*, which provides information about hospitals use medical imaging tests for outpatients based on the (1) protecting patients' safety, such as keeping patients' exposure to radiation and other risks as low as possible; (2) following up properly when screening tests such as mammograms show a possible problem; and (3) avoiding the risk, stress, and cost of doing imaging tests that patients may not need.

- *Survey of Patients' Hospital Experiences*, which is the Hospital Consumer Assessment of Healthcare Providers and Systems (HCAHPS) national, standardized survey of hospital patients. HCAHPS (pronounced "*H-caps*") was created to publicly report the patient's perspective of hospital care. The survey is administered to a random sample of recently discharged patients and asks questions about important aspects of their hospital experience (e.g., communication with doctors, communication with nurses, responsiveness of hospital staff, pain management, communication about medicines, discharge information, cleanliness of the hospital environment, and quietness of the hospital environment).

- *Medicare Payment and Volume*, which displays selected MS-DRG information for each hospital from a pre-determined range of dates (e.g., October 2007 through September 2008). Patients who have similar clinical characteristics and similar costs are assigned to an MS-DRG (Medicare severity diagnosis-related group). The MS-DRG is associated with a fixed payment amount based on the average cost of patients in the group. Patients are assigned to a MS-DRG based on diagnosis, surgical procedures, age, and other information. Medicare uses this information that is provided by hospitals on their bills to decide how much they should be paid.

INSTRUCTIONS

1. Go to http://www.hospitalcompare.hhs.gov.
2. Enter the ZIP Code or City, State of a location (e.g., hometown, city you will move to after graduation, and so on).
3. Select the search type, and click the Find Hospitals link.
4. Click on the Quality of Care tab, select hospitals to compare, and click the Compare link.
5. Review the results displayed, and compare data among the hospitals listed to determine if there is one that whose data is significantly higher or lower than the other.
6. Click on the View Graphs and/or View Tables links to review descriptive statistics about the hospitals.
7. As directed by your instructor, prepare a narrative summary of the results of your findings (e.g., word-processed document, discussion board posting).

ASSIGNMENT 5.7   Multiple Choice Review

---

1. **A provider was ordered by a judge to bring a patient's medical record to a court hearing. Which document was served on the provider instructing him to comply?**
   a. deposition
   b. interrogatory
   c. subpoena duces tecum
   d. subpoena

2. **The type of law passed by legislative bodies is known as _____ law.**
   a. common
   b. criminal
   c. regulatory
   d. statutory

3. **Which civil case document contains a list of questions that must be answered in writing?**
   a. deposition
   b. interrogatory
   c. precedent
   d. regulation

4. **Which federal law has regulated the conduct of any contractor submitting claims for payment to the federal government since 1863?**
   a. False Claims Act
   b. Federal Claims Collection Act
   c. Privacy Act
   d. Social Security Act

5. **The Federal Claims Collection Act requires Medicare administrative contractors to**
   a. attempt to recover any reimbursement funds sent as overpayment to providers and beneficiaries.
   b. enforce civil monetary penalties upon those who submit false or fraudulent claims to the government.
   c. protect the privacy of individuals identified in information systems maintained by government hospitals.
   d. provide free or reduced-charge medical services to persons unable to pay, in return for federal funds.

6. **The Hospital IQR program equips consumers with _____ information so they can make more informed decisions about healthcare options.**
   a. audit performance
   b. healthcare cost
   c. medically unlikely edit
   d. quality of care

7. **The Physicians at Teaching Hospitals (PATH) legislation was passed to**
   a. increase reimbursement amounts paid to teaching hospitals and other types of healthcare facilities.
   b. increase the number of physicians and other healthcare providers available to teach medical students.
   c. limit the types of patients that are seen by medical school residents in PATH healthcare settings.
   d. monitor Medicare rule compliance for payment of Part B services and proper coding and billing practices.

8. **The _____ combats fraud and abuse in health insurance and healthcare delivery by alerting users to conduct a comprehensive review of a practitioner's, provider's, or supplier's past actions.**
   a. Clinical Data Abstracting Center
   b. *Federal Register*
   c. Healthcare Integrity and Protection Data Bank
   d. Peer Review Improvement Act

9. **One of the provisions of HIPAA Title I designed to improve portability and continuity of healthcare coverage is**
   a. excluding enrollment of employees with a history of poor health.
   b. increasing exclusions for preexisting conditions.
   c. prohibiting a change from group to individual coverage.
   d. providing credit for prior health coverage.

10. **Which protects whistleblowers, who are individuals who make specified disclosures relating to funds covered by the Act?**
    a. ARRA
    b. HIPAA
    c. MMA
    d. TEFRA

11. **In addition to civil, criminal, and administrative penalties, those who commit healthcare fraud can also be tried for**
    a. breach of contract.
    b. criminal negligence.
    c. mail and wire fraud.
    d. medical malpractice.

12. **The first step a physician practice can take to identify areas in the practice that are vulnerable to fraud and abuse is to**
    a. conduct appropriate training and education sessions for employees.
    b. designate a compliance officer to monitor and enforce standards.
    c. enforce disciplinary standards through well-publicized guidelines.
    d. perform periodic audits to internally monitor billing processes.

13. **An example of an overpayment is**
    a. duplicate processing of a claim.
    b. incorrect application of EOB.
    c. payment based on reasonable charge.
    d. an unprocessed voided claim.

14. Unless the case involves fraud, administrative contractors are prohibited from seeking overpayment recovery when the
    a. amount paid in excess was less than or equal to $100.
    b. office manager sends a letter to request an exception.
    c. overpayment is not reopened within 48 months after payment.
    d. provider did not know the reasonable charge for the service.

15. CMS is authorized to enter into contracts with entities to perform cost report auditing, medical review, anti-fraud activities by the _____ program
    a. CERT
    b. Error prevention
    c. Hospital VBR
    d. Medicare integrity

16. Which government agency is responsible for investigating a Medicare provider who is suspected of committing fraud?
    a. Centers for Medicare and Medicaid Services
    b. Office of Inspector General
    c. Social Security Administration
    d. U.S. Attorney General

17. The agency that assigns the National Standard Employer Identification Number (EIN) is the
    a. Centers for Medicare and Medicaid Services.
    b. HHS Office of Inspector General.
    c. Internal Revenue Service.
    d. Social Security Administration.

18. PSCs were replaced by the Zone Program Integrity Contractor in _____.
    a. 2009
    b. 2010
    c. 2011
    d. 2012

19. Assigning passwords to users who are authorized to access patient records is a form of
    a. confidentiality.
    b. privacy.
    c. privilege.
    d. security.

20. What special handling is required to release medical information for a patient who is HIV-positive?
    a. A special notation should be made on the standard release of information.
    b. The insurance company must speak with the patient directly about the HIV diagnosis.
    c. The patient should sign an additional authorization statement for release of information.
    d. The provider must not release HIV-related information unless subpoenaed.

CHAPTER 6A
ICD-9-CM Coding

INTRODUCTION

This chapter familiarizes students with coding diseases and conditions using ICD-9-CM. Students will code diagnostic statements and case studies by applying ICD-9-CM coding conventions, principles, and rules.

ASSIGNMENT 6A.1   ICD-9-CM Index to Diseases

OBJECTIVES

At the conclusion of this assignment, the student should be able to:

1. Identify the condition in a diagnostic statement that would be considered the main term in the ICD-9-CM Index to Diseases.
2. Locate main terms in the ICD-9-CM Index to Diseases.

INSTRUCTIONS

In each of the following diagnostic statements, underline the condition that would be considered the main term in the ICD-9-CM Index to Diseases.

1. Acute confusion
2. Tension headache
3. Brain stem infarction
4. Allergic bronchitis
5. Bronchial croup
6. Newborn anoxia
7. Acute abdominal cramps
8. Insect bite
9. Radiation sickness
10. Car sickness

ASSIGNMENT 6A.2   Basic Coding

OBJECTIVES

At the conclusion of this assignment, the student should be able to:

1. Locate main terms in the ICD-9-CM Index to Diseases.
2. Identify codes in the ICD-9-CM Index to Diseases and verify them in the Tabular List of Diseases.

INSTRUCTIONS

Assign codes to the following conditions using the ICD-9-CM Index to Diseases. Be sure to verify the code(s) in the ICD-9-CM Tabular List of Diseases.

1. Herpes zoster _____
2. Parkinson's disease _____
3. Maxillary sinusitis _____
4. Pneumonia with influenza _____
5. Hiatal hernia _____
6. Skene's gland abscess _____
7. Skin eruption due to chemical product _____
8. Infectional erythema _____
9. Polydactyly of fingers _____
10. Blindness due to injury _____

ASSIGNMENT 6A.3   Multiple Coding

OBJECTIVES

At the conclusion of this assignment, the student should be able to:

1. Assign ICD-9-CM codes to conditions, using the Index to Diseases and Tabular List of Diseases.
2. Sequence codes in proper order according to ICD-9-CM coding principles and rules.

INSTRUCTIONS

Assign codes to each condition, and sequence the codes in proper order according to ICD-9-CM coding principles and rules (e.g., manifestation coding rule). Be sure to verify the code(s) in the ICD-9-CM Tabular List of Diseases.

1. Parasitic infestation of eyelid due to pediculus capitis _____
2. Post-infectious encephalitis due to measles (20 years ago) _____
3. Peripheral neuropathy in hyperthyroidism _____
4. Cerebral degeneration due to Fabry's disease _____
5. Myotonic cataract due to Thomsen's disease _____
6. Acute and chronic conjunctivitis _____
7. Xanthelasma of the eyelid due to lipoprotein deficiency _____
8. Cholesteatoma, middle ear and attic _____
9. Varicose vein with inflammation and ulcer due to pregnancy, patient at 30 weeks _____
10. Psoriatic arthropathy and parapsoriasis _____

ASSIGNMENT 6A.4   Combination Coding

OBJECTIVES

At the conclusion of this assignment, the student should be able to:

1. Use the Index to Diseases and Tabular List of Diseases to locate ICD-9-CM codes.
2. Interpret ICD-9-CM principles and rules to assign an appropriate combination code.

INSTRUCTIONS

Assign a combination code to each diagnostic statement below, using the ICD-9-CM Index to Diseases. Be sure to verify the code(s) in the ICD-9-CM Tabular List of Diseases.

1. Diabetes with ketoacidosis _____
2. Detached retina with giant tear _____
3. Rheumatic fever with heart involvement _____
4. Acute lung edema with heart disease _____
5. Atherosclerosis of the extremities with intermittent claudication _____
6. Emphysema with acute and chronic bronchitis _____
7. Acute gastric ulcer with perforation and hemorrhage _____
8. Diverticulosis with diverticulitis _____
9. Acute and chronic cholecystitis _____
10. Fractured fibula (closed) with tibia _____

ASSIGNMENT 6A.5 Coding Hypertension

OBJECTIVES

At the conclusion of this assignment, the student should be able to:

1. Interpret the ICD-9-CM hypertension table.
2. Assign ICD-9-CM codes to diagnostic statements that document hypertensive disease.

INSTRUCTIONS

Code the following diagnostic statements using the Hypertension table in the ICD-9-CM Index to Diseases. Be sure to verify the code(s) using the ICD-9-CM Tabular List of Diseases.

1. Hypertension, benign _____
2. Hypertension due to brain tumor, unspecified _____
3. Malignant hypertension with congestive heart failure _____
4. Newborn affected by maternal hypertension _____
5. Hypertensive disease due to pheochromocytoma _____
6. Chronic venous hypertension due to deep vein thrombosis _____
7. Malignant labile hypertension _____
8. Benign renovascular hypertension _____
9. Secondary hypertension due to Cushing's disease _____
10. Necrotizing hypertension _____

ASSIGNMENT 6A.6 Coding Neoplasms

OBJECTIVES

At the conclusion of this assignment, the student should be able to:

1. Interpret the ICD-9-CM Neoplasm table.
2. Assign ICD-9-CM codes to diagnostic statements that document neoplastic disease.

INSTRUCTIONS

Code the following diagnostic statements using the Neoplasm table in the ICD-9-CM Index to Diseases. Be sure to verify the code(s) in the ICD-9-CM Tabular List of Diseases.

1. Carcinoma of the right palatine tonsil _____
2. Metastatic ovarian cancer to the liver _____
3. Stomach cancer, primary site _____
4. Lipoma of muscle of forearm _____
5. Osteosarcoma of the left femoral head _____
6. Neurofibromatosis _____
7. Hodgkin's sarcoma _____
8. Chronic lymphocytic leukemia _____
9. Intrathoracic reticulosarcoma _____
10. Adenocarcinoma of the rectum and anus _____

ASSIGNMENT 6A.7 Assigning V Codes (Factors Influencing Health Status and Contact with Health Services)

OBJECTIVES

At the conclusion of this assignment, the student should be able to:

1. Interpret content in the V code supplementary classification of ICD-9-CM.
2. Assign ICD-9-CM V codes to diagnostic statements that document factors influencing health status and contact with health services.

INSTRUCTIONS

Code the following diagnostic statements using the ICD-9-CM Index to Diseases. Be sure to verify the code(s) in the ICD-9-CM supplemental classification for V codes (located in the Tabular List of Diseases). (Assign just the V code to each statement.)

1. Exercise counseling _____
2. Personal history of alcoholism _____
3. Counseling for parent-child conflict _____
4. Screening, cancer, unspecified _____
5. Follow-up exam, postsurgery _____
6. Health check, adult _____
7. Routine child health check up _____
8. Fitting of artificial eye _____
9. Flu shot (Vaccination) _____
10. Family history of breast cancer _____

ASSIGNMENT 6A.8   Coding Burns, Fractures, and Late Effects

OBJECTIVES

At the conclusion of this assignment, the student should be able to:

1. Use the Index to Diseases and Tabular List of Diseases to locate ICD-9-CM codes.
2. Interpret ICD-9-CM principles and rules to assign appropriate codes to burns, fractures, and late effects.

INSTRUCTIONS

Code the following diagnostic statements using the ICD-9-CM Index to Diseases. Be sure to verify the code(s) in the ICD-9-CM Tabular List of Diseases. Do not assign E codes.

1. Second-degree burn, right upper arm and shoulder _____
2. Burns of the mouth, pharynx, and esophagus _____
3. Third-degree burn, trunk _____
4. Open fracture of coccyx with other spinal cord injury _____
5. Bennett's fracture, closed _____
6. Fifth cervical vertebra fracture, closed _____
7. Scarring due to third-degree burn of left arm _____
8. Hemiplegia due to old cerebrovascular accident (CVA) _____
9. Arm injury due to car accident 10 years ago _____
10. Brain damage due to old cerebral abscess _____

ASSIGNMENT 6A.9   Assigning E Codes (External Causes of Injury and Poisoning)

OBJECTIVES

At the conclusion of this assignment, the student should be able to:

1. Use the *Index to External Causes of Injury and Poisoning* in ICD-9-CM.
2. Interpret ICD-9-CM principles and rules to assign appropriate codes for external causes of injury and poisonings.

INSTRUCTIONS

Code the following diagnostic statements using the ICD-9-CM Index to Diseases and the Index to External Causes. Be sure to verify the code(s) in the ICD-9-CM supplemental classification for E codes (located in the Tabular List of Diseases). Assign the E code only to each statement.

1. Assault by hanging and strangulation _____
2. Brain damage due to allergic reaction to penicillin _____
3. Self-inflicted injury by crashing of motor vehicle, highway _____
4. Exposure to noise at nightclub _____
5. Struck accidentally by falling rock at quarry _____
6. Dog bite _____
7. Accidental poisoning from shellfish at restaurant _____
8. Foreign object left in body during surgical operation _____
9. Fall from ladder at home _____
10. Accident caused by hunting rifle at rifle range _____

ASSIGNMENT 6A.10 Coding Procedures

OBJECTIVES

At the conclusion of this assignment, the student should be able to:
1. Use the Index to Procedures and Tabular List of Procedures to locate ICD-9-CM codes.
2. Interpret ICD-9-CM principles and rules to assign appropriate codes to procedures.

INSTRUCTIONS

Code the following procedural statements using the ICD-9-CM Index to Procedures. Be sure to verify the code(s) in the ICD-9-CM Tabular List of Procedures.

1. Culdotomy (female) _____
2. Cataract extraction with lens implant _____
3. Insertion of Swan-Ganz catheter _____
4. Jaboulay operation _____
5. Esophagogastroduodenoscopy (EGD) with closed biopsy _____
6. Insertion of vessel-to-vessel cannula (arteriovenous shunt) for renal dialysis; renal dialysis also performed during encounter _____
7. Insertion of bilateral myringotomy tubes _____
8. Extracorporeal shock wave lithotripsy (ESWL) of staghorn calculus, left kidney _____
9. Forceps delivery with partial breech extraction _____
10. Repair of claw toe by tendon lengthening _____

ASSIGNMENT 6A.11 Coding Patient Cases

OBJECTIVES

At the conclusion of this assignment, the student should be able to:
1. Identify diagnoses in case studies, and locate codes in the ICD-9-CM Index to Diseases.
2. Interpret ICD-9-CM principles and rules to assign appropriate diagnosis codes.

INSTRUCTIONS

Code the following case studies using the ICD-9-CM Index to Diseases. Be sure to verify the code(s) in the ICD-9-CM Tabular List of Diseases. Assign the diagnosis code <u>only</u> for each case study. Do <u>not</u> assign procedure or service codes.

1. **PATIENT CASE #1**

   HISTORY: The patient is an 87-year-old white male who has coronary artery disease, systolic hypertension, exogenous obesity, and peripheral venous insufficiency. He recently had a kidney stone removed. He claims that his only symptom of the stone was persistent back pain. Since the surgery, he has been doing fairly well.

   PHYSICAL EXAMINATION: The exam showed a well-developed, obese male who does not appear to be in any distress, but has considerable problems with mobility and uses a cane to ambulate. VITAL SIGNS: Blood pressure today is 158/86, pulse is 80 per minute, and weight is 204 pounds. He has no pallor. He has rather pronounced shaking of the arms, which he claims is not new. NECK: No jugular venous distention. HEART: Very irregular. LUNGS: Clear. EXTREMITIES: There is edema of both legs.

ASSESSMENT:

1. Coronary artery disease

2. Exogenous obesity

3. Degenerative joint disease involving multiple joints

4. History of congestive heart failure

5. Atrial fibrillation

6. History of myocardial infarction

PLAN: The patient will return to the clinic in four months.

---

2. **PATIENT CASE #2**

S: No change in gait instability. When the patient had to lie quietly with neck extended, gait instability was much worse for 20 to 30 minutes after the test. Medications: Warfarin, digoxin, verapamil.

O: Alert. Ataxic gait with foot slapping and instability in tandem walking. Mild distal weakness and wasting. Barely detectable DTRs. Impaired vibratory sense below the hips. Impaired position sense in toes. Head CT shows diffuse atrophic changes. EMG: Distal demyelinating axonal neuropathy.

A: Gait disorder with central/peripheral components in the context of cervical spondylosis and peripheral neuropathy.

P: Have patient obtain a B12/folate test. Reassess in one month.

---

3. **PATIENT CASE #3**

CHIEF COMPLAINT: Feels tired all the time and has no energy.

HISTORY OF PRESENT ILLNESS: The patient is an 80-year-old man with the following diagnoses: hyperlipidemia, coronary artery disease, cerebrovascular disease, esophageal reflux, and anxiety with depression. The patient was last seen in July of this year for the above problems. The patient is new to our clinic and is requesting follow-up for the fatigue and lack of energy, in addition to the problems noted above.

PHYSICAL EXAMINATION: The patient is 57 inches tall and weighs 184 pounds. Blood pressure is 122/70. Pulse is 60 per minute. Respiratory rate is 18 per minute. HEENT: Basically within normal limits. The patient wears glasses. Hearing aids are present bilaterally. NECK: Supple. Trachea is midline. LUNGS: Clear to auscultation and percussion. HEART: Regular, without murmur or ectopic beats noted. ABDOMEN: Slightly obese and nontender. Bowel sounds were normal. EXTREMITIES: The lower extremity pulses were present. He has good circulation with some very mild edema around the ankles.

ASSESSMENT:

1. Hyperlipidemia

2. Coronary artery disease

3. Cerebrovascular disease

4. Esophageal reflux

5. Anxiety with depression

PLAN: The patient will be referred to Psychiatry. I will see him again in three months.

---

4. **PATIENT CASE #4**

HISTORY OF PRESENT ILLNESS: The patient is an 88-year-old veteran with chronic constipation, mild dementia, and positive PPD test with negative x-ray. He complains of soreness around the anal region and incontinence of stool and sometimes urine.

PHYSICAL EXAMINATION: The patient is alert and well-oriented today. Vital signs as per the nursing staff. CHEST: Clear. HEART: Normal sinus rhythm. ABDOMEN: Soft and benign. RECTAL: The anal area and surrounding perianal area is erythematous and there is a tear going from the rectum to the anal region. Slight oozing of blood was noted. Rectal exam was done, and I could not feel any masses in the rectum; however, the exam was painful for the patient.

ASSESSMENT: Anal tear with hemorrhoids.

PLAN: Sitz bath. Protective ointment around the area. Surgical consult. Give donut ring to the patient to keep pressure off the area.

---

5. **PATIENT CASE #5**

S: The patient is still having pain in the right hip area. She has a new complaint of pain and pressure in the right orbital area.

O: Blood pressure today was 132/82. Pulse was 76 and regular. Temperature was 100.6 degrees. Pain and tenderness in the right frontal sinus region. The eyes appear slightly puffy. Examination of the right hip reveals point tenderness in the region of the head of the femur.

A: Sinus pain. Right hip pain; rule out trochanteric bursitis.

P: The patient will be sent for a sinus x-ray and right hip x-ray. I suspect the patient has a sinus infection due to the symptoms and fever. If the x-ray of the hip does not reveal any other pathology, will offer cortisone injection to the patient for relief of the right hip pain.

> **ASSIGNMENT 6A.12** ICD-9-CM Coding

OBJECTIVES

At the conclusion of this assignment, the student should be able to:

1. Locate correct ICD-9-CM codes using encoder software.
2. Recognize ICD-9-CM coding conventions.

OVERVIEW

ICD-9-CM is the current coding classification in use in the United States for diagnostic coding and hospital-based procedural coding. Students new to coding typically begin with learning and using a coding manual. However, there are various Web sites that can assist in code assignment. One of these sites is **www.ICD9coding.com.** This site allows the user to access encoder software for the application of ICD-9-CM codes.

INSTRUCTIONS

Go to the Web site for encoding software at **www.ICD9coding.com** to access free coding software. Review the diagnoses below, and provide your answer in the space provided.

1. Pneumonia, candidiasis of lung   _____
2. Histoplasmosis, pneumonia NOS   _____
3. Pneumonia, viral NEC   _____
4. Anemia, iron deficiency, unspecified   _____
5. Otitis media, nonsuppurative with stenosis of the eustachian tube   _____
6. Hypertension, essential, benign   _____
7. Diabetes, with ketoacidosis, type II, not stated as uncontrolled   _____
8. Hyperlipidemia, screening   _____
9. Abdominal pain, generalized   _____
10. Sinusitis, chronic, pansinusitis   _____

> **NOTE:** Navigate the encoder Web site using the terms provided in the above exercise to find the correct ICD-9-CM code. This will require click-ing on links to navigate to pages within the Web site to locate the correct code. The search text box at the Web site can also be used to locate codes. For example, type the term hyperlipidemia in the search text box at the site, scroll to "screening for hyperlipidemia" and click on that link.

ASSIGNMENT 6A.13   Multiple Choice Review

1. **Codes in slanted square brackets are _____ of other conditions.**
   a. eponyms
   b. manifestations
   c. modifiers
   d. subterms

2. **When coding a late effect, code the _____ first.**
   a. acute disease
   b. main symptom
   c. original cause
   d. residual condition

3. **Which is an example of an outpatient setting?**
   a. emergency department
   b. nursing home
   c. rehabilitation hospital
   d. residential care facility

4. **A concurrent condition that exists with the first-listed diagnosis is a**
   a. comorbidity.
   b. complication.
   c. manifestation.
   d. symptom.

5. **If a patient develops bleeding at the site of operative wound closure, this is a(n)**
   a. comorbidity.
   b. complication.
   c. encounter.
   d. manifestation.

6. A 45-year-old patient presents with polyuria and polydipsia. The physician documents "suspected diabetes mellitus." Which would be reported by the physician's office on the CMS-1500 claim?

    a. diabetes mellitus

    b. polydipsia only

    c. polyuria only

    d. polyuria and polydipsia

7. On May 1, a patient presents with a blood pressure of 150/90 and is asked to rest for 10 minutes. Upon reevaluation, the blood pressure is 130/80, and the patient is asked to return to the office on May 15 to rule out hypertension. Which would be reported by the physician's office on the CMS-1500 claim submitted for the May 1 office visit?

    a. benign hypertension

    b. elevated blood pressure

    c. malignant hypertension

    d. rule out hypertension

8. A patient presents with wheezing and a productive cough. The physician records "probable bronchitis, pending chest x-ray results." X-ray results confirms bronchitis. During this visit, the patient's glucose is checked to determine the status of his diabetes. The patient reports that his previous indigestion and diarrhea are currently not a problem. Which would be reported by the physician's office on the CMS-1500 claim?

    a. bronchitis, diabetes mellitus

    b. bronchitis, diabetes mellitus, indigestion, diarrhea

    c. bronchitis, indigestion, diarrhea

    d. productive cough

9. A patient presents complaining of tenderness in the left breast and a family history of breast cancer. Upon examination, the physician discovers a small lump in the left breast. The patient is referred to a breast surgeon and x-ray for mammogram. The physician documents "questionable breast cancer of the left breast." Which would be reported by the physician's office on the CMS-1500 claim?

    a. breast cancer

    b. breast lump; breast pain; family history of breast cancer

    c. breast pain; breast cancer

    d. personal history of breast cancer

10. A 19-year-old patient is brought to the emergency room from a fraternity party because of nausea, vomiting, and lethargy. The diagnosis is alcohol poisoning. Which E code should be reported for "alcohol poisoning"?

    a. accident

    b. assault

    c. therapeutic use

    d. undetermined

11. What general effect will reporting E codes have on CMS-1500 claims processing?

    a. The claim processing will be expedited because the circumstances related to an injury are indicated.

    b. The claim will automatically be denied; the claim should be paid by another payer if an E code is present.

    c. The claim will be automatically paid without difficulty because a higher level of detail has been included.

    d. The provider will receive a higher reimbursement amount due to the specificity of the information on the claim.

12. A neoplasm that is considered life-threatening and has spread outside its margins of origin is called

    a. benign.

    b. *in situ*.

    c. malignant.

    d. precancerous.

13. ICD-9-CM Index to Diseases has this format indented below the main term. This format of the classification provides quality terms related to the diagnostic information related to the code that is being assigned. What is this format called?

    a. eponyms

    b. essential modifiers

    c. nonessential modifiers

    d. notes

14. The condition "Lyme disease" is an example of a(n)

    a. category.

    b. eponym.

    c. manifestation.

    d. modifier.

15. Four-digit disease codes in ICD-9-CM are called _____ codes.

    a. category

    b. classification

    c. subcategory

    d. subclassification

16. A severe form of hypertension with vascular damage and a diastolic reading of 130 mm Hg or greater is called _____ hypertension.

    a. benign

    b. chronic

    c. malignant

    d. unspecified

17. When assigning an ICD-9-CM code from the Neoplasm table, which is referenced first?

    a. anatomic site

    b. behavior

    c. category

    d. specificity

18. The appearance of a pathologic condition caused by ingestion or exposure to a chemical substance properly administered is considered a(n)

    a. accident.

    b. adverse effect.

    c. assault.

    d. poisoning.

19. Begin the search process for an ICD-9-CM diagnosis code by using the _____.

    a. DRG grouper (software)

    b. index to diseases

    c. table of external effects

    d. tabular list of diseases

20. When coding late effects, the first code reported is the residual condition and the second code is the

    a. etiology.

    b. manifestation.

    c. sign.

    d. symptom.

CHAPTER 6B
ICD-10-CM Coding

INTRODUCTION

This chapter familiarizes students with coding diseases and conditions using ICD-10-CM. Students will code diagnostic statements and case studies by applying ICD-10-CM coding conventions, principles, and rules.

> **NOTE:** Content about ICD-10-PCS is located at the Student Resources online companion, including coding exercises and answer keys.

ASSIGNMENT 6B.1 ICD-9-CM Legacy Coding System: Interpreting General Equivalency Mappings

---

OBJECTIVES

At the conclusion of this assignment, the student should be able to:

1. Explain the purpose of general equivalence mappings.
2. Locate ICD-10-CM codes for their ICD-9-CM equivalents using general equivalence mappings.

OVERVIEW

NCHS and CMS annually publish *general equivalence mappings (GEMs)*, which are translation dictionaries or crosswalks of codes that can be used to roughly identify ICD-10-CM (and ICD-10-PCS) codes for their ICD-9-CM equivalent codes (and vice versa). GEMs facilitate the location of corresponding diagnosis (and procedure) codes between the two code sets.

INSTRUCTIONS

1. Re-enter each ICD-9-CM code from column 1 (of the table below) *without a decimal* in column 2.
2. Refer to Table 6B-1 to locate each ICD-9-CM diagnosis code (without decimals), and enter the GEM ICD-10-CM diagnosis code (without decimals) in column 3 (of the table below).
3. Then, enter the equivalent ICD-10-CM code *with* decimals in column 4 (of the table below).

	COLUMN 1 ICD-9-CM CODE	COLUMN 2 GEM ICD-9-CM CODE	COLUMN 3 GEM ICD-10-CM DIAGNOSIS CODE	COLUMN 4 ICD-10-CM DIAGNOSIS CODE
1.	003.24			
2.	001.9			
3.	002.3			
4.	001.0			
5.	003.22			

TABLE 6B-1 Portion of GEM for ICD-9-CM to ICD-10-CM Diagnoses Codes

GENERAL EQUIVALENCE MAPPING FOR DIAGNOSES	
ICD-9-CM DIAGNOSIS CODE	**ICD-10-CM DIAGNOSIS CODE**
0010	A001
0019	A0100
0021	A012
0023	A014
0030	A021
0032	A0221
00322	A0223
00324	A0229
0010	A001
0019	A0100

© Cengage Learning 2013

ASSIGNMENT 6B.2 Overview of ICD-10-CM: Comparing ICD-10-CM to ICD-9-CM

OBJECTIVES

At the conclusion of this assignment, the student should be able to:
1. Explain how ICD-10-CM was expanded (as compared with ICD-9-CM).
2. Locate ICD-9-CM and ICD-10-CM codes to demonstrate greater specificity in ICD-10-CM.

OVERVIEW

ICD-10-CM far exceeds ICD-9-CM in the number of codes provided, having been expanded to (1) include health-related conditions, (2) provide much greater specificity at the sixth digit level, and (3) add a seventh digit extension (for some codes). Assigning the sixth and seventh characters when available for ICD-10-CM codes is mandatory because they report information documented in the patient record.

INSTRUCTIONS

Refer to Table 6B-2, and enter the ICD-9-CM and ICD-10-CM code for each condition stated below. Be prepared to explain the results.

ICD-9-CM Code   ICD-10-CM Code

_____   _____ 1. Mechanical breakdown of aortic graft (replacement)

_____   _____ 2. Mechanical breakdown of carotid arterial graft (bypass)

_____   _____ 3. Mechanical breakdown of femoral arterial graft (bypass)

_____   _____ 4. Mechanical breakdown of other vascular grafts

_____   _____ 5. Mechanical breakdown of unspecified vascular grafts

TABLE 6B-2   Comparing ICD-9-CM and ICD-10-CM codes

ICD-9-CM TABULAR LIST OF DISEASES	ICD-10-CM TABULAR LIST OF DISEASES
996.1 Mechanical complication of other vascular device, implant, or graft 　　Mechanical complications involving: 　　　aortic (bifurcation) graft (replacement) 　　　arteriovenous: 　　　　dialysis catheter 　　　　fistula　} surgically created 　　　　shunt 　　　balloon (counterpulsation) device, intra-aortic 　　　carotid artery bypass graft 　　　femoral-popliteal bypass graft 　　　umbrella device, vena cava 　　EXCLUDES *atherosclerosis of biological graft (440.30-440.32)* 　　　　*embolism (occlusion NOS) (thrombus) of (biological) (synthetic) graft (996.74)* 　　　　*peritoneal dialysis catheter (996.56)*	**T82.3 Mechanical complication of other vascular grafts** 　**T82.31 Breakdown (mechanical) of other vascular grafts** 　　**T82.310 Breakdown (mechanical) of aortic (bifurcation) graft (replacement)** 　　**T82.311 Breakdown (mechanical) of carotid arterial graft (bypass)** 　　**T82.312 Breakdown (mechanical) of femoral arterial graft (bypass)** 　　**T82.318 Breakdown (mechanical) of other vascular grafts** 　　**T82.319 Breakdown (mechanical) of unspecified vascular grafts**

© Cengage Learning 2013

ASSIGNMENT 6B.3   ICD-10-CM Coding Conventions

OBJECTIVES

At the conclusion of this assignment, the student should be able to:

1. Interpret ICD-10-CM coding conventions.
2. Assign ICD-10-CM codes after applying coding conventions.

OVERVIEW

ICD-10-CM *coding conventions* are general rules that are incorporated into the index and tabular list instructional notes. The conventions include format, abbreviations, punctuation and symbols, includes and excludes notes, inclusion terms, other and unspecified codes, etiology and manifestation rules, and, with, *see,* and *see also.*

INSTRUCTIONS

Assign ICD-10-CM codes after interpreting coding conventions. Verify codes in the ICD-10-CM tabular list.

Format

_____ 1. Kaposi's sarcoma, left lung
_____ 2. Chronic blood loss anemia
_____ 3. Acute narrow angle glaucoma, right eye
_____ 4. Subarachnoid hematoma (newborn)
_____ 5. Acute cortical necrosis, left kidney

Eponyms

_____ **6.** Barlow's disease

_____ **7.** Christmas disease

_____ **8.** DaCosta's syndrome

_____ **9.** Eale's disease

_____ **10.** Faber's syndrome

NEC and NOS Abbreviations

_____ **11.** Bacterial enteritis

_____ **12.** Anemia

_____ **13.** Nonsyphilitic neurogenic spondylopathy

_____ **14.** Chronic granulomatous hepatitis

_____ **15.** Dry eye syndrome of right lacrimal gland

Punctuation

_____ **16.** Abasia

_____ **17.** Amyloidosis, heart

_____ **18.** Detachment of retina with retinal break, right eye

_____ **19.** Taboparesis

_____ **20.** Thyrotoxic heart disease with thyroid storm

Includes, Excludes1, Excludes2, and Inclusion Terms

_____ **21.** Portal vein thrombosis and phlebitis of portal vein

_____ **22.** Secondary lymphedema

_____ **23.** Acute sore throat due to streptococcus

_____ **24.** Acute subglottic laryngitis

_____ **25.** Oligodontia

Other, Other Specified, and Unspecified

_____ **26.** Polyalgia

_____ **27.** Bile duct adhesions

_____ **28.** Gout

_____ **29.** Hypertrophic tongue

_____ **30.** Venofibrosis

And, Due to, With

_____ **31.** Abscess of mediastinum

_____ **32.** Vitiligo due to pinta

_____ **33.** Fever with chills

_____ **34.** Furuncle of trunk

_____ **35.** Pneumonia due to pulmonary actinomycosis

Cross References: *See, See Also, See Category, See Condition*

_____ **36.** Retinitis, left eye

_____ **37.** Chronic valvulitis

_____ **38.** Duplication of teeth

_____ **39.** Acute osteitis of jaw

_____ **40.** Injury of right thumb, crushing (initial encounter)

_____ **41.** Fistula of right external ear canal

_____ **42.** Aortic valve aneurysm

_____ **43.** Corrosive burn of right hand (initial encounter)

_____ **44.** Gastric atrophia

_____ **45.** Type C cephalitis

ASSIGNMENT 6B.4   ICD-10-CM Index to Diseases and Injuries

OBJECTIVES

At the conclusion of this assignment, the student should be able to:

1. Identify the condition in a diagnostic statement that is used to locate the main term in the ICD-10-CM Index to Diseases and Injuries.
2. Locate main terms in the ICD-10-CM Index to Diseases and Injuries.
3. Use the Neoplasm Table to locate anatomic sites, cellular classifications (malignant, benign, uncertain behavior, unspecified nature), and malignant neoplasm divisions (primary, secondary, carcinoma _in situ_).
4. Use the Table of Drugs and Chemicals to locate medicinal, chemical, and biological substances that result in poisonings and adverse effects.
5. Use the Index to External Causes of Injuries to classify how an injury or health condition occurred, and the intent (e.g., accidental), place where the event occurred, activity of the patient at the time of an event, and person's status (e.g., military).

INSTRUCTIONS

Use the appropriate section of the ICD-10-CM Index to Diseases and Injuries to assign codes to each condition stated below, verifying each code in the ICD-10-CM Tabular List of Diseases and Injuries.

Identifying Main Terms and Assigning Codes

Instructions: Underline the main term in each condition, and use the ICD-10-CM Index to Diseases and Injuries to assign codes. Verify codes in the ICD-10-CM tabular list.

_____ **1.** Herpes zoster

_____ **2.** Parkinson's disease

_____ **3.** Maxillary sinusitis

_____ **4.** Pneumonia with influenza

_____ **5.** Hiatal hernia

_____ **6.** Skene's gland abscess

_____ **7.** Skin eruption due to chemical product

_____ **8.** Infectional erythema

_____ **9.** Polydactyly of fingers

_____ **10.** Blindness due to injury, initial encounter

Neoplasm Table

Instructions: Use the ICD-10-CM Neoplasm Table to assign codes. Verify codes in the ICD-10-CM tabular list.

_____ **11.** Carcinoma of right palatine tonsil

_____ **12.** Metastatic ovarian cancer to the liver

_____ **13.** Stomach cancer

_____ **14.** Lipoma of muscle, right forearm

_____ **15.** Osteosarcoma, left femoral head

_____ **16.** Neurofibromatosis

_____ **17.** Hodgkin's sarcoma

_____ **18.** Chronic lymphocytic leukemia of B-cell type

_____ **19.** Intrathoracic reticulosarcoma

_____ **20.** Adenocarcinoma of rectum and anus

Table of Drugs and Chemicals

Instructions: Use the ICD-10-CM Table of Drugs and Chemicals to assign codes. Verify codes in the ICD-10-CM tabular list. Add the seventh character for *initial encounter* to each applicable code.

_____ **21.** Allergic reaction to Benadryl

_____ **22.** Accidental food poisoning from lobster

_____ **23.** Accidental poisoning from ingesting toilet deodorizer

_____ **24.** Adverse effect of acetaminophen

_____ **25.** Suicide attempt, Ambien

_____ **26.** Accidental overdose of prednisone

_____ **27.** Rash due to therapeutic use of penicillin

_____ **28.** Underdosing of Synthroid in patient with enlarged thyroid

_____ **29.** Dizziness due to accidental overdose of Valerian tincture

_____ **30.** Suicide attempt due to carbon monoxide poisoning

Index to External Causes of Injuries

Instructions: Use the ICD-10-CM Index to External Causes to assign codes. Verify codes in the ICD-10-CM tabular list. Add the seventh character for *initial encounter* to each applicable code.

_____ **31.** Patient suffered mental cruelty

_____ **32.** Snowmobile occupant injured in nontraffic accident

_____ **33.** Altitude sickness

_____ **34.** Patient participated in a brawl, and blood alcohol level was 85 mg/100 ml

_____ **35.** Law enforcement officer injured during administration of capital punishment

_____ **36.** Patient's wedding band constricted ring finger, left hand

_____ **37.** Patient injured in earthquake

_____ **38.** Patient fell out of window and sustained minor injuries

_____ **39.** Patient was using nail gun and nailed hand to roof

_____ **40.** Malnourished adolescent was living in an abandoned house

---

ASSIGNMENT 6B.5 ICD-10-CM Tabular List of Diseases and Injuries

OBJECTIVES

At the conclusion of this assignment, the student should be able to:

1. Identify major topic headings in the ICD-10-CM Tabular List of Diseases and Injuries.
2. Explain the organization of 3-character disease categories within an ICD-10-CM chapter.
3. Differentiate among ICD-10-CM categories, subcategories, and codes.
4. Apply seventh characters to subcategory codes, as applicable.

OVERVIEW

The ICD-10-CM Tabular List of Diseases and Injuries is a chronological list of codes contained within 21 chapters, which are based on body system or condition. ICD-10-CM codes are organized within *major topic headings* (printed in bold uppercase letters) that are followed by groups of 3-character disease categories within a chapter. *Categories, subcategories, and codes* contain a combination of letters and numbers, and all categories contain 3 characters. A 3-character category that has no further subdivision is a valid code. Subcategories contain either 4 or 5 characters. Codes may contain 3, 4, 5, 6, or 7 characters; the final level of subdivision is a code and all codes in the ICD-10-CM tabular list are boldfaced. Codes that have an applicable seventh character are referred to as codes (not subcategories), and codes that have an applicable seventh character are considered invalid without the seventh character.

ICD-10-CM utilizes the character "x" as a fifth character *placeholder* for certain 6-character codes to allow for future expansion without disturbing the 6-character structure) (e.g., T36.0x1A, an initial encounter for accidental poisoning by penicillin). When a placeholder exists, the x must be entered in order for the code to be considered a valid code.

Certain ICD-10-CM categories contain applicable *seventh characters*, which are required for all codes within the category. The seventh character must always be located in the seventh-character data field. If a code that requires a seventh character is not 6 characters in length, the placeholder x is entered to fill in the empty character(s) (e.g., M48.46xS).

Injury, Poisoning, and Certain Other Consequences of External Causes and *External Causes of Morbidity* are incorporated into ICD-10-CM's Tabular List of Diseases and Injuries as Chapter 19 (S and T codes) and Chapter 20 (V-Y codes), respectively. External cause codes are also reported for environmental events, industrial accidents, injuries inflicted by criminal activity, and so on. While assigning the codes does not directly impact reimbursement to the provider, reporting them can expedite insurance claims processing because the circumstances related to an injury are indicated.

Factors Influencing Health Status and Contact with Health Services are incorporated into ICD-10-CM's Tabular List of Diseases and Injuries as Chapter 21 (Z codes), which is the last chapter of the ICD-10-CM tabular list. The Z codes are reported for patient encounters when a circumstance other than disease or injury is documented (e.g., well child visit).

INSTRUCTIONS

Use the ICD-10-CM Index to Diseases and Injuries to assign codes. Then, verify codes in the ICD-10-CM tabular list.

Multiple Coding and Combination Coding

> **NOTE:** Add the seventh character for initial encounter to each applicable code.

_____ 1. Parasitic infestation of eyelid due to pediculus capitis

_____ 2. Post-infectious encephalitis due to measles (20 years ago)

_____ 3. Peripheral neuropathy in hyperthyroidism

_____ 4. Cerebral degeneration due to Fabry's disease

_____ 5. Myotonic cataract due to Thomsen's disease

_____ 6. Acute and chronic conjunctivitis, right eye

_____ 7. Xanthelasma of the left upper eyelid due to lipoprotein deficiency

_____ 8. Cholesteatoma, right middle ear and attic

_____ 9. Varicose vein with inflammation, left lower extremity, complicating third-trimester pregnancy

_____ 10. Psoriatic arthropathy and parapsoriasis

_____ 11. Diabetes with ketoacidosis

_____ 12. Detached retina with giant tear

_____ **13.** Rheumatic fever with heart involvement

_____ **14.** Acute lung edema with heart disease

_____ **15.** Atherosclerosis of the extremities with intermittent claudication

_____ **16.** Emphysema with acute and chronic bronchitis

_____ **17.** Acute gastric ulcer with perforation and hemorrhage

_____ **18.** Diverticulosis with diverticulitis

_____ **19.** Acute and chronic cholecystitis

_____ **20.** Closed fractures of left fibula and tibia shafts

Injury, Poisoning, and Certain Other Consequences of External Causes and External Causes of Morbidity

> **NOTE:** Add the seventh character for initial encounter to each applicable code.

_____ **21.** Second-degree burn, right upper arm and shoulder

_____ **22.** Burns of mouth, pharynx, and esophagus

_____ **23.** Third-degree burn, trunk

_____ **24.** Open fracture of coccyx with cauda equina spinal cord injury

_____ **25.** Bennett's fracture, left hand, closed

_____ **26.** Fifth cervical vertebra fracture, closed

_____ **27.** Scarring due to third-degree burn of left arm

_____ **28.** Hemiplegia due to old cerebral infarction

_____ **29.** Pain due to left upper arm injury from car accident 10 years ago

_____ **30.** Brain damage due to old cerebral abscess

Factors Influencing Health Status and Contact with Health Services

_____ **31.** Exercise counseling

_____ **32.** Personal history of alcoholism

_____ **33.** Counseling for parent-child conflict

_____ **34.** Screening for bilateral breast cancer

_____ **35.** Postsurgical follow-up exam

_____ **36.** Adult health checkup

_____ **37.** Routine child (age 2) health checkup

_____ **38.** Fitting of artificial eye, right

_____ **39.** Flu shot

_____ **40.** Family history of breast cancer

> **ASSIGNMENT 6B.6** Diagnostic Coding and Reporting Guidelines for Outpatient Services

OBJECTIVES

At the conclusion of this assignment, the student should be able to:

1. List and explain the diagnostic coding and reporting guidelines for outpatient services.

2. Assign ICD-10-CM codes to diagnostic statements by interpreting the diagnostic coding and reporting guidelines for outpatient services.

3. Interpret abbreviations and lab values to assign ICD-10-CM diagnosis codes appropriately.

OVERVIEW

Diagnostic coding and reporting guidelines for outpatient services were developed by the federal government, and they were approved for use by hospitals and providers for coding and reporting hospital-based outpatient services and provider-based office visits. When reviewing the coding guidelines, remember that *encounter* and *visit* are used interchangeably when describing outpatient and physician office services.

INSTRUCTIONS

Assign ICD-10-CM codes to the following diagnostic statements and patient cases. When multiple codes are assigned, sequence them properly according to coding conventions and guidelines. Refer to diagnostic coding and reporting guidelines for outpatient services in your textbook, and verify codes in the ICD-10-CM tabular list.

Coding Diagnostic Statements

> **NOTE:** Add the seventh character for initial encounter to each applicable code.

_____ 1. Fever, difficulty swallowing, acute tonsillitis

_____ 2. Chest pain, rule out arteriosclerotic heart disease

_____ 3. Hypertension, acute bronchitis, family history of lung cancer

_____ 4. Lipoma, subcutaneous tissue of left thigh

_____ 5. Audible wheezing, acute exacerbation of asthma

_____ 6. Routine annual gynecological visit and exam with Pap smear

_____ 7. Laceration of right forearm. Pain, left ankle and left wrist. Possible left ankle fracture. Possible left wrist fracture

_____ 8. Pregnancy visit (normal female at second trimester, first pregnancy)

_____ 9. Renal calculi with hematuria

_____ 10. Status post colostomy

_____ 11. Fever, throat pain, acute otitis media, rule out thrush

_____ 12. Epstein-Barr mononucleosis

_____ 13. Severe nausea and vomiting, gastroenteritis due to salmonella food poisoning

_____ 14. Congestive heart failure with bilateral right leg edema

_____ 15. Elevated fasting blood glucose level of 145 mg/dL

_____ 16. Gastroesophageal reflux disease

_____ 17. Severe headache, stuffy nose, allergic sinusitis

_____ 18. Epigastric abdominal pain, fever, vomiting, tachycardia, acute pancreatitis

_____ 19. Pyogenic arthritis of right knee due to *H. influenzae* infection

_____ 20. Acute pericarditis due to tuberculosis

Coding Patient Cases

1. PATIENT CASE #1

HISTORY: The patient is an 87-year-old white male who has coronary artery disease, systolic hypertension, exogenous obesity, and peripheral venous insufficiency. He recently had a kidney stone removed. He claims that his only symptom of the stone was persistent back pain. Since the surgery, he has been doing fairly well.

PHYSICAL EXAMINATION: The exam showed a well-developed, obese male who does not appear to be in any distress, but has considerable problems with mobility and uses a cane to ambulate. VITAL SIGNS: Blood pressure today is 158/86, pulse is 80 per minute, and weight is 204 pounds. He has no pallor. He has rather pronounced shaking of the arms, which he claims is not new. NECK: No jugular venous distention. HEART: Very irregular. LUNGS: Clear. EXTREMITIES: There is edema of both legs.

ASSESSMENT:

1. Coronary artery disease
2. Exogenous obesity
3. Degenerative joint disease involving multiple joints
4. History of congestive heart failure
5. Atrial fibrillation
6. History of myocardial infarction

PLAN: The patient will return to the clinic in four months.

---

2. PATIENT CASE #2

S: No change in gait instability. When the patient had to lie quietly with neck extended, gait instability was much worse for 20 to 30 minutes after the test. Medications: Warfarin, digoxin, verapamil.

O: Alert. Ataxic gait with foot slapping and instability in tandem walking. Mild distal weakness and wasting. Barely detectable DTRs. Impaired vibratory sense below the hips. Impaired position sense in toes. Head CT shows diffuse atrophic changes. EMG: Distal demyelinating axonal neuropathy.

A: Gait disorder with central/peripheral components in the context of cervical spondylosis and peripheral neuropathy.

P: Have patient obtain a B12/folate test. Reassess in one month.

---

3. PATIENT CASE #3

CHIEF COMPLAINT: Feels tired all the time and has no energy.

HISTORY OF PRESENT ILLNESS: The patient is an 80-year-old man with the following diagnoses: hyperlipidemia, coronary artery disease, cerebrovascular disease, esophageal reflux, and anxiety with depression. The patient was last seen in July of this year for the above problems. The patient is new to our clinic and is requesting follow-up for the fatigue and lack of energy, in addition to the problems noted above.

PHYSICAL EXAMINATION: The patient is 57 inches tall and weighs 184 pounds. Blood pressure is 122/70. Pulse is 60 per minute. Respiratory rate is 18 per minute. HEENT: Basically within normal limits. The patient wears glasses. Hearing aids are present bilaterally. NECK: Supple. Trachea is midline. LUNGS: Clear to auscultation and percussion. HEART: Regular, without murmur or ectopic beats noted. ABDOMEN: Slightly obese and nontender. Bowel sounds were normal. EXTREMITIES: The lower extremity pulses were present. He has good circulation with some very mild edema around the ankles.

ASSESSMENT:

1. Hyperlipidemia
2. Coronary artery disease
3. Cerebrovascular disease

4. Esophageal reflux
5. Anxiety with depression

PLAN: The patient will be referred to Psychiatry. I will see him again in three months.

---

4. PATIENT CASE #4

HISTORY OF PRESENT ILLNESS: The patient is an 88-year-old veteran with chronic constipation, mild dementia, and positive PPD test with negative x-ray. He complains of soreness around the anal region and incontinence of stool and sometimes urine.

PHYSICAL EXAMINATION: The patient is alert and well-oriented today. Vital signs as per the nursing staff. CHEST: Clear. HEART: Normal sinus rhythm. ABDOMEN: Soft and benign. RECTAL: The anal area and surrounding perianal area is erythematous and there is a tear going from the rectum to the anal region. Slight oozing of blood was noted. Rectal exam was done, and I could not feel any masses in the rectum; however, the exam was painful for the patient.

ASSESSMENT: Anal tear with hemorrhoids.

PLAN: Sitz bath. Protective ointment around the area. Surgical consult. Give donut ring to the patient to keep pressure off the area.

---

5. PATIENT CASE #5

S: The patient is still having pain in the right hip area. She has a new complaint of pain and pressure in the right orbital area.

O: Blood pressure today was 132/82. Pulse was 76 and regular. Temperature was 100.6 degrees. Pain and tenderness in the right frontal sinus region. The eyes appear slightly puffy. Examination of the right hip reveals point tenderness in the region of the head of the femur.

A: Orbital pain. Right hip pain; rule out trochanteric bursitis.

P: The patient will be sent for a sinus x-ray and right hip x-ray. I suspect the patient has a sinus infection due to the symptoms and fever. If the x-ray of the hip does not reveal any other pathology, will offer cortisone injection to the patient for relief of the right hip pain.

ASSIGNMENT 6B.7   Multiple Choice Review

Instructions: Select the most appropriate response.

1. **Which is assigned when the provider documents a reason for a patient seeking health care that is not a disorder or disease?**
   a. external cause of injury
   b. factor influencing health status
   c. nonspecific condition
   d. qualified diagnosis

2. **Morphology codes indicate:**
   a. clinical prognosis of a patient diagnosed with a neoplasm.
   b. medication best used to treat a particular type of neoplasm.
   c. signs and/or symptoms of the patient diagnosed with a neoplasm.
   d. tissue type of the neoplasm as documented on the pathology report.

3. **Which is the correct format for morphology codes?**
   a. 90203/M
   b. M/90203
   c. M9020/3
   d. M90/203

4. **Review the ICD-10-CM Index to Diseases and Injuries entry (below), and identify the subterm.**
   a. aqueduct of Sylvius
   b. Stenosis
   c. Stricture
   d. with spina bifida

ICD-10-CM INDEX TO DISEASES AND INJURIES

 Stricture *(see also Stenosis)*

  aqueduct of Sylvius (congenital) Q03.0

   with spina bifida—*see* Spina bifida, by site, with hydrocephalus

---

5. **Which code is reported for *primary malignant neoplasm of cecum?***
   a. C18.0
   b. C7a.021
   c. C78.5
   d. D12.0

6. **The patient's final diagnosis is *mucopolysaccharidosis cardiopathy*. The coder locates main term *cardiopathy and* subterm *mucopolysaccharidosis* in the ICD-10-CM index, which has codes E76.3 [I52] next to the subterm. After verification in the tabular list _____.**
   a. code E76.3 only is reported
   b. code I52 only is reported
   c. codes E76.3 and I52, in that order, are reported
   d. codes I52 and E76.3, in that order, are reported

7. **The "x" character in an ICD-10-CM code is called a(n) _____.**
   a. eponym
   b. modifier
   c. placeholder
   d. qualifier

8. **Includes notes appear below ICD-10-CM _____ to further define, or give examples of, the content of the category.**
   a. 3-character code titles
   b. chapter headings
   c. subcategory descriptions
   d. tabular list classifications

9. An ICD-10-CM *Excludes1* note is interpreted as _____.
   a. code also
   b. *see* or *see also*
   c. not coded here
   d. use additional code

10. Certain conditions have both an underlying etiology and multiple body system manifestations due to the underlying etiology. In ICD-10-CM, the _____ is sequenced first.
    a. etiology
    b. manifestation
    c. pointer
    d. sign or symptom

11. ICD-10-CM codes can have up to _____ characters.
    a. 4
    b. 5
    c. 6
    d. 7

12. In ICD-10-CM, the word "and" is interpreted to mean _____.
    a. and
    b. and/or
    c. or
    d. probable

13. In ICD-10-CM, the word "with" is interpreted to mean _____.
    a. "associated with" only
    b. "associated with" or "due to"
    c. "due to" only
    d. possible, probable, and rule out

14. The _____ routinely associated with a disease should *not* be assigned as additional codes except when otherwise instructed by ICD-10-CM.
    a. etiologies and manifestations
    b. findings and prognoses
    c. procedures and services
    d. signs and symptoms

15. Impetigo with otitis externa, left ear.
    a. H62.42
    b. L01.00
    c. L01.00, H62.42
    d. L01.09

16. Hypertensive heart disease with left ventricular heart failure.
    a. I11.0
    b. I11.0, I50.1
    c. I50.1
    d. I50.9

17. Atrophic glossitis. Patient has long-term dependence on cigarettes.

   a. K14.0, F17.218

   b. K14.4, F17.218

   c. K14.8, F17.218, Z72.0

   d. K14.9, F17.218, Z87.891

18. Staphylococcal polyarthritis.

   a. B95.8, M00.00

   b. M00.09

   c. M00.09, B95.8

   d. M13.0, B95.8

19. Paranoid dementia.

   a. F03

   b. F05

   c. R41.0

   d. R41.81

20. Ankle fracture, right.

   a. M84.471

   b. S82.301A

   c. S82.831A

   d. S82.891A

CHAPTER 7
CPT Coding

INTRODUCTION

This chapter familiarizes students with coding procedures according to CPT. Students will code procedural statements and case studies by applying CPT coding conventions, principles, and rules.

ASSIGNMENT 7.1 CPT Index

OBJECTIVES

At the conclusion of this assignment, the student should be able to:

1. Identify the word in a procedural statement that would be considered the main term in the CPT Index.
2. Locate main terms in the CPT Index.

INSTRUCTIONS

In each of the following procedural statements, underline the word that would be considered the main term in the CPT Index according to type, which is indicated by the name of the heading located above each set of procedures.

Identification of Main Terms in CPT Index

1. Ankle amputation
2. Lower arm biopsy
3. Bone marrow aspiration
4. Laparoscopic jejunostomy
5. Bladder neck resection

Identification of Procedure or Service as Main Term in CPT Index

6. Postpartum dilation and curettage
7. Clamp circumcision of newborn
8. Arthrotomy of toe, interphalangeal joint
9. Gastrotomy with vagotomy
10. Bladder aspiration

Identification of Organ or Other Anatomic Site as Main Term in CPT Index

11. Artery angioplasty
12. Excision of heel spur
13. Repair of diaphragm laceration

14. Excision of cyst of pericardium

15. Excision of epiphyseal bar of radius

Identification of Condition as Main Term in CPT Index

16. Toe polydactyly reconstruction

17. Drainage of hip hematoma

18. Drainage of cyst of liver

19. Destruction of kidney calculus

20. Repair of sliding inguinal hernia

Identification of Synonym as Main Term in CPT Index

21. Albarran test

22. Binding globulin, testosterone-estradiol

23. Digital slit-beam radiograph

24. Urine test for epinephrine

25. Energies, electromagnetic

Identification of Eponym as Main Term in CPT Index

26. Dwyer procedure

27. Kasai procedure

28. Waldius procedure

29. Bloom-singer prosthesis

30. Ober-Yount procedure

Identification of Abbreviation as Main Term in CPT Index

31. Manual sedimentation rate of RBCs

32. MRA of the leg

33. Urine pH

34. Standard EEG

35. Complete MRI of the heart

ASSIGNMENT 7.2 Evaluation and Management (E/M) Coding

OBJECTIVES

At the conclusion of this assignment, the student should be able to:

1. Use the CPT Index to locate E/M codes.

2. Verify codes in the E/M section of CPT.

INSTRUCTIONS

Assign CPT Evaluation and Management codes to the following services. (Refer to Figures 7-8A through 7-8D in the textbook for assistance.)

1. Subsequent hospital care, expanded _____
2. Subsequent nursing facility care, problem focused _____
3. Initial office visit, problem focused _____
4. Office consultation, low complexity medical decision making _____
5. Initial inpatient hospital visit, level 2 _____
6. Initial home visit, detailed _____
7. Follow-up home visit, comprehensive _____
8. Observation care discharge _____
9. Initial observation care, comprehensive _____
10. Emergency department (ED) visit, detailed _____

ASSIGNMENT 7.3 Anesthesia Coding

OBJECTIVES

At the conclusion of this assignment, the student should be able to:

1. Use the CPT Index to locate Anesthesia codes.
2. Verify codes in the Anesthesia section of CPT.

INSTRUCTIONS

Assign CPT Anesthesia codes to the following procedures. Be sure to include the physical status modifier, which indicates information about the patient's physical status in relation to anesthesia services provided. Where appropriate, assign one or more of the four codes (99100–99140) from the Medicine section that report qualifying circumstances for anesthesia.

1. Coronary angioplasty of two vessels; patient has severe coronary artery disease. _____
2. Amniocentesis; patient has petit mal epilepsy. _____
3. Extracorporeal shock wave lithotripsy; patient has controlled hypertension. _____
4. Percutaneous liver biopsy; patient has chronic alcoholism. _____
5. Debridement of third-degree burns of right arm, 6 percent body surface area; patient is 2 years old and otherwise healthy. _____
6. Total hip replacement, open procedure; patient has controlled diabetes mellitus. _____
7. Biopsy of clavicle; patient is postoperative mastectomy two years ago and is undergoing biopsy procedure for suspected metastatic bone cancer. _____
8. Hand cast application; patient is otherwise healthy. _____
9. Arthroscopic procedure of the ankle joint; patient has generalized arthritis. _____
10. Total cystectomy; patient has bladder cancer, which is localized. _____

ASSIGNMENT 7.4 Surgery Coding

OBJECTIVES

At the conclusion of this assignment, the student should be able to:

1. Use the CPT Index to locate Surgery codes.
2. Verify codes in the Surgery section of CPT.

INSTRUCTIONS

Assign codes to the following procedural statements using the CPT Index. Be sure to verify the code(s) in the CPT Surgery section.

> **NOTE:** Convert inches to centimeters when calculating wound size. The formula is: inches x 2.54. Or, go to **www.manuelsweb.com/in_cm.htm** and use the online conversion calculator.

1. Excision, 1-inch benign lesion, left leg _____
2. Simple repair of 2-inch laceration on the right foot _____
3. Layer closure of 3-inch stab wound of the neck _____
4. Excision, half-inch malignant lesion, left first finger _____
5. Intermediate repair of 5-inch laceration of the right thigh _____
6. Open reduction with internal fixation of fracture of great toe phalanx _____
7. Closed reduction of nasal bone fracture with stabilization _____
8. Surgical elbow arthroscopy with removal of loose body _____
9. Segmental osteotomy of the mandible _____
10. Trigger finger release _____
11. Tracheobronchoscopy through existing tracheostomy incision _____
12. Secondary rhinoplasty with major reconstruction of nasal tip to correct results of an initial rhinoplasty done elsewhere _____
13. Surgical thoracoscopy with excision of pericardial tumor _____
14. Total pulmonary decortication _____
15. Extraplural enucleation of empyema _____
16. Direct repair of cerebral artery aneurysm _____
17. Femoral-popliteal bypass graft _____
18. Coronary artery bypass graft (using two arterial grafts) _____
19. Complete cardiac MRI without contrast _____
20. Insertion of dual-chamber pacemaker with electrodes _____
21. Complete cleft lip repair, primary bilateral, one-stage procedure _____
22. Laparoscopic cholecystectomy with exploration of the common duct _____
23. Umbilectomy _____
24. Pancreatectomy with Whipple procedure _____
25. Percutaneous drainage of subdiaphragmatic abscess _____
26. Inguinal hernia repair without hydrocelectomy; the patient is a 14-month-old male _____
27. Cystourethroscopy with fulguration of large (6.5 cm) bladder tumor _____
28. Manometric studies through pyelostomy tube _____
29. Nephrorrhaphy of right kidney wound _____

30. Injection of contrast for voiding urethrocystography   _____
31. Laser removal of three condylomata from penis   _____
32. Incisional biopsy of the prostate   _____
33. Marsupialization of Bartholin's gland cyst   _____
34. Total bilateral salpingectomy and oophorectomy   _____
35. Antepartum care, 10 visits   _____
36. Burr holes with evacuation and drainage of subdural hematoma   _____
37. Craniotomy for repair of cerebrospinal fluid leak and rhinorrhea   _____
38. Thoracic laminectomy with exploration, two vertebrae   _____
39. Stereotactic biopsy of spinal cord   _____
40. Neuroplasty of the sciatic nerve   _____
41. Evisceration of eye with implant   _____
42. Laser iridectomy for glaucoma   _____
43. Total dacryocystectomy   _____
44. Removal of bilateral cerumen impaction   _____
45. Successful cochlear implant   _____

ASSIGNMENT 7.5   Radiology Coding

OBJECTIVES

At the conclusion of this assignment, the student should be able to:
1. Use the CPT Index to locate Radiology codes.
2. Verify codes in the Radiology section of CPT.

INSTRUCTIONS

Assign codes to the following procedural statements using the CPT Index. Be sure to verify the code(s) in the CPT Radiology section.

1. Complete radiographic examination of the mandible   _____
2. Urography, retrograde   _____
3. Pelvimetry   _____
4. Orthoroentgenogram, scanogram   _____
5. Chest x-ray, two views, with fluoroscopy   _____
6. X-ray of the facial bones, four views   _____
7. CAT scan of the abdomen, with contrast   _____
8. Gastroesophageal reflux study   _____
9. X-ray of the cervical spine, two views   _____
10. Barium enema   _____

ASSIGNMENT 7.6   Pathology and Laboratory Coding

OBJECTIVES

At the conclusion of this assignment, the student should be able to:
1. Use the CPT Index to locate Pathology and Laboratory codes.
2. Verify codes in the Pathology and Laboratory section of CPT.

INSTRUCTIONS

Assign codes to the following procedural statements using the CPT Index. Be sure to verify the code(s) in the CPT Radiology and Laboratory section.

1. Red blood cell count, automated _____
2. Blood gases, pH only _____
3. Glucose-6-phosphate dehydrogenase screen _____
4. Glucose tolerance test, three specimens _____
5. KOH prep _____
6. HIV antibody and confirmatory test _____
7. HDL cholesterol _____
8. Rapid test for infection, screen, each antibody _____
9. Herpes simplex virus, quantification _____
10. Urine dip, nonautomated, without microscopy _____

ASSIGNMENT 7.7   Medicine Coding

OBJECTIVES

At the conclusion of this assignment, the student should be able to:

1. Use the CPT Index to locate Medicine codes.
2. Verify codes in the Medicine section of CPT.

INSTRUCTIONS

Assign codes to the following procedural statements using the CPT Index. Be sure to verify the code(s) in the CPT Medicine section.

1. Right heart catheterization, for congenital cardiac anomalies _____
2. Medical testimony _____
3. Services requested between 10:00 p.m. and 8:00 a.m. in addition to basic service, normal office hours 9:00 a.m. to 6:00 p.m. _____
4. Acupuncture, one or more needles, with electrical stimulation _____
5. Hypnotherapy _____
6. One hour of psychological testing by psychiatrist, with interpretation and report _____
7. Wheelchair management with propulsion training, 15 minutes _____
8. Massage therapy, 45 minutes _____
9. Nonpressurized inhalation treatment for acute airway obstruction _____
10. Educational videotapes provided to patient _____

ASSIGNMENT 7.8   Assigning CPT Modifiers

OBJECTIVES

At the conclusion of this assignment, the student should be able to:

1. Identify the phrase in a procedure statement that indicates a modifier is to be assigned.
2. Use the CPT Appendix to locate modifiers.
3. Assign the modifier that describes the special circumstances associated with a procedural statement.

INSTRUCTIONS

Assign the CPT code and appropriate modifier to the following procedural statements. Before assigning the modifier, underline the phrase in each procedure statement that indicates a modifier is to be assigned. (Refer to Table 7-1 in the textbook for assistance in assigning modifiers.)

1. Vasovasostomy discontinued after anesthesia due to heart arrhythmia, hospital outpatient _____

2. Decision for surgery during initial office visit, comprehensive _____

3. Expanded office visit for follow-up of mastectomy; new onset diabetes was discovered and treatment initiated _____

4. Cholecystectomy, postoperative management only _____

5. Hospital outpatient hemorrhoidectomy by simple ligature discontinued prior to anesthesia due to severe drop in blood pressure _____

6. Total urethrectomy including cystotomy, female, surgical care only _____

7. Simple repair of 2-inch laceration of the right foot, discontinued due to near-syncope, physician's office _____

8. Tonsillectomy and adenoidectomy, age 10, and laser wart removal from the patient's neck while in the operating room _____

9. Repeat left medial collateral ligament repair, same surgeon _____

10. At the patient's request, bilateral Silver procedures were performed for correction of bunion deformity. _____

11. A patient undergoes simple repair of multiple skin lesions and of left foot and toes and intermediate repair of left heel laceration. The patient is discharged home after suturing, bandaging, and placement of the left foot in a soft cast. Codes 12041 and 12002 are reported. Which modifier, if any, is added to code 12002? _____

12. An 80-year-old male patient undergoes bilateral posterior packing of the nasal cavity. Which modifier is added to code 30905? _____

13. A patient undergoes magnetic resonance imaging (MRI), lower left leg. Dr. Miller interprets the MRI and documents a report. Which modifier is added to the CPT code reported for the MRI? _____

14. On April 2, the patient underwent incision and drainage (I&D) of a Bartholin's gland abscess. The abscess recurred two weeks later, and on April 29, the patient underwent repeat I&D by the same surgeon. Code 56420 was reported for the April 2 procedure. Which modifier is added to code 56420 for the procedure performed on April 29? _____

15. A male patient underwent biopsy of the prostate gland on October 20, as performed by Dr. Smith. The global period for this surgical procedure is zero days. The pathology results were of uncertain behavior. Per the pathologist's recommendation, the patient underwent repeat biopsy to obtain a larger sample on November 13, performed by Dr. Jones. Code 55700 was reported for the October 20 procedure. Which modifier is added to code 55700 for the procedure performed on November 13? _____

ASSIGNMENT 7.9   Coding Case Studies

OBJECTIVES

At the conclusion of this assignment, the student should be able to:

1. Use the CPT Index to locate Procedure and Service codes.

2. Verify codes in the appropriate section of CPT.

3. Assign modifier(s) when special circumstances are documented in a case study.

INSTRUCTIONS

Code the following case studies using the CPT Index. Be sure to verify the code(s) in the appropriate section of CPT. Assign Procedure and Service codes *only* for each case study. Do *not* code diagnosis. Refer to textbook Figures 7-8A through 7-8D for assistance with E/M code selection and Table 7-1 for assistance with assigning modifiers.

1. PATIENT CASE #1

HISTORY OF PRESENT ILLNESS: The patient is a 37-year-old female who has complaints of severe fatigue, sore throat, headache, and acute bilateral ear pain. The symptoms have been gradually increasing over the past 7 to 10 days, to the point where she is not able to sleep at night due to coughing and intense bilateral ear pain. She was referred to me by her primary care provider for further evaluation and medical treatment.

PHYSICAL EXAMINATION: GENERAL: The patient appears tired and ill. HEENT: Eyes are within normal limits. Bilateral otoscopic examination shows erythematous, inflamed tympanic membranes with question of perforation on the right. Throat is red and tonsils appear mildly swollen. NECK: There is mild cervical lymphadenopathy. HEART: Within normal limits. LUNGS: Generally clear. The rest of the exam was within normal limits. LABORATORY: Rapid strep was negative. Poly Stat Mono test was positive.

ASSESSMENT: Mononucleosis, pharyngitis, bilateral otitis media, and probable sinusitis.

PLAN: CBC with differential. Sinus x-ray to rule out sinusitis. The patient will be placed on a Z-Pak and prednisone taper. Tussionex for cough. The patient is to be off work for the next 10 days, and is to return to this office in seven days; sooner if she does not begin to feel better or if symptoms worsen.

---

2. PATIENT CASE #2

OPERATIVE PROCEDURE: Cystoscopy.

PREOPERATIVE DIAGNOSES:

1. Benign prostatic hypertrophy.
2. Rule out stricture of the urethra.
3. Rule out bladder lesions.

POSTOPERATIVE DIAGNOSIS:

1. Benign prostatic hypertrophy.
2. Cystitis.

POSTOPERATIVE CONDITION: Satisfactory.

OPERATIVE PROCEDURE AND FINDINGS: The established patient was placed in the lithotomy position. Genital area was prepped with Betadine and draped in the usual sterile fashion. About 10 cc of 2 percent Xylocaine jelly was introduced into the urethra and a cystoscopy was performed using a #16 French flexible cystoscope. The urethra was grossly normal. The prostate gland was moderately enlarged. There was mild inflammation of the bladder mucosa, but there were no gross tumors or calculi seen in the bladder at this time. Cystoscope was removed. The patient tolerated the procedure well and left the procedure room in good condition.

3. PATIENT CASE #3

S: Chronic fatigue. No acute complaints. This established patient purchased an Advantage BG and sugars are 97 to 409; no pattern. (She did not bring copies of her sugars as requested.) Eats two meals a day; history of noncompliance. The patient was seen in GYN Clinic this morning. Has GI upset with oral estrogen and doctor recommended estrogen patch. Seen in ophthalmology in July; no retinopathy. Last mammography was in June. Noncompliant with six-month follow-up of calcified cluster in the right breast, upper outer quadrant. Four-year history of small, tender irregularity in the right breast five o'clock position. Feet: The patient still has occasional pain with over-the-counter B12 pills. No change in respiration; refuses to attempt to quit smoking. Self-catheterizes neurogenic bladder.

O: Obese white female in no acute distress. Lump found on breast self-exam, right. Left breast reveals no mass, no nodes, nipple okay. Right breast reveals tender spots at eight and ten o'clock, mobile. Patient believes this has been the same for the past four years. Patient routinely does breast self-exam. Heart reveals regular sinus rhythm.

A: Diabetes mellitus on oral therapy, poorly controlled. Chronic small airway disease. Nicotine dependent. Obesity. Menopause. Rule out breast disease.

P: Hemoglobin today. Fasting lipid profile today. Repeat both labs in three months. Schedule mammogram today. Counseled patient on the importance of keeping the mammography appointment and close watch of the masses. Return to clinic in six weeks if mammogram is okay. Will start estrogen patch 0.5 mg/24 hours, #8. All other meds refilled today.

4. PATIENT CASE #4

HISTORY: The patient presented today for evaluation of ulcers of the lower left leg, in the region of the tibia and also in the calf area. The patient reports discomfort with these areas. The patient agreed to be seen at the insistence of his wife and because of increasing pain in the areas of the ulcerations. The patient is a known diabetic with poor compliance and sugars are usually high. We discussed his blood sugar monitoring schedule, and his wife indicates that the patient is very stubborn about monitoring his blood sugars. The patient could benefit from an intensive education session regarding diabetes, diabetic care, and preventing or slowing diabetes disease progression. He is either in complete denial of his diagnosis or is simply not making the effort to take care of himself; either way, the situation needs to be addressed.

PHYSICAL EXAMINATION: The exam was limited to the lower extremities. The left lower leg shows stasis dermatitis with two ulcerations in the region of the calf. One is approximately 1 cm in diameter and the other is approximately 1.5 cm in diameter. There are varicosities present as well as mild edema noted. There is a small, shallow ulcer in the mid-tibia region as well. The right lower leg has mild edema but is free of ulcers at this time.

DIAGNOSES:

1. Stasis dermatitis with ulcerations.
2. Dependent edema.
3. Diabetes mellitus, uncontrolled.

PLAN: The patient underwent wound irrigation and application of Silvadene cream to the ulcerations. Wounds were dressed with sterile gauze and wrapped with Kerlix. The patient will return in one week for reevaluation. If there is no improvement in the ulcerations, an Unna boot will be the next step. Additionally, we will arrange for intensive diabetic education for this patient.

---

5. **PATIENT CASE #5**

PREOPERATIVE DIAGNOSIS: Pilonidal cyst.

POSTOPERATIVE DIAGNOSIS: Pilonidal cyst, cellulitis.

OPERATION: Pilonidal cystectomy, cyst tract exploration and irrigation.

HISTORY: The patient is a 42-year-old white male who has had intermittent flare-ups of the pilonidal cyst. He was seen in the office two days ago with an acute flare-up with acute pain and pressure. He reported he was running a fever. He was scheduled for office surgery for removal and presents today for the above.

OPERATION: The patient was premedicated with 10 mg of Versed. The patient was brought to the procedure room and placed in the jackknife position. The lower sacrum and coccygeal areas were prepped with Betadine, and the operative field was draped in a sterile fashion. Local anesthetic was administered with topical Hurricaine spray, and 1 percent Xylocaine was then injected into the margins of the wound. An incision was made into the area of the obvious pilonidal cyst formation and approximately 15 cc of foul, purulent drainage was expressed from the wound. The contents of the cyst were excised, labeled, and sent for pathology. There was cellulitis extending circumferentially around the cyst, extending approximately 1.5 cm outside the area of the cyst. Exploration of the sinus tract was performed and the tract extended down approximately 2.5 cm. It was felt at this time that no sutures would be required, and the tract was irrigated with normal saline and flushed with antibiotic solution. The wound was then packed and dressed. The patient tolerated the procedure well. The patient was observed for 30 minutes following the procedure, after which he was instructed on wound care and signs of infection. The patient was released to the care of his wife. He was given a prescription for Keflex 500 mg p.o. b.i.d. and Darvocet N-100, #20, 1 p.o. q.4h. as needed for pain. He will return to the office in two days for reevaluation.

ASSIGNMENT 7.10   CPT Code Verification

OBJECTIVES

At the conclusion of this assignment, the student should be able to:

1. Validate coding accuracy based on coding information.
2. Analyze results and make recommendations.

OVERVIEW

CPT codes are assigned for a variety of outpatient services. Auditing of the codes assigned can be done as a tool to verify correct code assignment.

INSTRUCTIONS

Below is a table of 10 Health Records with information on the coding statement that was used to assign a CPT code. Review the information provided in the table verifying that the code assigned is correct. If the code is correct, record it again in the coding verification column. If the code is **incorrect,** record the correct code in the coding verification column. Provide an analysis of your findings: What percentage of the codes were correct? What percentage were incorrect based on the 10 charts that were reviewed? What recommendations could you provide to the coder(s) of these charts? Provide your thoughts in a double-spaced, word-processed document that is at least one-half page in length.

HEALTH RECORD NUMBER	CODING STATEMENT	CODE ASSIGNED	CODING VERIFICATION
25899	Office visit level 2, established patient	99213	
60159	Flexible diagnostic bronchoscopy	31624	
30121	Biopsy of the oropharynx	42800	
11133	CT scan of the thoracic spine with contrast	72128	
45456	Hepatic panel	82040, 82247, 82248, 84075, 84155, 84460	
55667	Routine ECG tracing only	93000	
91912	Application of figure-of-eight cast	29049	
34343	Initial posterior nasal packing	30905	
55578	Extensive excision of a pilonidal cyst	11770	
12332	Fitting of bifocals	92340	

ASSIGNMENT 7.11   Relative Value Units

OBJECTIVES

At the conclusion of this assignment, the student should be able to:

1. Discuss relative value units (RVUs).
2. Discuss the American Medical Association (AMA) role in the administration and oversight of CPT.

OVERVIEW

The American Medical Association is a professional network that also oversees the administration and maintenance of the CPT coding system. The AMA provides many resources on the Internet to assist physicians and coders with this classification system. The Internet is also a resource that can be accessed to locate information on code changes, CPT code update process, and relative value units (RVUs).

INSTRUCTIONS

1. Go to the Web site for the American Medical Association at **www.ama-assn.org** and explore the site to find out information about this organization.

2. Locate the RVU search feature by clicking on the CPT link below the Featured Resources. Then, click on the CPT/RVU Search link, and click to Accept. Search for the non-facility Medicare payment rate for CPT code 99285 for the following locations:

   - Pennsylvania
   - Oklahoma
   - Arizona
   - Los Angeles, California
   - Nevada
   - District of Columbia (including Maryland and Virginia suburbs)
   - New York (Manhattan)

3. Review the payment amount for each location for CPT code 99285. What location has the highest payment amount for this CPT code? Which location has the lowest payment amount? What is the dollar amount difference from the highest payment to the lowest payment? What is the average amount for these six locations? Is there a pattern for the urban locations versus nonurban locations?

4. Provide your analysis of the payment amount and the questions posed above in a double-spaced, word-processed document.

> **NOTE:** Navigate the American Medical Association Web site to research information needed for your summary. This will help you learn how to locate information using the Internet as a research tool and using Web sites, which often requires using tool bars and pull-down menus.

ASSIGNMENT 7.12   Multiple Choice Review

1. **The CPT coding manual contains _____ sections?**

   a. three

   b. four

   c. five

   d. six

2. **Instructions provided at the beginning of each section, which define terms particular to that section and provide explanation for codes and services that apply to that section, are called _____.**

   a. guidelines

   b. instructional notes

   c. qualifiers

   d. special reports

3. **Rather than using unlisted procedure or service CPT codes, Medicare and other third-party payers require providers to**

   a. assign ICD-9 procedure codes.

   b. attach a special report.

   c. perform a known procedure.

   d. report HCPCS level II codes.

4. **CPT modifiers are used to indicate that**
   a. a special report need not be attached to the claim.
   b. the description of the procedure performed has been altered.
   c. the provider should receive a higher reimbursement rate.
   d. the technique of the procedure was performed differently.

5. **Which component is included in the surgical package?**
   a. assistant surgeon services
   b. epidural or spinal anesthesia
   c. prescription pain medications
   d. uncomplicated postoperative care

6. **Which modifier is reported if a third-party payer requires a second opinion for a surgical procedure?**
   a. -26 professional component
   b. -32 mandated services
   c. -59 distinct procedural service
   d. -62 two surgeons

7. **The time frame during which all postoperative services are included in the surgical package is the global _____.**
   a. billing
   b. package
   c. period
   d. surgery

8. **Use your CPT coding manual to identify the technique for removing a skin lesion that involves transverse incision or horizontal slicing to remove epidermal or dermal lesions, which is called**
   a. destruction.
   b. excision.
   c. repair.
   d. shaving.

9. **Use your CPT coding manual to locate and review coding notes that apply to Repair (Closure) codes (located in the Integumentary subsection of the Surgery section). The proper way to report the repair of multiple lacerations at the same anatomic site is to**
   a. add together the length of each laceration and report a single code.
   b. code each individual laceration based on the length of each wound.
   c. code each individual laceration based on the most complicated repair.
   d. report individual codes for each laceration if they involved trauma.

10. **Use your CPT coding manual to locate and review coding notes that apply to the Musculoskeletal System subsection of the Surgery section to identify the term for "the attempted reduction or restoration of a fracture or joint dislocation by the application of manually applied forces."**
    a. fixation
    b. manipulation
    c. traction
    d. treatment

11. **CPT codes that are optional and are used for tracking performance measurements are called _____ codes.**
    a. Category I
    b. Category II
    c. Category III
    d. Category IV

12. **A bullet located to the left of a code number identifies**
    a. a revised code description.
    b. codes exempt from modifier -51.
    c. new procedures and services.
    d. revised guidelines and notes.

13. An anesthesiologist provided general anesthesia services to a 70-year-old female with mild systemic disease who underwent total knee replacement. Which physical status modifier would be reported with procedure code 01402?

   a. -P1   c. -P3

   b. -P2   d. -P4

14. A series of very specific blood chemistry studies ordered at one time is called a(n)

   a. assay.   c. report.

   b. panel.   d. study.

15. A CRNA provided general anesthesia services to a healthy patient who underwent an appendectomy. The CRNA did not receive medical direction from a physician. Which HCPCS Level II modifier would be reported with procedure code 00944?

   a. –QS   c. –QY

   b. –QX   d. –QZ

16. If a patient is seen by the provider for a presenting problem that runs a definite and prescribed course, is transient in nature, and is not likely to alter the patient's permanent health status, the problem is considered

   a. low severity.   c. minor.

   b. minimal.   d. moderate severity.

17. A patient is admitted to the hospital through the emergency department for treatment and who is held for a period of eight hours to be monitored. This patient received hospital _____ services.

   a. critical care   c. observation

   b. inpatient   d. outpatient

18. A 92-year-old female patient received general anesthesia services during total left hip arthroplasty. Which qualifying circumstance code would be reported in addition to procedure code 01214?

   a. 99100   c. 99135

   b. 99116   d. 99140

19. Which service is reported for the care of patients who live in a boarding home?

   a. consultation services

   b. domiciliary care

   c. home services

   d. nursing facility services

20. Use your CPT coding manual to review the Medicine section guidelines, and identify the CPT code assigned to supplies and materials.

   a. 99201   c. 99070

   b. 99000   d. 99999

CHAPTER 8
HCPCS Level II Coding

INTRODUCTION

This chapter familiarizes students with coding procedures, services, and supplies according to HCPCS. Students will code procedural statements and case studies by applying HCPCS coding conventions, principles, and rules.

ASSIGNMENT 8.1 HCPCS Index

OBJECTIVES

At the conclusion of the assignment, the student should be able to:
1. Identify the word in a service or procedural statement that would be considered the main term in the HCPCS Index.
2. Locate main terms in the HCPCS Index.

INSTRUCTIONS

In each of the following statements, underline the word that would be considered the main term in the HCPCS Index.
1. Breast pump
2. Cardiac output assessment
3. Dialysate solution
4. External defibrillator electrode
5. Fracture orthotic devices
6. Liquid gas system
7. Oral antiemetic
8. Pneumatic nebulizer administration set
9. Pneumococcal vaccination administration
10. Wheelchair shock absorber

ASSIGNMENT 8.2 HCPCS Level II Coding

OBJECTIVES

At the conclusion of this assignment, the student should be able to:
1. Locate main terms in the HCPCS Index.
2. Identify codes in the HCPCS Index and verify them in the tabular section.

INSTRUCTIONS

Assign HCPCS level II codes to the following procedures and services:

Transportation Services Including Ambulance (A0000–A0999)

1. Advanced life support, Level 2 _____
2. Ambulance transport of newborn from rural hospital to a children's specialty hospital _____
3. Patient received basic life support (BLS) during emergency transport via ambulance _____
4. Patient received life-sustaining oxygen in ambulance during transport to hospital _____
5. Wheelchair van transporting patient from assisted living facility to doctor's office _____

Medical and Surgical Supplies (A4000–A8999)

6. Physician gave patient injection using a sterile 3 cc syringe with needle _____
7. One pint of pHisoHex solution _____
8. Diaphragm for contraceptive use _____
9. Replacement adapter for breast pump _____
10. One pound of paraffin _____
11. Male external catheter with adhesive coating _____
12. Two-way indwelling Foley catheter _____
13. Ostomy belt _____
14. Reusable enema bag with tubing _____
15. One pair of apnea monitor electrodes _____
16. Rubber pessary _____
17. Tracheostomy care kit for new tracheostomy _____
18. Automatic blood pressure monitor _____
19. Ammonia test strips for dialysis (50 count) _____
20. Patient with diabetes was fitted with a pair of shoes custom-molded from casts of the patient's feet _____

Administrative, Miscellaneous, and Investigational (A9000–A9999)

21. DME delivery and setup _____
22. Exercise equipment _____
23. I-131 sodium iodide capsule as radiopharmaceutical diagnostic agent (1 millicurie) _____
24. Injectable contrast material for use in echocardiography, one study _____
25. One dose technetium Tc99m sestamibi _____

Enteral and Parenteral Therapy (B4000–B9999)

26. Parenteral nutrition supply kit; home mix, per day _____
27. Enteral formula via feeding tube (100 calories/1 unit), manufactured blenderized natural foods with intact nutrients _____
28. Enteral infusion pump with alarm _____
29. Gravity-fed enteral feeding supply kit (one day) _____
30. Parenteral nutrition administration kit (two days) _____

Outpatient PPS (C Codes) (C1300–C9899)

31. Brachytherapy seed, high-dose rate iridium 192   _____

32. Cardiac event recorder (implantable)   _____

33. Implantable joint device   _____

34. Patient underwent left breast MRI without contrast, followed by left breast MRI with contrast   _____

35. Short-term hemodialysis catheter   _____

36. Single-chamber implantable cardioverter-defibrillator   _____

Durable Medical Equipment (E0100–E9999)

37. "Patient helper" trapeze bars, attached to bed, with grab bar   _____

38. Adult oxygen tent   _____

39. Bilirubin light with photometer   _____

40. Nebulizer with compressor   _____

41. Folding walker with adjustable height   _____

42. Four-lead TENS unit   _____

43. Free-standing cervical traction stand   _____

44. Heavy-duty, extra-wide hospital bed with mattress to accommodate patient who weighs 460 pounds   _____

45. Heparin infusion pump for hemodialysis   _____

46. Jug urinal (male)   _____

47. Lambswool sheepskin heel pad for decubitus prevention   _____

48. Low-intensity ultrasound osteogenesis stimulator   _____

49. Metal bed pan   _____

50. Non-electronic communication board   _____

51. Patient was fitted with a pair of underarm wooden crutches with pads, tips, and handgrips   _____

52. Portable paraffin bath (unit)   _____

53. Portable sitz bath   _____

54. Quad cane with tips   _____

55. Raised toilet seat   _____

56. Power wheelchair accessory, lithium-based battery, each   _____

57. Replacement brake attachment for wheeled walker   _____

58. Ultraviolet light therapy 6-foot panel, with bulbs, timer, and eye protection   _____

59. Variable height hospital bed with mattress and side rails   _____

60. Wheelchair anti-tipping device   _____

Procedures/Professional Services (Temporary) (G0008–G9147)

61. Automated CBC (complete) with automated WBC differential count   _____

62. Patient received antiviral treatment for hepatitis C   _____

63. Individual smoking cessation counseling (10 minutes)   _____

64. Initial E/M evaluation for patient with peripheral neuropathy with loss of protective sensation (LOPS)   _____

65. PET imaging for initial diagnosis of breast cancer   _____

Alcohol and/or Drug Abuse Treatment Services (H0001–H2037)

66. Behavioral health counseling and therapy, 30 minutes _____

67. Partial hospitalization for mental health crisis, 18 hours _____

68. Psychiatric health facility services (one day) _____

69. Respite care services, not in the home (*per diem*) _____

70. Thirty minutes of activity therapy _____

Temporary Durable Medical Equipment (K0000–K9999)

71. Complete front caster assembly for wheelchair
    with two semi-pneumatic tires _____

72. IV hanger (each) _____

73. Leg strap (for wheelchair) _____

74. Lightweight portable motorized wheelchair _____

75. Replacement alkaline battery, 1.5 volt, for patient-owned
    external infusion pump _____

Orthotic Procedures and Devices (L0000–L4999)

76. Cervical wire frame, semi-rigid, for occipital/mandibular support _____

77. Custom-fabricated thoracic rib belt _____

78. HALO procedure; cervical halo incorporated into Milwaukee orthosis _____

79. Neoprene heel and sole elevation lift (one inch) _____

80. Posterior solid ankle plastic AFO, custom fabricated _____

81. Spenco foot insert _____

Prosthetic Procedures (L5000–L9999)

82. Below-knee disarticulation prosthesis, molded socket,
    shin, with SACH foot _____

83. Electric hand, myoelectrical controlled, adult _____

84. Partial foot prosthesis, shoe insert with longitudinal arch, toe filler _____

85. Preparatory prosthesis for hip disarticulation-hemipelvectomy;
    pylon, no cover, solid ankle cushion heel foot, thermoplastic,
    molded to patient model _____

86. Silicone breast prosthesis _____

Medical Services (M0000–M0301)

87. Brief office visit to change prescription medication used for
    treating the patient's personality disorder _____

88. Cellular therapy _____

89. Chemical endarterectomy (IV chelation therapy) _____

90. Fabric wrapping of abdominal aneurysm _____

91. Prolotherapy _____

Pathology and Laboratory Services (P0000–P9999)

92. Catheterization for collection of specimen (one patient) _____

93. Congo red, blood _____

94. Platelets, each unit _____

95. Two units whole blood for transfusion _____

Q Codes: (Temporary) Diagnostic (Q0035–Q9968)

96. Chemotherapy administration by push _____
97. Collagen skin test _____
98. Oral magnetic resonance contrast agent, 100 ml _____
99. Injection, sermorelin acetate, 1 mcg _____
100. KOH preparation _____
101. Pinworm examination _____

Diagnostic Radiology Services (R0000–R5999)

102. Portable x-ray service transportation to nursing home, one trip, one patient seen _____
103. Transportation of portable ECG to nursing facility, one patient seen _____
104. Transportation of portable x-ray service to patient's home, two patients seen (husband and wife) _____

Temporary National Codes (Non-Medicare) (S0000–S9999)

105. Allogenic cord-blood-derived stem cell transplant _____
106. Echosclerotherapy _____
107. Gastrointestinal fat absorption study _____
108. Global fee for extracorporeal shock wave lithotripsy (ESWL) treatment of kidney stone _____
109. Harvesting of multivisceral organs from cadaver with preparation and maintenance of allografts _____
110. Vaginal birth after Caesarean (VBAC) classes _____

National T Codes Established for State Medicaid Agencies (T1000–T9999)

111. Family training and counseling for child development, 15 minutes _____
112. Human breast milk processing, storage, and distribution _____
113. Intramuscular medication administration by home health LPN _____
114. Private-duty nursing, 30 minutes _____
115. Waiver for utility services to support medical equipment _____

Vision Services (V0000–V2999)

116. Bifocal lenses, bilateral, 5.25 sphere, 2.12 cylinder _____
117. Deluxe frame _____
118. Photochromatic tint for two lenses _____
119. Processing, preserving, and transporting corneal tissue _____
120. Reduction of ocular prosthesis _____

Hearing Services (V5000–V5999)

121. Assessment for hearing aid _____
122. Binaural behind-the-ear hearing aid _____
123. Digitally programmable monaural hearing aid, analog _____
124. Dispensing fee, Bilateral Contra Lateral Routing of Signal (BICROS) _____
125. Telephone amplifier _____

ASSIGNMENT 8.3   Coding Drugs in HCPCS

OBJECTIVES

At the conclusion of this assignment, the student should be able to:
1. Interpret the HCPCS Table of Drugs.
2. Assign HCPCS level II codes to procedure or service statements that contain drugs.

INSTRUCTIONS

Code the following statements using the Table of Drugs in HCPCS. Be sure to verify the code(s) in the HCPCS tabular section.

> **NOTE:** Drugs in the HCPCS Table of Drugs are listed by the generic or chemical name. (Drugs are listed by the trade name only if no generic or chemical name is available.) If you search for a drug by its trade name in the table, you are instructed to "see" the generic or chemical name. For assistance with identifying generic or chemical drug names, go to **www.rxlist.com.**

_____ 1. Tetracycline 250 mg injection
_____ 2. Ancef 500 mg IV
_____ 3. Clonidine HCl, 1 mg
_____ 4. Botulinum toxin type B, 100 units
_____ 5. Injection, morphine sulfate, 100 mg
_____ 6. Kenalog-40 20 mg
_____ 7. Streptokinase 250,000 IU IV
_____ 8. Ranitidine HCl injection, 25 mg
_____ 9. 50 units of insulin for administration through insulin pump
_____ 10. Lasix 20 mg IM

ASSIGNMENT 8.4   HCPCS Level II National Modifiers

OBJECTIVES

At the conclusion of this assignment, the student should be able to:
1. Locate HCPCS level II national modifiers in the coding manual.
2. Assign HCPCS level II national modifiers to special circumstances associated with procedures, services, and supplies.

INSTRUCTIONS

Match the modifier in the left column to its appropriate description in the right column.

_____ 1. AH   a. Left hand, thumb
_____ 2. E4   b. Technical component
_____ 3. FA   c. Four patients served
_____ 4. NU   d. Registered nurse (RN)
_____ 5. RC   e. Lower right eyelid
_____ 6. SB   f. New equipment
_____ 7. TA   g. Clinical psychologist
_____ 8. TC   h. Right coronary artery
_____ 9. TD   i. Left foot, great toe
_____ 10. UQ   j. Nurse midwife

INSTRUCTIONS

Enter the appropriate modifier for each description.

11. Intern   _____

12. Court-ordered   _____

13. Monitored anesthesia services   _____

14. No infection present   _____

15. RN   _____

16. Right coronary artery   _____

17. Primary physician   _____

18. Left hand, 5th digit   _____

19. Dressing for 2 wounds   _____

20. Adult program, geriatric   _____

21. Medicare Secondary Payer   _____

22. CLIA-waived test   _____

23. Administered subcutaneously   _____

24. Mental health program   _____

25. Replacement of a DME, prosthetic item   _____

26. Rental   _____

27. Special payment rate, weekends   _____

28. Follow-up services   _____

29. Great toe, left foot   _____

30. Substance abuse program   _____

31. Patient with mild systemic disease   _____

32. Specialty physician   _____

33. New equipment   _____

34. Lower right eyelid   _____

35. Thumb, left hand   _____

36. Related to trauma   _____

37. Outside providers' customary service area   _____

38. Ambulance transport from physician's office   _____

39. Patient pronounced dead after ambulance called   _____

40. Emergency services   _____

ASSIGNMENT 8.5   Coding Case Studies

OBJECTIVES

At the conclusion of this assignment, the student should be able to:

1. Use the HCPCS Index to locate procedure and service codes.
2. Verify codes in the appropriate section of HCPCS.
3. Assign modifier(s) when special circumstances are documented in a case study.

INSTRUCTIONS

Code the following case studies using the HCPCS Index. Be sure to verify the code(s) in the appropriate section of HCPCS. Assign the HCPCS level II procedure and service codes *only* for each case study. Do *not* code diagnoses or assign CPT codes.

1. PATIENT CASE #1

S: The patient is an 89-year-old white female resident of the county nursing facility. I was asked to see her today because the nursing staff had noticed the patient having difficulty breathing and was coughing up purulent material. A chest x-ray was ordered, and the mobile x-ray service arrived and took the x-ray while I was seeing my other patients.

O: The patient appears ill. Temperature is 100.7. CHEST: Scattered rhonchi throughout all lung fields, with severely diminished breath sounds in the left lower lung. Expiratory and inspiratory wheezes present. HEART: Within normal limits. ABDOMEN: No tenderness on palpation. EXTREMITIES: Mild dependent edema is noted; otherwise within normal limits.

A: The chest x-ray revealed a density consistent with left lower lobe pneumonia.

P: The patient was given an injection of Zithromax 500 mg. The cough does not seem to be bothersome to the patient right now, so the nursing staff will wait and watch. The nursing staff is to monitor her for any signs of increased fever, lethargy, or medication reaction. They are to encourage fluids and keep the patient up in a chair as much as possible when she is not sleeping. They are to contact me immediately if the patient's symptoms worsen.

2. PATIENT CASE #2

S: This 45-year-old construction worker was seen in the office today on an emergency basis because he stepped on a sharp edge of steel and lacerated his right foot. He states he cannot recall his last tetanus shot.

O: Examination of the right foot reveals a laceration of approximately 3.5 cm at the lateral edge of the foot which extends medially across the heel. PROCEDURE: The right heel was cleansed with pHisoHex and prepped with Betadine. The wound edges were infiltrated with 1 percent Xylocaine. After adequate anesthesia was obtained, the laceration was repaired with 3-0 nylon sutures. The wound was dressed with gauze and secured with paper tape.

A: Laceration of right heel, repaired in the office.

P: The patient was given a tetanus shot today. He was given instructions on wound care and signs of infection, and was also given reference sheets on the same. He is to be non-weightbearing for the next three days, and was given a pair of wooden crutches. He will return to the office in three days for reevaluation. The patient was also reminded to call immediately if pain increases or if he shows any signs of fever.

3. PATIENT CASE #3

MAMMOGRAPHY CLINIC NOTE: The patient is a 72-year-old female who presented today for mammogram. She states she has remained up-to-date with her mammograms, and her record shows compliance with yearly screening exams. The patient stated that when performing her self-breast exam about five days ago, she felt a lump in the upper outer quadrant of the left breast. The technician asked her to identify the location of the lump, and it was marked with a BB for mammography. The patient was asked to wait until the radiologist had read the initial x-rays. Upon interpretation, there indeed was a suspicious lesion in the upper outer quadrant of the left breast, approximately 1.5 cm. The patient was then asked to undergo additional radiographic views of the left breast for further investigation of the lesion. It is felt that the lesion is consistent with malignancy, and the patient was counseled by the nurse practitioner regarding the results of the mammography. We contacted the surgeon's office, and the patient was scheduled tomorrow for biopsy and further evaluation as needed.

---

4. PATIENT CASE #4

S: The patient presents today for annual physical exam with Pap. She is now 34, has two healthy children, and is doing well except for some complaints of fatigue and recent weight gain.

O: VITAL SIGNS: Blood pressure is 124/72. Pulse is 64 and regular. Respiratory rate is 20. Temperature is 98.8. Weight is 156, which is up 12 pounds since her last visit. HEENT: Within normal limits. The patient wears glasses. NECK: No thyromegaly or lymphadenopathy. HEART: Regular sinus rhythm. CHEST: Clear breath sounds throughout all lung fields. ABDOMEN: No tenderness or organomegaly. PELVIC: Normal external genitalia. Vagina is pink and rugated. Pap specimen was obtained without difficulty. RECTAL: Exam was deferred. EXTREMITIES: Pulses were full and equal. NEUROLOGIC: No complaints; exam within normal limits. LABORATORY: Lab performed in the office today included a CBC with differential, thyroid panel, and complete metabolic panel.

A: Fatigue and weight gain in an otherwise healthy 34-year-old female.

P: Will await the results of the blood work and call the patient to discuss them. Instructed the patient to take a daily multivitamin and drink at least two glasses of milk daily. Discussed dietary modifications to help stop weight gain. If the patient's blood work indicates abnormal thyroid function, will refer to Endocrinology.

---

5. PATIENT CASE #5

PROSTHESIS CLINIC NOTE: The patient presents today because of complaints of discomfort from his right ocular prosthesis. The prosthesis is relatively new and may need some modification. Upon examination, the patient appeared otherwise generally well. The right eye prosthesis was removed and given to the technician for evaluation. The right eye socket had a very small patch of irritated tissue in the upper medial wall. The technician resurfaced and polished the prosthesis, and after refitting, the patient reported a noticeable improvement in his level of comfort. The patient and I then discussed the psychological struggles he has had with the loss of his eye, but overall he feels more optimistic and states he believes he will be able to fully resume his normal level of activity.

ASSIGNMENT 8.6 Coding Verification

OBJECTIVES

At the conclusion of this assignment, the student should be able to:

1. Validate coding accuracy based on coding information.
2. Analyze results and make recommendations.

OVERVIEW

HCPCS level II codes can be utilized to capture procedures and services that do not have a CPT level I code. Auditing of HCPCS level II code(s) will provide the opportunity for analysis to provide recommendations that will improve code reporting and reimbursement.

INSTRUCTIONS

Access the Web site for online HCPCS level II coding (**www.eicd.com**). Once at the site, locate the link to the HCPCS level II coding classification. Review the following information and read the information presented in the column stated "coding statements" and the corresponding HCPCS level II code assigned. Enter information into the Web site search, and determine if the correct HCPCS level II code was assigned. If this code is correct, record it again in the coding verification column; if the code is incorrect, record the correct code in the coding verification column. Provide an analysis of your findings: What percentage of the codes were correct? What percentage were incorrect based on the 10 charts that were reviewed? What recommendations or suggestions can you provide based on your verification process? Provide your thoughts in a double-spaced, word-processed document that is at least one-half page in length.

HEALTH RECORD NUMBER	CODING STATEMENT	CODE ASSIGNED	CODING VERIFICATION
585598	Azathioprine oral 50 mg	J7501	
111454	20 mg injection of methylprednisolone acetate	J1030	
313258	Injection of digoxin 0.3 mg	J1160	
899784	Zidovudine, 10 mg injection	S0104	
123456	Prochlorperazine, 10 mg injection	Q0164	
778541	200 mg injection of fluconazole	J1450	
549786	3 mg injection of hydromorphone	J1170	
343437	2 mg injection of Urecholine	J0520 x 2	
777845	6 mg injection of pegfilgrastim	J2440	
233233	500 mg injection of cefazolin sodium	J0690	

> **NOTE:** Navigate the HCPCS level II coding Web site to research information needed for your summary. This will help you learn how to locate information using the Internet as a research tool and using Web sites, which often requires using tool bars and pull-down menus.

ASSIGNMENT 8.7   Multiple Choice Review

1. **Which HCPCS codes were discontinued in December 2003?**
   a. level I
   b. level II
   c. level III
   d. level IV

2. **Which organization is responsible for developing and maintaining the HCPCS level II codes?**
   a. AMA
   b. CMS
   c. HHS
   d. WHO

3. **Which is a member of the HCPCS National Panel?**
   a. American Hospital Association
   b. American Medical Association
   c. Centers for Disease Control and Prevention
   d. Centers for Medicare and Medicaid Services

4. **Which organization is responsible for providing suppliers and manufacturers with assistance in determining HCPCS level II codes to be used?**
   a. BCBSA
   b. DMEPOS
   c. DMERC
   d. PDAC

5. **Which HCPCS level II codes are used by state Medicaid agencies and mandated by state law to separately identify mental health services?**
   a. G codes
   b. H codes
   c. K codes
   d. S codes

6. **The first alphabetic character in a HCPCS code identifies the code**
   a. as one established for Medicare.
   b. as one unique to Medicaid.
   c. section of HCPCS level I.
   d. section of HCPCS level II.

7. **Drugs are listed in the HCPCS Table of Drugs according to**
   a. dosage to be used.
   b. generic name.
   c. route of administration.
   d. brand name.

8. **A regional MAC will receive claims that contain which HCPCS level II codes?**
   a. A, J, Q, V
   b. B, E, K, L
   c. C, F, H, N, S
   d. D, G, M, P, R

9. **If a provider is not registered with a regional MAC, a patient will receive medical equipment when the**
   a. local hospital dispenses the equipment.
   b. patient places an order for the equipment.
   c. physician refers the patient to another doctor.
   d. prescription is taken to a local DMEPOS dealer.

10. **If a particular service has both a CPT code and a HCPCS level II code, the provider will**
    a. assign only the CPT code.
    b. follow instructions provided by the payer.
    c. report both codes on the CMS-1500 claim form.
    d. report only the HCPCS code.

11. **If a HCPCS drug code description states "per 50 mg" and is administered in an 80 mg dose, which quantity (e.g., units) is reported on the CMS-1500 claim form?**
    a. 1
    b. 2
    c. 50
    d. 80

12. **HCPCS level II is considered a _____ system.**
    a. coding
    b. nomenclature
    c. payment
    d. reimbursement

13. **Which professional organization maintains level II "D" codes?**
    a. American Billers Association
    b. American Dental Association
    c. American Hospital Association
    d. American Medical Association

14. **How many regional MACs are assigned by CMS to process DME claims?**
    a. two
    b. three
    c. four
    d. five

15. **Which is an example of durable medical equipment (DME)?**
    a. blood glucose monitor.
    b. irrigation solution.
    c. IV pain medication.
    d. liquid oxygen.

16. **Permanent HCPCS level II codes are updated annually on**
    a. January 1.
    b. March 1.
    c. June 1.
    d. October 1.

17. **Which code range is assigned to "Administrative, Miscellaneous, and Investigational" HCPCS procedures or services?**
    a. A4000–A8999
    b. A9000–A9999
    c. E0100–E9999
    d. S0000–S9999

18. **Which modifier is used to describe the services of a clinical psychologist?**
    a. –AH
    b. –AM
    c. –AP
    d. –AS

19. **Which modifier is used to describe the right upper eyelid?**
    a. –E1
    b. –E2
    c. –E3
    d. –E4

20. **HCPCS level II codes are organized by type, depending on the purpose of the codes and the entity responsible for establishing and maintaining them. The four types include _____.**
    a. Permanent, Vision, Medical, Modifiers
    b. Miscellaneous, Temporary, Permanent, Drugs
    c. Diagnostic, Vision, Hearing, Medical
    d. Permanent national, Miscellaneous, Temporary codes, and Modifiers

CHAPTER 9
CMS Reimbursement Methodologies

ASSIGNMENT 9.1 Outpatient Prospective Payment System (OPPS)

OBJECTIVES

At the completion of this assignment, the student should be able to:

1. Explain the difference between coinsurance and copayment.
2. Calculate the patient's share of charges for an outpatient service.

INSTRUCTIONS

Under the OPPS, Medicare allows patients to pay either a coinsurance amount (20 percent of the charge for procedures and services) *or* a fixed copayment amount, whichever is less. For each of the following cases, calculate the amount the patient is required to pay to the hospital for the outpatient service provided.

> **NOTE:** In each of the following cases, the patient has already met the annual deductible required by the payer.

_____ 1. Sally Jones underwent outpatient surgery to have one mole removed from her upper back. The charge was $65. The fixed copayment amount for this type of procedure, adjusted for wages in the geographic area, is $15.

_____ 2. Cherie Brown underwent an outpatient chest x-ray that cost $75. The fixed copayment for this type of procedure, adjusted for wages in the geographic area, is $25.

_____ 3. James Hill underwent an outpatient oral glucose tolerance test. The charge for this procedure was $122. The fixed copayment for this type of procedure, adjusted for wages in the geographic area, is $20.

_____ 4. Scott Wills underwent toenail removal as an outpatient. The charge was $81. The fixed copayment for this type of procedure, adjusted for wages in the geographic area, is $25.

_____ 5. George Harris had a suspicious lesion removed from his left temple as an outpatient. The charge was $78. The fixed copayment amount for this type of procedure, adjusted for wages in the geographic area, is $15.

ASSIGNMENT 9.2 Diagnosis-Related Groups

OBJECTIVES

At the conclusion of this assignment, the student should be able to:

1. Interpret a diagnosis-related group (DRG) decision tree.
2. Differentiate between medical partitioning and surgical partitioning DRG decision trees.
3. Determine which DRG is assigned when a secondary diagnosis such as a complication or comorbidity is documented in the patient record.

INSTRUCTIONS

Diagnoses and procedures are grouped according to a particular DRG, and DRG decision trees (Figures 9-1 and 9-2) visually represent the process of assigning a DRG within a medical diagnostic category (MDC). The decision trees use a flowchart design to facilitate the decision-making logic for assigning a DRG. (Only ICD-9-CM or ICD-10-CM diagnosis codes are grouped according to a medical partitioning DRG decision tree. ICD-9-CM or ICD-10-PCS surgical procedure codes are grouped according to a surgical partitioning DRG decision tree.)

1. Interpret the DRG decision tree in Figure 9-1 to answer the following questions.

> **EXAMPLE:** Which neoplasm DRG is assigned to a patient whose provider has documented a complication or comorbidity?
>
> **Answer:** DRG 10.

_____ a. Which DRG is assigned when the provider documents "transient ischemia" as the patient's principal diagnosis?

_____ b. For a patient who has cranial and peripheral nerve disorders and a documented comorbidity, which DRG is assigned?

_____ c. Which DRG is assigned for a patient whose principal diagnosis is multiple sclerosis?

_____ d. A patient was diagnosed with trigeminal neuralgia. This is the only diagnosis reported in the record. Which DRG is assigned?

_____ e. For a patient with cerebrovascular disease that is classified as nonspecific, which DRG is assigned when the patient has a secondary diagnosis of insulin-dependent diabetes mellitus?

2. Interpret the DRG decision tree in Figure 9-2 to answer the following questions.

_____ a. For a 25-year-old patient who undergoes craniotomy for implantation of a chemotherapeutic agent, which DRG is assigned?

_____ b. Which DRG is assigned to a 5-year-old patient who underwent a procedure for a ventricular shunt?

_____ c. A 56-year-old patient underwent a craniotomy and suffered a cerebrovascular accident after the procedure. Which DRG is assigned?

_____ d. Which DRG is assigned for an otherwise healthy patient who underwent sciatic nerve biopsy?

_____ e. A patient underwent lumbar laminectomy because of injury from a fall. The patient recently completed a course of chemotherapy for non-Hodgkin's lymphoma. Which DRG is assigned?

ASSIGNMENT 9.3 Data Reports

OBJECTIVES

At the conclusion of this assignment, the student should be able to:

1. Locate data from a governmental report.
2. Calculate percentages using data from a report.
3. Verify data reporting.

OVERVIEW

The Centers for Medicare and Medicaid Services (CMS) has many resources available on its Web site. CMS provides data on Medicare Utilization for both Part A and Part B services. The data are presented in table format, ranked in order from the highest to the lowest allowed charge and allowed services. The types of data available at the Web site include E/M codes by specialty, lab procedures, level II codes, level I codes, and type of service codes.

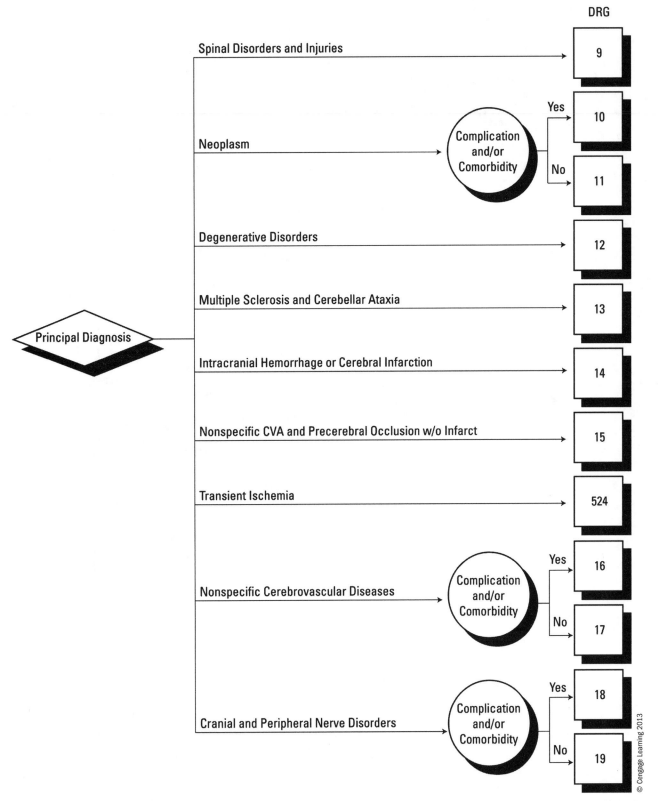

FIGURE 9-1 Major Diagnostic Category I: Diseases and Disorders of the Nervous System (Medical Partitioning)

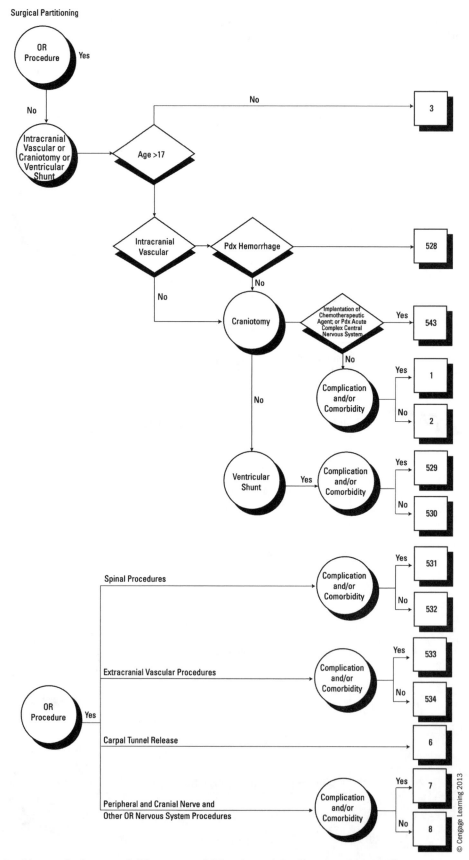

FIGURE 9-2 Major Diagnostic Category I: Diseases and Disorders of the Nervous System (Surgical Partitioning)

INSTRUCTIONS

Access the Web site for the Centers for Medicare and Medicaid Services (**www.cms.gov**). Once at the site, locate the link to the Research, Statistics, Data, & Systems area. Scroll to the Statistics, Trends & Reports Section and review the information under Medicare-Fee-For-Service Statistics, Medicare Utilization for Part B. Locate calendar year 2009 data under the headings Top 200 Level I (CPT) Codes and Top 200 Level II (HCPCS) Codes ranked by *Charges*. After reviewing the data tables, answer the following questions.

1. What CPT level I code is ranked number one in services?
2. What was the total allowed services for CPT code 99285?
3. What is the percentage of non E/M codes in the top 20 ranking?
4. What was the total allowed charges for HCPCS level II code A0425?
5. What is the percentage of transport HCPCS level II codes in the top 20 ranking?
6. In his annual meeting, a CFO at a local hospital stated that CMS paid $4.2 million for services in critical care units under CPT code 99291. Is this correct?
7. What was the national allowed charge for a diagnostic flexible colonoscopy?
8. List the highest ranking CPT surgical code and description?
9. What HCPCS level II code(s) had an allowed charge of $21.1 million?
10. What is the radiology procedure code with the highest allowed charge amount? What is the yearly total allowed charge for this procedure code? What is this radiology procedure code for?

> **NOTE:** Navigate the CMS Web site to research information needed to answer the questions in this assignment. This will help you learn how to locate information using the Internet as a research tool and using Web sites. It will also require you to find and verify information on a table.

ASSIGNMENT 9.4   Medicare Severity DRGs

OBJECTIVES

At the conclusion of this assignment, the student should be able to:

1. Enter data to calculate MS DRGs (Medicare Severity Diagnosis-Related Groups).
2. Interpret MS DRG data (e.g., reimbursement rate, weight).

OVERVIEW

The Centers for Medicare and Medicaid Services has developed a severity DRG calculation system. **IRP.com** is a Web site where you can access Medicare Severity DRG methodology information.

INSTRUCTIONS

Access the Web site by going to **http://www.irp.com** and clicking on the Medicare DRG Calculator link. Review the following paragraphs and enter the ICD-9-CM code(s) and other data at the site. Compare the information retrieved from the site to answer the questions in this assignment. (At the publication of this edition, ICD-10-CM/PCS codes could not yet be entered in the Medicare DRG Calculator.)

1. John L. Berry is a 70-year-old male, seen and admitted for congestive heart failure. The patient is discharged after developing pneumonia during the hospital stay. Total inpatient days this patient was in the hospital is seven days. Mr. Berry is discharged to his home with follow-up at his internist's office in three days. Discharge diagnoses codes (after review of the record by the coder): 428.0, 250.01, 486, and 401.9.

   a. What is the MS DRG weight for this patient?_____

   b. What is the major complication or comorbidity (MCC) diagnosis?_____

   c. How does the MCC diagnosis compare to the principal diagnosis as assigned by the coder?

   _____

2. Sally Parsons is an 85-year-old female admitted after being seen in the emergency department with a painful and swollen lower right leg. She is admitted for further treatment and evaluation. She is found to have an osteomyelitis of her leg. Discharge diagnoses codes are 730.06, 731.3, 733.00, and 244.9. Mrs. Parsons has osteoporosis and hypothyroidism, which are treated and evaluated during this inpatient admission. Mrs. Parsons is discharged to home with IV home health services.

   a. What is the MS DRG?_____

   b. What is the MS DRG reimbursement rate? _____

3. Lawrence Texfield is a 90-year-old man who is admitted due to his uncontrolled diabetes. He is in the hospital for eight days due to his additional complaint of chest pain on admission day three. He is discharged to home with home health services. Codes assigned after review of the record and physician documentation are 250.72, 443.81, 600.11, and 413.9.

   a. What is the MS DRG reimbursement rate? _____

4. Maria Martin is a 65-year-old female admitted after falling at home. She is diagnosed with a femur fracture and requires an ORIF (open reduction with internal fixation). After having the operation, she has a cardiac arrest, which is converted from, and she is found to have cardiomyopathy. Discharge for this patient is to a skilled nursing facility (SNF). ICD-9-CM codes assigned by coder after chart review: 820.8, 427.5, 425.4, 429.0, and 79.35.

   a. What is the MS DRG? _____

   b. What is the MS DRG reimbursement rate? _____

5. Abe Dillon is a 75-year-old male currently under treatment for anal sphincter cancer. He is admitted for inpatient surgery to remove his diseased gallbladder; this is done via an open procedure. Mr. Dillon is discharged from the hospital after four days to an intermediate care facility. ICD-9-CM codes assigned are 574.11, 403.90, 585.3, 154.2, 51.22, and 51.10.

   a. What is the MS DRG weight? _____

   b. What is the MS DRG reimbursement rate? _____

   c. Does this patient have a CC per the grouper? _____

ASSIGNMENT 9.5   Ambulatory Payment Classifications

OBJECTIVES

At the completion of this assignment, the student should be able to:

1. Explain the difference between Medicare *status indicators* and *procedure discounting*.
2. Locate and interpret data in an ambulatory payment classification table.
3. Verify procedure and service codes in the appropriate section of CPT manual.

INTRODUCTION

Ambulatory payment classifications (APCs) are used by Medicare's outpatient prospective payment system (OPPS) to calculate reimbursement rates for hospital outpatient procedures and services. APC payments are made to hospitals when a Medicare outpatient is discharged from the emergency department or outpatient clinic or when the patient is transferred to another hospital (or other facility) that is not affiliated with the initial hospital where the patient originally received outpatient services. If the patient is admitted to the hospital (as an inpatient) from the hospital's emergency department or outpatient, there is no APC payment; instead, Medicare reimburses the hospital according to its inpatient prospective payment system (IPPS) that uses Medicare severity diagnosis-related groups (MS-DRGs).

INSTRUCTIONS

Review each ambulatory payment classification (APC) tables, and answer the questions listed below each table. Be sure to verify the description of procedure/service code(s) in the CPT manual.

TABLE 9-1 Level I Skin Repair

MEDICARE STATUS INDICATORS AND PROCEDURE DISCOUNTING	
STATUS INDICATOR	**DESCRIPTION**
T	Significant procedure, multiple procedure reduction applies
S	Significant procedure, and is not discounted when you report multiple CPT codes that group to APCs with multiple "S" status indicators
Level I Skin Repair	
Codes in Range	11760
	11950
	11952
	11954
	12001
Status Indicator:	T
Relative Weight:	1.330
Payment Rate:	$98.81
National Adjusted Coinsurance:	$25.67
Minimum Unadjusted Coinsurance:	$18.37

© Cengage Learning 2013

_____ 1. What is the level I skin repair payment rate?
_____ 2. What is the relative weight for level I skin repair?
_____ 3. What is the Medicare status indicator for level I skin repair?
_____ 4. How many codes are contained in the range for level I skin repair?
_____ 5. What is the national adjusted coinsurance for level I skin repair?

TABLE 9-2 Fine Needle Biopsy/Aspiration

MEDICARE STATUS INDICATORS AND PROCEDURE DISCOUNTING	
STATUS INDICATOR	**DESCRIPTION**
T	Significant procedure, multiple procedure reduction applies
S	Significant procedure, and is not discounted when you report multiple CPT codes that group to APCs with multiple "S" status indicators
Fine Needle Biopsy/Aspiration	
Codes in Range	10021
	19001
	36680
Status Indicator:	T
Relative Weight:	1.5703
Payment Rate:	$108.16
National Adjusted Coinsurance:	N/A
Minimum Unadjusted Coinsurance:	$21.64

© Cengage Learning 2013

_____ 6. What is the level I skin repair minimum unadjusted coinsurance?

_____ 7. What is the payment rate for fine needle biopsy/aspiration?

_____ 8. What is the relative weight for fine needle biopsy/aspiration?

_____ 9. Which code is reported for placement of a needle for intraosseous infusion?

_____ 10. What is the Medicare status indicator for fine needle biopsy/aspiration?

TABLE 9-3 Level II Breast Surgery

MEDICARE STATUS INDICATORS AND PROCEDURE DISCOUNTING	
STATUS INDICATOR	**DESCRIPTION**
T	Significant procedure, multiple procedure reduction applies
S	Significant procedure, and is not discounted when you report multiple CPT codes that group to APCs with multiple "S" status indicators
Level II Breast Surgery	
Codes in Range	19105
	19303
	19304
	19316
	19328
Status Indicator:	T
Relative Weight:	33.9253
Payment Rate:	$2,336.64
National Adjusted Coinsurance:	$581.52
Minimum Unadjusted Coinsurance:	$467.33

© Cengage Learning 2013

_____ 11. What is the Medicare status indicator for level II breast surgery?

_____ 12. What is the national adjusted coinsurance for level II breast surgery?

_____ 13. What is the minimum unadjusted coinsurance for level II breast surgery?

_____ 14. What is the payment rate for level II breast surgery?

_____ 15. What is the relative weight for level II breast surgery?

TABLE 9-4 Cardiac Rehabilitation

MEDICARE STATUS INDICATORS AND PROCEDURE DISCOUNTING	
STATUS INDICATOR	**DESCRIPTION**
T	Significant procedure, multiple procedure reduction applies
S	Significant procedure, and is not discounted when you report multiple CPT codes that group to APCs with multiple "S" status indicators
Cardiac Rehabilitation	
Codes in Range	93797
	93798
	G0422
	G0423
Status Indicator:	S
Relative Weight:	0.9991
Payment Rate:	$68.81
National Adjusted Coinsurance:	$13.86
Minimum Unadjusted Coinsurance:	$13.77

© Cengage Learning 2013

_____ **16.** What is the payment rate for cardiac rehabilitation?

_____ **17.** What is the national adjusted coinsurance for cardiac rehabilitation?

_____ **18.** What is the Medicare status indicator for cardiac rehabilitation?

_____ **19.** What is the relative weight for cardiac rehabilitation?

_____ **20.** Which code is reported for "intensive cardiac rehabilitation; with or without continuous ECG monitoring with exercise, per session?"

TABLE 9-5 Small Intestine Endoscopy

MEDICARE STATUS INDICATORS AND PROCEDURE DISCOUNTING	
STATUS INDICATOR	**DESCRIPTION**
T	Significant procedure, multiple procedure reduction applies
S	Significant procedure, and is not discounted when you report multiple CPT codes that group to APCs with multiple "S" status indicators
Small Intestine Endoscopy	
Codes in Range	44360
	44361
	44363
	44364
	44365
Status Indicator:	T
Relative Weight:	10.1857
Payment Rate:	$701.55
National Adjusted Coinsurance:	$152.78
Minimum Unadjusted Coinsurance:	$140.31

© Cengage Learning 2013

_____ **21.** How many codes are contained in the range for small intestine endoscopy?

_____ **22.** What is the relative weight for small intestine endoscopy?

_____ **23.** What is the national adjusted coinsurance for small intestine endoscopy?

_____ **24.** What is the payment rate for small intestine endoscopy?

_____ **25.** What is the minimum unadjusted coinsurance for small intestine endoscopy?

ASSIGNMENT 9.6 Multiple Choice Review

1. **The Resource-Based Relative Value Scale (RBRVS) system is also known as**

   a. Clinical Laboratory Fee Schedule.

   b. Long-Term Care Diagnosis-Related Groups.

   c. Medicare Physician Fee Schedule.

   d. Resource Utilization Groups.

2. **Which reimbursement system establishes rates in advance of services and is based on reported charges from which a *per diem* rate is determined?**

   a. fee-for-service cost-based

   b. prospective price-based

   c. prospective cost-based

   d. retrospective reasonable cost

3. Review the following ambulance fee schedule and calculate the Medicare payment rate in year 6 (for an ambulance company reasonable charge of $600).

	AMBULANCE FEE SCHEDULE						
YEAR	AMBULANCE COMPANY (REASONABLE) CHARGE (a)	% OF REASONABLE CHARGE (b)	AMOUNT (c)	AMBULANCE FEE SCHEDULE RATE (d)	PHASE IN % (e)	AMOUNT (f)	MEDICARE PAYMENT (g)
	Formula: [(a) x (b) = (c)] + [(d) x (e) = (f)] = Medicare payment (g)						
1	$600	80%	$480	n/a	n/a	n/a	
2	$600	80%	$480	$425	20%	$85	
3	$600	60%	$360	$425	40%	$170	
4	$600	40%	$240	$425	60%	$255	
5	$600	20%	$120	$425	80%	$340	
6	$600	0%	$0	$425	100%	$425	

a. $425

b. $460

c. $480

d. $495

4. Review the following ambulance fee schedule and calculate the amount Medicare paid in year 5 (for an ambulance company reasonable charge of $720).

	AMBULANCE FEE SCHEDULE						
YEAR	AMBULANCE COMPANY (REASONABLE) CHARGE (a)	% OF REASONABLE CHARGE (b)	AMOUNT (c)	AMBULANCE FEE SCHEDULE RATE (d)	PHASE IN % (e)	AMOUNT (f)	MEDICARE PAYMENT (g)
	Formula: [(a) x (b) = (c)] + [(d) x (e) = (f)] = Medicare payment (g)						
1	$720	80%	$576	n/a	n/a	n/a	
2	$720	80%	$576	$425	20%	$85	
3	$720	60%	$432	$425	40%	$170	
4	$720	40%	$288	$425	60%	$255	
5	$720	20%	$144	$425	80%	$340	
6	$720	0%	$0	$425	100%	$425	

a. $425

b. $460

c. $484

d. $576

5. The Deficit Reduction Act of _____ established the Medicare clinical laboratory fee schedule.

a. 1980

b. 1984

c. 1999

d. 2005

6. Sally Brown registered as an outpatient at the hospital for three encounters: chest x-ray, gait training physical therapy, and excision of lesion from right upper arm. Ambulatory patient classification (APC) reimbursement will be based on the

a. APC that provides the hospital with the highest reimbursement amount possible.

b. assignment of multiple APCs that reflect all services provided, with discounting.

c. calculation of four APC rates after codes are assigned to calculate the payment.

d. reimbursement determined by the APC that the primary care provider documents.

7. An *episode of care* in the home health prospective payment system (HHPPS) is _____ days.
   a. 21
   b. 30
   c. 60
   d. 90

8. In which year was the inpatient prospective payment system implemented?
   a. 1973
   b. 1976
   c. 1983
   d. 1986

9. Which type of hospital is excluded from the inpatient prospective payment system?
   a. cancer
   b. coronary
   c. osteopathic
   d. university

10. The IPPS window requires outpatient preadmission services provided by a hospital up to _____ prior to a patient's inpatient admission to be covered by the IPPS MS-DRG payment.
    a. 12 hours
    b. 36 hours
    c. 48 hours
    d. 72 hours

11. Which is a relative value unit (RVU) in the Medicare physician fee schedule payment system?
    a. geographic location
    b. payroll expenditures
    c. physician experience
    d. practice expense

12. Medicare Part B radiology services payments vary according to
    a. cost of supplies.
    b. place of service.
    c. relative value units.
    d. time with the patient.

13. The physician fee schedule for CPT code 99214 is $75. Calculate the nonPAR *limiting charge* for this service.
    a. $56.25
    b. $71.25
    c. $75.00
    d. $81.94

14. The physician fee schedule for CPT code 99214 is $75. Calculate the nonPAR *allowed charge* for this service.
    a. $56.25
    b. $71.25
    c. $75.00
    d. $81.94

15. The intent of establishing a limiting charge for nonPARs is to
    a. increase the patient case load of Medicare PARs.
    b. protect Medicare enrollees financially.
    c. penalize providers who do not participate in Medicare.
    d. reduce fraud and abuse of the Medicare system.

16. Jeffrey Border received care from his participating physician, who charged $300 for her services. (Mr. Border has already met his Medicare Part B deductible.) Mr. Border has primary coverage with his employer group health plan (EGHP). The EGHP's allowed charge for the service was $260, of which 80 percent was paid by the EGHP ($208). The Medicare physician fee schedule for the procedure is $240. Using the rules to determine the amount of Medicare secondary benefits, calculate the Medicare secondary payment.
    a. $32
    b. $42
    c. $52
    d. $92

17. **Which is classified as a nonphysician practitioner?**
    a. laboratory technician
    b. medical assistant
    c. physician assistant
    d. radiologic technologist

18. **Which publication communicates new or changed policies and procedures that are being incorporated into a specific CMS manual?**
    a. benefit policy manual
    b. coverage determinations manual
    c. program transmittal
    d. quarterly provider update

19. **When an office-based service is performed in a health care facility, payment is affected by the use of**
    a. additional CPT modifier(s).
    b. a case-mix adjustment.
    c. ICD-9-CM/ICD-10-PCS procedure code(s).
    d. a site of service differential.

20. **Medicare is primary to**
    a. BCBS EGHP.
    b. homeowner liability insurance.
    c. Medicaid.
    d. workers' compensation.

CHAPTER 10
Coding for Medical Necessity

ASSIGNMENT 10.1   Choosing the First-Listed Diagnosis

OBJECTIVES

At the conclusion of this assignment, the student should be able to:

1. Define *first-listed diagnosis* as it is reported on the CMS-1500 claim.
2. Identify the first-listed diagnosis upon review of conditions, diagnoses, and signs or symptoms.

INSTRUCTIONS

Review each case and underline the first-listed diagnosis.

> **EXAMPLE:** The patient was seen in the office to rule out cervical radiculopathy. The patient has a recent history of pain in both scapular regions along with spasms of the left upper trapezius muscle. The patient has limited range of motion, neck and left arm. X-rays reveal significant cervical osteoarthritis. FIRST-LISTED DIAGNOSIS: <u>Cervical osteoarthritis</u>.

> **NOTE:** Do not select differentiated diagnoses, such as "rule out cervical radiculopathy," as the answer because such diagnoses are not coded and reported on the CMS-1500 claim for outpatient cases. Also, do not report symptoms such as spasms of the left upper trapezius muscle and limited range of motion, neck and left arm, because they are due to the cervical osteoarthritis that is reported as the first-listed diagnosis in Block 21, #1, of the CMS-1500 claim.

1. Pain, left knee. History of injury to left knee 20 years ago. The patient underwent arthroscopic surgery and medial meniscectomy, right knee (10 years ago). Probable arthritis, left knee.
2. The patient was admitted to the emergency department (ED) with complaints of severe chest pain. Possible myocardial infarction. EKG and cardiac enzymes revealed normal findings. Diagnosis upon discharge was gastroesophageal reflux disease.
3. A female patient was seen in the office for follow-up of hypertension. The nurse noticed upper arm bruising on the patient and asked how she sustained the bruising. The physician renewed the patient's hypertension prescription, hydrochlorothiazide.
4. A 10-year-old male was seen in the office for sore throat. The nurse swabbed the patient's throat and sent swabs to the hospital lab for a strep test. The physician documented "likely strep throat" on the patient's record.
5. The patient was seen in the outpatient department to have a lump in his abdomen evaluated and removed. The surgeon removed the lump, and the pathology report revealed that the lump was a lipoma.

ASSIGNMENT 10.2   Linking Diagnoses with Procedures/Services

OBJECTIVES

At the conclusion of this assignment, the student should be able to:

1. Define *medical necessity*.
2. Link diagnoses with procedures/services to justify medical necessity.

INSTRUCTIONS

Match the diagnosis in the right-hand column with the procedure/service in the left-hand column that justifies medical necessity.

_____	**1.** allergy test	**a.**	bronchial asthma
_____	**2.** EKG	**b.**	chest pain
_____	**3.** inhalation treatment	**c.**	family history, cervical cancer
_____	**4.** Pap smear	**d.**	fractured wrist
_____	**5.** removal of ear wax	**e.**	hay fever
_____	**6.** sigmoidoscopy	**f.**	hematuria
_____	**7.** strep test	**g.**	impacted cerumen
_____	**8.** urinalysis	**h.**	fibroid tumor
_____	**9.** biopsy	**i.**	rectal bleeding
_____	**10.** x-ray, radius and ulna	**j.**	sore throat

ASSIGNMENT 10.3   National Coverage Determinations

OBJECTIVES

At the conclusion of this assignment, the student should be able to:

1. Define *national coverage determinations*.
2. Locate national coverage determination policies at the CMS Web site.
3. Interpret national coverage determination policies to determine whether Medicare will reimburse for procedures/services provided.

INSTRUCTIONS

Assign ICD-9-CM (or ICD-10-CM) and CPT or HCPCS level II (procedure/service) codes to the following outpatient scenarios. (Do *not* assign ICD procedure codes.) Go to **www.cms.hhs.gov/mcd,** click on the **Indexes** link, and click on the National Coverage Determinations (NCDs) Alphabetical Listing link to review the item/service description and determine indications and limitations of coverage for each case. Indicate whether the procedure/service is covered by Medicare.

1. A 65-year-old white female underwent apheresis of red blood cells for the treatment of Guillain-Barré syndrome.
2. A 70-year-old male underwent blood glucose testing to monitor his diabetes mellitus.
3. A 45-year-old female with a mental disability underwent Roux-en-Y gastric bypass (RYGBP) surgery for treatment of morbid obesity. (The NCD for RYGBP is entitled "bariatric surgery for treatment of morbid obesity."). The patient also has hypertension and uncontrolled diabetes mellitus.
4. A 75-year-old female participated in a cardiac rehabilitation program for three months immediately following inpatient hospital discharge for an initial acute myocardial infarction.
5. A 72-year-old female underwent her annual screening mammogram, bilateral.

ASSIGNMENT 10.4   Coding from Case Scenarios

OBJECTIVES

At the conclusion of this assignment, the student should be able to:

1. Select diagnoses, procedures, and services upon review of case scenarios.
2. Assign ICD-9-CM (or ICD-10-CM), CPT, and HCPCS level II codes (and appropriate modifiers) to diagnoses, procedures, and services.

INSTRUCTIONS

Assign ICD-9-CM (or ICD-10-CM) codes to diagnoses and CPT or HCPCS level II codes to procedures and services in each case scenario. Be sure to report CPT and HCPCS modifiers where appropriate.

1. A 35-year-old established patient came to the office for excessive menstruation and irregular menstrual cycle. The physician performed an expanded problem-focused evaluation and cervical biopsy.

   CPT/HCPCS Level II Codes   **ICD-9-CM (or ICD-10-CM) Codes**

   _____   _____

2. The patient was referred by his primary care physician to see Dr. Pearson because of severe back pain. Dr. Pearson feels he should have surgery, but the patient states the pain is relieved by regular chiropractic care and doesn't want to have back surgery. After a problem-focused examination and a complete radiologic examination of the lumbosacral spine, including bending views, I consulted with Dr. Pearson and concluded the patient's degenerative disc disease is probably doing as well with a chiropractor as with orthopedic treatment. I did not recommend surgery at this time.

   CPT/HCPCS Level II Codes   **ICD-9-CM (or ICD-10-CM) Codes**

   _____   _____

3. The patient underwent a barium enema which included air contrast. The request form noted severe abdominal pain and diarrhea for the past two weeks. The radiology impression was diverticulitis of the colon.

   CPT/HCPCS Level II Codes   **ICD-9-CM (or ICD-10-CM) Codes**

   _____   _____

4. The patient presented for follow-up of COPD. At this time the patient is experiencing no significant cough, no sputum, no fever, and no respiratory distress. However, there is dyspnea only with exertion, which is accompanied by angina. A detailed examination was performed and the physician spent approximately 25 minutes with the patient. Chest is clear, no wheeze or rales. Chest x-rays, frontal and lateral, were taken to determine status of COPD. No additional treatment is required at this time.

   CPT/HCPCS Level II Codes   **ICD-9-CM (or ICD-10-CM) Codes**

   _____   _____

5. A surgeon is called to the hospital by the emergency department physician to see a 59-year-old male who presented with an abdominal mass, left lower quadrant. The surgeon performed a comprehensive examination, admitted the patient, and scheduled an exploratory laparotomy.

   CPT/HCPCS Level II Codes   **ICD-9-CM (or ICD-10-CM) Codes**

   _____   _____

ASSIGNMENT 10.5   Coding from SOAP Notes and Operative Reports

OBJECTIVES

At the conclusion of this assignment, the student should be able to:

1. Interpret SOAP notes and the contents of operative reports to identify diagnoses, procedures, and services that should be reported on the CMS-1500 claim.
2. Assign ICD-9-CM (or ICD-10-CM), CPT, and HCPCS level II codes (and appropriate modifiers) to diagnoses, procedures, and services.

INSTRUCTIONS

Review the following SOAP notes and operative reports to select the diagnoses, procedures, and services that should be reported on the CMS-1500 claim. Then assign ICD-9-CM (or ICD-10-CM) codes to diagnoses and CPT or HCPCS level II codes (and appropriate modifiers) to procedures and services. (The level of service is indicated for each visit.)

1. ## CASE STUDY #1

S: A new patient was seen today in the GI clinic for a level 2 visit. She complains of one week of severe epigastric pain and burning, especially after eating.

O: On examination there is extreme guarding and tenderness, epigastric region, with no rebound. Bowel sounds are normal. BP 110/70.

A: Rule out gastric ulcer.

P: The patient is to have upper gastrointestinal series. Start on Zantac and eliminate alcohol, fried foods, and caffeine. Return to clinic in one week.

CPT/HCPCS Level II Codes   **ICD-9-CM (or ICD-10-CM) Codes**

_____   _____

2. ## CASE STUDY #2

S: The patient returned to the clinic for a level 2 visit after undergoing an upper gastrointestinal series. She states she is still experiencing epigastric pain.

O: Upper gastrointestinal series revealed areas of ulceration.

A: Acute gastric ulcer.

P: Omeprazole 10 mg q.d. Return for follow-up visit in three weeks.

CPT/HCPCS Level II Codes   **ICD-9-CM (or ICD-10-CM) Codes**

_____   _____

3. ## CASE STUDY #3

S: The patient was seen in the orthopedic clinic today for an urgent level 3 visit. He was walking up his driveway when he slipped and fell, landing on his left arm and striking his head against the car. He was unconscious for less than 10 minutes, experienced dizziness and vomiting, and felt severe pain in his left arm. The patient's wife was actually coming here today for follow-up of her rheumatoid arthritis, and asked that we evaluate her husband's injuries.

O: Examination of the head reveals a 2.5 cm superficial laceration of the scalp, temporal region, left side. Examination of the left arm reveals restriction of motion and acute pain upon palpation and with attempted range of motion of the upper arm and shoulder. The patient underwent a skull x-ray to rule out fracture and x-ray of the left arm and shoulder for evaluation of the pain. The patient was taken to the radiography department where x-ray was negative for skull fracture, revealing only swelling in the area of the laceration. An x-ray of the left arm and shoulder, however, revealed an undisplaced fracture of the proximal left humerus at the greater tuberosity.

A: Concussion. Superficial laceration of scalp, 2.5 cm. Nondisplaced fracture of proximal left humerus at the greater tuberosity.

P: The patient underwent simple repair of the scalp laceration with sutures. The left arm was manipulated slightly to achieve proper anatomic alignment of the proximal humerus. The arm and shoulder were immobilized with sling and binder. The patient was given pain medication, and the patient's wife was instructed on how to perform neuro checks every two hours on the patient for the next 24 hours. The patient will be seen back in the clinic in two days. The patient and wife were instructed to contact the office if any problems arise in the meantime.

CPT/HCPCS Level II Codes   **ICD-9-CM (or ICD-10-CM) Codes**

_____   _____

4. **CASE STUDY #4**

S: An established patient was seen today for a level 2 visit. The patient complains of rectal discomfort, rectal bleeding, and severe itching.

O: Rectal examination reveals multiple soft external hemorrhoids.

A: Multiple soft, thrombosed external hemorrhoids.

P: Suppositories are to be used after each bowel movement. The patient will return to the office in four weeks for reevaluation.

CPT/HCPCS Level II Codes   **ICD-9-CM (or ICD-10-CM) Codes**

_____   _____

5. **CASE STUDY #5**

S: A 53-year-old new patient was seen today for a level 2 visit. The female patient presents with complaints of polyuria, polydipsia, and weight loss.

O: Urinalysis by dip, automated, with microscopy reveals elevated glucose.

A: Possible diabetes.

P: The patient is to have a glucose tolerance test and return in three days for her blood work results and applicable management of care.

CPT/HCPCS Level II Codes   **ICD-9-CM (or ICD-10-CM) Codes**

_____   _____

6. **CASE STUDY #6**

PREOPERATIVE DIAGNOSIS: Pterygium of the right eye

POSTOPERATIVE DIAGNOSIS: Pterygium of the right eye

PROCEDURE PERFORMED: Pterygium excision with conjunctival autograft of the right eye

ANESTHESIA: General endotracheal anesthesia

PROCEDURE: After the patient was prepped and draped in the usual sterile fashion, attention was directed to his right eye under the operating microscope. The area of the pterygium was viewed and an injection of lidocaine with Marcaine was placed subconjunctivally to infiltrate the area of the pterygium and surrounding conjunctiva. Then, using a combination of sharp and blunt dissection with 57 Beaver blade Westcott scissors, the pterygium was lifted away from the cornea, making a plane to the cornea to achieve clarity to the cornea. Next, an area was marked with a hand-held cautery nasally through the conjunctiva. A muscle hook was inserted to identify the medial rectus muscle. Then, using Westcott scissors and .12, the head and body of the pterygium were removed noting where the medial rectus muscle was at all times. Cautery was used to achieve hemostasis. An area of conjunctiva superior to the area of the prior pterygium under the lid was isolated and an incision was made through the conjunctiva. This section of conjunctiva was then transposed and placed into position over the area of the prior pterygium, thus forming an autograft. This was sutured into place with multiple single 8-0 Vicryl sutures. The autograft was noted to be in good position. Hemostasis was noted to be well achieved. The cornea was noted to be smooth and clear in the area of the prior pterygium with the epithelial defect secondary to removal of the pterygium. Maxitrol drops were placed. The patient's eye was patched. The patient tolerated the procedure well without complications and is to follow up in our office tomorrow.

CPT/HCPCS Level II Codes   **ICD-9-CM (or ICD-10-CM) Codes**

_____   _____

7. **CASE STUDY #7**

PREOPERATIVE DIAGNOSIS: Subcutaneous mass, posterior scalp

POSTOPERATIVE DIAGNOSIS: Subcutaneous mass, posterior scalp

PROCEDURE PERFORMED: Excision, subcutaneous mass, posterior scalp

ANESTHESIA: General

PROCEDURE: After instillation of 1 percent Xylocaine, a transverse incision was made directly over this elongated posterior scalp lesion. Hemostasis was obtained with electrocautery and suture ligature. A fatty tumor was encountered and sharp dissection used in completely excising this lesion. Hemostasis was obtained with ties, suture ligatures, and electrocautery. The 3 cm lesion was removed in its entirety. The wound was irrigated and the incision closed in layers. The skin was closed with a running nylon suture for hemostasis.

CPT/HCPCS Level II Codes   **ICD-9-CM (or ICD-10-CM) Codes**

_____   _____

8. CASE STUDY #8

PREOPERATIVE DIAGNOSIS: Ventral hernia

POSTOPERATIVE DIAGNOSIS: Ventral hernia

PROCEDURE PERFORMED: Repair of ventral hernia with mesh

ANESTHESIA: General

PROCEDURE: The vertical midline incision was opened. Sharp and blunt dissection was used in defining the hernia sac. The hernia sac was opened and the fascia examined. The hernia defect was sizable. Careful inspection was utilized to uncover any additional adjacent fascial defects. Small defects were observed on both sides of the major hernia and were incorporated into the main hernia. The hernia sac was dissected free of the surrounding subcutaneous tissues and retained. Prolene mesh was then fashioned to size and sutured to one side with running #0 Prolene suture. Interrupted Prolene sutures were placed on the other side and tagged untied. The hernia sac was then sutured to the opposite side of the fascia with Vicryl suture. The Prolene sutures were passed through the interstices of the Prolene mesh and tied into place, ensuring that the Prolene mesh was not placed under tension. Excess mesh was excised. Jackson-Pratt drains were placed, one on each side. Running subcutaneous suture utilizing Vicryl was placed, after which the skin was stapled.

CPT/HCPCS Level II Codes   **ICD-9-CM (or ICD-10-CM) Codes**

_____   _____

9. CASE STUDY #9

PREOPERATIVE DIAGNOSIS: Intermittent exotropia, alternating fusion with decreased stereopsis

POSTOPERATIVE DIAGNOSIS: Intermittent exotropia, alternating fusion with decreased stereopsis

PROCEDURE PERFORMED: Bilateral lateral rectus recession of 7.0 mm

ANESTHESIA: General endotracheal anesthesia

PROCEDURE: The patient was brought to the operating room and placed in the supine position where she was prepped and draped in the usual sterile fashion for strabismus surgery. Both eyes were exposed to the surgical field. After adequate anesthesia, one drop of 2.5 percent Neosynephrine was placed in each eye for vasoconstriction. Forced ductions were performed on both eyes, and the lateral rectus was found to be normal. An eye speculum was placed in the right eye and surgery was begun on the right eye. An inferotemporal fornix incision was performed. The right lateral rectus muscle was isolated on a muscle hook. The muscle insertion was isolated, and checked ligaments were dissected back. After a series of muscle hook passes using the Steven's hook and finishing with two passes of a Green's hook, the right lateral rectus was isolated. The epimesium, as well as Tenon's capsule, was dissected from the muscle insertion and the checked ligaments were lysed. The muscle was imbricated on a 6-0 Vicryl suture with an S29 needle with locking bites at either end. The muscle was detached from the globe, and a distance of 7.0 mm posterior to the insertion of the muscle was marked. The muscle was then reattached 7.0 mm posterior to the original insertion using a cross-swords technique. The conjunctiva was closed using two buried sutures. Attention was then turned to the left eye where an identical procedure was performed. At the end of the case the eyes seemed slightly exotropic in position in the anesthetized state. Bounce back tests were normal. Both eyes were dressed with tetracaine drops and Maxitrol ointment. There were no complications. The patient tolerated the procedure well, was awakened from anesthesia without difficulty, and was sent to the recovery room. The patient was instructed in the use of topical antibiotics, and detailed postoperative instructions were provided. The patient will be followed up within a 48-hour period in my office.

CPT/HCPCS Level II Codes　　　　　**ICD-9-CM (or ICD-10-CM) Codes**

_____　　　_____

10. **CASE STUDY #10**

PREOPERATIVE DIAGNOSIS: Right trigger thumb

POSTOPERATIVE DIAGNOSIS: Right trigger thumb

OPERATION: Right trigger thumb release, midlateral incision technique

ANESTHESIA: Local digital block

ESTIMATED BLOOD LOSS: Minimal

DESCRIPTION OF PROCEDURE: A local digital block anesthetic was administered to allow the patient to actively flex the thumb after release. After exsanguination of the extremity, a tourniquet cuff on the right upper arm was inflated. A longitudinal skin incision was marked along the radial side of the metacarpophalangeal crease, approximately 1 cm from the midline and measuring 2.5 cm in length.

The skin incision was made with a #15 blade scalpel. Care was taken to extend the incision only through the dermal layer, and skin hooks were used for retraction. Blunt dissection was performed to identify the radial digital nerve. The nerve was retracted away from the flexor tendon and protected throughout the procedure. Blunt dissection was continued to expose the first annular pulley and its boundaries. Retraction allowed full visualization of the pulley to perform the longitudinal release. The patient was asked to flex and extend the thumb to confirm the absence of triggering. The wound was irrigated, and the skin was closed with nonabsorbable suture. The patient tolerated the procedure well and was discharged to the outpatient observation area in good condition.

CPT/HCPCS Level II Codes　　　　　**ICD-9-CM (or ICD-10-CM) Codes**

_____　　　_____

ASSIGNMENT 10.6 VistA-Office Electronic Health Record

OBJECTIVES

At the conclusion of this assignment, the student should be able to:

1. Discuss the goal of VistA-Office Electronic Health Record (EHR).
2. Discuss the additions to this software specifically for a physician office setting.

OVERVIEW

An electronic health record (EHR) is a digital method of creating and storing medical information on a patient. The Department of Health and Human Services announced in 2004 its goal of having a US EHR network in 10 years. One step toward this goal is the creation of EHR systems that are functional for the outpatient setting.

INSTRUCTIONS

Go to the WorldVistA Organization Web site at **www.worldvista.org,** and locate the link to WorldVistA EHR. Using the Web site as a reference tool, fill in your answers to the questions below in the space provided.

1. What parties developed the VistA-Office EHR? _____

_____

2. List features of both the core VistA and WorldVistA EHR. _____

_____

3. This EHR has a report feature that allows for data to be presented. List types of reports that this EHR can generate. _____

_____

4. Define and briefly explain the acronym DOQ-IT. _____

_____

5. What is the goal of VistA-Office EHR? _____

_____

> **NOTE:** Navigate the WorldVista Web site to research information needed to answer the questions listed in this assignment. This will help you learn how to locate information using the Internet as a research tool and using Web sites, which often requires using tool bars, pull-down menus, and web page links.

ASSIGNMENT 10.7 Multiple Choice Review

1. **A patient was seen today for pain in his right foot. During the evaluation, the physician also documented that the patient was last seen for pneumonia four months ago. How is the pneumonia reported on the CMS-1500 claim?**
   a. as the ICD-9-CM (or ICD-10-CM) code for "status post pneumonia"
   b. by reporting modifier -25 with the appropriate E/M code
   c. the pneumonia history is not documented on the claim
   d. by using an E/M code that reflects an extended evaluation

2. **A secondary diagnosis is also known as a _____ condition.**
   a. coexisting
   b. complicating
   c. reference
   d. verified

3. **An acceptable reason to delay a documentation entry in the patient record is to**
   a. authenticate provided services.
   b. change an erroneous entry.
   c. provide additional information for clarification.
   d. substantiate medical necessity of care provided.

4. **Local coverage determinations (LCDs) contain**
   a. auditing instructions.
   b. coding guidelines.
   c. covered and noncovered codes.
   d. reimbursement rates.

5. **An *Advance Beneficiary Notice (ABN)* is required by _____ for all outpatient and physician office procedures/services that are not covered.**
   a. Medicaid
   b. Medicare
   c. TRICARE
   d. Worker's compensation

6. **The objective section of a SOAP note includes the**
   a. chief complaint and the patient's description of the presenting problem.
   b. diagnostic statement and the physician's rationale for the diagnosis.
   c. documentation of measurable observations made during a physical exam.
   d. statement of the physician's future plans for work-up and management.

7. **Which of the following belongs in the "review of systems" section of the history and physical examination report?**

   a. Blood pressure 113/70; pulse 80 and regular; temperature 97.9; respiratory rate 18.

   b. No complaints of nausea, vomiting, diarrhea, bloody stools, reflux, or constipation.

   c. Patient has a long-standing history of atrial fibrillation and is on Coumadin therapy.

   d. The patient's mother died from leukemia when the patient was 25; father is living and well.

8. **After a fall at home, a 77-year-old woman was brought to the emergency department by her daughter. The patient sustained a 2 cm laceration of the thigh and a small, 0.5 cm laceration of the wrist. The thigh wound was closed with sutures and the wrist laceration underwent butterfly closure. The patient was discharged from the emergency department in satisfactory condition.**

   Select the appropriate CPT and HCPCS procedure code(s) and modifier(s) for this case.

   a. 12001, G0168-59

   b. 99281-25, 12001

   c. 99281-25, 12001, G0168-59

   d. 99281-25, 12001-59, G0168-59

9. **A patient was seen in the physician's office with complaints of rapid heartbeat. The patient has no known history of cardiac problems. The physician ordered an electrolyte panel. After receiving the results, the physician ordered a repeat potassium level.**

   Select the appropriate CPT code(s) and modifier(s) for this case.

   a. 80051, 84132

   b. 80051, 84132, 84132

   c. 80051, 84132-59

   d. 80051, 84132-91

10. **A 42-year-old male was referred to an ophthalmologist for evaluation of two lesions of his left eye, and was scheduled for surgery a week after the evaluation. The patient presented for surgery, and was prepped and draped in the usual sterile fashion. The patient underwent two separate procedures: the first was excision of a chalazion of the left lower eyelid. The second procedure performed was biopsy of a lesion of the left upper eyelid.**

    Select the appropriate CPT code(s) and modifier(s) for this case.

    a. 67800, 67810

    b. 67800, 67810-59

    c. 67800-E2, 67810-59-E1

    d. 67800-E2, 67810-E1

11. **A 58-year-old male presented for screening colonoscopy. The patient received premedication per protocol. The scope was inserted and advanced, but despite multiple attempts, could not pass beyond the splenic flexure. For the patient's comfort, the procedure was terminated.**

    Select the appropriate CPT code(s) and modifier(s) for this case.

    a. 45330

    b. 45330-21

    c. 45378

    d. 45378-52

12. **A patient was admitted to the day surgery unit to undergo a laparoscopic cholecystectomy. The patient was prepped and draped in the usual sterile fashion for laparoscopy. Upon laparoscopic examination, the patient's gallbladder was noted to be extremely friable, and there was also question of obstruction or torsion of the common bile duct. The decision was made to perform an open cholecystectomy. The patient still had excellent general anesthetic response and the open procedure was begun. The gallbladder was removed without much difficulty. The surgeon also performed exploration of the common bile duct and although it had appeared abnormal under laparoscopic viewing, the common bile duct was normal and free of stone or obstruction. The patient tolerated the procedure well.**

    Select the appropriate CPT code for this case.

    a. 47562-57

    b. 47562

    c. 47600

    d. 47610

13. The patient was seen by General Surgery and scheduled for removal of a worrisome lump behind the right knee. The patient stated he had no idea how long it had been there; he noticed it while trying to "rub out" a cramp of his calf muscle. The patient underwent excision of what was identified as a Baker's cyst of the left popliteal fossa. The patient tolerated the procedure well, and was understandably relieved by the definitive benign diagnosis.

    Select the appropriate CPT code for this case.
    a. 27334   c. 27347
    b. 27345   d. 27360

14. HISTORY: The patient is a very vibrant 82-year-old woman seen today for routine physical examination. She states she has been very busy with local travel with her seniors group and also with spending time with her grandchildren and great-grandchildren. She is status post CABG six years ago and is doing wonderfully. Her only complaint today is that of arthritis of the left hip, which she manages with an over-the-counter anti-inflammatory. She is conscientious about taking the tablets with food or milk to prevent stomach irritation. Otherwise, she is well. REVIEW OF SYSTEMS: Essentially unchanged since last visit. EXAMINATION: HEENT: pupils equal, round, reactive to light and accommodation (PERRLA). Neck: Clear. Chest: No wheezes, rubs, or rhonchi. Heart: Regular rate and rhythm, with no murmurs. Abdomen: Soft, flat, without hepatosplenomegaly or tenderness. Pelvic: Not performed today. Rectal: Not performed today. Extremities: There are varicosities of both lower extremities which are nontender, otherwise unremarkable. Neurologic: Cranial nerves II through XII are intact. The patient amazingly does not require glasses and has good hearing. ASSESSMENT: Delightful, healthy 82-year-old female with osteoarthritis of the left hip, essentially unchanged. PLAN: The patient will return in six months for routine evaluation; sooner if problems arise.

    Select the appropriate CPT code for this case.
    a. 99201   c. 99211
    b. 99202   d. 99212

15. The patient is a 40-year-old male who is known to me and was seen in the office today on an urgent basis because he believed he had collapsed his right lung. He has a history of collapsed lung and was confident it had happened again. On examination, the patient's breath sounds on the right were nonexistent. An emergency two-view (frontal and lateral) chest x-ray was performed which demonstrated the collapsed lung on the right. The patient was sent to the local hospital emergency department. The on-call surgeon was contacted and met the patient in the emergency department, where she performed a right tube thoracoscopy.

    Select the appropriate CPT code(s) and modifier(s) for the office visit only for this case.
    a. 99212-57, 71020   c. 99241, 71020
    b. 99213-57, 71020   d. 99281, 71020

16. The patient presents to the office after a five-year absence with complaints of abdominal pain, diarrhea, and rectal bleeding, which began three weeks ago. A detailed examination revealed a tense abdomen with some guarding in the right upper quadrant. Tomorrow, the patient will undergo a flexible sigmoidoscopy to rule out colon cancer.

    Select the appropriate CPT code(s) and modifier(s) for this case.
    a. 99202   c. 99203
    b. 99202-57   d. 99203-57

17. On 08/12/YY, a patient underwent an exploratory laparotomy, left partial hepatic resection for malignant hepatoma, and a cholecystectomy.

    Select the CPT code for the first-listed procedure in this case.
    a. 47120   c. 47125
    b. 47122   d. 47141

18. A 65-year-old patient underwent bronchoscopy and biopsy for a left lower lobe lung mass. The biopsy was sent to pathology immediately and revealed adenocarcinoma of the left lower lobe. The patient then underwent a left lower lobectomy and thoracic lymphadenopathy.

    Select the CPT code for the first-listed procedure in this case.
    a. 31625   c. 32663
    b. 32480   d. 38746

19. A 33-year-old patient with a strong family history of breast cancer underwent excision of a right breast mass in the outpatient surgery center. The pathology report was returned immediately and revealed a malignant neoplasm, central portion of the right breast. The patient then underwent a right modified radical mastectomy.

    Select the CPT code and modifier for the first-listed procedure in this case.
    a. 19301   c. 19307
    b. 19301-58   d. 19307-78

20. An 80-year-old patient was admitted to the outpatient surgery center for dilation of a urethral stricture with insertion of urethral stent. A cystourethroscope was inserted through the urethral meatus and advanced through the urethra into the bladder. It was able to pass through the site of stricture successfully, although with some difficulty. Examination of the urethra showed the area of stricture. Examination of the bladder revealed the bladder appeared to be essentially unremarkable. A urethral stent was introduced into the urethra and placed at the point of stricture. Improved urinary flow was immediately noted. The procedure was concluded and the patient tolerated the procedure well.

    Select the CPT code for the first-listed procedure in this case.
    a. 52000   c. 52281
    b. 52005   d. 52282

CHAPTER 11
Essential CMS-1500 Claim Instructions

INTRODUCTION

This chapter familiarizes students with special instructions that apply to completion of CMS-1500 claims.

ASSIGNMENT 11.1 National Provider Identifier (NPI) Standard

OBJECTIVES

At the conclusion of this assignment, the student should be able to:

1. Discuss electronic file interchange (EFI).
2. Discuss the national provider identifier (NPI).

OVERVIEW

The Centers for Medicare and Medicaid Services (CMS) has many resources available on its Web site related to the NPI: overview, fact sheets, tip sheets, PowerPoint presentation, and a question resource sheet, just to list a few. The NPI replaced the PIN and UPIN used in the past by healthcare providers. One advantage of the NPI is that it will provide identification for all healthcare plans and insurance payers.

INSTRUCTIONS

Access the Centers for Medicare and Medicaid Services Web site to answer questions about its content. Write your answers in the space provided at the end of each question.

1. Go to **www.cms.hhs.gov,** and click on the National Provider Identifier Standard link. Then, click on the EFI link, and scroll down and click on the EFI Summary PDF file to answer the following questions about electronic file interchange (EFI).

   a. What is the electronic file interchange (EFI)?

   _____

   b. Why was the EFI implemented?

   _____

2. Go to **www.cms.hhs.gov,** and click on the National Provider Identifier (NPI) Standard link. Then, click on the Medicare NPI Implementation link and the Frequently Asked Questions (FAQ) link.

   a. What is the purpose of the national provider identifier (NPI)?

   _____

   b. Who must use the NPI, and when?

   _____

ASSIGNMENT 11.2 Medically Unlikely Edits (MUE) Project

OBJECTIVE

At the conclusion of this assignment, the student should be able to:

1. Discuss the MUE project.

OVERVIEW

The Centers for Medicare and Medicaid Services (CMS) has resources available on its Web site related to the MUE project. As outlined in the chapter text, the MUE project is a method that CMS has implemented to improve claim accuracy and decrease errors in billing.

INSTRUCTIONS

Access the Web site for the Centers for Medicare and Medicaid Services (**www.cms.hhs.gov**). Once at the site, click on the Medicare link, click on the National Correct Coding Initiative link, and click on the Medically Unlikely Edits link. Review the following questions related to information on the site. Write your answers in the space provided at the end of each question.

1. Why did CMS develop MUEs?

   _____

2. What is an MUE?

   _____

3. When were MUEs edits implemented?

   _____

4. To whom are inquiries about a specific claim addressed?

   _____

5. To whom should inquiries about the rationale for an MUE value be addressed?

   _____

> **NOTE:** Navigate the CMS Web site to research information needed to answer the questions in this assignment. This will help you learn how to locate information using the Internet as a research tool and using Web sites. It will also require you to find and verify information on a table.

ASSIGNMENT 11.3   Identifying CMS-1500 Claims Completion Errors

OBJECTIVES

At the conclusion of this assignment, the student should be able to:

1. Explain how optical scanning guidelines impact CMS-1500 claims completion.
2. Identify CMS-1500 claims completion errors.

OVERVIEW

The CMS-1500 paper claim was designed to accommodate *optical scanning* of paper claims. This process uses a device (e.g., scanner) to convert printed or handwritten characters into text that can be viewed by an *optical character reader (OCR)* (a device used for optical character recognition). Entering data into the computer using this technology greatly increases productivity associated with claims processing because the need to manually enter data from the claim into a computer is eliminated. OCR guidelines were established when the HCFA-1500 (now called CMS-1500) claim was developed and are now used by all payers that process claims using the official CMS-1500 claim.

> **NOTE:** When completing this assignment, refer to optical scanning guidelines located in Chapter 11 in your textbook.

INSTRUCTIONS

1. The CMS-1500 claims in Figures 11-1, 11-2, and 11-3 contain optical scanning errors.
2. Review each claim to identify the optical scanning errors.
3. Circle each optical scanning error.

1500

HEALTH INSURANCE CLAIM FORM

INSTRUCTIONAL FORM ONLY - NOT APPROVED FOR USE

PICA — PICA — CARRIER

1. MEDICARE (Medicare #) / MEDICAID (Medicaid #) / TRICARE CHAMPUS (Sponsor's SSN) / CHAMPVA (Member ID#) / GROUP HEALTH PLAN (SSN or ID) [X] / FECA BLK LUNG (SSN) / OTHER (ID)

1a. INSURED'S I.D. NUMBER (For Program in Item 1): 123456798

2. PATIENT'S NAME (Last Name, First Name, Middle Initial): CHRIS P. CREAM

3. PATIENT'S BIRTH DATE MM DD YY: 09 08 60 — SEX M [X] F [ ]

4. INSURED'S NAME (Last Name, First Name, Middle Initial): CREAM, CHRIS, P

5. PATIENT'S ADDRESS (No., Street): 8890 ECLAIR LANE

6. PATIENT'S RELATIONSHIP TO INSURED: Self [X] Spouse [ ] Child [ ] Other [ ]

7. INSURED'S ADDRESS (No., Street): 8880 ECLAIR LANE

CITY: ANYWHERE — STATE: US

8. PATIENT STATUS: Single [X] Married [ ] Other [ ]

CITY: ANYWHERE — STATE: US

ZIP CODE: 12345 — TELEPHONE (Include Area Code): (101)476-1145

Employed [X] Full-Time Student [ ] Part-Time Student [ ]

ZIP CODE: 12345 — TELEPHONE (Include Area Code): (101)4761145

9. OTHER INSURED'S NAME (Last Name, First Name, Middle Initial):

10. IS PATIENT'S CONDITION RELATED TO:

11. INSURED'S POLICY GROUP OR FECA NUMBER:

a. OTHER INSURED'S POLICY OR GROUP NUMBER:

a. EMPLOYMENT? (Current or Previous) YES [ ] NO [X]

a. INSURED'S DATE OF BIRTH MM DD YY: 09 08 1960 — SEX M [X] F [ ]

b. OTHER INSURED'S DATE OF BIRTH MM DD YY — SEX M [ ] F [ ]

b. AUTO ACCIDENT? YES [ ] NO [X] PLACE (State)

b. EMPLOYER'S NAME OR SCHOOL NAME: EDIBLE CRUMBS

c. EMPLOYER'S NAME OR SCHOOL NAME:

c. OTHER ACCIDENT? YES [ ] NO [X]

c. INSURANCE PLAN NAME OR PROGRAM NAME: AETNA

d. INSURANCE PLAN NAME OR PROGRAM NAME:

10d. RESERVED FOR LOCAL USE

d. IS THERE ANOTHER HEALTH BENEFIT PLAN? YES [ ] NO [X] *If yes,* return to and complete item 9 a-d.

READ BACK OF FORM BEFORE COMPLETING & SIGNING THIS FORM.

12. PATIENT'S OR AUTHORIZED PERSON'S SIGNATURE I authorize the release of any medical or other information necessary to process this claim. I also request payment of government benefits either to myself or to the party who accepts assignment below.

SIGNED SIGNATURE ON FILE — DATE

13. INSURED'S OR AUTHORIZED PERSON'S SIGNATURE I authorize payment of medical benefits to the undersigned physcian or supplier for services described below.

SIGNED SIGNATURE ON FILE

— PATIENT AND INSURED INFORMATION —

14. DATE OF CURRENT: ILLNESS (First symptom) OR INJURY (Accident) OR PREGNANCY (LMP) MM DD YY: 07 04 YYYY

15. IF PATIENT HAS HAD SAME OR SIMILAR ILLNESS GIVE FIRST DATE MM DD YY

16. DATES PATIENT UNABLE TO WORK IN CURRENT OCCUPATION FROM MM DD YY TO MM DD YY

17. NAME OF REFERRING PROVIDER OR OTHER SOURCE — 17a. — 17b. NPI

18. HOSPITALIZATION DATES RELATED TO CURRENT SERVICES FROM MM DD YY TO MM DD YY

19. RESERVED FOR LOCAL USE

20. OUTSIDE LAB? YES [ ] NO [X] — $ CHARGES

21. DIAGNOSIS OR NATURE OF ILLNESS OR INJURY (Relate Items 1, 2, 3 or 4 to Item 24E by Line)

1. 716.94 — 3. ___ — 2. ___ — 4. ___

22. MEDICAID RESUBMISSION CODE — ORIGINAL REF. NO.

23. PRIOR AUTHORIZATION NUMBER

	24. A DATE(S) OF SERVICE From MM DD YY	To MM DD YY	B. PLACE OF SERVICE	C. EMG	D. PROCEDURES, SERVICES, OR SUPPLIES (Explain Unusual Circumstances) CPT/HCPCS	MODIFIER	E. DIAGNOSIS POINTER	F. $ CHARGES	G. DAYS OR UNITS	H. EPSDT Family Plan	I. ID. QUAL.	J. RENDERING PROVIDER ID. #
1	07 04 YY		11		99212			45 00	1		NPI	
2											NPI	
3											NPI	
4											NPI	
5											NPI	
6											NPI	

25. FEDERAL TAX I.D. NUMBER: 11-1234562 — SSN [ ] EIN [X]

26. PATIENT'S ACCOUNT NO.: 11-A

27. ACCEPT ASSIGNMENT? (For govt. claims, see back) [X] YES [ ] NO

28. TOTAL CHARGE: $ 45 00 — 29. AMOUNT PAID: $ — 30. BALANCE DUE: $ 45 00

31. SIGNATURE OF PHYSICIAN OR SUPPLIER INCLUDING DEGREES OR CREDENTIALS (I certify that the statements on the reverse apply to this bill and are made a part thereof.)

DONALD L GIVINGS MD

SIGNED — DATE MM DD YY

32. SERVICE FACILITY LOCATION INFORMATION — a. NPI — b.

33. BILLING PROVIDER INFO & PH # (101)1115555

DONALD L GIVINGS MD
11350 MEDICAL DRIVE
ANYWHERE US 12345

a. 1234567890 — b.

— PHYSICIAN OR SUPPLIER INFORMATION —

NUCC Instruction Manual available at: www.nucc.org — INSTRUCTIONAL USE ONLY - NOT APPROVED FOR USE

FIGURE 11-1 Chris P. Cream CMS-1500 with optical scanning errors

1500

HEALTH INSURANCE CLAIM FORM

INSTRUCTIONAL FORM ONLY - NOT APPROVED FOR USE

PICA | PICA | CARRIER

1. MEDICARE (Medicare #) / MEDICAID (Medicaid #) / TRICARE CHAMPUS (Sponsor's SSN) / CHAMPVA (Member ID#) / GROUP HEALTH PLAN (SSN or ID) / FECA BLK LUNG (SSN) / OTHER (ID) [X]	1a. INSURED'S I.D. NUMBER (For Program in Item 1) 42915750
2. PATIENT'S NAME (Last Name, First Name, Middle Initial) BRIGHT, BRITTANY	3. PATIENT'S BIRTH DATE MM DD YY: 04 07 1988 SEX M [ ] F [X]
4. INSURED'S NAME (Last Name, First Name, Middle Initial) WRIGHT, BRITTANY	
5. PATIENT'S ADDRESS (No., Street) 8731 NOVELS AVENUE	6. PATIENT'S RELATIONSHIP TO INSURED: Self [X] Spouse [ ] Child [ ] Other [ ]
7. INSURED'S ADDRESS (No., Street) 8731 NOVELS AVENUE	
CITY: ANYWHERE STATE: US	8. PATIENT STATUS: Single [X] Married [ ] Other [ ]
CITY: ANYWHERE STATE: US	
ZIP CODE: 12345 TELEPHONE (Include Area Code): ( )6285296	Employed [X] Full-Time Student [ ] Part-Time Student [ ]
ZIP CODE: 12345 TELEPHONE (Include Area Code): (101)6285296	
9. OTHER INSURED'S NAME (Last Name, First Name, Middle Initial)	10. IS PATIENT'S CONDITION RELATED TO:
11. INSURED'S POLICY GROUP OR FECA NUMBER	
a. OTHER INSURED'S POLICY OR GROUP NUMBER	a. EMPLOYMENT? (Current or Previous) YES [ ] NO [X]
a. INSURED'S DATE OF BIRTH MM DD YY: 04 07 1988 SEX M [ ] F [X]	
b. OTHER INSURED'S DATE OF BIRTH MM DD YY SEX M [ ] F [ ]	b. AUTO ACCIDENT? YES [ ] NO [X] PLACE (State)
b. EMPLOYER'S NAME OR SCHOOL NAME THE BIG BOOK STORE	
c. EMPLOYER'S NAME OR SCHOOL NAME	c. OTHER ACCIDENT? YES [ ] NO [X]
c. INSURANCE PLAN NAME OR PROGRAM NAME US HEALTH	
d. INSURANCE PLAN NAME OR PROGRAM NAME	10d. RESERVED FOR LOCAL USE
d. IS THERE ANOTHER HEALTH BENEFIT PLAN? YES [ ] NO [X] *If yes,* return to and complete item 9 a-d.	

PATIENT AND INSURED INFORMATION

READ BACK OF FORM BEFORE COMPLETING & SIGNING THIS FORM.

12. PATIENT'S OR AUTHORIZED PERSON'S SIGNATURE I authorize the release of any medical or other information necessary to process this claim. I also request payment of government benefits either to myself or to the party who accepts assignment below.

SIGNED SIGNATURE ON FILE DATE

13. INSURED'S OR AUTHORIZED PERSON'S SIGNATURE I authorize payment of medical benefits to the undersigned physcian or supplier for services described below.

SIGNED SIGNATURE ON FILE

14. DATE OF CURRENT: ILLNESS (First symptom) OR INJURY (Accident) OR PREGNANCY (LMP) MM DD YY: 10 31 YYYY	15. IF PATIENT HAS HAD SAME OR SIMILAR ILLNESS. GIVE FIRST DATE MM DD YY
16. DATES PATIENT UNABLE TO WORK IN CURRENT OCCUPATION FROM MM DD YY TO MM DD YY	
17. NAME OF REFERRING PROVIDER OR OTHER SOURCE	17a. / 17b. NPI
18. HOSPITALIZATION DATES RELATED TO CURRENT SERVICES FROM MM DD YY TO MM DD YY	
19. RESERVED FOR LOCAL USE	20. OUTSIDE LAB? YES [ ] NO [X] $ CHARGES
21. DIAGNOSIS OR NATURE OF ILLNESS OR INJURY (Relate Items 1, 2, 3 or 4 to Item 24E by Line) 1. 493 90 3. ___ . ___ 2. ___ . ___ 4. ___ . ___	22. MEDICAID RESUBMISSION CODE ORIGINAL REF. NO. 23. PRIOR AUTHORIZATION NUMBER

	24. A DATE(S) OF SERVICE From MM DD YY	To MM DD YY	B. PLACE OF SERVICE	C. EMG	D. PROCEDURES, SERVICES, OR SUPPLIES (Explain Unusual Circumstances) CPT/HCPCS	MODIFIER	E. DIAGNOSIS POINTER	F. $ CHARGES	G. DAYS OR UNITS	H. EPSDT Family Plan	I. ID. QUAL.	J. RENDERING PROVIDER ID. #
1	10 31 YY		11		99212	24	1	55	1		NPI	
2											NPI	
3											NPI	
4											NPI	
5											NPI	
6											NPI	

PHYSICIAN OR SUPPLIER INFORMATION

25. FEDERAL TAX I.D. NUMBER SSN EIN 111234562	26. PATIENT'S ACCOUNT NO. 11-B	27. ACCEPT ASSIGNMENT? (For govt. claims, see back) YES [X] NO [ ]	28. TOTAL CHARGE $ 55 00	29. AMOUNT PAID $	30. BALANCE DUE $ 55 00
31. SIGNATURE OF PHYSICIAN OR SUPPLIER INCLUDING DEGREES OR CREDENTIALS (I certify that the statements on the reverse apply to this bill and are made a part thereof.) DONALD L GIVINGS SIGNED DATE MM DD YY	32. SERVICE FACILITY LOCATION INFORMATION a. NPI b.		33. BILLING PROVIDER INFO & PH # (101)1115555 DONALD L GIVINGS MD 11350 MEDICAL DRIVE ANYWHERE US 12345 a. 1234567890 b.		

NUCC Instruction Manual available at: www.nucc.org

INSTRUCTIONAL USE ONLY - NOT APPROVED FOR USE

FIGURE 11-2 Brittany Bright CMS-1500 with optical scanning errors

1500

HEALTH INSURANCE CLAIM FORM

INSTRUCTIONAL FORM ONLY - NOT APPROVED FOR USE

PICA | PICA

CARRIER

1. MEDICARE (Medicare #) | MEDICAID (Medicaid #) | TRICARE CHAMPUS (Sponsor's SSN) | CHAMPVA (Member ID#) | GROUP HEALTH PLAN (SSN or ID) X | FECA BLK LUNG (SSN) | OTHER (ID)

1a. INSURED'S I.D. NUMBER (For Program in Item 1): 321987456

2. PATIENT'S NAME (Last Name, First Name, Middle Initial): DUNNETT, ANTHONY. L

3. PATIENT'S BIRTH DATE MM DD YY: 7 30 1990 SEX M X F

4. INSURED'S NAME (Last Name, First Name, Middle Initial): DUNNETT, ANTHONY, L

5. PATIENT'S ADDRESS (No., Street): 555 MILKY WAY

6. PATIENT'S RELATIONSHIP TO INSURED: Self X Spouse Child Other

7. INSURED'S ADDRESS (No., Street): 555 MILKY WAY

CITY: ANYWHERE STATE: US

8. PATIENT STATUS: Single X Married Other; Employed X Full-Time Student Part-Time Student

CITY: ANYWHERE STATE: US

ZIP CODE: 12345 TELEPHONE (Include Area Code): (101)8294312

ZIP CODE: 12345 TELEPHONE (Include Area Code): (101)8294312

9. OTHER INSURED'S NAME (Last Name, First Name, Middle Initial)

10. IS PATIENT'S CONDITION RELATED TO:

11. INSURED'S POLICY GROUP OR FECA NUMBER: 411

a. OTHER INSURED'S POLICY OR GROUP NUMBER

a. EMPLOYMENT? (Current or Previous) YES X NO

a. INSURED'S DATE OF BIRTH MM DD YY: 07 30 1990 SEX M X F

b. OTHER INSURED'S DATE OF BIRTH MM DD YY SEX M F

b. AUTO ACCIDENT? YES X NO PLACE (State)

b. EMPLOYER'S NAME OR SCHOOL NAME: HOT LAVA CAFE

c. EMPLOYER'S NAME OR SCHOOL NAME

c. OTHER ACCIDENT? YES X NO

c. INSURANCE PLAN NAME OR PROGRAM NAME: METROPLITAN

d. INSURANCE PLAN NAME OR PROGRAM NAME

10d. RESERVED FOR LOCAL USE

d. IS THERE ANOTHER HEALTH BENEFIT PLAN? YES X NO *If yes,* return to and complete item 9 a-d.

READ BACK OF FORM BEFORE COMPLETING & SIGNING THIS FORM.

12. PATIENT'S OR AUTHORIZED PERSON'S SIGNATURE I authorize the release of any medical or other information necessary to process this claim. I also request payment of government benefits either to myself or to the party who accepts assignment below.

SIGNED SIGNATURE ON FILE DATE

13. INSURED'S OR AUTHORIZED PERSON'S SIGNATURE I authorize payment of medical benefits to the undersigned physcian or supplier for services described below.

SIGNED SIGNATURE

PATIENT AND INSURED INFORMATION

14. DATE OF CURRENT: MM DD YY 04 01 YYYY ILLNESS (First symptom) OR INJURY (Accident) OR PREGNANCY (LMP)

15. IF PATIENT HAS HAD SAME OR SIMILAR ILLNESS GIVE FIRST DATE MM DD YY

16. DATES PATIENT UNABLE TO WORK IN CURRENT OCCUPATION MM DD YY FROM TO

17. NAME OF REFERRING PROVIDER OR OTHER SOURCE 17a. 17b. NPI

18. HOSPITALIZATION DATES RELATED TO CURRENT SERVICES MM DD YY FROM TO

19. RESERVED FOR LOCAL USE

20. OUTSIDE LAB? YES X NO $ CHARGES

21. DIAGNOSIS OR NATURE OF ILLNESS OR INJURY (Relate Items 1, 2, 3 or 4 to Item 24E by Line)

1. 78841 3. 2. 4.

22. MEDICAID RESUBMISSION CODE ORIGINAL REF. NO.

23. PRIOR AUTHORIZATION NUMBER

	24. A DATE(S) OF SERVICE From MM DD YY	To MM DD YY	B. PLACE OF SERVICE	C. EMG	D. PROCEDURES, SERVICES, OR SUPPLIES (Explain Unusual Circumstances) CPT/HCPCS	MODIFER	E. DIAGNOSIS POINTER	F. $ CHARGES	G. DAYS OR UNITS	H. EPSDT Family Plan	I. ID. QUAL.	J. RENDERING PROVIDER ID. #
1	04 01 YY		11		99211		1	350 00	1		NPI	
2											NPI	
3											NPI	
4											NPI	
5											NPI	
6											NPI	

PHYSICIAN OR SUPPLIER INFORMATION

25. FEDERAL TAX I.D. NUMBER: 111234524 SSN EIN X

26. PATIENT'S ACCOUNT NO.: 11-C

27. ACCEPT ASSIGNMENT? (For govt. claims, see back) X YES NO

28. TOTAL CHARGE: $ 350 00

29. AMOUNT PAID: $

30. BALANCE DUE: $ 350 00

31. SIGNATURE OF PHYSICIAN OR SUPPLIER INCLUDING DEGREES OR CREDENTIALS (I certify that the statements on the reverse apply to this bill and are made a part thereof.)

ERIN A HELPER MD

SIGNED DATE MM DD YY

32. SERVICE FACILITY LOCATION INFORMATION

a. NPI b.

33. BILLING PROVIDER INFO & PH # (101)1111234

ERIN A HELPER MD
101 MEDIC STREEET
ANYWHERE US 12345

a. NPI b.

NUCC Instruction Manual available at: www.nucc.org

INSTRUCTIONAL USE ONLY - NOT APPROVED FOR USE

FIGURE 11-3 Anthony Dunnett CMS-1500 with optical scanning errors

ASSIGNMENT 11.4 Multiple Choice Review

1. **HIPAA privacy standards require providers to notify patients about their right to**
   a. appeal.
   b. care.
   c. confidentiality.
   d. privacy.

2. **Development of an insurance claim begins when the**
   a. health insurance specialist reviews the encounter form for CPT codes.
   b. patient contacts the provider's office and schedules an appointment.
   c. patient pays his or her share of the treatment costs (e.g., the coinsurance).
   d. provider completes the patient's history and physical examination.

3. **Which of the following is true?**
   a. An inpatient admission can be converted to outpatient observation care.
   b. If a patient is admitted after observation, the charges are billed separately.
   c. Outpatient observation care can be converted to inpatient admission.
   d. Outpatient observation services are the same as critical care services.

4. **When Block 27 contains an X in the YES box, the provider agrees to**
   a. accept assignment and collect a co-payment from the patient.
   b. accept assignment, and collect deductible/co-payment/coinsurance amounts from the patient.
   c. collect deductible and coinsurance payments from the patient.
   d. collect deductible/copayment/coinsurance amounts from the policyholder.

5. **Optical character reader (OCR) guidelines were established when the**
   a. Balanced Budget Act was passed.
   b. CMS-1500 claim form was developed.
   c. HCFA changed to CMS in 2001.
   d. HIPAA legislation was passed.

6. **When typewritten data in a CMS-1500 claim run over into adjacent blocks, the claim will be**
   a. corrected by the payer and processed.
   b. rejected (and the provider should correct and resubmit).
   c. reviewed manually and sent to the payer.
   d. sent to the patient with a denial letter.

7. **Which is the correct way to enter the amount of $125.75 on the CMS-1500 claim?**
   a. $125.75
   b. 125.75
   c. $125 75
   d. 125 75

8. **A patient's name on the insurance card reads Marvin L. Blue III. How is this entered on the CMS-1500 claim?**
   a. BLUE III, MARVIN, L
   b. BLUE, MARVIN, L III
   c. MARVIN, BLUE, L III
   d. MARVIN, L, BLUE III

9. **Which is the proper way to report a patient's birth date of June 16, 1967, on the CMS-1500 claim?**
   a. 06-16-67
   b. 06 16 67
   c. 06-16-1967
   d. 06 16 1967

10. **Which is the proper way to prepare a rejected claim for resubmission?**
    a. Correct the error and submit a photocopy of the corrected claim.
    b. Create the corrected claim on an original (red-print) claim form.
    c. Use correction fluid on the original returned claim and resubmit the claim.
    d. Write the correction on the original claim and submit it manually.

11. **Which is the proper format for entering the name of a provider in Block 33 of the CMS-1500 claim?**
    a. Dr. Howard Hurtz
    b. Dr. Howard Hurtz, M.D.
    c. Howard Hurtz MD
    d. Hurtz, Howard M.D.

12. **Which is issued by CMS to individual providers and healthcare organizations?**
    a. EIN
    b. NPI
    c. PIN
    d. UPIN

13. **If the patient does not sign Block 13 of the CMS-1500 claim, the payer sends reimbursement to the**
    a. billing entity.   c. patient.
    b. facility.   d. provider.

14. **When more than one diagnosis reference number is reported on a CMS-1500 claim, the first-listed code is the**
    a. condition that has been treated most regularly.
    b. diagnosis with the highest reimbursement rate.
    c. illness most likely to require hospital admission.
    d. reason the patient was treated by the provider.

15. **What type of data are required by all payers in Block 24B of the CMS-1500 claim?**
    a. date of service   c. type of service
    b. place of service   d. units of service

CHAPTER 12
Commercial Insurance

INTRODUCTION

This chapter familiarizes students with completion of the CMS-1500 claim form for primary and secondary commercial payers.

> **NOTE:** When the subscriber's employer and a group number are included on the case study, enter an X in the Group Health Plan box in Block 1. If there is no employer or group number, enter an X in the Other box in Block 1.

> **NOTE:** When completing CMS-1500 claims for case studies in this workbook, enter just one diagnosis pointer number in Block 24E.

> **NOTE:** When completing claims for patients who have both primary and secondary insurance coverage, enter a P (primary) next to the case number on the primary claim (e.g., 12-A-P), and enter an S (secondary) (e.g., 12-A-S) next to the case number on the secondary claim.

ASSIGNMENT 12.1   Commercial Primary CMS-1500 Claims Completion

OBJECTIVES

At the conclusion of this assignment, the student should be able to:

1. Assign ICD-9-CM (or ICD-10-CM) diagnosis and CPT or HCPCS level II procedure/service codes.
2. Prepare commercial insurance CMS-1500 claims.

INSTRUCTIONS

Use optical scanning guidelines to complete CMS-1500 claims for case studies 12-A and 12-B. Obtain a blank claim by making a copy of the CMS-1500 claim in Appendix III of the textbook. Refer to the CMS-1500 claims completion instructions (primary) in the textbook.

ASSIGNMENT 12.2   Commercial Primary/Secondary Same Payer CMS-1500 Claims Completion

OBJECTIVES

At the conclusion of this assignment, the student should be able to:

1. Assign ICD-9-CM (or ICD-10-CM) diagnosis codes and CPT or HCPCS level II procedure/service codes.
2. Prepare a commercial insurance CMS-1500 claim.

INSTRUCTIONS

Use optical scanning guidelines to complete the CMS-1500 claim for case study 12-C. Obtain a blank claim by making a copy of the CMS-1500 claim in Appendix III of the textbook. Refer to the textbook CMS-1500 claims completion instructions when third-party payer is the same for primary and secondary health insurance coverage.

Donald L. Givings, M.D.

11350 Medical Drive ■ Anywhere NY 12345 ■ (101) 111-5555

EIN: 11-1234562
NPI: 1234567890

Case Study 12-A

PATIENT INFORMATION:

Name:	Dawn L. Zapp
Address:	663 Hilltop Drive
City:	Anywhere
State:	NY
Zip Code:	12345
Telephone:	(101) 333-4445
Gender:	Female
Date of Birth:	02-12-1967
Occupation:	Cashier
Employer:	Superfresh Foods
Spouse's Employer:	

INSURANCE INFORMATION:

Patient Number:	12-A
Place of Service:	Office
Primary Insurance Plan:	NorthWest Health
Primary Insurance Plan ID #:	444556666
Group #:	
Primary Policyholder:	Dawn L. Zapp
Policyholder Date of Birth:	02-12-1967
Relationship to Patient:	Self
Secondary Insurance Plan:	
Secondary Insurance Plan ID #:	
Secondary Policyholder:	

Patient Status ☐ Married ☐ Divorced ☒ Single ☐ Student ☐ Other

DIAGNOSIS INFORMATION

Diagnosis	Code	Diagnosis	Code
1. Headache		5.	
2. Cough		6.	
3.		7.	
4.		8.	

PROCEDURE INFORMATION

Description of Procedure or Service	Date	Code	Charge
1. Est. patient OV level II	05-10-YYYY		$65.00
2.			
3.			
4.			
5.			

SPECIAL NOTES:
    Return visit: 2 weeks

Donald L. Givings, M.D.

Case Study 12-B

11350 Medical Drive ■ Anywhere NY 12345 ■ (101) 111-5555

EIN: 11-1234562
NPI: 1234567890

PATIENT INFORMATION:

Name:	Albert E. Stein
Address:	2011 Shore Drive
City:	Anywhere
State:	NY
Zip Code:	12345
Telephone:	(101) 651-9388
Gender:	Male
Date of Birth:	07-25-1968
Occupation:	Driver
Employer:	Home Decor Today
Spouse's Employer:	

INSURANCE INFORMATION:

Patient Number:	12-B
Place of Service:	Office
Primary Insurance Plan:	Aetna
Primary Insurance Plan ID #:	4291974911
Group #:	
Primary Policyholder:	Albert E. Stein
Policyholder Date of Birth:	07-25-1968
Relationship to Patient:	Self
Secondary Insurance Plan:	
Secondary Insurance Plan ID #:	
Secondary Policyholder:	

Patient Status ☐ Married ☐ Divorced ☒ Single ☐ Employed ☐ Student ☐ Other

DIAGNOSIS INFORMATION

Diagnosis	Code	Diagnosis	Code
1. Annual Physical Exam		5.	
2.		6.	
3.		7.	
4.		8.	

PROCEDURE INFORMATION

Description of Procedure or Service	Date	Code	Charge
1. Office visit, established visit, level II	02-23-YYYY		$65.00
2.			
3.			
4.			
5.			

SPECIAL NOTES:

© Cengage Learning 2013

Donald L. Givings, M.D.

11350 Medical Drive ■ Anywhere NY 12345 ■ (101) 111-5555

EIN: 11-1234562
NPI: 1234567890

Case Study 12-C

PATIENT INFORMATION:

Name:	Bethany L. Branch
Address:	401 Cartvalley Court
City:	Anywhere
State:	NY
Zip Code:	12345
Telephone:	(101) 333-4445
Gender:	Female
Date of Birth:	05-03-1986
Occupation:	Student (Full time)
Employer:	
Spouse's Employer:	

INSURANCE INFORMATION:

Patient Number:	12-C
Place of Service:	Office
Primary Insurance Plan:	Metropolitan
Primary Insurance Plan ID #:	212224545
Group #:	
Primary Policyholder:	John L. Branch
Policyholder Date of Birth:	10-10-54
Relationship to Patient:	Father
Primary Policyholder's Employer:	Alstom
Secondary Insurance Plan:	Metropolitan
Secondary Insurance Plan ID #:	315661111
Secondary Policyholder:	Karen M. Branch
Policyholder Date of Birth:	09-01-1955
Secondary Policyholder's Employer:	Gateway

Patient Status   ☐ Married   ☐ Divorced   ☒ Single   ☒ Student   ☐ Other

DIAGNOSIS INFORMATION

Diagnosis	Code	Diagnosis	Code
1. Acute bronchitis		5.	
2. Strep pharyngitis		6.	
3.		7.	
4.		8.	

PROCEDURE INFORMATION

Description of Procedure or Service	Date	Code	Charge
1. Office consult level II	12-04-YYYY		$75.00
2. Rapid strep test	12-04-YYYY		$12.00
3.			
4.			
5.			

SPECIAL NOTES:
Return visit: PRN
Referring physician: James R. Feltbetter, M.D.
NPI: 7778878789

© Cengage Learning 2013

ASSIGNMENT 12.3   Commercial Secondary CMS-1500 Claims Completion

OBJECTIVES

At the conclusion of this assignment, the student should be able to:

1. Assign ICD-9-CM (or ICD-10-CM) diagnosis and CPT or HCPCS level II procedure/service codes.
2. Prepare a commercial insurance secondary payer CMS-1500 claim.

INSTRUCTIONS

Use optical scanning guidelines to complete a CMS-1500 claim for case study 12-D. Obtain a blank claim by making a copy of the CMS-1500 claim form in Appendix III of the textbook. Refer to the CMS-1500 claims completion instructions (secondary) in the textbook.

ASSIGNMENT 12.4   Group Health Plan CMS-1500 Claims Completion

OBJECTIVES

At the conclusion of this assignment, the student should be able to:

1. Assign ICD-9-CM (or ICD-10-CM) diagnosis and CPT or HCPCS level II procedure/service codes.
2. Prepare a commercial insurance group health plan CMS-1500 claim.

INSTRUCTIONS

Use optical scanning guidelines to complete a CMS-1500 claim for case study 12-E. Obtain a blank claim by making a copy of the CMS-1500 claim form in Appendix III of the textbook. Refer to the CMS-1500 claims completion instructions (group health plans) in the textbook.

> **NOTE:** Case study 12-E is located on page 167.

ASSIGNMENT 12.5   Multiple Choice Review

1. **Which is considered a commercial health insurance company?**
   a. Medicaid
   b. Medicare
   c. Prudential
   d. TRICARE

2. **Another term that can be used to indicate a fee-for-service plan is a _____ plan.**
   a. liability
   b. noncapitated
   c. prepaid
   d. sliding scale

3. **When a patient is covered by a large employer group health plan (EGHP), *and* the patient is also a Medicare beneficiary, _____ is primary.**
   a. EGHP
   b. EGHP or Medicare
   c. Medicare
   d. Neither EGHP nor Medicare

Donald L. Givings, M.D.

Case Study 12-D

11350 Medical Drive ■ Anywhere NY 12345 ■ (101) 111-5555

EIN: 11-1234562
NPI: 1234567890

PATIENT INFORMATION:

Name:	Laurie P. Reed
Address:	579 Vacation Drive
City:	Anywhere
State:	NY
Zip Code:	12345
Telephone:	(101) 333-5555
Gender:	Female
Date of Birth:	06-05-1964
Occupation:	Tutor
Employer:	The Learning Center
Spouse's Employer:	Recycling R US

INSURANCE INFORMATION:

Patient Number:	12-D
Place of Service:	Office
Primary Insurance Plan:	US Health
Primary Insurance Plan ID #:	C748593
Group #:	
Primary Policyholder:	John P. Reed
Policyholder Date of Birth:	09-08-1962
Relationship to Patient:	Spouse
Secondary Insurance Plan:	Cigna
Secondary Insurance Plan ID #:	345679999
Secondary Policyholder:	Laurie P. Reed

Patient Status ☒ Married   ☐ Divorced   ☐ Single   ☐ Student   ☐ Other

DIAGNOSIS INFORMATION

Diagnosis	Code	Diagnosis	Code
1. Allergic rhinitis		5.	
2.		6.	
3.		7.	
4.		8.	

PROCEDURE INFORMATION

Description of Procedure or Service	Date	Code	Charge
1. Est. patient OV level II	10-28-YYYY		$55.00
2.			
3.			
4.			
5.			

SPECIAL NOTES:
    Return visit: PRN

© Cengage Learning 2013

Donald L. Givings, M.D.

Case Study 12-E

11350 Medical Drive ■ Anywhere NY 12345 ■ (101) 111-5555

EIN: 11-1234562
NPI: 1234567890

PATIENT INFORMATION:

Name:	Sandy Marks
Address:	101 West State Street
City:	Anywhere
State:	NY
Zip Code:	12345
Telephone:	(101) 333-9876
Gender:	Female
Date of Birth:	05-10-1990
Occupation:	Teacher
Employer:	Carnelian Middle School
Spouse's Employer:	

INSURANCE INFORMATION:

Patient Number:	12-E
Place of Service:	Office
Primary Insurance Plan:	Empire Plan
Primary Insurance Plan ID #:	890102568
Group #:	
Primary Policyholder:	Sandy Marks
Policyholder Date of Birth:	05-10-1990
Relationship to Patient:	Self
Secondary Insurance Plan:	
Secondary Insurance Plan ID #:	
Secondary Policyholder:	

Patient Status ☐ Married ☐ Divorced ☒ Single ☐ Student ☐ Other

DIAGNOSIS INFORMATION

Diagnosis	Code	Diagnosis	Code
1. Hypertension		5.	
2.		6.	
3.		7.	
4.		8.	

PROCEDURE INFORMATION

Description of Procedure or Service	Date	Code	Charge
1. New patient OV, level III	07-20-YYYY		$75.00
2.			
3.			
4.			
5.			

SPECIAL NOTES:

© Cengage Learning 2013

4. Logan is the daughter of Amy (DOB 3/29/68) and Bill (DOB 11/15/70), and is covered by both parents' health insurance plans. According to the birthday rule, a medical claim for Logan will be submitted to
   a. Amy's plan as primary payer and Bill's plan as secondary payer.
   b. Amy's plan only, as she is two years older than her husband.
   c. Bill's plan as primary payer and Amy's plan as secondary payer.
   d. Bill's plan only, as he has been employed with his company longer.

5. When the patient is the domestic partner of the primary policyholder, this is indicated on the CMS-1500 claim form by
   a. entering "DP" after the patient's name in Block 2.
   b. entering the patient's full name in Block 9.
   c. placing an X in the OTHER box of Block 6.
   d. placing an X in the SINGLE box of Block 8.

6. Reimbursement for income lost as a result of a temporary or permanent illness or injury is covered by _____ insurance.
   a. automobile
   b. disability
   c. health
   d. liability

7. The patient was seen in the provider's office on 12/03/2006. The patient's history reflects that the patient was injured four months earlier. What is entered in Block 14 of the CMS-1500 claim form?
   a. 04 03 2006
   b. 08 03 2006
   c. 11 03 2006
   d. 12 03 2006

8. What is entered in Block 17b of the CMS-1500 claim?
   a. Employer Identification Number (EIN)
   b. National Provider Identifier (NPI)
   c. Provider Identification Number (PIN)
   d. Provider's Social Security Number (SSN)

9. Dr. Smith evaluates Marcia Brady during a three-month recheck of her diabetes mellitus. He performs venipuncture and sends the patient's blood sample to an outside laboratory for testing of the blood glucose level. Dr. Smith's insurance specialist enters the outside laboratory's _____ in Block 24J because the blood glucose test is reported in Block 24D on that line.
   a. EIN
   b. NPI
   c. SSN
   d. Group #

10. If the patient has paid a copayment on the claim being submitted, this is indicated on the CMS-1500 claim form by entering the
    a. amount paid in Block 19.
    b. amount paid in Block 29.
    c. patient's name in Block 13.
    d. letter Y in Block 27.

11. The patient was required to obtain an authorization number before being treated by a specialist. Where is the authorization number entered in the CMS-1500 claim form?
    a. Block 10d
    b. Block 17a
    c. Block 19
    d. Block 23

12. **When an insurance claim is submitted to an insurance company that covers the treatment of injuries sustained in a motor vehicle accident, the _____ reviews the claim and determines coverage for the injured person.**
    a. claims analyst
    b. health care broker
    c. medical adjuster
    d. negligence attorney

13. **Beatrice Blue holds a private commercial health care policy, and she wishes to have payment from the health insurance company sent directly to her provider. How is this reported on the CMS-1500 claim form?**
    a. Beatrice Blue will sign Block 12.
    b. Beatrice Blue will sign Block 13.
    c. The provider will sign Block 12.
    d. The provider will sign Block 13.

14. **Which claims are submitted to cover the cost of medical care for traumatic injuries, lost wages, pain, and suffering?**
    a. disability
    b. automobile
    c. liability
    d. medical

15. **A balance of $12.55 is due to the patient for services provided by Dr. Brown. What is entered in *Block 30* of the CMS-1500 claim?**
    a. Leave blank
    b. 12 55
    c. −12 55
    d. CREDIT

16. **When the same commercial payer issues the primary and secondary or supplemental policies, it is *generally* acceptable to submit _____ claim(s).**
    a. one
    b. two
    c. three
    d. three or more

17. **When laboratory tests are performed in the office enter an X in the NO box of**
    a. Block 9d.
    b. Block 11d.
    c. Block 20.
    d. Block 27.

18. **Reimbursement for loss of or damage to a vehicle (e.g., caused by fire, flood, hail, theft, vandalism, or wind) is covered by _____ (automobile) insurance.**
    a. collision
    b. comprehensive
    c. liability
    d. medical

19. **Which health plan is required to accept employees and their family members?**
    a. dental
    b. group
    c. individual
    d. medical

20. **What is entered in Block 24j if the provider is a member of a group practice?**
    a. Employer Identification Number (EIN)
    b. National Provider Identifier (NPI)
    c. Preauthorization number
    d. Social Security Number (SSN)

CHAPTER 13
Blue Cross Blue Shield

INTRODUCTION

This chapter familiarizes students with completion of CMS-1500 claim forms for primary and secondary Blue Cross and Blue Shield (BCBS) payers.

> **NOTE:** When the subscriber's employer and a group number are included on the case study, enter an X in the Group Health Plan box in Block 1. If there is no employer or group number, enter an X in the Other box in Block 1.

> **NOTE:** When completing CMS-1500 claims for case studies in this workbook, enter just one diagnosis pointer number in Block 24E.

> **NOTE:** When completing claims for patients who have both primary and secondary insurance coverage, enter a P (primary) next to the case number on the primary claim (e.g., 13-A-P), and enter an S (secondary) (e.g., 13-A-S) next to the case number on the secondary claim. When completing claims for patients who have BCBS insurance for both primary and secondary coverage, enter BB as part of the case number (e.g., 13-C-BB).

ASSIGNMENT 13.1 BCBS Primary CMS-1500 Claims Completion

OBJECTIVES

At the conclusion of this assignment, the student should be able to:

1. Assign ICD-9-CM (or ICD-10-CM) diagnosis and CPT or HCPCS level II procedure/service codes.
2. Prepare a BCBS insurance primary payer CMS-1500 claim.

INSTRUCTIONS

Use optical scanning guidelines to complete a CMS-1500 for case studies 13-A and 13-B. Obtain a blank claim by making a copy of the CMS-1500 claim form in Appendix III of the textbook. Refer to the CMS-1500 claims completion instructions (primary) in the textbook.

ASSIGNMENT 13.2 BCBS Primary/Secondary Same Payer CMS-1500 Claims Completion

OBJECTIVES

At the conclusion of this assignment, the student should be able to:

1. Assign ICD-9-CM (or ICD-10-CM) diagnosis codes and CPT or HCPCS level II procedure/service codes.
2. Prepare BCBS CMS-1500 insurance claims.

INSTRUCTIONS

Use optical scanning guidelines to complete CMS-1500 claims for case studies 13-C and 13-D. Obtain a blank claim by making a copy of the CMS-1500 claim in Appendix III of the textbook. Refer to the CMS-1500 claims completion instructions (Primary and Secondary when payer is the same) in the textbook.

Donald L. Givings, M.D.

Case Study 13-A

11350 Medical Drive ■ Anywhere NY 12345 ■ (101) 111-5555

EIN: 11-1234562
NPI: 1234567890

PATIENT INFORMATION:

Name:	Monty L. Booker
Address:	47 Snowflake Road
City:	Anywhere
State:	NY
Zip Code:	12345
Telephone:	(101) 333-5555
Gender:	Male
Date of Birth:	12-25-1966
Occupation:	Editor
Employer:	Atlanta Publisher
Spouse's Employer:	

INSURANCE INFORMATION:

Patient Number:	13-A
Place of Service:	Office
Primary Insurance Plan:	BCBS US
Primary Insurance Plan ID #:	NXY678223434
Group #:	
Primary Policyholder:	Monty L. Booker
Policyholder Date of Birth:	12-25-1966
Relationship to Patient:	Self
Secondary Insurance Plan:	
Secondary Insurance Plan ID #:	
Secondary Policyholder:	

Patient Status   ☒ Married   ☐ Divorced   ☐ Single   ☐ Student   ☐ Other

DIAGNOSIS INFORMATION

Diagnosis	Code	Diagnosis	Code
1. Abnormal loss of weight		5.	
2. Polydipsia		6.	
3. Polyphagia		7.	
4.		8.	

PROCEDURE INFORMATION

Description of Procedure or Service	Date	Code	Charge
1. New patient OV level II	01-19-YYYY		$100.00
2. Urinalysis, with microscopy	01-19-YYYY		$10.00
3.			
4.			
5.			

SPECIAL NOTES:
   Return visit: 3 weeks

© Cengage Learning 2013

Donald L. Givings, M.D.

Case Study 13-B

11350 Medical Drive ■ Anywhere NY 12345 ■ (101) 111-5555

EIN: 11-1234562
NPI: 1234567890

PATIENT INFORMATION:

Name:	Anita B. Strong
Address:	124 Prosper Way
City:	Anywhere
State:	NY
Zip Code:	12345
Telephone:	(101) 333-5555
Gender:	Female
Date of Birth:	04-25-1959
Occupation:	Author
Employer:	Anywhere Weekly News
Spouse's Employer:	

INSURANCE INFORMATION:

Patient Number:	13-B
Place of Service:	Office
Primary Insurance Plan:	BCBS US
Primary Insurance Plan ID #:	XWG214556666
Group #:	
Primary Policyholder:	Anita B. Strong
Policyholder Date of Birth:	04-25-1960
Relationship to Patient:	Self
Secondary Insurance Plan:	
Secondary Insurance Plan ID #:	
Secondary Policyholder:	

Patient Status   ☒ Married   ☐ Divorced   ☐ Single   ☐ Student   ☐ Other

DIAGNOSIS INFORMATION

Diagnosis	Code	Diagnosis	Code
1. Migraine, classical		5.	
2.		6.	
3.		7.	
4.		8.	

PROCEDURE INFORMATION

Description of Procedure or Service	Date	Code	Charge
1. Est. patient OV level I	11-07-YYYY		$55.00
2.			
3.			
4.			
5.			

SPECIAL NOTES:
   Return visit: PRN
   Patient paid $20.00 toward today's bill.

Donald L. Givings, M.D.

Case Study 13-C

11350 Medical Drive ■ Anywhere NY 12345 ■ (101) 111-5555

EIN: 11-1234562
NPI: 1234567890

PATIENT INFORMATION:

Name:	Virginia A. Love
Address:	61 Isaiah Circle
City:	Anywhere
State:	NY
Zip Code:	12345
Telephone:	(101) 333-5555
Gender:	Female
Date of Birth:	07-04-1962
Occupation:	Decorator
Employer:	Home Designs
Spouse's Employer:	Imperial Bayliners

INSURANCE INFORMATION:

Patient Number:	13-C
Place of Service:	Office
Primary Insurance Plan:	BCBS
Primary Insurance Plan ID #:	XWN212567972
Group #:	123
Primary Policyholder:	Charles L. Love
Policyholder Date of Birth:	10-06-60
Relationship to Patient:	Spouse
Secondary Insurance Plan:	BCBS
Secondary Insurance Plan ID #:	XMP111451111
Secondary Policyholder:	Virginia A. Love

Patient Status ☒ Married ☐ Divorced ☐ Single ☐ Student ☐ Other

DIAGNOSIS INFORMATION

Diagnosis	Code	Diagnosis	Code
1. Chronic conjunctivitis		5.	
2. Contact dermatitis		6.	
3.		7.	
4.		8.	

PROCEDURE INFORMATION

Description of Procedure or Service	Date	Code	Charge
1. Est. patient OV level II	07-03-YYYY		$55.00
2.			
3.			
4.			
5.			

SPECIAL NOTES:
   If conjunctivitis does not clear within one week refer to Dr. Glance.
   Return visit: PRN

© Cengage Learning 2013

Iris A. Glance, M.D. OPHTHALMOLOGIST

66 Granite Drive ■ Anywhere NY 12345 ■ (101) 111-5555

EIN: 11-6161612
NPI: 6789137892

Case Study 13-D

PATIENT INFORMATION:

Name:	Virginia A. Love
Address:	61 Isaiah Circle
City:	Anywhere
State:	NY
Zip Code:	12345
Telephone:	(101) 333-5555
Gender:	Female
Date of Birth:	07-04-1962
Occupation:	Decorator
Employer:	Home Designs
Spouse's Employer:	Imperial Bayliners

INSURANCE INFORMATION:

Patient Number:	13-D
Place of Service:	Office
Primary Insurance Plan:	BCBS
Primary Insurance Plan ID #:	XWN212567372
Group #:	123
Primary Policyholder:	Charles L. Love
Policyholder Date of Birth:	10-06-60
Relationship to Patient:	Spouse
Secondary Insurance Plan:	BCBS
Secondary Insurance Plan ID #:	XMP111451111
Secondary Policyholder:	Virginia A. Love

Patient Status   ☒ Married   ☐ Divorced   ☐ Single   ☐ Student   ☐ Other

DIAGNOSIS INFORMATION

Diagnosis	Code	Diagnosis	Code
1. Chronic conjunctivitis		5.	
2. Conjunctival degeneration		6.	
3.		7.	
4.		8.	

PROCEDURE INFORMATION

Description of Procedure or Service	Date	Code	Charge
1. Office consult level I	07-13-YYYY		$65.00
2.			
3.			
4.			
5.			

SPECIAL NOTES:
Onset of symptoms: 07-03-YYYY.

ASSIGNMENT 13.3   BCBS Secondary CMS-1500 Claims Completion

OBJECTIVES

At the conclusion of this assignment, the student should be able to:
1. Assign ICD-9-CM (or ICD-10-CM) diagnosis and CPT or HCPCS level II procedure/service codes.
2. Prepare a BCBS insurance secondary payer CMS-1500 claim.

INSTRUCTIONS

Use optical scanning guidelines to complete a CMS-1500 for case study 13-E. Obtain a blank claim by making a copy of the CMS-1500 claim form in Appendix III of the textbook. Refer to the CMS-1500 claims completion instructions (secondary) in the textbook.

ASSIGNMENT 13.4   Multiple Choice Review

1. **Prior to the joint venture between Blue Cross and Blue Shield, the Blue Shield plans covered only**
   a. hospital charges.
   b. physician services.
   c. prescription costs.
   d. therapy services.

2. **Blue Cross facilities that had signed contracts to provide services to subscribers for special rates were known as _____ hospitals.**
   a. benefit
   b. member
   c. plan
   d. subscriber

3. **In what year was the BlueCross BlueShield Association (BCBSA) created?**
   a. 1929
   b. 1938
   c. 1977
   d. 1986

4. **Which is a function of the BlueCross BlueShield Association (BCBSA)?**
   a. hiring local personnel
   b. membership enrollment
   c. national advertising
   d. processing Medicaid claims

5. **The difference between for-profit status and nonprofit status is that**
   a. for-profit corporations pay taxes on profits generated by the corporation.
   b. for-profit corporations pay their shareholders with before-tax profits.
   c. nonprofit corporations do not have stocks, shareholders, or officers.
   d. nonprofit corporations return earned profits to stock shareholders.

6. **When a policyholder moves into an area served by a different BCBS corporation than the policyholder previously used, the plan must**
   a. allow conversion and guarantee transfer of membership.
   b. immediately cancel the individual's policy.
   c. locate a primary provider for the member.
   d. prohibit the member from seeking urgent care.

Donald L. Givings, M.D.

11350 Medical Drive ■ Anywhere NY 12345 ■ (101) 111-5555

EIN: 11-1234562
NPI: 1234567890

Case Study 13-E

PATIENT INFORMATION:

Name:	Keith S. Kutter
Address:	22 Pinewood Avenue
City:	Anywhere
State:	NY
Zip Code:	12345
Telephone:	(101) 333-5555
Gender:	Male
Date of Birth:	12-01-1955
Occupation:	Manager
Employer:	First League
Spouse's Employer:	Anderson Music

INSURANCE INFORMATION:

Patient Number:	13-E
Place of Service:	Office
Primary Insurance Plan:	AETNA
Primary Insurance Plan ID #:	FLX313007777
Group #:	
Primary Policyholder:	Keith S. Kutter
Policyholder Date of Birth:	12-01-1955
Relationship to Patient:	Self
Secondary Insurance Plan:	BCBS
Secondary Insurance Plan ID #:	GPW212446868
Secondary Policyholder:	Linda Kutter
Secondary Policyholder DOB:	05-22-1956

Patient Status   ☒ Married   ☐ Divorced   ☐ Single   ☐ Student   ☐ Other

DIAGNOSIS INFORMATION

Diagnosis	Code	Diagnosis	Code
1. Muscle spasms		5.	
2.		6.	
3.		7.	
4.		8.	

PROCEDURE INFORMATION

Description of Procedure or Service	Date	Code	Charge
1. Est. patient OV level II	09-03-YYYY		$65.00
2.			
3.			
4.			
5.			

SPECIAL NOTES:
   Refer to a chiropractor.

© Cengage Learning 2013

7. **The preferred provider network (PPN) allowed rate is generally**
   a. 10 percent higher than the participating provider rate.
   b. 10 percent lower than the participating provider rate.
   c. based on the Medicare Physician Fee Schedule.
   d. equal to the participating provider payment.

8. **Which is an incentive for a provider to sign a PPN contract?**
   a. higher reimbursement rates than those of participating providers
   b. no quality assurance or cost-containment program requirements
   c. PPN providers are not held to any managed care provisions
   d. written notification of new employer groups and hospitals

9. **Small businesses are likely to select which BCBS coverage?**
   a. fee-for-service
   b. indemnity
   c. managed care
   d. supplemental

10. **An example of a benefit provided by BCBS basic coverage is**
    a. assistant surgeon fees.
    b. mental health visits.
    c. occupational therapy.
    d. private-duty nursing.

11. **The BCBS plan type that offers choice and flexibility to subscribers is**
    a. Healthcare Anywhere.
    b. indemnity coverage.
    c. major medical coverage.
    d. managed care.

12. **A special accidental injury rider provides which benefit?**
    a. Chronic conditions are covered if treatment is sought within the contract's established guidelines.
    b. Medical care is paid at 100 percent if treatment is received within 24 to 72 hours of accident or injury.
    c. Nonsurgical care is paid at 100 percent if treatment is received within the contract's established time frame.
    d. Surgical care is paid at 100 percent if treatment is received within the contract's established time frame.

13. **What special handling is required for BCBS claims filed under the medical emergency care rider?**
    a. Claims require all six procedure/service codes to be entered in Block 24D.
    b. CPT codes must reflect critical care services provided to the patient.
    c. Health insurance specialists must enter four diagnosis codes in Block 21.
    d. ICD-9-CM (or ICD-10-CM) codes must reflect a condition that requires immediate care.

14. **The outpatient pretreatment authorization plan (OPAP) is also known as**
    a. preapproval.
    b. preauthorization.
    c. precertification.
    d. prevention.

15. **What title is listed on the BCBS identification cards for federal employees?**
    a. BCBS Federal Program
    b. BCBS National Account for Federal Employees
    c. Federal Employee Health Benefits Program
    d. Government-Wide Service Benefit Plan

16. BCBS Medicare supplemental plans are also known as _____ plans.
    a. MediBlue
    b. Medicare
    c. Medigap
    d. MediSup

17. The BlueCard Program allows members to obtain health services while in another BCBS service area. The patient will also
    a. pay a higher copayment or coinsurance for care.
    b. pay a higher premium for the flexible coverage.
    c. receive the benefits of the other BCBS contract.
    d. receive the benefits of his or her home plan contract.

18. Which BCBS program or plan would be most appropriate for a student who is attending school out of state?
    a. Away from Home Care Program
    b. BlueCard Program
    c. indemnity plan
    d. point-of-service plan

19. What information is entered in Block 13 of a BCBS CMS-1500 claim form?
    a. nothing; the box is left blank
    b. SIGNATURE ON FILE
    c. the patient's signature
    d. the provider's signature

20. What information is entered in Block 29 of the CMS-1500 claim when the patient pays a $15.00 copayment?
    a. 0 00
    b. 20 00
    c. $20.00
    d. Nothing; the box is left blank.

CHAPTER 14
Medicare

INTRODUCTION

This chapter familiarizes students with completion of CMS-1500 claims for Primary Medicare, Medicare as Secondary Payer (MSP), Medicare/Medigap, and Medicare/Medicaid.

> **NOTE:** When completing CMS-1500 claims for case studies in this workbook, enter just one diagnosis pointer number in Block 24E.

> **NOTE:** When completing claims for patients who have both primary and secondary insurance coverage, enter a P (primary) next to the case number on the primary claim (e.g., 14-A-P), and enter an S (secondary) (e.g., 14-A-S) next to the case number on the secondary claim. For patients who have Medicare and Medicaid crossover coverage, add MM to the patient account number (e.g., 14-B-MM).

ASSIGNMENT 14.1 Medicare Primary CMS-1500 Claims Completion

OBJECTIVES

At the conclusion of this assignment, the student should be able to:

1. Assign ICD-9-CM (or ICD-10-CM) diagnosis and CPT or HCPCS level II procedure/service codes.
2. Prepare a Medicare insurance primary payer CMS-1500 claim.

INSTRUCTIONS

Use optical scanning guidelines to complete a CMS-1500 for case studies 14-A and 14-B. Obtain a blank claim by making a copy of the CMS-1500 claim form in Appendix III of the textbook. Refer to the CMS-1500 claims completion instructions (primary) in the textbook.

ASSIGNMENT 14.2 Medicare as Secondary Payer CMS-1500 Claims Completion

OBJECTIVES

At the conclusion of this assignment, the student should be able to:

1. Assign ICD-9-CM (or ICD-10-CM) diagnosis and CPT or HCPCS level II procedure/service codes.
2. Prepare a Medicare as Secondary Payer (MSP) CMS-1500 claim.

INSTRUCTIONS

Use optical scanning guidelines to complete a CMS-1500 for case studies 14-C and 14-D. Obtain a blank claim by making a copy of the CMS-1500 claim form in Appendix III of the textbook. Refer to the CMS-1500 claims completion instructions (secondary) in the textbook.

ASSIGNMENT 14.3 Medicare/Medigap CMS-1500 Claims Completion

OBJECTIVES

At the conclusion of this assignment, the student should be able to:

1. Assign ICD-9-CM (or ICD-10-CM) diagnosis and CPT or HCPCS level II procedure/ service codes.
2. Prepare a Medicare/Medigap CMS-1500 claim.

INSTRUCTIONS

Use optical scanning guidelines to complete a CMS-1500 for case study 14-E. Obtain a blank claim by making a copy of the CMS-1500 claim form in Appendix III of the textbook. Refer to the CMS-1500 claims completion instructions (secondary) in the textbook.

ASSIGNMENT 14.4 Medicare/Medicaid CMS-1500 Claims Completion

OBJECTIVES

At the conclusion of this assignment, the student should be able to:

1. Assign ICD-9-CM (or ICD-10-CM) diagnosis and CPT or HCPCS level II procedure/service codes.
2. Prepare a Medicare/Medicaid CMS-1500 claim.

INSTRUCTIONS

Use optical scanning guidelines to complete a CMS-1500 for case studies 14-F and 14-G. Obtain a blank claim by making a copy of the CMS-1500 claim form in Appendix III of the textbook. Refer to the CMS-1500 claims completion instructions (secondary) in the textbook.

ASSIGNMENT 14.5 Roster Billing

OBJECTIVES

At the conclusion of this assignment, the student should be able to:

1. Assign ICD-9-CM (or ICD-10-CM) diagnosis and CPT or HCPCS level II procedure/service codes.
2. Prepare a Medicare CMS-1500 claim for roster billing for vaccines.

INSTRUCTIONS

Use optical scanning guidelines to complete a CMS-1500 for case studies 14-H and 14-I. Obtain a blank claim by making a copy of the CMS-1500 claim form in Appendix III of the textbook. Refer to the CMS-1500 claims completion instructions (roster billing) in the textbook.

Donald L. Givings, M.D.

Case Study 14-A

11350 Medical Drive ■ Anywhere NY 12345 ■ (101) 111-5555

EIN: 11-1234562
NPI: 1234567890

PATIENT INFORMATION:

Name:	Alice E. Worthington
Address:	3301 Sunny Day Drive
City:	Anywhere
State:	NY
Zip Code:	12345
Telephone:	(101) 333-5555
Gender:	Female
Date of Birth:	02-16-1926
Occupation:	
Employer:	None
Spouse's Employer:	

INSURANCE INFORMATION:

Patient Number:	14-A
Place of Service:	Office
Primary Insurance Plan:	Medicare
Primary Insurance Plan ID #:	444223333A
Group #:	
Primary Policyholder:	Alice E. Worthington
Policyholder Date of Birth:	02-16-1926
Relationship to Patient:	Self
Secondary Insurance Plan:	
Secondary Insurance Plan ID #:	
Secondary Policyholder:	

Patient Status ☐ Married ☐ Divorced ☒ Single ☐ Student ☐ Other

DIAGNOSIS INFORMATION

Diagnosis	Code	Diagnosis	Code
1. Breast lump, left		5.	
2. Breast pain, left		6.	
3. Family history of breast cancer		7.	
4.		8.	

PROCEDURE INFORMATION

Description of Procedure or Service	Date	Code	Charge
1. Est. patient OV level II	07-12-YYYY		$65.00
2.			
3.			
4.			
5.			

SPECIAL NOTES:
Refer to Jonathan B. Kutter, M.D.

Jonathan B. Kutter, M.D. SURGERY

Case Study 14-B

339 Woodland Place ■ Anywhere NY 12345 ■ (101) 111-5555

EIN: 11-1234562
NPI: 2345675678

PATIENT INFORMATION:

Name:	Alice E. Worthington
Address:	3301 Sunny Day Drive
City:	Anywhere
State:	NY
Zip Code:	12345
Telephone:	(101) 333-5555
Gender:	Female
Date of Birth:	02-16-1926
Occupation:	
Employer:	None
Spouse's Employer:	

INSURANCE INFORMATION:

Patient Number:	14-B
Place of Service:	Office
Primary Insurance Plan:	Medicare
Primary Insurance Plan ID #:	444223333A
Group #:	
Primary Policyholder:	Alice E. Worthington
Policyholder Date of Birth:	02-16-1926
Relationship to Patient:	Self
Secondary Insurance Plan:	
Secondary Insurance Plan ID #:	
Secondary Policyholder:	

Patient Status ☐ Married ☐ Divorced ☒ Single ☐ Student ☐ Other

DIAGNOSIS INFORMATION

Diagnosis	Code	Diagnosis	Code
1. Breast lump, left		5.	
2. Breast pain, left		6.	
3. Family history of breast cancer		7.	
4.		8.	

PROCEDURE INFORMATION

Description of Procedure or Service	Date	Code	Charge
1. Office consult level II	07-15-YYYY		$75.00
2.			
3.			
4.			
5.			

SPECIAL NOTES:
Onset of symptoms: 07-12-YYYY. Referred by Donald L. Givings, M.D., NPI: 1234567890.

Donald L. Givings, M.D.

Case Study 14-C

11350 Medical Drive ■ Anywhere NY 12345 ■ (101) 111-5555

EIN: 11-1234562
NPI: 1234567890

PATIENT INFORMATION:

Name:	Rebecca Nichols
Address:	384 Dean Street
City:	Anywhere
State:	NY
Zip Code:	12345
Telephone:	(101) 333-5555
Gender:	Female
Date of Birth:	10-12-1925
Occupation:	
Employer:	Retired
Spouse's Employer:	

INSURANCE INFORMATION:

Patient Number:	14-C
Place of Service:	Inpatient hospital
Primary Insurance Plan:	BCBS
Primary Insurance Plan ID #:	667143344
Group #:	
Primary Policyholder:	Rebecca Nichols
Policyholder Date of Birth:	10-12-1925
Relationship to Patient:	Self
Secondary Insurance Plan:	Medicare
Secondary Insurance Plan ID #:	667143344A
Secondary Policyholder:	Rebecca Nichols

Patient Status ☐ Married ☐ Divorced ☒ Single ☐ Student ☐ Other

DIAGNOSIS INFORMATION

Diagnosis	Code	Diagnosis	Code
1. Rectal bleeding		5.	
2. Diarrhea		6.	
3. Abnormal loss of weight		7.	
4.		8.	

PROCEDURE INFORMATION

Description of Procedure or Service	Date	Code	Charge
1. Initial hosp. level III	08-06-YYYY		$175.00
2. Subsq. hosp. level III	08-07-YYYY		85.00
3. Subsq. hosp. level III	08-08-YYYY		85.00
4. Subsq. hosp. level II	08-09-YYYY		75.00
5. Hosp. discharge, 30 min.	08-10-YYYY		75.00

SPECIAL NOTES:
  Goodmedicine Hospital, 1 Provider Street, Anywhere Street, Anywhere NY 12345. NPI: 1123456789
  Dr. Gestive saw the patient for a consult on August 7 & August 8.

© Cengage Learning 2013

Lisa M. Mason, M.D. FAMILY PRACTICE

547 Antigua Road ■ Anywhere NY 12345 ■ (101) 111-5555

EIN: 11-4958672
NPI: 4567897890

Case Study 14-D

PATIENT INFORMATION:

Name:	Samuel T. Mahoney Jr.
Address:	498 Meadow Lane
City:	Anywhere
State:	NY
Zip Code:	12345
Telephone:	(101) 333-5555
Gender:	Male
Date of Birth:	09-04-1930
Occupation:	
Employer:	None
Spouse's Employer:	

INSURANCE INFORMATION:

Patient Number:	14-D
Place of Service:	Office
Primary Insurance Plan:	Aetna
Primary Insurance Plan ID #:	312785894
Group #:	
Primary Policyholder:	Samuel T. Mahoney Jr.
Policyholder Date of Birth:	09-04-1930
Relationship to Patient:	Self
Secondary Insurance Plan:	Medicare
Secondary Insurance Plan ID #:	312785894A
Secondary Policyholder:	Samuel T. Mahoney Jr.

Patient Status   ☒ Married   ☐ Divorced   ☐ Single   ☐ Student   ☐ Other

DIAGNOSIS INFORMATION

Diagnosis	Code	Diagnosis	Code
1. Asthma		5.	
2. Acute upper respiratory infection		6.	
3.		7.	
4.		8.	

PROCEDURE INFORMATION

Description of Procedure or Service	Date	Code	Charge
1. Est. patient OV level II	10-03-YYYY		$25.00
2.			
3.			
4.			
5.			

SPECIAL NOTES:
Dr. Mason is nonPAR with Medicare
Onset of disease: 01-01-YYYY

© Cengage Learning 2013

Donald L. Givings, M.D.

Case Study 14-E

11350 Medical Drive ■ Anywhere NY 12345 ■ (101) 111-5555

EIN: 11-1234562
NPI: 1234567890

PATIENT INFORMATION:

Name:	Abraham N. Freed
Address:	12 Nottingham Circle
City:	Anywhere
State:	NY
Zip Code:	12345
Telephone:	(101) 333-5555
Gender:	Male
Date of Birth:	10-03-1922
Occupation:	
Employer:	Retired Johnson Steel
Spouse's Employer:	

INSURANCE INFORMATION:

Patient Number:	14-E
Place of Service:	Office
Primary Insurance Plan:	Medicare
Primary Insurance Plan ID #:	645454545A
Group #:	
Primary Policyholder:	Abraham N. Freed
Policyholder Date of Birth:	10-03-1922
Relationship to Patient:	Self
Secondary Insurance Plan:	BCBS Medigap
Secondary Insurance Plan ID #:	NXY645454545
Secondary Policyholder:	Abraham N. Freed

Patient Status   ☒ Married   ☐ Divorced   ☐ Single   ☐ Student   ☐ Other

DIAGNOSIS INFORMATION

Diagnosis	Code	Diagnosis	Code
1. Hypertension, malignant		5.	
2. Dizziness		6.	
3.		7.	
4.		8.	

PROCEDURE INFORMATION

Description of Procedure or Service	Date	Code	Charge
1. New patient OV level IV	03-07-YYYY		$100.00
2. EKG	03-07-YYYY		50.00
3. Venipuncture	03-07-YYYY		8.00
4.			
5.			

SPECIAL NOTES:
   Return visit: 2 weeks

© Cengage Learning 2013

Donald L. Givings, M.D.

11350 Medical Drive ■ Anywhere NY 12345 ■ (101) 111-5555

EIN: 11-1234562
NPI: 1234567890

Case Study 14-F

PATIENT INFORMATION:

Name:	Patricia S. Delaney
Address:	45 Garden Lane
City:	Anywhere
State:	NY
Zip Code:	12345
Telephone:	(101) 333-5555
Gender:	Female
Date of Birth:	04-12-1931
Occupation:	
Employer:	
Spouse's Employer:	

INSURANCE INFORMATION:

Patient Number:	14-F
Place of Service:	Office
Primary Insurance Plan:	Medicare
Primary Insurance Plan ID #:	485375869A
Group #:	
Primary Policyholder:	Patricia S. Delaney
Policyholder Date of Birth:	04-12-1931
Relationship to Patient:	Self
Secondary Insurance Plan:	Medicaid
Secondary Insurance Plan ID #:	22886644XT
Secondary Policyholder:	Self

Patient Status ☐ Married ☐ Divorced ☒ Single ☐ Student ☐ Other

DIAGNOSIS INFORMATION

Diagnosis	Code	Diagnosis	Code
1. Rosacea		5.	
2.		6.	
3.		7.	
4.		8.	

PROCEDURE INFORMATION

Description of Procedure or Service	Date	Code	Charge
1. Est. patient OV level I	12-15-YYYY		$55.00
2.			
3.			
4.			
5.			

SPECIAL NOTES:
Refer patient to dermatologist
Return visit: PRN

© Cengage Learning 2013

Claire M. Skinner, M.D. DERMATOLOGY

50 Clear View Drive ■ Anywhere NY 12345 ■ (101) 111-5555

EIN: 11-5555552
NPI: 5671238901

Case Study 14-G

PATIENT INFORMATION:

Name:	Patricia S. Delaney
Address:	45 Garden Lane
City:	Anywhere
State:	NY
Zip Code:	12345
Telephone:	(101) 333-5555
Gender:	Female
Date of Birth:	04-12-1931
Occupation:	
Employer:	
Spouse's Employer:	

INSURANCE INFORMATION:

Patient Number:	14-G
Place of Service:	Office
Primary Insurance Plan:	Medicare
Primary Insurance Plan ID #:	485375869A
Group #:	
Primary Policyholder:	Patricia S. Delaney
Policyholder Date of Birth:	04-12-1931
Relationship to Patient:	Self
Secondary Insurance Plan:	Medicaid
Secondary Insurance Plan ID #:	22886644XT
Secondary Policyholder:	Self

Patient Status   ☐ Married   ☐ Divorced   ☒ Single   ☐ Student   ☐ Other

DIAGNOSIS INFORMATION

Diagnosis	Code	Diagnosis	Code
1. Rosacea		5.	
2.		6.	
3.		7.	
4.		8.	

PROCEDURE INFORMATION

Description of Procedure or Service	Date	Code	Charge
1. Office consult level III	12-18-YYYY		$85.00
2.			
3.			
4.			
5.			

SPECIAL NOTES:
Return visit PRN
Onset of symptoms: 12-15-YYYY Referred by Donald L. Givings, M.D., NPI: 1234567890.

© Cengage Learning 2013

Mingo River Clinic

Case Study 14-H

103 Park Road ■ Anywhere NY 12345 ■ (101) 111-5555

EIN: 34-6121151
NPI: 7375433213

HICN	Name	DOB	Sex	Address	Signature
4545667777	Marshall, Quinn	03/01/35	M	45 Black Road Anywhere, NY 12345	Quinn Marshall
337889961	Morales, Lucy	10/01/29	F	1841 Hillcrest Lane Anywhere, NY 12345	Lucy A Morales
894443377	Hansberry, John	10/12/31	M	1421 Lawson Road Anywhere, NY 12345	John Hansberry
331222121	Hershey, March	02/15/33	F	301 Deer Lane Anywhere, NY 12345	March Hershey
555332226	Fields, Langston	05/16/28	M	8 Marble Rock Road Anywhere, NY 12345	Langston Fields

DIAGNOSIS INFORMATION

Diagnosis	Code	Diagnosis	Code
1. Flu vaccine		5.	
2.		6.	
3.		7.	
4.		8.	

PROCEDURE INFORMATION

Description of Procedure or Service	Date	Code	Charge
1. Flu vaccine	03-12-YYYY		$10.00
2. Administration of flu vaccine	03-12-YYYY		$ 5.00
3.			
4.			
5.			

SPECIAL NOTES:
   ($50 to be billed to Medicare) for flu vaccine
   ($5 to be billed to Medicare) for the administration of flu vaccine

Mingo River Clinic

Case Study 14-I

103 Park Road ■ Anywhere NY 12345 ■ (101) 111-5555

EIN: 34-6121151
NPI: 7375433213

HICN	Name	DOB	Sex	Address	Signature
998337777	Jones, Karen	03/01/35	F	75 Main Street Anywhere, NY 12345	*Karen Jones*
4444553333	Williams, Pia	08/08/28	F	17 Ski Top Lane Anywhere, NY 12345	*Pia Williams*
1111223333	Gooding, Maria	05/01/25	F	103 Carrier Street Anywhere, NY 12345	*Maria Gooding*
2222115555	Hennessy, Michael	06/10/41	M	55678 Browne Road Anywhere, NY 12345	*Michael Hennessy*
5588996321	White, Mary	03/03/29	F	25 Yeager Road Anywhere, NY 12345	*Mary White*
1895457733	Martin, Majors	05/15/31	M	1503 Williamstown Spring Road Anywhere, NY 12345	*MAJORS MARTIN*

DIAGNOSIS INFORMATION

Diagnosis	Code	Diagnosis	Code
1. Pneumonia vaccine		5.	
2.		6.	
3.		7.	
4.		8.	

PROCEDURE INFORMATION

Description of Procedure or Service	Date	Code	Charge
1. Pneumonia vaccine	05-03-YYYY		$15.00
2. Administration of pneumonia vaccine	05-03-YYYY		$ 6.00
3.			
4.			
5.			

SPECIAL NOTES:

$48 to be billed to Medicare for pneumonia vaccine.

$6 to be billed to Medicare for the administration of pneumonia vaccine.

© Cengage Learning 2013

ASSIGNMENT 14.6   Multiple Choice Review

1. **Medicare Part A coverage is available to individuals under the age of 65 who**
   a. have end-stage renal disease and meet requirements.
   b. are not disabled and are willing to pay the premium.
   c. have received RRB disability benefits for one year.
   d. have received SSA disability benefits for one year.

2. **Which information must be obtained about the beneficiary to confirm Medicare eligibility over the phone?**
   a. date of birth
   b. mailing address
   c. marital status
   d. social security number

3. **What length of time is the Medicare initial enrollment period (IEP)?**
   a. 1 year
   b. 12 months
   c. 7 months
   d. 90 days

4. **The Medicare "spell of illness" is also known as the**
   a. benefit period.
   b. elective days.
   c. reserve days.
   d. sickness period.

5. **Patients may elect to use their Medicare lifetime reserve days after how many continuous days of hospitalization?**
   a. 14
   b. 45
   c. 60
   d. 90

6. **For a beneficiary to qualify for Medicare's skilled nursing benefit, the individual must have**
   a. enrolled in Medicare Part B in addition to Medicare Part A.
   b. had a 90-day hospitalization in an acute care facility.
   c. had at least three inpatient days of an acute hospital stay.
   d. lifetime reserve days available for nursing facility care.

7. **Temporary hospitalization of a patient for the purpose of providing relief from duty for the nonpaid primary caregiver of a patient is called _____ care.**
   a. boarding
   b. hospice
   c. relief
   d. respite

8. **All terminally ill Medicare patients qualify for _____ care.**
   a. home health
   b. hospice
   c. private-duty
   d. respite

9. **Medicare Part B will cover some home healthcare services if the patient**
   a. has been disabled more than two years.
   b. has enrolled in Medicare Advantage.
   c. does not have Medicare Part A.
   d. is terminally ill and at the end of life.

10. **How much is a beneficiary with Medicare Part B expected to pay for durable medical equipment (DME)?**
    a. 20 percent of the Medicare-approved amount
    b. 50 percent of the retail cost of the equipment
    c. a copay of $20 per each DME item
    d. the full Medicare-approved amount

11. **Which component of the Medicare Modernization Act of 2003 was created to provide tax-favored treatment for individuals covered by a high-deductible health plan?**
    a. extra coverage plans
    b. health savings accounts
    c. Medicare Part D
    d. Medicare savings accounts

12. **Dr. Cummings has been practicing in town for nearly 30 years. As a courtesy to his loyal Medicare patients, he does not charge the coinsurance. How can this affect Dr. Cummings's practice?**
    a. It will increase the doctor's patient base because new residents will want the savings.
    b. The billing process will be smoother for the doctor's health insurance specialists.
    c. The doctor may be subject to large fines and exclusion from the Medicare program.
    d. This will only affect the doctor's bottom line; he will earn less profit with this practice.

13. **One of the benefits of becoming a Medicare participating provider (PAR) is**
    a. faster processing and payment of assigned claims.
    b. that providers can balance-bill the beneficiaries.
    c. that there is no Advance Beneficiary Notice requirement.
    d. that there is no limit on fees or charges for services.

14. **The maximum fee a nonPAR may charge for a covered service is called the**
    a. allowed fee.
    b. limiting charge.
    c. maximum benefit.
    d. usual fee.

15. **Which practitioner who submits claims for services must accept assignment?**
    a. anesthesiologist
    b. orthopedic surgeon
    c. psychiatrist
    d. physician assistant

16. **Dr. Taylor has instructed you, as the health insurance specialist, to obtain an Advance Beneficiary Notice (ABN) on all surgical cases in the practice just in case Medicare denies the claim. How should you handle this situation?**
    a. At the next practice meeting, solicit ideas on how best to obtain signatures from each Medicare patient.
    b. Discuss the ABN with every Medicare surgical patient, and persuade the patient to sign the form.
    c. Explain to Dr. Taylor that the practice cannot do this, as Medicare considers this activity fraudulent.
    d. Print out a list of all Medicare patients in the practice and send each an ABN to sign.

17. **What is entered in Block 11 of the CMS-1500 claim when a reference lab provides services to a Medicare patient in the absence of a face-to-face encounter?**
    a. MSP CLAIM
    b. NONE
    c. ON FILE
    d. SAME

18. **Although they may do so more frequently, how often are providers required to collect or verify Medicare as Secondary Payer (MSP) information?**

    a. after a primary Medicare claim has been denied

    b. at the time of the initial beneficiary encounter only

    c. each time the beneficiary is seen by the provider

    d. each time the patient re-registers with the practice

19. **Medicare can assign a claim conditional primary payer status for payment processing. Which of the following would warrant this type of conditional status?**

    a. A patient who is mentally impaired failed to file a claim with the primary payer.

    b. A workers' compensation claim was denied and has been successfully appealed.

    c. The patient did not provide MSP information and the provider submits a request.

    d. The liability payer has not provided a response within 60 days of filing the claim.

20. **If a service was performed on June 30, the Medicare claim must be submitted for payment and postmarked no later than**

    a. December 31 of the same year.

    b. January 31 of the next year.

    c. June 30 of the next year.

    d. December 31 of the next year.

CHAPTER 15
Medicaid

INTRODUCTION

This chapter familiarizes students with completion of CMS-1500 claims for primary and mother/baby Medicaid payers.

> **NOTE:** When completing CMS-1500 claims for case studies in this workbook, enter just one diagnosis pointer number in Block 24E.

> **NOTE:** When completing claims for patients who have both primary and secondary insurance coverage, enter a P (primary) next to the case number on the primary claim (e.g., 15-A-P), and enter an S (secondary) (e.g., 15-A-S) next to the case number on the secondary claim.

ASSIGNMENT 15.1   Medicaid Primary CMS-1500 Claims Completion

OBJECTIVES

At the conclusion of this assignment, the student should be able to:

1. Assign ICD-9-CM (or ICD-10-CM) diagnosis and CPT or HCPCS level II procedure/service codes.
2. Prepare a Medicaid insurance primary payer CMS-1500 claim.

INSTRUCTIONS

Use optical scanning guidelines to complete a CMS-1500 for case studies 15-A and 15-B. Obtain a blank claim by making a copy of the CMS-1500 claim form in Appendix III of the textbook. Refer to the CMS-1500 claims completion instructions (primary) in the textbook.

ASSIGNMENT 15.2   Medicaid as Secondary Payer CMS-1500 Claims Completion

OBJECTIVES

At the conclusion of this assignment, the student should be able to:

1. Assign ICD-9-CM (or ICD-10-CM) diagnosis and CPT or HCPCS level II procedure/service codes.
2. Prepare a Medicaid as secondary payer CMS-1500 claim.

INSTRUCTIONS

Use optical scanning guidelines to complete a CMS-1500 for case studies 15-C and 15-D. Obtain a blank claim by making a copy of the CMS-1500 claim form in Appendix III of the textbook. Refer to the CMS-1500 claims completion instructions (secondary) in the textbook.

ASSIGNMENT 15.3   Medicaid Mother/Baby CMS-1500 Claims Completion

OBJECTIVES

At the conclusion of this assignment, the student should be able to:

1. Assign ICD-9-CM (or ICD-10-CM) diagnosis and CPT or HCPCS level II procedure/service codes.
2. Prepare a Medicaid mother/baby CMS-1500 claim.

INSTRUCTIONS

Use optical scanning guidelines to complete a CMS-1500 for case study 15-E. Obtain a blank claim by making a copy of the CMS-1500 claim form in Appendix III of the textbook. Refer to the CMS-1500 claims completion instructions (mother/baby) in the textbook.

Donald L. Givings, M.D.

11350 Medical Drive ■ Anywhere NY 12345 ■ (101) 111-5555

EIN: 11-1234562
NPI: 1234567890

Case Study 15-A

PATIENT INFORMATION:

Name:	Sharon W. Casey
Address:	483 Oakdale Avenue
City:	Anywhere
State:	NY
Zip Code:	12345
Telephone:	(101) 333-5555
Gender:	Female
Date of Birth:	10-06-1970
Occupation:	
Employer:	
Spouse's Employer:	

INSURANCE INFORMATION:

Patient Number:	15-A
Place of Service:	Office
Primary Insurance Plan:	Medicaid
Primary Insurance Plan ID #:	22334455
Group #:	
Primary Policyholder:	Sharon W. Casey
Policyholder Date of Birth:	10-06-1970
Relationship to Patient:	Self
Secondary Insurance Plan:	
Secondary Insurance Plan ID #:	
Secondary Policyholder:	

Patient Status   ☐ Married   ☐ Divorced   ☒ Single   ☐ Student   ☐ Other

DIAGNOSIS INFORMATION

Diagnosis	Code	Diagnosis	Code
1. Excessive menstruation		5.	
2. Irregular menstrual cycle		6.	
3.		7.	
4.		8.	

PROCEDURE INFORMATION

Description of Procedure or Service	Date	Code	Charge
1. Est. patient OV level III	11-13-YYYY		$75.00
2.			
3.			
4.			
5.			

SPECIAL NOTES:
    Refer patient to GYN
    Return visit: PRN

Maria C. Section, M.D. OB/GYN

11 Maden Lane ■ Anywhere NY 12345 ■ (101) 111-5555

EIN: 11-6699772
NPI: 6781239012

Case Study 15-B

PATIENT INFORMATION:

Name:	Sharon W. Casey
Address:	483 Oakdale Avenue
City:	Anywhere
State:	NY
Zip Code:	12345
Telephone:	(101) 333-5555
Gender:	Female
Date of Birth:	10-06-1970
Occupation:	
Employer:	
Spouse's Employer:	

INSURANCE INFORMATION:

Patient Number:	15-B
Place of Service:	Office
Primary Insurance Plan:	Medicaid
Primary Insurance Plan ID #:	22334455
Group #:	
Primary Policyholder:	Sharon W. Casey
Policyholder Date of Birth:	10-06-1970
Relationship to Patient:	Self
Secondary Insurance Plan:	
Secondary Insurance Plan ID #:	
Secondary Policyholder:	

Patient Status ☐ Married ☐ Divorced ☒ Single ☐ Student ☐ Other

DIAGNOSIS INFORMATION

Diagnosis	Code	Diagnosis	Code
1. Excessive menstruation		5.	
2. Irregular menstrual cycle		6.	
3.		7.	
4.		8.	

PROCEDURE INFORMATION

Description of Procedure or Service	Date	Code	Charge
1. Office consult level III	11-20-YYYY		$85.00
2.			
3.			
4.			
5.			

SPECIAL NOTES:
Onset of symptoms: 11-13-YYYY
Referred by Donald L. Givings, M.D., NPI: 1234567890
Return visit: One month

© Cengage Learning 2013

Donald L. Givings, M.D.

Case Study 15-C

11350 Medical Drive ■ Anywhere NY 12345 ■ (101) 111-5555

EIN: 11-1234562
NPI: 1234567890

PATIENT INFORMATION:

Name:	Fred R. Jones
Address:	444 Taylor Avenue
City:	Anywhere
State:	NY
Zip Code:	12345
Telephone:	(101) 333-5555
Gender:	Male
Date of Birth:	01-05-1949
Occupation:	
Employer:	
Spouse's Employer:	

INSURANCE INFORMATION:

Patient Number:	15-C
Place of Service:	Office
Primary Insurance Plan:	Aetna
Primary Insurance Plan ID #:	55771122
Group #:	
Primary Policyholder:	Fred R. Jones
Policyholder Date of Birth:	01-05-1949
Relationship to Patient:	Self
Secondary Insurance Plan:	Medicaid
Secondary Insurance Plan ID #:	55771122
Secondary Policyholder:	Fred R. Jones

Patient Status ☐ Married ☒ Divorced ☐ Single ☐ Student ☐ Other

DIAGNOSIS INFORMATION

Diagnosis	Code	Diagnosis	Code
1. Difficulty walking		5.	
2.		6.	
3.		7.	
4.		8.	

PROCEDURE INFORMATION

Description of Procedure or Service	Date	Code	Charge
1. Est. patient OV level III	06-19-YYYY		$75.00
2.			
3.			
4.			
5.			

SPECIAL NOTES:
   Refer patient to a podiatrist
   Return visit 3 months

© Cengage Learning 2013

John F. Walker, D.P.M. PODIATRY

Case Study 15-D

546 Foothill Place ■ Anywhere NY 12345 ■ (101) 111-5555

EIN: 11-9933772
NPI: 8901231234

PATIENT INFORMATION:

Name:	Fred R. Jones
Address:	444 Taylor Avenue
City:	Anywhere
State:	NY
Zip Code:	12345
Telephone:	(101) 333-5555
Gender:	Male
Date of Birth:	01-05-1949
Occupation:	
Employer:	
Spouse's Employer:	

INSURANCE INFORMATION:

Patient Number:	15-D
Place of Service:	Office
Primary Insurance Plan:	Aetna
Primary Insurance Plan ID #:	55771122
Group #:	
Primary Policyholder:	Fred R. Jones
Policyholder Date of Birth:	01-05-1949
Relationship to Patient:	Self
Secondary Insurance Plan:	Medicaid
Secondary Insurance Plan ID #:	55771122
Secondary Policyholder:	Fred R. Jones

Patient Status ☐ Married   ☒ Divorced   ☐ Single   ☐ Student   ☐ Other

DIAGNOSIS INFORMATION

Diagnosis	Code	Diagnosis	Code
1. Fracture, great toe (initial encounter)		5.	
2.		6.	
3.		7.	
4.		8.	

PROCEDURE INFORMATION

Description of Procedure or Service	Date	Code	Charge
1. Office consult level II	06-23-YYYY		$75.00
2. Toe x-ray 2 views	06-23-YYYY		50.00
3. Closed treatment of fracture, great toe	06-23-YYYY		65.00
4.			
5.			

SPECIAL NOTES:
Onset of symptoms: 06-19-YYYY
Referred by Donald L. Givings, M.D., NPI:1234567890

© Cengage Learning 2013

Donald L. Givings, M.D.

11350 Medical Drive ■ Anywhere NY 12345 ■ (101) 111-5555

EIN: 11-1234562
NPI: 1234567890

Case Study 15-E

PATIENT INFORMATION:

Name:	Jackson, Newborn
Address:	375 Ravenwood Avenue
City:	Anywhere
State:	NY
Zip Code:	12345
Telephone:	(101) 333-5555
Gender:	Male
Date of Birth:	03-10-2011
Occupation:	
Employer:	
Spouse's Employer:	

INSURANCE INFORMATION:

Patient Number:	15-E
Place of Service:	Inpatient hospital
Primary Insurance Plan:	Medicaid
Primary Insurance Plan ID #:	77557755 (mother)
Group #:	
Primary Policyholder:	Sandy Jackson
Policyholder Date of Birth:	02-15-1985
Relationship to Patient:	Mother
Secondary Insurance Plan:	
Secondary Insurance Plan ID #:	
Secondary Policyholder:	

Patient Status ☐ Married ☐ Divorced ☒ Single ☐ Student ☐ Other

DIAGNOSIS INFORMATION

Diagnosis	Code	Diagnosis	Code
1. Healthy single liveborn infant (vaginal delivery)		5.	
2.		6.	
3.		7.	
4.		8.	

PROCEDURE INFORMATION

Description of Procedure or Service	Date	Code	Charge
1. History of examination of normal newborn	03-10-YYYY		$150.00
2. Attendance at delivery	03-10-YYYY		400.00
3. Subsequent care for normal newborn	03-11-YYYY		100.00
4.			
5.			

SPECIAL NOTES:
Inpatient care provided at Goodmedicine Hospital, 1 Provider Street, Anywhere NY 12345. NPI: 1123456789
Application for infant's Medicaid ID number has been submitted.

© Cengage Learning 2013

ASSIGNMENT 15.4   SCHIP CMS-1500 Claims Completion

OBJECTIVES

At the conclusion of this assignment, the student should be able to:

1. Assign ICD-9-CM (or ICD-10-CM) diagnosis and CPT or HCPCS level II procedure/ service codes.
2. Prepare a SCHIP CMS-1500 claim.

INSTRUCTIONS

Use optical scanning guidelines to complete a CMS-1500 claim for case study 15-F. Obtain a blank claim by making a copy of the CMS-1500 claim form in Appendix III of the textbook. Refer to the CMS-1500 claims completion instructions (primary) in the textbook.

Goodmedicine Clinic

1 Provider Street ■ Anywhere NY 12345 ■ (101) 111-2222
NPI: 3312345678   EIN: 33-1234567

Case Study 15-F

Provider: Nancy J. Healer, M.D.   **EIN:** 44-1234567   **NPI:** 6789012345

PATIENT INFORMATION:

Name:	Ryan Michaels
Address:	101 Pinewood Drive
City:	Anywhere
State:	NY
Zip Code:	12345
Telephone:	(101) 111-9898
Gender:	Male
Date of Birth:	04-29-2011
Occupation:	
Employer:	
Spouse's Employer:	

INSURANCE INFORMATION:

Patient Number:	15-F
Place of Service:	Office
Primary Insurance Plan:	SCHIP
Primary Insurance Plan ID #:	BJZ06070908D
Group #:	
Primary Policyholder:	Ryan Michaels
Policyholder Date of Birth:	04-29-2011
Relationship to Patient:	Self
Secondary Insurance Plan:	
Secondary Insurance Plan ID #:	
Secondary Policyholder:	

Patient Status   ☐ Married   ☐ Divorced   ☒ Single   ☐ Student   ☐ Other

DIAGNOSIS INFORMATION

Diagnosis	Code	Diagnosis	Code
1. Acute sinusitis, frontal		5.	
2. Acute sore throat		6.	
3.		7.	
4.		8.	

PROCEDURE INFORMATION

Description of Procedure or Service	Date	Code	Charge
1. New patient office visit, level II	12-18-YYYY		$75.00
2.			
3.			
4.			
5.			

SPECIAL NOTES:
   Patient paid $5.00 for today's visit.

© Cengage Learning 2013

ASSIGNMENT 15.5   Multiple Choice Review

1. **The Medicaid program is**
   a. federally funded and state mandated.
   b. federally mandated and state administered.
   c. state funded and federally administered.
   d. state mandated and federally administered.

2. **The Temporary Assistance to Needy Families (TANF) program provides**
   a. cash assistance on a limited-time basis for children deprived of support.
   b. cash assistance to low-income families who need to purchase groceries.
   c. financial assistance for food, utilities, healthcare, and school expenses.
   d. temporary financial support for housing and household-related costs.

3. **What is included in a couple's combined resources, according to the Spousal Impoverishment Protection legislation?**
   a. automobile
   b. burial funds
   c. home
   d. summer home

4. **When a patient has become retroactively eligible for Medicaid benefits, any payments made by the patient during the retroactive period must be**
   a. applied toward future medical care.
   b. recorded as additional practice income.
   c. refunded to the patient by Medicaid.
   d. refunded to the patient by the practice.

5. **To receive matching funds through Medicaid, states must offer what coverage?**
   a. inpatient hospital services
   b. prescription drug benefits
   c. private-duty nursing care
   d. surgical dental services

6. **Early and Periodic Screening, Diagnostic, and Treatment (EPSDT) services are offered for which Medicaid-enrolled population?**
   a. home health patients
   b. individuals under age 21
   c. persons over the age of 65
   d. rehabilitation facility inpatients

7. **Programs of All-Inclusive Care for the Elderly (PACE) work to limit out-of-pocket costs to beneficiaries by**
   a. limiting participants to care only from contract providers.
   b. providing only very basic medical and preventive care.
   c. requiring a flat $10 copayment for every service provided.
   d. not applying deductibles, copayments, or other cost-sharing.

8. **Which is subject to Medicaid preauthorization guidelines?**
   a. any minor surgery performed in the provider's procedure room
   b. medically necessary inpatient admission with documentation
   c. any extension of inpatient acute care hospital days
   d. patient hospitalization within the expected length of stay

9. **Which services are exempt from Medicaid copayments?**

   a. family planning services

   b. office visits

   c. outpatient urgent care

   d. prescription drug costs

10. **An individual whose income is at or below 100 percent of the federal poverty level (FPL) and has resources at or below twice the standard allowed under the SSI program may receive assistance from Medicaid to pay for Medicare premiums, deductibles, and coinsurance amounts as a**

    a. qualified disabled and working individual (QDWI).

    b. qualified Medicare beneficiary (QMB).

    c. qualifying individual (QI).

    d. specified low-income Medicare beneficiary (SLMB).

11. **A primary care provider in a Medicaid primary care case management (PCCM) plan differs from an HMO primary care provider in that the Medicaid primary care provider is**

    a. at higher risk for the cost of care provided.

    b. never permitted to authorize specialty care.

    c. not at risk for the cost of care provided.

    d. responsible for coordinating patient care.

12. **A Medicaid voided claim**

    a. has an additional payment to the provider.

    b. is in suspense and awaiting approval.

    c. must be corrected and resubmitted.

    d. should not have been paid originally.

13. **One way the federal government verifies receipt of Medicaid services by a patient is by use of**

    a. an annual audit of each state's Medicaid offices to validate expenditures.

    b. a monthly audit of all the provider's remittance advice notices and receipts.

    c. a monthly survey sent to a sample of Medicaid recipients requesting verification.

    d. a survey provided to each Medicaid recipient upon completion of treatment.

14. **Medicaid reimbursement is expedited when the provider**

    a. authenticates each CMS-1500 claim form filed with a manual signature.

    b. enters an X in the YES box in Block 27 to accept assignment.

    c. enters the required insurance information in Blocks 11 through 11d.

    d. enters the required insurance information in Blocks 9 through 9d.

15. **A Medicaid card issued for the "unborn child of . . ." is good for**

    a. hospitalization services for the newborn child and the mother.

    b. medical care rendered to the mother, such as for a back strain.

    c. physician office visits for the mother for care other than prenatal.

    d. services that promote the life and health of the unborn child.

16. **What is required in Block 32 if an X is entered in the YES box of Block 20?**

    a. name and address of the outside laboratory

    b. name and address of the referring provider

    c. the same information as was entered in Block 31

    d. the same information as was entered in Block 33

17. **Medicaid is not always the payer of last resort if the patient also has what type of coverage?**
    a. CHAMPVA
    b. Medicare
    c. TRICARE
    d. workers' compensation

18. **Which is considered a valid entry in Block 24H of a Medicaid claim?**
    a. the letter B, if the service was for both EPSDT and family planning
    b. the letter F, if the service provided was for a family planning
    c. the number of days the Medicaid patient was treated for the current problem
    d. the number of times the Medicare patient has been treated for the problem

19. **When a Medicaid patient has third-party payer coverage and a claim has been rejected, the rejection code is recorded in which block of the Medicaid CMS-1500 claim?**
    a. Block 11
    b. Block 19
    c. Block 22
    d. Block 24H

20. **When payment has been received by a primary payer, the payment amount is entered in which block of the Medicaid CMS-1500 claim?**
    a. Block 19
    b. Block 20
    c. Block 29
    d. Block 30

CHAPTER 16
TRICARE

INTRODUCTION

This chapter familiarizes students with completion of CMS-1500 claims for primary TRICARE payers.

> **NOTE:** When completing CMS-1500 claims for case studies in this workbook, enter just one diagnosis pointer number in Block 24E.

> **NOTE:** When completing claims for patients who have both primary and secondary insurance coverage, enter a P (primary) next to the case number on the primary claim (e.g., 16-A-P), and enter an S (secondary) (e.g., 16-A-S) next to the case number on the secondary claim.

ASSIGNMENT 16.1   TRICARE Primary CMS-1500 Claims Completion

OBJECTIVES

At the conclusion of this assignment, the student should be able to:

1. Assign ICD-9-CM (or ICD-10-CM) diagnosis and CPT or HCPCS level II procedure/ service codes.
2. Prepare a TRICARE insurance primary payer CMS-1500 claim.

INSTRUCTIONS

Use optical scanning guidelines to complete a CMS-1500 for case studies 16-A through 16-C. Obtain a blank claim by making a copy of the CMS-1500 claim form in Appendix III of the textbook. Refer to the CMS-1500 claims completion instructions (primary) in the textbook.

ASSIGNMENT 16.2   TRICARE Secondary CMS-1500 Claims Completion

OBJECTIVES

At the conclusion of this assignment, the student should be able to:

1. Assign ICD-9-CM (or ICD-10-CM) diagnosis codes and CPT or HCPCS level II procedure/ service codes.
2. Prepare a TRICARE CMS-1500 claim.

INSTRUCTIONS

Use optical scanning guidelines to complete the CMS-1500 claim for case study 16-D and 16-E. Obtain a blank claim by making a copy of the CMS-1500 claim form in Appendix III of the textbook. Refer to the textbook CMS-1500 claims completion instructions when payer is the same for primary and secondary health insurance coverage.

Donald L. Givings, M.D.

11350 Medical Drive ■ Anywhere NY 12345 ■ (101) 111-5555

EIN: 11-1234562
NPI: 1234567890

Case Study 16-A

PATIENT INFORMATION:

Name:	Jeffrey D. Heem
Address:	333 Heavenly Place
City:	Anywhere
State:	NY
Zip Code:	12345
Telephone:	(101) 333-5555
Gender:	Male
Date of Birth:	05-05-1964
Occupation:	
Employer:	US Army
Spouse's Employer:	

INSURANCE INFORMATION:

Patient Number:	16-A
Place of Service:	Office
Primary Insurance Plan:	TRICARE Standard
Primary Insurance Plan ID #:	234556789
Group #:	
Primary Policyholder:	Jeffrey D. Heem
Policyholder Date of Birth:	05-05-1964
Relationship to Patient:	Self
Secondary Insurance Plan:	
Secondary Insurance Plan ID #:	
Secondary Policyholder:	

Patient Status [X] Married ☐ Divorced ☐ Single ☐ Student ☐ Other

DIAGNOSIS INFORMATION

Diagnosis	Code	Diagnosis	Code
1. Acute sinusitis, frontal		5.	
2. Sore throat		6.	
3.		7.	
4.		8.	

PROCEDURE INFORMATION

Description of Procedure or Service	Date	Code	Charge
1. New patient OV level II	11-05-YYYY		$70.00
2.			
3.			
4.			
5.			

SPECIAL NOTES:

Donald L. Givings, M.D.

Case Study 16-B

11350 Medical Drive ■ Anywhere NY 12345 ■ (101) 111-5555

EIN: 11-1234562
NPI: 1234567890

PATIENT INFORMATION:

Name:	Dana S. Bright
Address:	28 Upton Circle
City:	Anywhere
State:	NY
Zip Code:	12345
Telephone:	(101) 333-5555
Gender:	Female
Date of Birth:	07-05-1971
Occupation:	
Employer:	
Spouse's Employer:	US Navy (See duty address below)

INSURANCE INFORMATION:

Patient Number:	16-B
Place of Service:	Office
Primary Insurance Plan:	TRICARE Extra
Primary Insurance Plan ID #:	567565757
Group #:	
Primary Policyholder:	Ron L. Bright
Policyholder Date of Birth:	08-12-1970
Relationship to Patient:	Spouse
Secondary Insurance Plan:	
Secondary Insurance Plan ID #:	
Secondary Policyholder:	

Patient Status   ☒ Married   ☐ Divorced   ☐ Single   ☐ Student   ☐ Other

DIAGNOSIS INFORMATION

Diagnosis	Code	Diagnosis	Code
1. Chronic cholecystitis		5.	
2.		6.	
3.		7.	
4.		8.	

PROCEDURE INFORMATION

Description of Procedure or Service	Date	Code	Charge
1. Est. patient OV level IV	06-22-YYYY		$85.00
2.			
3.			
4.			
5.			

SPECIAL NOTES:
   Spouse's Employer's Address: Duty Station Address: 21 Naval Station, Anywhere NY 23456
   Refer patient to Jonathan B. Kutter, M.D.

© Cengage Learning 2013

Jonathan B. Kutter, M.D. SURGERY

Case Study 16-C

339 Woodland Place ■ Anywhere NY 12345 ■ (101) 111-5555

EIN: 11-5566772
NPI: 4567891132

PATIENT INFORMATION:		INSURANCE INFORMATION:	
Name:	Dana S. Bright	Patient Number:	16-C
Address:	28 Upton Circle	Place of Service:	Outpatient hospital
City:	Anywhere	Primary Insurance Plan:	TRICARE Extra
State:	NY	Primary Insurance Plan ID #:	567565757
Zip Code:	12345	Group #:	
Telephone:	(101) 333-5555	Primary Policyholder:	Ron L. Bright
Gender:	Female	Policyholder Date of Birth:	08-12-1970
Date of Birth:	07-05-1971	Relationship to Patient:	Spouse
Occupation:	Homemaker	Secondary Insurance Plan:	
Employer:		Secondary Insurance Plan ID #:	
Spouse's Employer:	US Navy	Secondary Policyholder:	

Patient Status   [X] Married   ☐ Divorced   ☐ Single   ☐ Student   ☐ Other

DIAGNOSIS INFORMATION

Diagnosis	Code		Diagnosis	Code
1. Chronic cholecystitis		5.		
2.		6.		
3.		7.		
4.		8.		

PROCEDURE INFORMATION

Description of Procedure or Service	Date	Code	Charge
1. Laparoscopic cholecystectomy	06-29-YYYY		$2,300.00
2.			
3.			
4.			
5.			

SPECIAL NOTES:
Referred by Donald L. Givings, M.D., NPI: 1234567890
Onset of symptoms: 06-22-YYYY Admitted/Discharged: 6/29/YYYY
Goodmedicine Hospital, 1 Provider Street, Anywhere NY 12345. NPI: 1123456789.
Spouse's Employer's Address: Duty Station
Address: 21 Naval Station, Anywhere NY 23456

© Cengage Learning 2013

Donald L. Givings, M.D.

11350 Medical Drive ■ Anywhere NY 12345 ■ (101) 111-5555

EIN: 11-1234562
NPI: 1234567890

Case Study 16-D

PATIENT INFORMATION:

Name:	Odel M. Ryer, Jr.
Address:	484 Pinewood Ave.
City:	Anywhere
State:	NY
Zip Code:	12345
Telephone:	(101) 333-5555
Gender:	Male
Date of Birth:	04-28-1969
Occupation:	
Employer:	US Air Force
Spouse's Employer:	Paws and Tails

INSURANCE INFORMATION:

Patient Number:	16-D
Place of Service:	Office
Primary Insurance Plan:	AETNA
Primary Insurance Plan ID #:	464444646B
Group #:	
Primary Policyholder:	Rose M. Ryer
Policyholder Date of Birth:	01-01-1970
Relationship to Patient:	Spouse
Secondary Insurance Plan:	TRICARE Standard
Secondary Insurance Plan ID #:	464444646
Secondary Policyholder:	Odel M. Ryer, Jr.

Patient Status ☒ Married ☐ Divorced ☐ Single ☐ Student ☐ Other

DIAGNOSIS INFORMATION

Diagnosis	Code	Diagnosis	Code
1. Heartburn		5.	
2.		6.	
3.		7.	
4.		8.	

PROCEDURE INFORMATION

Description of Procedure or Service	Date	Code	Charge
1. Est. patient OV level I	04-12-YYYY		$55.00
2.			
3.			
4.			
5.			

SPECIAL NOTES:

Return visit: PRN

Primary insurance paid: $44.00.

© Cengage Learning 2013

Donald L. Givings, M.D.

11350 Medical Drive ■ Anywhere NY 12345 ■ (101) 111-5555

EIN: 11-1234562
NPI: 1234567890

Case Study 16-E

PATIENT INFORMATION:

Name:	Annalisa M. Faris
Address:	394 Myriam Court
City:	Anywhere
State:	NY
Zip Code:	12345
Telephone:	(101) 333-5555
Gender:	Female
Date of Birth:	04-04-1999
Occupation:	Full-Time Student
Employer:	US Marines (Father)
Spouse's Employer:	Borders Publishing (Mother)

INSURANCE INFORMATION:

Patient Number:	16-E
Place of Service:	Inpatient hospital
Primary Insurance Plan:	BCBS
Primary Insurance Plan ID #:	323233333X
Group #:	
Primary Policyholder:	Mari L. Faris
Policyholder Date of Birth:	06-21-1975
Relationship to Patient:	Mother
Secondary Insurance Plan:	TRICARE Prime
Secondary Insurance Plan ID #:	621334444
Secondary Policyholder:	Nacir R. Faris
Secondary Policyholder DOB:	10-12-1976

Patient Status ☐ Married ☐ Divorced ☒ Single ☒ Student ☐ Other

DIAGNOSIS INFORMATION

Diagnosis	Code	Diagnosis	Code
1. Chills with fever		5.	
2. Lethargy		6.	
3. Loss of appetite		7.	
4. Loss of weight		8.	

PROCEDURE INFORMATION

Description of Procedure or Service	Date	Code	Charge
1. Initial hosp. level III	06-02-YYYY		$200.00
2. Subsq hosp. level III	06-03-YYYY		85.00
3. Subsq hosp. level II	06-04-YYYY		75.00
4. Discharge day management, 30 minutes	06-04-YYYY		75.00

SPECIAL NOTES:
Goodmedicine Hospital, 1 Provider Street, Anywhere NY 12345. NPI: 1123456789.
Father's Employer's Address: Duty Station Address: 555 Regiment Way, Anywhere NY 12345
Patient was discharged 06/04/YYYY but not seen
Primary insurance paid: $344.00.

© Cengage Learning 2013

ASSIGNMENT 16.3 Multiple Choice Review

1. **The conversion of CHAMPUS to TRICARE was the result of a(n)**
   a. act of legislation that was passed in 1967 at the request of the military.
   b. need to limit the amount of money paid for military dependents' care.
   c. reorganization of each branch of the United States uniformed services.
   d. successful CHAMPUS Reform Initiative (CRI) demonstration project.

2. **Lead agents of selected military treatment facilities (MTFs) hold what rank?**
   a. captain
   b. commander
   c. lieutenant
   d. major

3. **The entire healthcare system of the U.S. uniformed services is known as the**
   a. CHAMPUS Reform Initiative (CRI).
   b. Department of Defense Health System.
   c. Military Health Services System (MHSS).
   d. TRICARE Demonstration Project.

4. **The organization responsible for coordinating and administering the TRICARE program is the**
   a. Military Health Services System.
   b. TRICARE Management Activity.
   c. U.S. Department of Defense.
   d. U.S. Office of Health Affairs.

5. **The term *sponsor* is used to describe**
   a. active duty, retired, or deceased military personnel.
   b. beneficiaries of military personnel.
   c. dependents of military personnel.
   d. remarried former spouses of military personnel.

6. **Claims are submitted to the TRICARE**
   a. Management Activity.
   b. Program Integrity Office.
   c. regional contractors.
   d. service centers.

7. **TRICARE plans are primary to**
   a. employer-sponsored HMOs.
   b. liability insurance claims.
   c. Medicaid.
   d. workers' compensation.

8. **TRICARE nurse advisors are available 24/7 to assist with**
   a. preauthorizations and referrals for healthcare services.
   b. providing information to beneficiaries about TRICARE.
   c. rendering emergency care to TRICARE beneficiaries.
   d. treatment alternatives and recommendations for care.

9. **The entity responsible for the prevention, detection, investigation, and control of TRICARE fraud, waste, and abuse is the**
   a. Military Health Services System.
   b. Program Integrity Office.
   c. TRICARE Management Activity.
   d. TRICARE Service Center.

10. **Which TRICARE option is a fee-for-service plan?**
    a. TRICARE Extra
    b. TRICARE Premium
    c. TRICARE Prime
    d. TRICARE Standard

11. **In which TRICARE option are active military personnel required to enroll?**
    a. TRICARE Extra
    b. TRICARE Premium
    c. TRICARE Prime
    d. TRICARE Standard

12. **A military treatment facility (MTF) *catchment area* is**
    a. also known as a TRICARE Region, and is managed by lead agents.
    b. defined by code boundaries within a 40-mile radius of an MTF.
    c. an area where healthcare services are not available to military personnel.
    d. an area that contains civilian healthcare professionals to render care.

13. **If a TRICARE Prime beneficiary seeks care from a facility outside of the treatment area without prior approval, the point-of-service option is activated. This will result in what cost(s) to the beneficiary?**
    a. a coinsurance payment of 50 percent for each service or treatment and no deductible
    b. an annual deductible plus 50 percent or more of visit or treatment fees
    c. beneficiary payment for all services out-of-pocket
    d. the same annual deductible as TRICARE Extra and Standard

14. **Which TRICARE option has the highest out-of-pocket costs of all the TRICARE plans?**
    a. TRICARE Extra
    b. TRICARE Premium
    c. TRICARE Prime
    d. TRICARE Standard

15. **TRICARE outpatient claims will be denied if they are filed more than**
    a. one year after the patient's discharge.
    b. one year after the date of service.
    c. six months after the date of service.
    d. 30 days after the date of service.

16. **If the physician's charges for care of a TRICARE beneficiary, as the result of an accidental injury, are $500 or higher, the insurance specialist must submit a**
    a. DD Form 2527 that was completed by the patient.
    b. DD Form 2527 that was completed by the provider.
    c. DD Form 2642 that was completed by the patient.
    d. DD Form 2642 that was completed by the provider.

17. **TRICARE has established a good-faith policy for assigned claims to protect the provider when**
    a. a claim submitted to TRICARE contains charges for a noncovered service.
    b. a patient presented an ID card and it turned out to be invalid.
    c. the health insurance specialist entered an incorrect charge on the claim.
    d. the provider has abused the TRICARE program and is under investigation.

18. **What special handling is required for TRICARE hospice claims?**
    a. Enter the words HOSPICE CLAIM at the top of the CMS-1500 claim form.
    b. Enter the words HOSPICE CLAIMS on the envelope.
    c. Hospice claims can only be submitted every four weeks.
    d. No special handling is required; processing is the same.

19. **What information is entered in Block 13 of the TRICARE CMS-1500 claim form?**
    a. SEE AUTHORIZATION FORM
    b. SIGNATURE ON FILE
    c. the patient's full signature
    d. the provider's full signature

20. **When the TRICARE patient has been referred by a military treatment facility, attach a(n) _____ to the CMS-1500 claim form.**
    a. DD Form 2527
    b. DD Form 2161
    c. DD Form 2642
    d. MTF referral form

CHAPTER 17
Workers' Compensation

INTRODUCTION

This chapter familiarizes students with completion of CMS-1500 claims for primary workers' compensation payers.

> **NOTE:** When completing CMS-1500 claims for case studies in this workbook, enter just one diagnosis pointer number in Block 24E.

> **ASSIGNMENT 17.1** Workers' Compensation Primary CMS-1500 Claims Completion

OBJECTIVES

At the conclusion of this assignment, the student should be able to:

1. Assign ICD-9-CM (or ICD-10-CM) diagnosis and CPT or HCPCS level II procedure/service codes.
2. Prepare a workers' compensation insurance primary payer CMS-1500 claim.

INSTRUCTIONS

Use optical scanning guidelines to complete a CMS-1500 for case studies 17-A and 17-B. Obtain a blank claim by making a copy of the CMS-1500 claim in Appendix III of the textbook. Refer to the CMS-1500 claims completion instructions (primary) in the textbook.

Donald L. Givings, M.D.

Case Study 17-A

11350 Medical Drive ■ Anywhere NY 12345 ■ (101) 111-5555

EIN: 11-1234562
NPI: 1234567890

PATIENT INFORMATION:

Name:	Sandy S. Grand
Address:	109 Darling Road
City:	Anywhere
State:	NY
Zip Code:	12345
Telephone:	(101) 333-5555
Gender:	Female
Date of Birth:	12-03-1972
Occupation:	Personal trainer
Employer:	Starport Fitness Center
Address:	257 Treadmill Way
City:	Anywhere
State:	NY
Zip Code:	12345

INSURANCE INFORMATION:

Patient Number:	17-A
Place of Service:	Office
WC Insurance Plan:	Workers Trust
WC Claim #:	CLR545701
WC Policyholder:	Starport Fitness Center
Address:	257 Treadmill Way
City:	Anywhere
State:	NY
Zip Code:	12345
Relationship to Patient:	Employer

Patient Status ☐ Married ☐ Divorced ☒ Single ☐ Student ☐ Other

DIAGNOSIS INFORMATION

Diagnosis	Code	Diagnosis	Code
1. Wrist fracture, closed (initial encounter)		5.	
2. Fall from chair (initial encounter)		6.	
3. Fall at work (office building)		7.	
4.		8.	

PROCEDURE INFORMATION

Description of Procedure or Service	Date	Code	Charge
1. New patient OV level IV	02-03-YYYY		$100.00
2.			
3.			
4.			
5.			

SPECIAL NOTES:

Patient's SSN is 425-99-1188: Date of injury: 02-03-YYYY

Employer's phone number: (101) 333-6565. Case Manager's name is June Ward.

Donald L. Givings, M.D.

11350 Medical Drive ■ Anywhere NY 12345 ■ (101) 111-5555

EIN: 11-1234562
NPI: 1234567890

Case Study 17-B

PATIENT INFORMATION:

Name:	Marianna D. Holland
Address:	509 Dutch Street
City:	Anywhere
State:	NY
Zip Code:	12345
Telephone:	(101) 383-8761
Gender:	Female
Date of Birth:	11-05-1977
Occupation:	Hairstylist
Employer:	Hair Etc.
Address:	8731 Miracle Mile
City:	Anywhere
State:	NY
Zip Code:	12345

INSURANCE INFORMATION:

Patient Number:	17-B
Place of Service:	Office
WC Insurance Plan:	Workers Shield
WC Claim #:	BA678802
WC Policyholder:	Hair Etc.
Address:	8731 Miracle Mile
City:	Anywhere
State:	NY
Zip Code:	12345
Relationship to Patient:	Employer

Patient Status ☒ Married   ☐ Divorced   ☐ Single   ☐ Student   ☐ Other

DIAGNOSIS INFORMATION

Diagnosis	Code	Diagnosis	Code
1. Open wound of finger		5.	
2. Injured by hair cutting scissors (initial encounter)		6.	
3. Injured at work (hair salon)		7.	
4.		8.	

PROCEDURE INFORMATION

Description of Procedure or Service	Date	Code	Charge
1. New patient OV level III	05-12-YYYY		$80.00
2.			
3.			
4.			
5.			

SPECIAL NOTES:

Patient may return to work 5/16/YYYY.

Employer's phone number: (101) 383-6700. Case manager's is Julie Kindle.

Patient's SSN is 521-15-0429. Date of injury: 05-12-YYYY

© Cengage Learning 2013

ASSIGNMENT 17.2 Workers' Compensation Intake Form

INTRODUCTION

A workers' compensation intake form is completed for each new patient who seeks care for a work-related accident so that appropriate services are provided.

OBJECTIVES

At the conclusion of this assignment, the student should be able to:

1. Determine the patient information necessary for workers' compensation third-party billing.
2. Accurately complete insurance verification forms.

INSTRUCTIONS

1. Review case study 17-A for patient Sandy S. Grand, and complete the workers' compensation intake form.
2. Review case study 17-B for patient Marianna D. Holland, and complete the workers' compensation intake form.
3. Enter only the data included on each case study. (Some data may not be available at the patient's first office visit and would need to be entered at a later time.)

CASE STUDY 17-A	
WORKERS' COMPENSATION INTAKE FORM DR. DONALD L. GIVINGS, M.D. · 11350 MEDICAL DRIVE · ANYWHERE NY 12345 · (101) 111-5555	
TODAY'S DATE:	
PATIENT NAME:	
PATIENT NUMBER:	
DATE OF INJURY:	
CLAIM NUMBER:	
TYPE OF INJURY/BODY PART:	
EMPLOYER NAME:	
ADDRESS:	
INSURANCE COMPANY:	
PHONE NUMBER:	
FAX NUMBER:	
CLAIM ADJUSTER:	
TREATMENT AUTHORIZED:	
COMPLETED BY:	
NOTES:	

CASE STUDY 17-B	
WORKERS' COMPENSATION INTAKE FORM DR. DONALD L. GIVINGS, M.D. ▪ 11350 MEDICAL DRIVE ▪ ANYWHERE NY 12345 ▪ (101) 111-5555	
TODAY'S DATE:	
PATIENT NAME:	
PATIENT NUMBER:	
DATE OF INJURY:	
CLAIM NUMBER:	
TYPE OF INJURY/BODY PART:	
EMPLOYER NAME:	
ADDRESS:	
INSURANCE COMPANY:	
PHONE NUMBER:	
FAX NUMBER:	
CLAIM ADJUSTER:	
TREATMENT AUTHORIZED:	
COMPLETED BY:	
NOTES:	

ASSIGNMENT 17.3 Multiple Choice Review

1. **The Division of Coal Mine Workers' Compensation administers and processes claims for the**
   a. Federal Black Lung Program.
   b. Federal Employees' Compensation Act Program.
   c. Federal Employment Liability Act.
   d. Longshore and Harbor Workers' Compensation Program.

2. **Federal and state laws require employers to maintain workers' compensation coverage to meet minimum standards, covering a majority of employees for work-related illnesses and injuries**
   a. only for companies that have a history of occupational deaths.
   b. for employers who are able to afford coverage.
   c. if the employee was not negligent in performing assigned duties.
   d. for companies with high-risk occupations only.

3. **The medical term for black lung disease is**
   a. pneumoconiosis.
   b. pneumocystitis.
   c. pneumonia.
   d. pneumothorax.

4. **The Mine Safety and Health Administration (MSHA) is similar in purpose and intent to the**
   a. Energy Employees Occupational Illness Compensation Program.
   b. Federal Occupational Illness Compensation Program.
   c. Longshore and Harbor Workers' Compensation Program.
   d. Occupational Safety and Health Administration (OSHA).

5. **Material Safety Data Sheets (MSDS) contain data regarding**
   a. chemical and hazardous substances used at a worksite.
   b. how to implement an effective safety program at work.
   c. medicinal and therapeutic substances used at a worksite.
   d. the yearly number of occupational injuries and illness.

6. **How long must records of employee vaccinations and accidental exposure incidents be retained?**
   a. 10 years
   b. 20 years
   c. 7 years
   d. 5 years

7. **The Federal Employment Liability Act (FELA) and the Merchant Marine Act were designed to**
   a. develop a compensation fund for occupational injuries and deaths.
   b. increase the salaries of persons in certain high-risk occupations.
   c. offer medical and healthcare benefits to federal employees.
   d. provide employees with protection from employer negligence.

8. **Which agency is responsible for handling appeals for denied workers' compensation claims?**
   a. Occupational Safety and Health Administration
   b. Office of Workers' Compensation Programs
   c. State Insurance Commissioner
   d. State Workers' Compensation Commission

9. **In which scenario would an employee be eligible for workers' compensation benefits?**
   a. An angry worker was injured in the warehouse when he tried to attack a coworker.
   b. An employee broke her ankle while walking with a coworker during their lunch hour.
   c. An employee was injured in an accident while driving to the bank to deposit her employer's checks.
   d. The employee was injured in a fall after drinking too much alcohol at a dinner meeting.

10. **Workers' compensation survivor benefits are calculated according to the**
    a. degree of risk that was involved in the employee's occupation.
    b. employee's earning capacity at the time of illness or injury.
    c. number of survivors in the household under the age of 18.
    d. period of time the employee was disabled before death.

11. **A patient was treated by his primary care physician on 01/25/YYYY for a wrist fracture that occurred on the job. On 02/02/YYYY, the patient was evaluated for symptoms of severe high blood pressure and a recheck of the wrist fracture. Where should the provider document treatment from the visit on 02/02/YYYY?**
    a. Both services should be recorded in the patient's medical record.
    b. Both services should be recorded in the workers' compensation record.
    c. Only the fracture recheck is to be recorded in the workers' compensation record.
    d. Only the visit from 01/25/YYYY is to be recorded in the workers' compensation record.

12. **The First Report of Injury form is completed by the**
    a. employer.
    b. patient.
    c. provider.
    d. witness.

13. **The treating physician's personal signature is required**
    a. if the patient has requested report copies.
    b. on all original reports and photocopies.
    c. only on original reports.
    d. only on photocopied reports.

14. **After the claim has been acknowledged, the information that must be included on all correspondence to the employer, payer, billings, and the Commission Board is the**
    a. file/case number assigned to the claim.
    b. patient's employee number.
    c. patient's social security number.
    d. treating physician's provider EIN number.

15. **What information is entered in Block 11 of the worker's compensation CMS-1500 claim?**
    a. claim number
    b. date of injury
    c. employer
    d. social security number

16. **Which of the following can be a designated state workers' compensation fiscal agent?**
    a. a private, commercial insurance company
    b. the Office of Workers' Compensation Programs
    c. the state's compensation board
    d. the state's Department of Labor

17. **Workers' compensation plans that allow an employer to set aside a state-mandated percentage of capital funds to cover employee compensation and benefits are**
    a. combination programs.
    b. commercial insurance.
    c. self-insurance plans.
    d. state-funded plans.

18. **If a patient fails to alert the provider that an injury was work-related, and then changes his mind later and tries to receive workers' compensation benefits, the claim will most likely be**
    a. denied by the workers' compensation payer, and the patient will have to appeal.
    b. held in suspense for an indefinite period of time until documentation is reviewed.
    c. paid by workers' compensation beginning with the date of the most recent treatment.
    d. paid out-of-pocket by the patient first, then reimbursed by workers' compensation.

19. **Which box is marked in Block 6 of the workers' compensation CMS-1500 claim?**
    a. CHILD
    b. OTHER
    c. SELF
    d. SPOUSE

20. **Which box is marked in Block 1 of the workers' compensation CMS-1500 claim if the patient is a federal employee?**
    a. FECA
    b. Medicaid
    c. Medicare
    d. Other

APPENDIX A
Mock CMRS Examination

The Certified Medical Reimbursement Specialist (CMRS) examination is a voluntary, national credential awarded by the Certifying Board of the American Medical Billers Association (AMBA). The CMRS credential recognizes the competency of a member who has met the AMBA's high standards of proficiency through certification testing, and the CMRS is skilled in facilitating the claims-paying process from the time a service is rendered by a healthcare provider until the balance is paid.

The CMRS examination contains the following 16 sections (and is taken online through AMBA's secure learning management system): medical terminology, anatomy and physiology, information technology, Web and information technology, ICD-9-CM coding, CPT coding, clearinghouses, CMS (HCFA) 1500 form, insurance, insurance carriers, acronyms, compliance, fraud and abuse, managed care, general, and case study. The mock CMRS examination included in this appendix serves as practice for the actual examination. When preparing to take the CMRS certification examination, be sure to reference textbooks and other materials that cover content tested in the 16 sections, including the study guide available for purchase from AMBA's Web site by going to **www.ambanet.net** and clicking on the CMRS Exam link.

> ## MOCK CMRS EXAMINATION

INSTRUCTIONS

Select the most appropriate response. You are permitted to use ICD-9-CM, CPT, and HCPCS level II coding manuals to answer coding questions.

Medical Terminology

1. **The creation of an opening of a portion of the colon through the abdominal wall to an outside surface is called a(n)**

   a. lithotripsy.

   b. anastomosis.

   c. colostomy.

   d. biopsy.

2. **A physician suspects that his patient, Mr. Jones, may have bladder cancer. He wants to visually examine Mr. Jones' bladder. This procedure is called a(n)**

   a. cystoscopy.

   b. endoscopy.

   c. bladderemetry.

   d. cystogram.

3. **Three-year-old Alyssa Walker was referred to an endocrinologist by her pediatrician with symptoms of chronic respiratory infections, pancreatic insufficiency, and a growing intolerance to heat. The endocrinologist plans to order a series of tests including a sweat test, hoping to rule out a hereditary disorder called**

   a. Reyes syndrome.

   b. cystic fibrosis.

   c. sickle cell anemia.

   d. hemophilia.

4. **When a thrombus travels through the vascular system it is called a(n)**

   a. atherosclerosis.

   b. atheroma.

   c. lumen.

   d. embolus.

5. **A leiomyoma is a tumor of the**
   a. bone.
   b. smooth muscle.
   c. cartilage.
   d. blood.

6. **A patient is prescribed albuterol. The patient has been experiencing SOB during times of stress and during exercise. When this occurs, audible wheezing is another sign. Which of the disorders listed below could be the medical term to describe this patient's medical condition?**
   a. cystic fibrosis
   b. pneumonia
   c. pneumothorax
   d. asthma

7. **Karen Davis presents to the ED with severe abdominal pain. It is determined after laboratory and ultrasound testing that she has an abdominal pregnancy. This type of pregnancy could also be termed**
   a. primigravida.
   b. ectopic.
   c. retroversion.
   d. abruptio placentae.

8. **An allergic reaction of the skin that is manifested by the presence of hives is called**
   a. ecchymosis.
   b. hirsutism.
   c. urticaria.
   d. verruca.

9. **The removal of foreign material, dead tissue, or damaged tissue is called**
   a. cryosurgery.
   b. debridement.
   c. fulguration.
   d. incision and drainage.

10. **SPECT, PET, MRI, and CT scan are all types of**
    a. diseases.
    b. endoscopic procedures.
    c. radiology procedures.
    d. surgical procedures.

Anatomy and Physiology

11. **Which group of organs listed below is associated with the lymph system?**
    a. spleen, thymus gland, and pancreas
    b. thymus gland, tonsils, and adenoids
    c. spleen, thymus gland, and tonsils
    d. blood, spleen, and tonsils

12. **The formed elements of plasma include**
    a. monocytes, lymphocytes, and eosinophils.
    b. water, thrombocytes, and platelets.
    c. neutrophils, eosinophils, and lymphocytes.
    d. thrombocytes, erythrocytes, and leukocytes.

13. **Which organ listed below is known as the "master gland"?**
    a. heart
    b. liver
    c. pituitary
    d. thymus

14. **Which of the following is the first part of the small intestine?**
    a. duodenum
    b. jejunum
    c. ileum
    d. pylorus

15. **Melanin is produced by skin epithelial cells called melanocytes. Where are melanocytes located?**
    a. stratum basale
    b. epidermal skin layer
    c. dermal skin layer
    d. subcutaneous skin layer

16. **Which of the following structures is part of the lower respiratory tract?**
    a. bronchi
    b. nasopharynx
    c. larynx
    d. trachea

17. **The large arteries of the human cardiovascular system have three layers. What is the function of arteries?**
    a. carry blood from the veins to the capillaries
    b. carry blood from the heart directly to the veins
    c. carry blood from the heart to the body cells
    d. return blood from the body back to the heart

18. **The axial skeleton is composed of**
    a. cranial bones and facial bones.
    b. skull and extremity bones.
    c. skull, rib cage, and vertebral column.
    d. tarsal, tibia, and fibula bones.

19. **Nephrons are present in kidney tissue. What is the function of nephrons?**
    a. maintaining blood flow in kidneys
    b. maintaining homeostasis by regulating water, salts, and glucose
    c. maintaining function of adrenal glands
    d. removing old red blood cells

20. **Which of the following is an internal structure of the female reproductive system?**
    a. Bartholin's glands
    b. labia minora
    c. oviducts
    d. vulva

Information Technology

21. **What is the name used to identify medical coding software? This software assists in the assignment of ICD-9-CM and/or HCPCS codes.**
    a. application software
    b. encoder
    c. transaction
    d. file retrieval

22. **What is the definition of the acronym LAN?**
    a. local-area network
    b. land-area network
    c. local-application network
    d. local-access network

23. **Which group listed below are input devices?**
    a. printers, monitors, and speakers
    b. computer desk and monitor
    c. printers, monitors, and keyboards
    d. keyboards, scanners, pointing devices, and light pens

24. **What is the acronym used to define a health record that is stored in a digital format and is accessible to providers and healthcare professionals via computer software? This format is able to record and have medical data entered into it for updating medical events and as a record of care.**
    a. DVR
    b. EHR
    c. HHR
    d. PHI

25. **What is the term given to a computerized information station that allows facility visitors and patients to access information on health-related topics or a map of the facility?**
    a. Web site
    b. fax on demand
    c. telephone interface system
    d. information kiosk

26. **What federal legislation details provisions for the transmission of health data electronically?**
    a. EMTALA
    b. TEFTRA
    c. HIPAA
    d. Conditions of Participation

27. **What is the acronym given to a group or network in a community or region that is sharing clinical information? This group may not be within the same healthcare facility or hospital.**
    a. RIO
    b. RHIO
    c. LAN
    d. ONIC

28. **Virus protection software and data recovery software are considered what type of computer programs?**
    a. operating system programs
    b. utility programs
    c. communication programs
    d. educational programs

29. **Which of the following is a secondary storage device?**
    a. hard drive
    b. floppy disc drive
    c. optical disc drive
    d. all of the above

30. **Which of the following is correct for defining an Intranet?**
    a. An Intranet connects devices across a large geographical area.
    b. An Intranet is a specialized client-serve network that uses Internet technology.
    c. An Intranet is a local connection of input and output devices.
    d. An Intranet is a wide area connection of output devices.

Web and Information Technology

31. **What is the definition of the acronym ISP?**
    a. Internet Service Processor
    b. Internet Service Provider
    c. Internet Service Platform
    d. Internet Service Program

32. **Which Web address below is the correct one for the Centers for Medicare and Medicaid Services?**
    a. www.cmms.net
    b. www.cms.org
    c. www.cms.hhs.gov
    d. www.cmms.hss.gov

33. **What is the definition of the acronym FTP?**
    a. File Transfer Protocol
    b. File That Paperwork
    c. File The Provider
    d. Final Transfer Provider

34. **Which Web address below is the correct one for the AMBA?**
    a. www.amba.net
    b. www.amba.com
    c. www.ambanet.com
    d. www.ambanet.net/AMBA.htm

35. **What is the definition of the acronym ASCII?**
    a. American Standard Code Interchange Information
    b. American Standard Code Information Interchange
    c. American Standard Code Information Internet
    d. American Standard Code Internet Information

36. **To find out the latest information on NPI (National Provider Identifier), to which Web site should you refer?**
    a. www.cms.gov
    b. www.ahima.org
    c. www.npi.gov
    d. www.cms.hhs.gov

37. Which of the following is the correct Web address for the Department of Health and Human Services?

   a. www.dhhs.com

   b. www.dhh.org

   c. www.hhs.gov

   d. www.hhs.org

38. At which Web address would you find information on the mission of the American Medical Billing Association?

   a. www.ambanet.net/cmrs.htm

   b. www.information.amba.org

   c. www.information.amba.net

   d. www.missionAMBA.net

39. Which address is correct for the American Medical Association?

   a. www.ama-assn.org

   b. www.ama.org

   c. www.ama.net

   d. www.ama.com

40. The *Federal Register* can be found at which of the following Web sites?

   a. www.amba.net

   b. www.cms.gov

   c. www.archives.gov

   d. www.cms.archives.gov

ICD-9-CM Coding

41. A patient is diagnosed with viral pneumonia. Which ICD-9-CM code(s) is correct for this condition?

   a. 486

   b. 480.9, 486

   c. 480.9

   d. 488.1

42. A type 2 diabetic has a cataract. It is noted in the patient's chart that the cataract is due to the patient's diabetes, which is controlled with medication. What is the correct coding of this patient's condition?

   a. 250.00

   b. 250.50, 366.41

   c. 366.9, 250.00

   d. 366.9

43. What is the correct ICD-9-CM code for dermatitis due to cat hair?

   a. 692.0

   b. 692.9, 692.84

   c. 692.9

   d. 692.84

44. A 16-year-old presents after falling while ice skating with the complaint of pain in the right ankle. The patient is examined in the emergency department by the physician. Radiology films of the ankle are done, and the patient is found to have a fracture of the malleolus bone of the right ankle. The patient is placed in a temporary cast and referred to an orthopedic physician for further treatment. What would be the correct ICD-9-CM diagnosis code(s) to report for this patient?

   a. 719.47

   b. 824.8

   c. 824.8, 719.47

   d. 824.9

45. What is the ICD-9-CM code(s) for hypertrophic tonsillitis?

   a. 463

   b. 463, 474.00

   c. 474

   d. 474.00

46. What is the ICD-9-CM code(s) for personal history of malignant neoplasm of the kidney?

   a. V16.51

   b. V16.51, 239.5

   c. V10.52

   d. 180.8

47. **A patient is diagnosed with keratitis; the code assigned is 370.9. This code means that**

    a. the patient has an infection of the eye due to snow blindness.

    b. the patient has an unspecified cause for the keratitis.

    c. the patient has a corneal ulcer.

    d. the patient has an infection due to a vitamin deficiency.

48. **What do E codes describe?**

    a. personal history of disease

    b. family history of disease

    c. cause of injury or adverse effect

    d. late effect

49. **Which of the following code(s) is correct for the documented condition of periumbilic abdominal pain?**

    a. 789.0

    b. 789.00

    c. 789.05

    d. 789.09

50. **A 45-year-old female patient is diagnosed with acute maxillary sinusitis by her family physician. The patient is given prescription medication and told to revisit the office in two weeks for a follow-up visit. What is the correct ICD-9-CM diagnosis code for this office bill?**

    a. 473.9

    b. 461.9

    c. 461.8

    d. 461.0

CPT Coding

51. **Which of the following codes is from the E/M section of CPT?**

    a. 90801

    b. 99281

    c. 78812

    d. 59015

52. **A patient presents to the physician's office with a laceration of her finger. The laceration is repaired in the office. The physician documents the size of the laceration as 2.0 cm. What is the correct CPT code to be assigned for this repair?**

    a. 12001

    b. 12002

    c. 12031

    d. 13100

53. **A patient has a chest x-ray done. The code on the bill is 71022. Per the radiology report, the patient had a chest x-ray with frontal and lateral views. The claim has not been paid. What is the correct CPT code for this radiology exam?**

    a. 71010

    b. 71020

    c. 71022

    d. 71034

54. **A patient has a laparoscopic cholecystectomy. What is the correct CPT code for this surgical procedure?**

    a. 47560

    b. 47562

    c. 47579

    d. 47600

55. **What is code 80061 used for?**

    a. E/M service established patient in the office

    b. nail debridement

    c. allergy testing

    d. lipid panel

56. **CPT code 90641 has a plus sign (+) in front of it; this means that**

    a. this procedure is typically done under conscious sedation.

    b. this is a new code for this year's edition of CPT.

    c. this procedure is an add-on code.

    d. the product related to this code is pending FDA approval.

57. **What does CPT code 45380 describe?**
    a. a sigmoidoscopy
    b. a proctosigmoidoscopy with biopsy
    c. a colonoscopy with single or multiple biopsies
    d. a colonoscopy with removal of polyp

58. **If a patient has CPT code 99205 circled on his encounter form, that means that the patient was seen**
    a. in an acute care hospital.
    b. at home.
    c. in the office.
    d. in an assisted living facility.

59. **What level of exam is required for a 99215 E/M code to be assigned?**
    a. expanded problem focused
    b. problem focused
    c. detailed
    d. comprehensive

60. **Code 4002F is what type of CPT code?**
    a. Category III
    b. Category II
    c. E/M code
    d. Laboratory code

Clearinghouses

61. **What is a clearinghouse?**
    a. a type of file format for electronic claims
    b. a company that processes paper claims into electronic claims
    c. the largest U.S. medical billing software vendor
    d. a company that changes CMS-1500 forms to UB-04 forms

62. **What is an advantage of a value-added network (VAN)?**
    a. automatic submission of all claim attachments
    b. processing of claims within 48 hours
    c. 100 percent clean claims
    d. efficiency and less cost to the provider

63. **What agency can providers check with to see if a clearinghouse is accredited?**
    a. AMBA
    b. CMS
    c. EHNAC
    d. The Joint Commission

64. **What is the third stage of a claim's life cycle?**
    a. submission
    b. payment
    c. transfer to flat file
    d. adjudication

65. **What federal legislation mandated national standards for electronic data?**
    a. *Federal Register*
    b. HIPAA
    c. ERISA
    d. Hill Burton Act

66. **A CMS-1500 claim form must be converted into what type of file for electronic processing?**
    a. VAN file
    b. CMS File
    c. electronic flat file
    d. adjudication file

67. **Which of the following would be performed during the claim adjudication process?**
    a. The claim is screened to ensure that it is not a duplicate claim.
    b. The claim is converted from a CMS-1500 format to an electronic flat file.
    c. The claim is stamped with the date of receipt during clearinghouse processing.
    d. The check for the covered amount is mailed to the provider.

68. **Which item would result in the denial of a claim?**
    a. patient having paid her co-pay to the office
    b. patient having coverage with another insurance payer
    c. missing digit in the patient's birth date
    d. noncovered benefit

69. **Which definition best describes a claim attachment?**
    a. a copy of the office encounter form from the date of service
    b. a copy of the privacy notice that was given to the patient
    c. a set of supporting information taken from the patient's chart
    d. an authorization letter from the insurance company

70. **What is the difference between an Extranet claims submission and Internet claims submission?**
    a. If using an Extranet, the provider can access information about payers and various data elements on a claim.
    b. If using an Internet, the provider must have extra magnetic tapes to download claim information.
    c. If using an Extranet, the network is not secure, so there is a potential for protected health information (PHI) to be accessed by non-authorized individuals.
    d. If using an Internet, there is a 35 percent reduction in error rates.

CMS (HCFA) 1500 Form

71. **Which statement could be listed in Box 12 of the CMS-1500 claim form?**
    a. HIPAA COMPLIANT
    b. SIGNATURE ON FILE
    c. NPI NUMBER PENDING
    d. CO-INSURANCE AMOUNT PAID ON DATE OF SERVICE

72. **If a procedure is done multiple times during an office visit, how is this reflected on the CMS-1500 claim form?**
    a. The CPT code for the procedure is listed with the modifier of -50.
    b. The CPT code for the procedure is listed twice.
    c. Days of service is completed in Box 24G.
    d. Number of units is completed in Box 24G.

73. **CMS-1500 claim forms are designed for**
    a. electronic flat file.
    b. optical scanning.
    c. imaging technology.
    d. benefit scanning.

74. **What is the unique 10-digit number that identifies a provider and is placed on a CMS-1500 claim form?**
    a. PIN
    b. UPIN
    c. NPI
    d. NUPIN

75. **Where are ICD-9-CM diagnosis(es) code(s) entered on a CMS-1500 claim form?**
    a. Box 20
    b. Box 21
    c. Box 22
    d. Box 24

76. **The abbreviation POS, which is used on a CMS-1500 claim form, is defined as**
    a. provider on service.
    b. provider of service.
    c. plan of service.
    d. place of service.

77. The legal business name of the practice that is entered in Box 33 is called
   a. billing entity.
   b. practice.
   c. provider.
   d. facility.

78. What is the maximum number of procedures that can be reported on one CMS-1500 claim form?
   a. four
   b. five
   c. six
   d. seven

79. Which of the following is the correct date pattern to be used on a CMS-1500 claim form?
   a. YY MM DD
   b. DD MM YY
   c. MMDDYY
   d. MMDDYYYY

80. When entering information on a CMS-1500 claim form, which of the following statements is true?
   a. Enter spaces for all punctuation that is related to the address.
   b. Only 9-digit zip code should be entered.
   c. Temporary addresses can be used on the form.
   d. When entering a 9-digit zip code enter the hyphen.

Insurance

81. The rule stating that a policyholder whose birth day and month occur earlier in the year is the primary policyholder for dependent children is called the _____ rule.
   a. dependent
   b. parent
   c. birthday
   d. gender

82. Which Medicare program is designed to pay for prescription drugs?
   a. Part A
   b. Part B
   c. Part C
   d. Part D

83. Mr. Joseph Martin is injured on the job when he falls 30 feet from a platform. He is taken to the hospital and examined and found to have a fractured foot and ankle. What form is important for Mr. Martin to complete for workers' compensation coverage?
   a. CMS-1500
   b. Medical Necessity
   c. First Report of Injury
   d. Temporary Disability

84. Marta Wilson is a 66-year-old female patient at a skilled nursing facility. Mrs. Wilson is there receiving care and physical therapy treatment due to a recent brain hemorrhage. Mrs. Wilson has Medicare as her primary insurance. To which part of Medicare should the billing specialist submit the claims for Mrs. Wilson's care in this facility?
   a. Medicare Part A
   b. Medicare Part C
   c. Medicare Part D
   d. Medigap

85. For hospital billing, what form is used to file medical claims?
   a. CMS-1500
   b. UB-97
   c. UB-02
   d. UB-04

86. **What was the impact of TEFRA on medical billing?**
    a. TEFRA established national standard code sets to be reported for medical claims in the United States.
    b. TEFRA required the implementation of PPS systems in the U.S. healthcare reimbursement arena.
    c. TEFRA required the use of a national provider identification number for all providers of care, physicians, and facilities.
    d. TEFRA established security safeguards for electronic data.

87. **What situation may be covered by liability insurance?**
    a. claim for $1,000 for office treatment of basal cell carcinoma
    b. claim for $50,000 for treatment of malunion of fracture (patient fell at home while repairing kitchen ceiling)
    c. claim for $100,000 in lost wages
    d. claim for $5,000 for abdominal surgery due to appendicitis

88. **Medicare provides healthcare coverage to Americans over the age of 65. Medicare is a type of _____ health plan.**
    a. private
    b. self-pay
    c. government
    d. third-party

89. **What legislation impacted managed care plans by requiring them to follow reporting and disclosure requirements?**
    a. HIPAA
    b. ERISA
    c. EMTALA
    d. OSHA

90. **What was the impact of HIPAA on medical billing?**
    a. HIPAA has implemented national standard reporting guidelines for all medical claims.
    b. HIPAA has established national code sets, which include ICD-9-CM and CPT.
    c. HIPAA has required the implementation of APCs.
    d. HIPAA has required the use of patient consents for all medical care.

Insurance Carriers

91. **Which of the following is a feature unique to a BCBS plan?**
    a. In their negotiated contract with providers, they agree to process all medical claims within 48 hours of receipt.
    b. In their negotiated contract with providers, they agree to provide educational seminars on health topics to providers and enrollees.
    c. BCBS plans only cover individuals under the age of 65.
    d. BCBS plans cover individuals with terminal illnesses for 50 percent of charges submitted.

92. **What is a QMBP? What services does it provide for an individual?**
    a. QMBP is legislation that is part of HIPAA and requires every state to provide healthcare coverage to its residents.
    b. QMBP is a private health plan that provides Medigap coverage to Medicare enrollees.
    c. QMBP is a program that is governed by the state and pays funds for Medicaid coverage of individuals.
    d. QMBP is a program that provides funds to pay for individuals' Medicare Part A and Part B premiums.

93. **What has replaced the EOMB form from Medicare?**
    a. ABN
    b. Waiver
    c. MSN
    d. EOB

94. **What are the four factors of medical necessity?**
    a. critical pathway, practice guidelines, ICD-9-CM guidelines, and CCI edits
    b. purpose, scope, evidence, and value
    c. scope, value, cost, and charge
    d. cost, charge, location of service, and practice guidelines

95. **Which of the following is a managed care option health plan for military officers and their dependents?**
    a. CHAMPVA
    b. CHAMPUS
    c. TRICARE Prime
    d. MTF Plan

96. **What is the term used for updated medical information on a patient who is receiving workers' compensation coverage and/or workers' disability coverage?**
    a. progress report
    b. second report of injury
    c. status update
    d. injury update

97. **Which of the following is the insurance program administrated by states that expands healthcare coverage for children?**
    a. Medicaid
    b. SCHIP
    c. Medicare Part C
    d. PACE

98. **Which of the following is a typically covered service under Medicare Part B?**
    a. inpatient hospital care, hospice care, and DME
    b. skilled nursing facility care, hospice care, and outpatient therapy
    c. DME, prescriptions, and skilled nursing facility care
    d. DME, ambulatory hospital care, and physician services

99. **Which patient could be a Medicare eligible recipient?**
    a. a 60-year-old man with a diagnosis of cardiomyopathy who needs a heart transplant
    b. a 45-year-old woman diagnosed as terminal with chronic lymphocytic leukemia
    c. a 35-year-old diagnosed with end-stage renal disease
    d. a 66-year-old man who is in the United States under a visa

100. **What is the focus of PACE?**
    a. to provide clinical and administrative oversight for U.S. nursing homes
    b. to provide skilled nursing care facilities in areas that do not have this type of facility
    c. to provide community-based services for individuals who require nursing care
    d. to expand dental services, vision services, and so forth for the elderly population covered under Medicaid and Medicare

Acronyms

INSTRUCTIONS

Define the listed acronym in the space provided.

101. EGHP _____

102. ABN _____

103. OCE _____

104. LCD _____

105. APC _____

106. FCA _____

107. HIPAA _____

108. MCO _____

109. HMO _____

110. CPT _____

Compliance

111. **Which of the governmental agencies or departments provides compliance program guidelines?**
    a. American Medical Association   c. Office of Inspector General
    b. State Insurance Inspector   d. Federal Bureau of Investigation

112. **Per the OIG, what is the first step of a compliance plan?**
    a. establishment of an audit program for claims review
    b. establishment of a compliance training program for employees
    c. appointment of a compliance officer
    d. written policies and procedures

113. **Which of the following is an important component of a compliance plan?**
    a. appointment of the owner of the practice as the compliance officer
    b. establishment of a reporting method for employees to report alleged compliance violations
    c. establishment of a fund to pay for legal fees associated with HIPAA violations
    d. hiring of a legal consultant to oversee the office/practice compliance plan

114. **Dr. Lawrence is being investigated by the OIG. It is alleged that he has been referring all of his patients who need DME to a company called Medical Supply Depot. This company is owned by Dr. Lawrence, his brother Allen, and his cousin Jenny. Dr. Lawrence may have violated the provisions of what legislation?**
    a. HIPAA   c. CoP
    b. Stark   d. CCI

115. **Which of the following was established to provide CPT coding information, especially on the issue of unbundling?**
    a. CCI   c. APC
    b. encoding software   d. APG

116. **What is meant by the term *upcoding*?**

    a. separating components of a surgical procedure into two or more CPT codes when the procedure should have been billed with one CPT code

    b. using unspecified ICD-9-CM code(s) when more specific information is documented in the health record, and applicable code(s) are in the ICD-9-CM classification

    c. submitting a claim for a level of reimbursement that is not documented in the health record

    d. submitting a claim for services that were not rendered to a patient

117. **Accreditation by The Joint Commission or another healthcare agency is**

    a. required by federal law.

    b. required by state law.

    c. required for a facility to provide healthcare services.

    d. voluntary.

118. **Per OIG compliance guidelines for small group physician practices, which statement is true?**

    a. Conduction of audits by an external source or vendor is recommended.

    b. Conduction of audits internally is recommended.

    c. Appointment of an oversight or advisory board on compliance issues is required.

    d. Hiring a consultant to provide compliance training to all employees of the practice is required.

119. **What is a focus of the OIG work plan?**

    a. E/M consult codes

    b. wound care claims

    c. pathology claims

    d. duplicate patient claims

120. **What is meant by the term *unbundling*?**

    a. using ICD-9-CM NOS and NEC codes

    b. separating the components of a surgical procedure into multiple CPT codes when it should have been billed under one CPT code

    c. billing for E/M service on the day of a surgery

    d. billing for an office consult E/M code on all new patients to the office

Fraud and Abuse

121. **What federal legislation governs improper billing practices?**

    a. HIPAA

    b. FCA

    c. *qui tam*

    d. Stark I and II

122. **Peer Review Organizations, which are contracted by CMS to perform claim audits, are now known as**

    a. IDS.

    b. JC.

    c. QIO.

    d. Compliance Auditors.

123. **Which of the following could be considered abuse under the False Claims Act?**

    a. falsifying certificates of medical necessity for PT and OT treatments

    b. soliciting kickbacks for laboratory procedures

    c. intentionally unbundling CPT codes on abdominal surgery procedures to increase reimbursement

    d. E/M documentation in patient record that agrees with CPT code level billed to CMS only 2.5 percent of the time

124. **Which of the following could be considered fraud under the False Claims Act?**
    a. solicitation of kickbacks for referrals to an outpatient physical therapy clinic
    b. submission of claims for office visits that were not rendered
    c. submission of claims for DME that was medically necessary based on medical diagnosis
    d. submission of claims for E/M services at a higher level than documented in the record 0.7 percent of the time in a 12 month period

125. **Which healthcare provider system or employer has the largest settlement to date under the False Claims Act?**
    a. Tenet Healthcare Corporation
    b. BCBS of Illinois
    c. Shell Oil Company
    d. Highmark Inc.

126. **Which Web address is correct to report suspected Medicare fraud?**
    a. www.cms.gov
    b. hhstips@oig.hhs.gov
    c. www.oig.gov
    d. www.fraudhotline.gov

127. **The simplified _____ billing process was developed to enable Medicare beneficiaries to participate in mass PPV and influenza virus vaccination programs offered by public health clinics and other entities that bill Medicare payers.**
    a. default
    b. group health
    c. Medi/Medi
    d. roster

128. **What is a Medicare Ombudsman?**
    a. an individual who works for Medicare and performs claim audits
    b. an individual who provides training to physician practices on compliance programs and tips to avoid fraud and abuse charges
    c. an individual who works with Medicare beneficiaries to provide them with information on their options under the Medicare system
    d. an individual who introduces legislation for the standardization of health care in the United States

129. *Qui tam* **is a legal phrase that relates to**
    a. *Federal Register.*
    b. subpoena duces tecum.
    c. Federal False Claims Act.
    d. CPT coding.

130. **What is the definition of UCR?**
    a. unusual, costly, and revenue
    b. uniform, customary, and revenue
    c. uncovered, costly, and reasonable
    d. usual, customary, and reasonable

Managed Care

131. **Mr. Spencer sees Dr. Hansfield on 08/03/YY for an office visit. Mr. Spencer has a managed care plan as his only insurance coverage. On 09/30/YY Mr. Spencer receives a document in the mail from his insurance payer. This document has CPT and ICD-9-CM codes listed on it along with payment information. What is this document?**
    a. EOB
    b. remittance advice
    c. waiver
    d. notice

132. **There are three major types of managed care plans; one of them is a point of service plan. What are the other two major types?**
    a. HMO and GP
    b. HMO and PPO
    c. PPO and POS
    d. HMO and Medicaid

133. **Which of the following is a component of an HMO?**
    a. PCP
    b. enrollees not required to choose a PCP
    c. PCP as gatekeeper
    d. no need for referrals for in-network providers or services

134. **What is an actuarial calculation?**
    a. calculation used to determine the managed care companies' rates and premiums
    b. calculation used to determine overhead cost for a physician practice
    c. calculation used to determine physician specialty differential
    d. calculation used to determine geographical differential for a physician practice

135. **How can relative value units be used by physician practice management?**
    a. to determine cost of practice services (E/M, office procedures, etc.)
    b. to determine cost of running practice including salaries and equipment needs
    c. to compare physician performance within a group practice
    d. to compare practice performance with world data

136. **What is a Management Service Organization?**
    a. a company owned by a hospital that audits medical claims
    b. a company owned by a hospital or a physician practice that hires clinical staff
    c. a company owned by a hospital or a physician practice that provides administrative and managerial services
    d. a company owned by a hospital that provides ABN and EOB to patients

137. **Which of the following is a component of a health risk appraisal?**
    a. number of medical claims for an enrollee in the last 12 months
    b. amount of co-payment requested by employer for employee coverage
    c. geographical location of where the enrollee lives
    d. personal and family health history of an enrollee

138. **When employees have the opportunity to choose which benefit(s) they want under an employer sponsored plan, this is called**
    a. POS.   c. HMO.
    b. cafeteria plan.   d. PPO.

139. **What is the purpose of underwriting?**
    a. assumption of cost   c. assumption of risk
    b. assumption of charges   d. assumption of quality management

140. **What is the role of a case manager?**
    a. to coordinate care for a patient after a hospital stay
    b. to coordinate care of a patient that is transferred from acute care to long-term care
    c. to coordinate office visits for elderly patients with multiple specialty physicians
    d. to coordinate level of care for a patient by working with doctors and insurance for a plan that meets the patient's needs based on medical necessity

General

141. CPT codes are what level of the HCPCS classification?

   a. one
   b. two
   c. three
   d. four

142. Malpractice expense, physician work, and overhead for a practice are all components of

   a. APCs.
   b. PPS.
   c. DRGs.
   d. RVUs.

143. NEC and NOS are found in the ICD-9-CM coding classification system. What is the term used to refer to NEC and NOS?

   a. coding guidelines
   b. coding abbreviations
   c. coding conventions
   d. coding rules

144. A physician requests pre-authorization of a sixth round of chemotherapy for a patient with an aggressive form of breast cancer. The patient had been treated with chemotherapy, radiation therapy, and alternative treatments in the past 12 months. Her health insurance plan does not authorize this request based on the grounds of

   a. coverage limits and HIPAA guidelines.
   b. FCA guidelines.
   c. medical necessity and the component of evidence.
   d. unauthorized use of alternative treatment.

145. A patient, Ms. Julia Kelly, is seen in the emergency department of a local hospital. She is treated for a 2.0 cm cut of her finger, which is sutured. Ms. Kelly also complains of facial pain. She is examined for this issue and receives a prescription medication for her documented diagnosis of sinusitis. Ms. Kelly is discharged home after the visit to follow-up with her personal physician on the sinusitis and for suture removal. What coding classification system(s) would be used to report all of the services given to Ms. Kelly in the emergency department?

   a. CPT
   b. CPT and HCPCS
   c. ICD-9-CM
   d. ICD-9-CM and CPT

146. What is the term given to physicians that maintain their own offices and share services with a group of physicians?

   a. Health Maintenance Organization
   b. Group Practice Without Walls
   c. Provider Network
   d. Preferred Provider Organization

147. Dr. Lawson owns three surgical practices with a group of physicians in two neighboring states. She is looking for a new managed care insurance plan for her 20 employees. She has narrowed her choices down to five companies. Before she makes a presentation to her partners, she wants to compare these five companies on two areas: access to services and wellness education. What organization can Dr. Lawson contact to get this type of information?

   a. The Joint Commission
   b. Insurance Boards of the two states
   c. Centers for Medicare and Medicaid Services
   d. National Committee on Quality Assurance

148. Which of the following is a common documentation method used by physicians for progress notes or office notes?

   a. SOAP
   b. PHI
   c. DRG
   d. RBRVS

149. Karen Murray is a private in the U.S. Army. While on active duty, she is injured during a combat training exercise and suffers a broken leg. The claim for her health care for this injury should be submitted to which payer?

    a. TRICARE

    b. Medicare

    c. Workers' Compensation

    d. BCBS

150. A patient has a cystoscopy done in an ambulatory surgery unit for a complaint of hematuria. During the procedure a lesion is found and biopsied. The patient is discharged to home from the ambulatory surgery unit. The billing specialist bills the claim for the doctor services to the patient's insurance payer with the following codes: 599.70 for hematuria and code 57.33 for the cystoscopy, which was done by the doctor. The claim is denied for payment by the insurance payer. Which of the following is the most likely reason for this denial?

    a. The patient should have been admitted as a hospital inpatient for this procedure.

    b. Medical necessity was not met in this case.

    c. Hematuria is not a valid diagnostic reason for this procedure.

    d. The cystoscopy should have been coded with a CPT code.

ICD-10-CM Coding

151. Viral pneumonia.

    a. J12.0

    b. J12.89

    c. J12.9

    d. P23.0

152. Type 2 (insulin-controlled) diabetic cataract, right eye.

    a. E11.36

    b. E11.36, Z79.4

    c. T38.3x5, H26.31

    d. Z79.4

153. Dermatitis due to cat hair.

    a. L23.81

    b. L30.9

    c. L30.9, T49.4x5

    d. T49.4x5

154. Patient treated in emergency department for pain, right ankle. Preliminary diagnosis was ankle fracture, right. X-rays were negative. Patient placed in temporary cast and referred to orthopedic physician for further treatment.

    a. M25.571

    b. M25.571, S82.899A

    c. S82.899A

    d. S82.899A, M25.571

155. Hypertrophic tonsillitis.

    a. J03.90

    b. J03.91

    c. J35.01

    d. J35.03

156. Personal history of malignant neoplasm of right kidney.

    a. C64.1

    b. C79.01

    c. Z85.520

    d. Z85.528

157. ICD-10-CM code H16.11 is reported for

    a. iridocyclitis.

    b. keratitis.

    c. neovascularization.

    d. rubeosis.

158. Periumbilical abdominal pain.
    a. R10.30
    b. R10.31
    c. R10.32
    d. R10.33

159. Acute maxillary sinusitis.
    a. J01.00
    b. J01.01
    c. J01.80
    d. J01.90

160. Secondary neoplasm of descending colon.
    a. C18.6
    b. C78.5
    c. D01.0
    d. D37.4

APPENDIX B
Mock CPC-P Examination

The American Academy of Professional Coders is a national organization that offers many coding examinations an individual can take to achieve coding certification. One of these exams is the Certified Professional Coder-Payer (CPC-P). This exam is focused on the U.S. payer environment, which includes the correct assignment of the two major U.S. classification systems used for medical coding: HCPCS and ICD-9-CM. The CPC-P exam is divided into three sections. The first section is composed of questions on medical terminology and human anatomy. The second section is composed of questions on payment systems, HIPAA, general insurance, payment impacts, and inpatient reimbursement concepts. The third section of this exam is composed of 70 questions on the following topics: ICD-9-CM coding guidelines, HCPCS coding, CPT coding and guidelines, hospital coding guidelines, applying ICD-9-CM and HCPCS codes, and correctly applying CPT modifiers. The total number of questions on the CPC-P exam is 150. On the examination date, candidates are allowed to use all coding manuals: ICD-9-CM, CPT, and HCPCS level II. AAPC does have a study guide for this examination that can be purchased at their Web site. Also at the Web site is more information on the exam, the application requirements, and the application to take the exam. The Web site for AAPC is **www.aapc.com.** Once at the site, click on the link marked "certification" for access to the exam area.

> **MOCK CPC-P EXAMINATION**

INSTRUCTIONS

Select the most appropriate response. You are permitted to use ICD-9-CM, CPT, and HCPCS level II coding manuals to answer coding questions.

Medical Terminology

1. **If tissue is documented as friable, this means that the tissue is**
   - a. healthy.
   - b. pulverized.
   - c. bleeding.
   - d. cancerous.

2. **A patient is having cryotherapy to address severe actinic keratosis. How is this skin condition being treated?**
   - a. excision of the keratosis
   - b. shaving of the keratosis
   - c. freezing of the keratosis
   - d. incision and draining of the keratosis

3. **In this laboratory test, oxygen, carbon dioxide, and pH of an arterial blood sample are measured and quantified. What is this test?**
   - a. ABC
   - b. CBC
   - c. Sweat Test
   - d. ABG

4. **What organ has the major function of bile storage?**
   - a. gallbladder
   - b. liver
   - c. stomach
   - d. pancreas

5. A patient presents with red elevated skin patches. The patient refers to them as hives from visiting a friend who has several cats. What term could be used correctly to describe this patient's skin condition?

   a. erythema

   b. urticaria

   c. vitiligo

   d. verruca

6. What is the correct medical term used to describe a burn of partial thickness?

   a. first degree

   b. second degree

   c. third degree

   d. eschar

7. If a patient has a disease that has an idiopathic etiology, what does this mean?

   a. The patient has a disease with an unknown cause.

   b. The patient has a hospital-acquired infection.

   c. The patient has a hereditary disease.

   d. The patient has a genetic disease.

8. What part of the body is most distal from the head?

   a. stomach

   b. thigh

   c. foot

   d. hand

9. A cytologist specializes in the

   a. heart.

   b. brain.

   c. cell.

   d. lymph organs.

10. To what location does the term *infracostal* refer?

    a. above the chest

    b. above the face

    c. below the stomach

    d. below the ribs

11. What does the term *buccal* refer to?

    a. tongue

    b. teeth

    c. cheek

    d. esophagus

12. What term is correct to describe a patient vomiting blood?

    a. hematemesis

    b. hemoptysis

    c. hematoma

    d. hemophilia

13. Which of the following is the correct abbreviation for a radiological procedure that uses a magnetic field to produce images?

    a. ECHO

    b. MRI

    c. CT scan

    d. EKG

14. What is the medical term for the shaft portion of a long bone?

    a. epiphysis

    b. diaphysis

    c. cartilage

    d. epicondyle

15. What is meant by the term *contracture*?

    a. The patient has limited speech due to a stroke.

    b. The patient has hearing loss due to a birth injury.

    c. The patient has limited mobility due to a condition of the muscle and/or joint.

    d. The patient has limited growth due to a hereditary condition.

16. **What disease can be identified by a DEXA scan?**
    a. Graves' disease
    b. Parkinson's disease
    c. osteoporosis
    d. muscular dystrophy

17. **In a nephrolithotomy, what is being done?**
    a. A diseased kidney is being removed.
    b. A shunt is being placed for kidney dialysis.
    c. Kidney stones are being removed using shockwaves.
    d. An incision is being made to remove kidney stones.

18. **What is meant by the phrase "breech presentation"?**
    a. A baby is born shoulder first.
    b. A baby is born either feet or buttocks first.
    c. A baby is born head first with the brow showing.
    d. A baby is delivered via Cesarean section.

19. **If a patient reports polyphagia, what does this mean?**
    a. The patient has excessive urination.
    b. The patient has excessive urination at night.
    c. The patient has difficulty eating.
    d. The patient has excessive hunger.

20. **What is the medical term given to a condition where there is an opening in the spinal cord of an infant? This condition is often seen at birth.**
    a. poliomyelitis
    b. hydrocephalus
    c. spina bifida
    d. asthenia

Anatomy

21. **A patient with psoriasis is suffering from what type of skin lesion?**
    a. scabies
    b. bulla
    c. plaque
    d. wheal

22. **What is the largest and upper portion of the brain?**
    a. cerebellum
    b. cerebrum
    c. diencephalon
    d. brainstem

23. **What of the following is the white of the eye?**
    a. cornea
    b. sclera
    c. tunic
    d. choroid

24. **The dura mater, arachnoid, and pia mater are all components of the**
    a. brainstem.
    b. endocrine system.
    c. peripheral nervous system.
    d. meninges.

25. **Where is an areola located?**
    a. breast
    b. stomach
    c. muscle
    d. uterus

26. **In what organ will you find a Bowman capsule?**
    a. kidney
    b. heart
    c. bladder
    d. pancreas

27. **What are the three major muscle types found in the human body?**
    a. striated, smooth, and visceral
    b. cardiac, smooth, and skeletal
    c. cardiac, smooth, and visceral
    d. visceral, adduction, and striated

28. **Where do the two branches of the trachea lead?**
    a. to the bronchi and the heart
    b. to the bronchi and the cilia
    c. to the right and left lung
    d. to the diaphragm

29. **What statement correctly describes the liver?**
    a. This organ is used for endocrine and exocrine functions.
    b. This organ is located posteriorly to the stomach.
    c. This organ is located near the kidneys and used to produce insulin.
    d. This organ is located beneath the diaphragm and used to produce bile.

30. **In a nail, where does new growth occur?**
    a. nail root
    b. lunula
    c. nail bed
    d. nail body

31. **What is the visible part of hair?**
    a. follicle
    b. root
    c. shaft
    d. papilla

32. **The large intestine begins at the**
    a. stomach.
    b. duodenum.
    c. ileum.
    d. sigmoid junction.

33. **What lies between the chest cavity and the abdominal cavity?**
    a. pleura
    b. diaphragm
    c. visceral
    d. bronchi

34. **Where is a myelin sheath located?**
    a. internal space between the skull and the brain
    b. in blood cells in the brain
    c. covering axons of the PNS and ANS
    d. internal area of the spinal cord

35. **Where is the pons located?**
    a. in the brainstem
    b. in the stomach
    c. in the intestine
    d. in the cerebellum

36. **Where is the fibrous tunic located?**
    a. ear
    b. intestinal tract
    c. nose
    d. eye

37. **Eye muscles control movement of the eye. How many muscles are there for one eye?**
    a. five
    b. six
    c. seven
    d. eight

38. **The pinna, labyrinth, and cochlea are all structures of the**
    a. eye.
    b. femur bone.
    c. nose.
    d. ear.

39. **What are the components of a kidney?**
    a. cortex, meninges, medulla, and orifice
    b. cortex, medulla, and hilum
    c. orifice, urethra, meatus, and nephron
    d. nephron, medulla, and meatus

40. **Where is your parietal bone?**
    a. on either side of your skull, behind the frontal bone
    b. on either side of your skull, in front of the ethmoid bones
    c. at the back of the skull, below the temporal bone
    d. at the front of the skull, in front of the sphenoid bone

General Insurance

41. **APACHE is a tool used in the insurance industry. What information does this tool provide?**
    a. risk of dying
    b. risk of injury
    c. risk of malpractice
    d. risk of chronic illness

42. **What agency oversees the investigation of cases under the False Claims Act?**
    a. Centers for Medicare and Medicaid Services
    b. The Joint Commission
    c. Office of Inspector General
    d. TRICARE

43. **What is an IDS?**
    a. a type of cafeteria benefits plan
    b. a group of facilities that provide comprehensive medical care and services
    c. a type of health insurance that requires payment of a premium
    d. a type of insurance plan that requires a physician be identified as a gatekeeper

44. **What is the main difference between an HMO health plan and a POS health plan?**
    a. In a POS health plan, the enrollee can choose what provider to see for care without the need for a referral or a designated primary care physician.
    b. In an HMO health plan, the enrollee can choose what provider to see for care without the need for a referral or a designated primary care physician.
    c. In a POS health plan, the enrollee must designate a primary care physician.
    d. In an HMO health plan, the enrollee must designate a primary hospital for services.

45. **What data set is managed by the National Committee for Quality Assurance (NCQA)?**
    a. UHDDS
    b. DEEDS
    c. HEDIS
    d. UACDS

46. **What is the term used in the insurance industry for the lump sum payment of a set dollar amount for each covered person on a specific health plan?**
    a. *per diem*
    b. deductible
    c. copayment
    d. capitation

Payment Systems

47. What is the abbreviation given to the prospective payment system used for skilled nursing facilities?
    a. DRGs
    b. RUGs
    c. RBRVUs
    d. APCs

48. What was the result of the Balanced Budget Act of 1997?
    a. the implementation of the DRG payment system for hospitals
    b. the implementation of the DME fee schedule
    c. the implementation of the APC system
    d. the implementation of the DRG severity system

49. What is the current name for the Resource Based Relative Value Scale System?
    a. PPS
    b. DRG
    c. PFS
    d. APC

50. Under the Home Health Resource Group (HHRG) guidelines, how often must a patient's care be recertified?
    a. every 30 days
    b. every 60 days
    c. every 90 days
    d. every 120 days

51. In which situation could the use of case mix information be helpful?
    a. deciding if a facility should open an urgent care center
    b. deciding if a facility should build a new parking structure for employee parking
    c. deciding if a facility should seek accreditation from CARF
    d. deciding if a facility should seek accreditation from The Joint Commission

HIPAA

52. What was the impact of HIPAA on the HCPCS coding classification system?
    a. HIPAA required the standardization of this system and implementation of new G codes.
    b. HIPAA resulted in the implementation of a new work plan to audit correct usage of HCPCS codes.
    c. HIPAA requires all insurance payers to recognize HCPCS codes.
    d. HIPAA resulted in the deletion of HCPCS level III or national codes.

53. What specific type of data has HIPAA security provisions?
    a. patient to physician data
    b. information from a health record that is faxed
    c. information handwritten in a health record
    d. data transmitted electronically

54. ICD-10-CM is the next version of the current ICD-CM system used in the United States. Before ICD-10-CM can be implemented in the United States, what must occur?
    a. training of all HIM professionals on this system
    b. training of all physicians on this system
    c. legislation of ICD-10-CM as an approved code set under HIPAA
    d. legislation of ICD-10-CM as an alternative code set under HIPAA

Payment Impacts

55. **What has been impacted by the Correct Coding Initiative?**
    a. identification of fraudulent claims
    b. identification of abuse of Medicare coding practices
    c. defining of hospital focused terms for diagnosis and procedures
    d. defining of cases of upcoding and unbundling

56. **In August of 2006, what decision was made by the Office of Management and Budget that will impact hospital-based billing?**
    a. decision to implement National Provider Identifier (NPI)
    b. decision to implement ICD-10-CM
    c. decision to implement UB-04 claim
    d. decision to implement coding and billing compliance guidelines

57. **Which of the following documents should be updated at least on an annual basis to incorporate ICD-9-CM and CPT code changes?**
    a. UB-92
    b. encounter form
    c. CMS-1500 form
    d. facesheet

58. **What legislation resulted in the NPI?**
    a. HIPAA
    b. EMTALA
    c. TEFRA
    d. False Claims Act

59. **Use of the revised CMS-1500 (08/05) claim was required effective April 1, 2007 due to**
    a. coding guideline changes.
    b. Medicare administrative contractors.
    c. implementation of NPI.
    d. corresponding use of the UB-04.

Inpatient

60. **Mr. Larry North is seen in the emergency department (ED) with the complaint of abdominal pain, fever, and fatigue. Various laboratory tests are performed in the ED, and he has an abdominal ultrasound. Mr. North is admitted for further testing and possible surgery. The next day, the patient reports worsening pain and is taken to the operating room for exploratory surgery. The surgeon finds a ruptured appendix that was not seen on the ultrasound. The patient's appendix is removed, and he is placed on high dose IV antibiotics to avoid peritonitis. After three additional days in the hospital, Mr. North is discharged to home with home health for continued IV medication. What is the principal diagnosis for this hospital admission?**
    a. abdominal pain
    b. peritonitis
    c. ruptured appendix
    d. abdominal pain, fever, and fatigue

61. **The Deficit Reduction Act of 2005 has required hospitals to report what type of diagnostic information on all inpatient Medicare patients?**
    a. Complications and Comorbidities
    b. Present on Admission (POA) diagnosis(es)
    c. Significant Procedures
    d. Principal Procedures

62. **What is the term used to describe a preexisting condition that affects the hospital stay of 75 percent of patients who have this condition?**
    a. complication
    b. severity of illness
    c. disposition
    d. comorbidity

63. **What is the newest payment methodology that will impact hospital billing and coding and is based on the idea of severity of illness?**
    a. APR DRG
    b. OPPS
    c. CMI DRG
    d. POA

64. **What is the acronym given to an electronic data report that trends data on specific DRGs?**
    a. QIO
    b. PEPPER
    c. EMTALA
    d. APR DRG

65. **A patient is admitted to a local acute care hospital and receives the following procedures and treatments during his three-day hospital stay. Which one is reportable based on UHDDS guidelines and definition of a *significant procedure*?**
    a. MRI of the chest
    b. blood transfusion of packed cells
    c. blood pressure checks every four hours by nursing staff
    d. blood sugar lab test every day

66. **A patient is admitted to a local hospital. Admission diagnosis is severe fatigue. The patient also reports weight loss. The patient is worked up and found to have abnormal blood testing and enlarged lymph nodes. After two days in the hospital, the patient is discharged to follow up with a specialist. The final diagnosis documented on the patient's discharged health record is probable non-Hodgkin's lymphoma. Given this information what should be coded for this record?**
    a. weight loss
    b. all admission diagnoses
    c. admission diagnoses and non-Hodgkin's lymphoma
    d. non-Hodgkin's lymphoma

67. **Which diseases have a presumed cause and effect relationship based on ICD-9-CM coding guidelines?**
    a. cataracts and diabetes mellitus
    b. hypertension and renal disease
    c. autism and premature birth
    d. atherosclerosis and Parkinson's disease

68. **A patient is admitted to an acute care hospital and is found to have cholecystitis with a blockage. The patient has a laparoscopic cholecystectomy on the day of admission. That evening the patient complains of severe pain in the throat. The patient is found to have a positive strep test for which he is placed on oral antibiotics. The next day, the patient is up walking and falls, suffering a Colles' fracture. He is taken to the operating room for an open reduction of the fracture. Discharge diagnoses are cholecystitis with cholelithiasis obstruction, strep throat, Colles' fracture reduced. What is the principal procedure for this admission?**
    a. ORIF
    b. cannot determine based on information provided
    c. laparoscopic cholecystectomy
    d. need to query physician to determine principal procedure

ICD-9-CM Coding Rules

69. A patient is documented as having acute and chronic actinic dermatitis. After indexing this condition, the coder should

    a. code 692.9.

    b. code 692.72.

    c. code 692.74.

    d. code 692.72 and 692.74.

70. Which condition is included in ICD-9-CM code category 308?

    a. combat fatigue

    b. prolonged posttraumatic emotional disturbance

    c. adjustment disorder

    d. chronic stress reaction

71. Which disease is excluded under code category 442?

    a. cirsoid aneurysm

    b. false aneurysm

    c. acquired arteriovenous aneurysm

    d. aneurysmal varix

72. When indexing polyneuropathy caused by disseminated lupus erythematosus, the following is found: 710.0 *[357.1]*. What does this mean for the coding of this condition?

    a. The coding of 357.1 is optional, based on documentation in the health record.

    b. The coding 357.1 is required based on ICD-9-CM guidelines.

    c. The coding of 357.1 is optional, and if coded, it should be sequenced first before code 710.0.

    d. The coding of this condition requires two codes listed in the following sequence: 357.1 and 710.0.

73. Which situation would be classified as an adverse effect under ICD-9-CM guidelines?

    a. a 15-year-old who took medication prescribed correctly and developed a full body rash

    b. a 26-year-old who took her husband's medication by mistake

    c. a 70-year-old who was given the wrong medication by the pharmacy and developed tachycardia

    d. a 40-year-old who took two aspirins every hour for six hours for back pain and developed hematemesis

74. A newborn record is assigned the following codes: V27.0, 774.30. What, if anything, is incorrect about this code assignment based on ICD-9-CM coding guidelines?

    a. Record also needs a newborn code from category V30 added to codes listed.

    b. Codes are correct, no errors in what is listed.

    c. A code from category 650 needs to be included on this newborn record.

    d. Outcome of delivery code should not be on a newborn record.

75. Code 780.39 is assigned for convulsions NOS. What does NOS mean?

    a. The patient is having convulsions due to an unknown drug the patient took.

    b. The patient is having convulsions, but the reason for this sign is not clearly documented in the health record.

    c. The patient is having convulsions due to fever, but the record does not have the exact temperature of the patient.

    d. The patient is having seizures and convulsions.

76. An inpatient record has the following on the final diagnoses line: severe pitting edema, severe shortness of breath, fatigue, congestive heart failure. What should be coded based on this information and ICD-9-CM coding guidelines?

   a. severe pitting edema

   b. shortness of breath

   c. fatigue and severe pitting edema

   d. congestive heart failure

77. A patient has the following diagnostic information listed on the hospital facesheet upon discharge: open fracture of trimalleous, history of osteomalacia due to vitamin deficiency, hyperlipidemia, history of breast cancer (10 years ago), family history of colon cancer and lung cancer. Given the "open fracture of trimalleous" diagnosis and ICD-9-CM coding guidelines, after reviewing the record for verification, which of the following is coded?

   a. history of osteomalacia

   b. history of breast cancer

   c. family history of colon cancer

   d. family history of lung cancer

78. A patient with kidney cancer is admitted to the hospital for monitoring and blood transfusions for malignancy treatment anemia. In this case, what ICD-9-CM condition would be the principal diagnosis?

   a. kidney cancer

   b. history of kidney cancer

   c. anemia

   d. blood transfusions

79. When a patient is documented to have a diabetic complication, which digit of the diabetes code will reflect this?

   a. third

   b. fourth

   c. fifth

   d. sixth

80. When a patient has been found to be HIV positive but has no signs or symptoms of HIV, what classification terminology is given to this patient?

   a. AIDS

   b. asymptomatic HIV

   c. testing for HIV

   d. HIV-related

HCPCS

81. What do HCPCS codes that begin with the letter J represent?

   a. DME

   b. ambulance services

   c. orthotics

   d. drug substance that was administered

82. Which entity is responsible for overseeing the maintenance of HCPCS classification system?

   a. AHA

   b. CMS

   c. HHS

   d. WHO

83. What legislation made HCPCS one of the recognized national code sets?

   a. TEFRA

   b. Stark II

   c. Balanced Budget Act

   d. HIPAA

84. What is unique about HCPCS codes that begin with the letter T?

   a. They are temporary codes.

   b. They are DME codes for home health services.

   c. They are national codes for state Medicaid agencies.

   d. They are local codes for providers to use.

CPT Rules

85. A patient has a 2.0 cm laceration of the forearm and a 1.5 cm laceration of the scalp. Both wounds are repaired at the intermediate level. Using your CPT coding book, which of these statements is true?

    a. Multiple codes from the 12001 to 12007 code range should be used.

    b. One code from the 12001 to 12007 code range should be used.

    c. One code from the 12031 to 12037 code range should be used.

    d. Multiple codes from the 12031 to 12037 code range should be used.

86. What is included in the code for a Z-plasty?

    a. skin grafting

    b. excision of the lesion

    c. tissue transfer

    d. skin closure

87. If a patient has a colonoscopy with the removal of polyp of the transverse colon via bipolar cautery and another polyp of the descending colon via snare technique, which CPT coding guideline should be followed?

    a. Two codes from the code range of 45378 to 45392 should be applied.

    b. One code from the code range of 45378 to 45392 should be applied.

    c. Three codes from the code range of 45378 should be applied.

    d. The physician performing the procedure should be queried to find out which polyp was more difficult to remove.

88. A patient has the following lab test ordered on a blood sample: albumin, total bilirubin, direct bilirubin, alkaline phosphatase, total protein, and ALT. Which statement would apply to the coding of this lab test?

    a. The bilirubin should only be coded once, even though it was tested twice.

    b. Only the albumin and ALT should be coded.

    c. Each test should be coded separately for a total of six codes.

    d. A CPT panel code should be used.

89. What type of code is assigned to a record when 85 minutes of critical care is given to a patient in the emergency department?

    a. Emergency Department E/M code

    b. Hospital Inpatient E/M code

    c. Critical Care code

    d. Emergency Department E/M code and a prolonged E/M service code

90. A patient has a humeral shaft fracture. This injury is manipulated, and a cast is applied. The codes assigned were 24500 and 29358. Is this correct coding based on CPT guidelines?

    a. Yes, codes are correct.

    b. No, codes are incorrect. The code for the cast should be 29425.

    c. No, codes are incorrect. The total procedure should be coded with 24505 only.

    d. Maybe—codes are correct but the casting code needs a modifier.

91. **A coding consultant is reviewing charts coded by Suzie New. Suzie is a new coder at a large surgical practice. The consultant identifies the following coding errors:**

Patient ID #	Date of Procedure	Codes Listed	Physician
4545897	05/08/YYYY	22100, 22103-51	Dr. Brown
8788907	05/10/YYYY	58100, 58110-51	Dr. Wayne

What error is Suzie making?

a. applying the modifier -51 to add-on codes

b. applying the modifier -51 when the modifier -59 should be used

c. applying the modifier -51 when the modifier -54 should be used

d. applying the modifier -51 when the modifier -25 should be used

92. **What type of code is 1034F?**

a. temporary code

b. HCPCS level II code

c. performance measurement code

d. HCPCS level III code

93. **What statement is true when coding multiple benign skin lesion excisions?**

a. Intermediate closure of the skin is included in the excision code.

b. Adding together the sizes of the lesions excised is correct, in order to assign one code.

c. Each lesion is assigned one code; lesion size cannot be added together.

d. The shaving and use of electricity for removal is included in excision codes.

94. **What statement is true when coding excision of lesions?**

a. Any margins excised with the lesion should be included in the total size.

b. The lesion size should be taken from the pathology report.

c. The morphology of the lesion is not a factor in code determination.

d. The location of the lesion on the body is not a factor in code determination.

95. **What do category III codes represent?**

a. tracking of outcomes

b. codes that will be deleted

c. emerging technologies

d. vascular families

96. **A patient presents to his cardiologist office on 04/03/YYYY, which is 10 days after he had a permanent cardiac dual-chamber pacemaker inserted. The cardiologist, after examining the patient, determines that the pacemaker needs repositioning to get a better capture. The patient is seen the next day by Dr. Moore, who did the original insertion, for the repositioning. Based on CPT guidelines, which statement is true for this situation?**

a. Dr. Moore's service of repositioning should be billed with a -76 modifier for repeat procedure.

b. Dr. Moore's service of repositioning is not billable within 14 days of the original pacemaker insertion.

c. Dr. Moore's service of repositioning should be billed with an unlisted CPT code.

d. Dr. Moore's service needs to be preauthorized by the AMA to ensure payer payment.

CPT Sections/Applied Coding

Choose the correct code(s) for each of the following situations.

97. **A patient has a 3.5 cm lipoma of the thigh removed. The physician documents that 0.5 margins were also excised. The surgical defect was closed with 3.0 nylon sutures of the dermis and 1.5 sutures of the epidermis.**

a. 11406

b. 11406, 12032-51

c. 11604

d. 11606, 12002-51

98. A patient has a 5.0 cm basal cell carcinoma of the neck excised. The physician performs a W-plasty type closure of the 4 sq cm defect.
    a. 14040
    b. 14040, 11626-51
    c. 14040, 11626-59
    d. 14040, 11626-51, 12042-51

99. A patient has a chest tube inserted for the condition of hemothorax.
    a. 32560
    b. 32035
    c. 32551
    d. 32422

100. Thoracoscopy with lung biopsy, approach via a chest tube.
    a. 32551
    b. 32602
    c. 32602, 32551
    d. 32602, 32551-51

101. Mitchell bunionectomy with osteotomy, tenotomy, and capsulotomy.
    a. 28296
    b. 28296, 28234-51, 28260-51
    c. 28296, 28261-51
    d. 28288, 28260-51, 28230-51

102. Right ankle arthroscopy with extensive debridement.
    a. 29894-RT
    b. 29898-RT
    c. 29898-RT, 11004-51
    d. 29894-RT, 29898-51, 11004-51

103. Application of temporary short leg cast on a patient with an ankle fracture.
    a. 27786
    b. 29405
    c. 27786, 29405
    d. 27886, 29405-51

104. Debridement of sacral decubitus ulcer with suture closure.
    a. 15931
    b. 11000
    c. 11004
    d. 15931, 11004-51

105. 2.8 cm wound of the hand (intermediate repair) and 1.0 cm wound of the ear (simple repair).
    a. 12042
    b. 12052
    c. 12013
    d. 12042, 12011-51

106. Application of acellular dermal allograft of a patient's forearm, covering 25 sq cm.
    a. 15330
    b. 15300
    c. 15320
    d. 15430

107. Cryosurgery removal of 17 actinic keratoses.
    a. 11400
    b. 11200
    c. 17004
    d. 17000, 17003-51, 17003-51, 17003-51

108. Bilateral reduction mammoplasty.
    a. 19318
    b. 19318-50
    c. 19318, 19318-51
    d. 19303

109. Bronchoscopy with placement of bronchial stent with dilation and multiple endobronchial biopsies.
    a. 31625
    b. 31625, 31622-51
    c. 31636, 31625-51
    d. 31625-50, 31622-51, 31622-51

ICD-9-CM Hospital Coding/Applied Coding

110. A 75-year-old patient is admitted to the hospital with a 48-hour history of nausea and vomiting. The patient also has type 2 diabetes and is admitted for evaluation of her complaints. After workup and testing, the patient is discharged home in an improved condition. During her hospital stay, the patient requires subcutaneous insulin injections due to elevated blood sugar levels. Final discharge diagnoses include nausea and vomiting due to either food poisoning or gastroenteritis. What are the correct ICD-9-CM codes for this case?

   a. 250.01, 787.04

   b. 005.9, 569.71, 250.01

   c. 787.04, 005.9, 569.71, 250.01

   d. 055.9, 569.71, 250.02

111. Under the current proposal, ICD-10-CM codes will be

   a. a maximum of seven numeric characters.

   b. a maximum of seven alphanumeric characters.

   c. a minimum of two characters.

   d. a minimum of four alphanumeric characters.

112. A patient is experiencing dizziness resulting from the interaction of Aldomet and St. John's Wort. The Aldomet was taken as prescribed by the physician. However, the physician did not know that the patient was taking St. John's Wort. This would be a case of

   a. adverse effect.

   b. poisoning.

   c. complication.

   d. late effect.

113. Carl Jackson is a 75-year-old man brought to the ED by his daughter after he fell. Mr. Jackson is complaining of severe knee pain. After examination and x-rays, Mr. Jackson is admitted with the diagnosis of DJD of the knee and is scheduled for knee replacement surgery. The surgery is performed on 05/04/YYYY. On 05/07/YYYY, Mr. Jackson is transferred to an inpatient rehab facility for two weeks of intensive physical therapy. On 05/10/YYYY, he presents to the ED with complaints of fever, chills, and warmth of the surgical site. He is found to have an infection of the prosthetic implanted knee joint. On 05/12/YYYY, the infected artificial knee joint is removed. Mr. Jackson is placed on a course of IV antibiotics and discharged to an SNF on 05/15/YYYY. On 05/24/YYYY, Mr. Jackson is readmitted to the hospital for a second knee joint replacement surgery. What is the classification for the admission on 05/24 for Mr. Jackson?

   a. DJD and total knee replacement

   b. DJD with infectious complication and total knee replacement

   c. infectious complication of surgery and knee revision

   d. acquired deformity of knee and joint revision

114. A patient delivered twins at 33 weeks due to premature rupture of membranes. Twin A Apgar scores were 8 and 9; twin B scores were 7 and 8. The twins were taken to NICU for observation. The mother had a postpartum embolism that was treated with medication. After five days in the hospital, mother and babies were discharged home. The following codes were reported for the mother: 650, V27.2, 673.21, 651.01. These codes were identified in an audit as being incorrect. What is incorrect about the applied ICD-9-CM codes?

   a. 644.21 should be listed as principal diagnosis code.

   b. 658.11 should be listed as a secondary diagnosis code.

   c. Postpartum embolism is coded to 673.22, not 673.21.

   d. All of the above (a, b, and c) are correct.

115. A patient is admitted through the ED of a local hospital. The patient is a nursing home resident and is 86 years of age. The patient's complaint is stated by the nurse that is with her as "non-healing ulcer of the left foot." The patient also has a peripheral circulatory disorder due to non-insulin dependent diabetes. After evaluation and examination, the patient is admitted for surgical debridement of a gangrenous ulcer of her foot. The debridement is done on the second hospital admission day. Final discharge diagnoses per physician documentation in the health record: diabetic gangrenous ulcer, diabetic peripheral circulatory disorder, type 2 diabetes. Which code set below is correct based on this information?

 a. 707.14, 785.4, 86.22

 b. 707.14, 785.4, 250.00, 86.22

 c. 250.70, 707.14, 785.4, 86.22

 d. 250.70, 785.4, 86.22

116. A patient was scheduled for a laparoscopic cholecystectomy. The first incision and trocar were inserted, but after the second incision, the patient developed bradycardia. The procedure was aborted, and the incisions were sutured close. In this case

 a. the chart should be coded with the ICD-9-CM code for a laparoscopic cholecystectomy.

 b. the chart should only have diagnosis codes reported.

 c. the chart should have diagnosis codes and the administration of anesthesia codes as the procedure.

 d. the chart should have diagnosis codes and procedure code of abdominal incision reported.

ICD-9-CM Sections

Choose the correct code(s) for each of the following situations.

117. A 45-year-old patient is admitted to the hospital for treatment of malignant lymphoma. The patient was diagnosed as HIV positive 13 years ago and has two episodes of PCP pneumonia in the past. After five days in the hospital, the patient is discharged to at-home hospice care.

 a. 201.9

 b. 042, 201.90

 c. 201.90

 d. 201.9, 042

118. Ms. Carter is a 38-year-old female who is admitted due to swelling and pain in her upper right arm. She doesn't recall any injury or insect bite. After diagnostic workup, it is determined that she has acute lymphangitis. Blood cultures confirm that this is due to a group A streptococci.

 a. 682.0

 b. 682.8, 041.01

 c. 682.3

 d. 682.3, 041.01

119. A woman at 40 weeks gestation is admitted in labor. The baby is found by ultrasound view to have the umbilical cord wrapped tightly around its neck. The baby is quickly delivered vaginally, resuscitated for moderate asphyxia, and given oxygen in the delivery. The infant is taken to the NICU for continued oxygen treatment for the first day. The baby has no further complications, and the mother and child are discharged on the second day after delivery.

 a. V27.0, 762.5, 93.93, 93.96

 b. V30.00, 786.6, 93.93, 93.96

 c. V30.00, 762.5, 768.6, 93.93, 93.96

 d. 762.5, 768.6, V30.00, 93.96, 93.93

120. Mrs. Lopez comes to the hospital in labor at term. Upon evaluation by the physician, she is fully effaced and has suffered a second-degree laceration of her perineum. A healthy baby is born via cephalic presentation. Her laceration is repaired in the delivery room.

 a. 650, 664.11, V27.0, 75.69

 b. 664.11, V27.0, 75.69

 c. 664.11, 75.69

 d. 650, V27.0, 75.69

121. A patient presents to the office with the complaint of gross hematuria. The patient has been taking Coumadin for the past three years. The patient reports that he has been taking the medication as prescribed. The patient's wife has the bottle, and it is reviewed and found to be correct. The patient is directed to stop taking the Coumadin for one week and return for a repeat urinalysis and blood work at that time.

a. 599.70, E934.2

b. 964.2, E858.2

c. 964.2, 599.70, E934.2

d. 599.70, 964.2, E934.2

122. A patient presents for evaluation of hemiplegia. The patient suffered a CVA 15 months ago on the left side. The patient is right-handed. The patient also has marked dysphasia at this time. Both conditions are documented as late effects by the physician.

a. 438.22, 438.12

b. 438.21, 436, 787.20

c. 342.91, 787.20, 486

d. 438.12, 342.91

123. A patient is admitted to the burn unit for treatment. The patient has second and third degree burns of both hands, second and third degree burns of both forearms, and first and second degree burns of both upper arms. The total percentage of the patient's body that is burned is 12 percent; the total of third degree burn is 4 percent.

a. 943.09, 944.08

b. 943.09, 948.01

c. 944.30, 943.31, 943.23, 948.11

d. 944.30, 944.28, 941.37, 943.21, 943.23, 943.13

124. A patient is admitted with severe abdominal pain. The patient reports that she took some of her husband's medication by mistake. Her husband has testicular cancer and is taking Bleomycin for treatment. The patient is admitted and treated for her complaints. Discharge diagnosis: Bleomycin taken by accident.

a. 789.7, E930.7

b. 960.7, 789.7, E856

c. 789.7, E856

d. 789.7, 960.7, E930.7

125. A patient is seen in the ED for complaints of photophobia and blurred vision. The patient is examined and admitted for further evaluation. At first, the patient has an abnormal finding on a brain CT scan, but that is ruled out as the cause of his symptoms. The patient is seen by an ophthalmologist and is diagnosed with iridocyclitis. The patient is discharged to follow up with the ophthalmologist in the office after one week of intraocular steroid drops.

a. 379.90

b. 364.03

c. 368.13, 368.8

d. 379.90, 368.13, 368.8

126. A patient presents to the ED with severe fatigue and mild shortness of breath. The patient is under chemotherapy for breast cancer treatment. The patient is admitted after her hemoglobin is found to be low at 9.5 gm/dL, and her hematocrit is 29 percent. She is admitted for a blood transfusion of packed cells. After the transfusion and one day in the hospital, the patient is discharged. She will continue her chemotherapy treatments as an outpatient as scheduled.

a. 285.9, 99.04

b. 285.9, V10.3, 99.04

c. 285.9, 174.9, 99.04

d. 174.9, V57.1, 285.9, 99.04

127. A 25-year-old woman presents at 39 weeks of pregnancy. After four hours of labor, she delivers a seven-pound baby that was presented in the cephalic position. The mother had an episiotomy with repair during the delivery. After one day in the hospital, the mother and child are discharged to home.

a. 650, 73.6

b. 650, V27.0, 73.6

c. 664.01, 650, V27.9, 73.5, 73.6

d. 652.41, V27.0, 73.5

128. A patient is admitted for IV antibiotic treatment of cellulitis of the hand. The patient suffered a laceration of the hand while working in his garage. At first, the cut did not seem deep or severe, and the patient did not seek treatment until three days later when the cut was still not healing and was starting to hurt. At that time, the patient was seen by his physician, who, after examination, escorted the patient to the hospital for inpatient admission. After two days of antibiotic treatment, the patient was discharged to home in improved condition.

  a. 682.4

  b. 882.1, 682.4

  c. 882.0, 682.9

  d. 882.1, 682.4, 136.9

129. A patient is admitted, treated, and discharged. The final diagnosis is hypertensive nephrosclerosis, stage I.

  a. 403.90

  b. 403.90, 585.1

  c. 585.1, 401.9

  d. 585.1, 401.9, 403.91

130. A patient is discharged in improved condition after treatment for acute osteomyelitis of the foot due to blastomyces dermatitidis fungal infection.

  a. 730.07

  b. 730.07, 116.1

  c. 730.28

  d. 730.07, 116.0

131. A 2-year-old child is admitted per Child Services after having been found in an unsafe environment. The child is admitted for observation and examination for suspected abuse and neglect. Per examination, no physical findings are apparent. The child is discharged to the care of the Child Service Agency.

  a. V71.81

  b. 995.50

  c. 995.52, 995.54

  d. V71

132. A 15-year-old type 2 diabetic is admitted with diabetic acidosis, uncontrolled.

  a. 250.01, 250.02

  b. 276.2, 250.01

  c. 250.12

  d. 250.02

133. A patient is involved in an MVA and is admitted due to several open fractures. After examination and x-rays, the patient is found to also have an internal injury of his basilica vein of his upper arm due to one of the fractures. The patient has an open fracture of the humeral shaft and an open fracture of the radius at the proximal end. The patient's fractures are stabilized, and he is transferred to a university hospital for further treatment.

  a. 812.20, 813.81

  b. 812.21, 813.21

  c. 812.31, 813.17

  d. 903.1, 812.31, 813.17

134. A patient is admitted for chemotherapy treatment for diagnosis of primary carina lung cancer.

  a. 162.9, 17.70

  b. 162.2, 17.70

  c. V58.11, 162.2, 17.70

  d. V58.12, 162.2, 17.70

135. After two days of inpatient medical treatment, Mr. Fox is discharged home. Final discharge diagnosis is acute exacerbation of chronic obstructive pulmonary disease.

  a. 491.21

  b. 491.22

  c. 491.20

  d. 496

136. A 25-year-old patient is admitted for surgical treatment of congenital mitral valve insufficiency. The surgical replacement of the valve with a prosthetic is done without complication, and the patient is discharged home after three days in the hospital.

  a. 396.3, 35.24

  b. 424.0, 746.6, 35.24

  c. 424.0, 35.24

  d. 746.6, 35.24

137. A patient with a two-year history of HTN is admitted. Discharge diagnoses are cardiomyopathy and hypertension.

    a. 402.90

    b. 402.91

    c. 425.4, 401.9

    d. 402.90, 425.4

138. A patient is admitted for medical treatment and care of viral double pneumonia due to RSV.

    a. 480.1

    b. 486

    c. 486, 079.6

    d. 480.9, 079.6

HCPCS Level II

Choose the correct code(s) for each of the following situations.

139. Injection of Nebcin, 50 mg.

    a. J3246

    b. J3260

    c. J3260 $\times$ 8

    d. J3260 $\times$ 80

140. ALS level I service from scene of MVA to trauma hospital. Patient was in cardiac afibrillation during transport, which was via an ambulance.

    a. A0426

    b. A0427

    c. A0428

    d. A0429

141. The physician of a patient with ALS has ordered and received a hydraulic seat lift. How would this DME be coded?

    a. E0625

    b. E0627

    c. E0630

    d. E0635

142. Metal crutches with hand grips.

    a. E0110

    b. E0111

    c. E0111 $\times$ 2

    d. E0113

143. John Adams is a 70-year-old man with primary insurance payer of Medicare. Mr. Adams has his annual screening sigmoidoscopy. Mr. Adams had several benign colon polyps removed five years ago.

    a. G0104

    b. G0105

    c. G0106

    d. G0121

144. Portable parenteral infusion pump for delivery of nutrition.

    a. B9000

    b. B9002

    c. B9004

    d. B9006

145. A patient, Ms. James, is seen in the dentist office of Dr. Brown. Ms. James has been a patient in this office for the past four years. Today, Ms. James complains of pain in her left lower molar. Dr. Brown performs a problem-focused oral exam and has two bitewing x-rays taken by the technician in the office. [CMS does not include D codes on its Web site; however, publishers (e.g., Ingenix) obtain permission from the ADA to include D codes at www.EncoderPro.com and in paper-based HCPCS Level II coding manuals.]

    a. D0160, D0272

    b. D0170, D0272

    c. D0180, D0272

    d. D0170, D0270 $\times$ 2

Modifiers

146. When comparing HCPCS level II modifiers to CPT modifiers, what is different?

    a. HCPCS modifiers are entirely numeric.

    b. HCPCS modifiers are either alphanumeric or entirely alpha characters.

    c. CPT modifiers are entirely alphanumeric.

    d. There are no HCPCS level II modifiers.

147. A patient has a colonoscopy with bipolar cautery for control of bleeding in the sigmoid junction and polypectomy of the splenic flexure area using snare technique. The codes reported are 45385 and 45382. What is the correct modifier to attach to the second reported CPT code?

    a. −51   c. −52

    b. −59   d. −32

148. Choose the correct code for this procedure: Repair of a diaphragmatic hernia in a 25-day-old infant.

    a. 39503   c. 43336-63

    b. 39503-63   d. 49491-52

149. Choose the correct code for this procedure: Removal of right lobe of thyroid. Patient had left lobe removed 30 days prior. Global period for thyroid lobectomy is 45 days. The right lobectomy was performed by the same physician that did the left lobectomy.

    a. 60260-78   c. 60220-77

    b. 60220-76   d. 60240-79

150. Which of the following is a CPT modifier approved for hospital outpatient use?

    a. −26   c. −91

    b. −51   d. −99

ICD-10-CM

151. Actinic dermatitis due to exposure to the sun.

    a. L55.9   c. L57.8

    b. L57.0   d. L58.0, L58.1

152. Which of the following conditions is excluded from ICD-10-CM category I72?

    a. Acquired aneurysm   c. False aneurysm

    b. Cirsoid aneurysm   d. Ruptured aneurysm

153. Which is the interpretation of index entry *polyneuropathy, in (due to), deficiency (of) B(-complex) vitamins* E53.9 [G63]?

    a. Both codes are reported, sequencing code G63 before code E53.9.

    b. Code E53.9 is reported first, followed by code G63.

    c. Code G63 is reported first, followed by code E53.9.

    d. Reporting code G63 is optional because it is within brackets.

154. Codes Z37.0 and P59.8 were reported for a single liveborn infant, born in the hospital (vaginal delivery). Which explains the reporting of these codes?

    a. A code from category O80 should also be reported for any newborn case.

    b. The assigned codes are correct, and there are no reporting errors.

    c. Outcome of delivery codes are reported for the mother's case only.

    d. Code Z37.0 is erroneously reported, and code Z38.00 is reported instead.

155. Code R56.9 is assigned for *convulsions NOS*. The NOS abbreviation means that the patient is having convulsions

    a. and provider documentation is not specified in the patient record.

    b. because of unknown over-the-counter drugs taken by the patient.

    c. due to fever, but the patient's exact temperature is not recorded.

    d. in addition to seizures, which resulted in the patient's convulsions.

156. A 75-year-old patient was admitted to the hospital with a 48-hour history of nausea and vomiting. The patient also has type 2 diabetes and underwent an evaluation of her complaints during the inpatient admission. After workup and testing, the patient was discharged home in an improved condition. During her hospital stay, the patient required subcutaneous insulin injections due to elevated blood sugar levels. Final discharge diagnoses include nausea and vomiting due to either food poisoning or gastroenteritis; type 2 diabetes mellitus.

    a. E11.9, K52.9, T62.9, R11.2

    b. K52.9, T62.9, E11.9, R11.2

    c. T62.9, K52.9, R11.2, E11.9

    d. R11.2, T62.9, K52.9, E11.9

157. A patient delivered a liveborn infant whose APGAR score was 9. After two days in the hospital, mother and baby were discharged home. The following codes were reported for the mother's chart, in this order: Z37.2, O80. A coding audit revealed that

    a. both codes were reported accurately and in the appropriate sequence.

    b. code O80 should be reported as the principal diagnosis on the mother's chart.

    c. code Z38.30 should be reported as a secondary diagnosis code for the mother's chart.

    d. code Z38.30 should be reported in addition to code Z37.2 on the mother's record.

158. An 86-year-old female patient was admitted as an inpatient through the emergency department of a local hospital from a nursing facility. The patient's complaint was stated by the nursing facility nurse as *nonhealing ulcer of the left foot*. The patient also has peripheral angiopathy due to type 2 diabetes mellitus for which she is administered insulin. After evaluation and examination, the patient was admitted for surgical debridement of a gangrenous ulcer of her left foot. The excisional debridement was performed on the second day of the inpatient hospital admission. Final discharge diagnoses per physician documentation in the patient record include diabetic gangrenous ulcer, diabetic peripheral angiopathy, and type 2 diabetes.

    a. E11.52, E11.59, I96, 0H9NZZZ

    b. E11.52, I96, 0H9NZZZ

    c. E11.52, Z79.4, 0H9NZZZ

    d. I96, E11.52, Z79.4, 0H9NZZZ

159. A 45-year-old patient was admitted to the hospital for treatment of classic Hodgkin's lymphoma, neck. The patient was diagnosed as HIV positive 13 years ago and has two episodes of *Pneumocystis carinii* pneumonia in the past. After five days in the hospital, the patient was discharged to at-home hospice care. Final diagnosis was classic Hodgkin's lymphoma, neck, and AIDS.

    a. C81.71, B20

    b. C81.71, B20, B59

    c. C81.71, Z21

    d. C81.71, Z21, B20, B59

160. Ms. Carter is a 38-year-old woman admitted to the hospital due to swelling and pain in her upper right arm. She does not recall any injury or insect bite. After diagnostic workup, it was determined that she has acute lymphangitis due to group A streptococci.

    a. L03.113

    b. L03.113, B95.0

    c. L03.123

    d. L03.123, B95.0

161. A 45-year-old woman was seen in the office for management of her benign hypertension. The provider renewed her hypertension medication.

    a. G93.2

    b. I10

    c. I15.8

    d. I87.309

162. A 75-year-old male patient was admitted for inpatient treatment of acute congestive heart failure.

   a. I50.31

   b. I50.32

   c. I50.41

   d. I50.42

163. A patient presents to the office with the complaint of gross hematuria. The patient has been taking Coumadin for the past three years. The patient reports that he has been taking the medication as prescribed. The patient's wife has the bottle, which was reviewed and found to be correct. The patient was directed to stop taking the Coumadin for one week and return for repeat urinalysis and blood work at that time.

   a. T45.511A, R31.0

   b. T45.514A, R31.0

   c. T45.515A, R31.0

   d. T45.516A, R31.0

164. A patient presents for evaluation of hemiplegia. The patient suffered a cerebral infarction over one year ago on the left side. The patient is right-handed. The patient also has marked dysphasia at this time. Both conditions were documented as late effects by the physician.

   a. G81.9, R47.02

   b. I63.9, G81.9, R47.02

   c. I69.354, I69.321

   d. I69.854, I69.391

165. A patient was admitted to the burn unit for treatment. The patient has second- and third-degree burns of both hands, second- and third-degree burns of both forearms, and first- and second-degree burns of both upper arms. The total percentage of the patient's body that was burned is 12 percent; the total third-degree burn is 4 percent.

   a. T22.099A, T23.099A

   b. T22.099A, T31.0

   c. T23.309A, T23.299A, T20.36xA, T22.219A, T22.239A, T22.139A

   d. T23.301A, T23.302A, T22.311A, T22.312A, T22.231A, T22.232A, T31.11

166. A patient was admitted with severe abdominal pain. The patient reported that she took some of her husband's medication by mistake. Her husband has testicular cancer and is taking Bleomycin for treatment. The patient was admitted and treated for her complaints. Discharge diagnoses were Bleomycin taken by accident and severe abdominal pain.

   a. T45.1x1, R10.0

   b. T45.1x4, R10.0

   c. T45.1x5A, R10.0

   d. T45.1x6A, R10.0

167. A patient was treated in the emergency department for complaints of bilateral photophobia and blurred vision. After evaluation, the patient was diagnosed with acute iridocyclitis. The patient was discharged to follow up with the ophthalmologist in the office after one week of intraocular steroid drops.

   a. H20.013

   b. H20.013, H53.19

   c. H20.013, H53.19, H53.8

   d. H53.19, H53.8

168. A patient was treated in the emergency department for mild shortness of breath and severe fatigue.

   a. R06.00, R53.81

   b. R06.01, R53.82

   c. R06.02, R53.83

   d. R53.83, R06.00

169. A 2-month-old female baby underwent scheduled newborn examination in the pediatrician's office during which cradle cap was diagnosed.

   a. L21.0

   b. Z00.121

   c. Z00.121, L21.0

   d. Z00.129

170. A 70-year-old female patient received home health intravenous antibiotic treatment of cellulitis, left hand.

   a. L03.11

   b. L03.113

   c. L03.114

   d. L03.90

171. **Hypertensive nephrosclerosis, stage I.**
    a. I12.9
    b. I12.9, N18.1
    c. N18.1, I10
    d. N18.1, I10, I12.9

172. **Acute osteomyelitis of the right tibia due to *Bastomyces dermatitidis* fungal infection.**
    a. M86.10, B40.89
    b. M86.161, B40.3
    c. M86.169, B40.7
    d. M86.9, B40.9

173. **A 2-year-old child was admitted per local child services agency for evaluation of suspected abuse and neglect. Per examination, no physical findings are apparent. It was determined that the child's parents are in a child custody battle, and one parent accused the other of abuse and neglect. Child abuse and neglect was ruled out, and the child was discharged to the care of his mother with weekly follow-up by the local child services agency.**
    a. T76.92xA
    b. T76.02xA
    c. Z03.89
    d. Z04.72

174. **A 15-year-old was treated for type I diabetic acidosis.**
    a. E10.10
    b. E10.8
    c. E11.69, E87.2
    d. E87.2, E10.10

175. **Patient underwent inpatient treatment for comminuted open fracture of left humeral shaft and closed torus fracture of left radius at proximal end.**
    a. M84.422, M84.433
    b. S42.351, S52.112
    c. S42.351B, S52.112
    d. S42.351B, S52.112B

176. **A patient underwent outpatient chemotherapy treatment for primary carina lung cancer.**
    a. C34.00
    b. C34.90
    c. Z51.11, C34.00
    d. Z51.12, C34.00

177. **Acute exacerbation of chronic obstructive pulmonary disease.**
    a. J44.0
    b. J44.1
    c. J44.1, J44.9
    d. J44.9

178. **Inpatient open surgical replacement of mitral valve with prosthetic for congenital mitral valve insufficiency.**
    a. I08.0, 02RG3KZ
    b. I34.8, 02RG4KZ
    c. Q23.3, 02RG0JZ
    d. Q23.3, I34.8, 02RG0KZ

179. **Constrictive cardiomyopathy and hypertension.**
    a. I11.9
    b I11.9, I42.5
    c. I42.2
    d. I42.5, I10

180. **Double pneumonia due to respiratory syncytial virus.**
    a. J12.1, B97.4
    b. J12.9, B97.4
    c. J18.9, B97.4
    d. P23.0, B97.4

APPENDIX C
Case Studies for Medical Office Simulation Software 2.0 (MOSS)

MEDICAL OFFICE SIMULATION SOFTWARE 2.0 (MOSS)

- Introduction
- How to Access MOSS
- How to Log in to MOSS
- MOSS Tutorial
- MOSS Case Studies

INTRODUCTION

Medical Office Simulation Software 2.0 (MOSS) software is included free with the *Workbook to Accompany Understanding Health Insurance.* MOSS simulates medical practice management software used in a provider's office by allowing students to:

- Register new and established patients.
- Post procedures and/or services performed.
- Generate CMS-1500 claims.
- Post payments to patient accounts.

HOW TO ACCESS MOSS

To access the *Medical Office Simulation Software 2.0* (MOSS) student practice software program online, refer to the information on the printed access card located in the front of this workbook. You will download the MOSS software program on your personal computer.

> **NOTE:** Consult with your instructor before installing the software and completing the case studies located in this appendix.

HOW TO LOG IN TO MOSS

1. Double click the MOSS icon, which is located on your personal computer desktop.
2. In the *Name:* field, enter the student number assigned by your instructor (e.g., Student1) as one word without spaces. In the *Password:* field, enter your student number the first time you log in. (The password can be changed to whatever you choose, but be sure to remember what it is.)

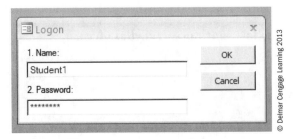

3. At the *Main Menu*, verify that the radio button for *Feedback Mode* is clear, which means it is "turned off" (Figure 1). If the radio button is blackened, click to clear it.

MOSS TUTORIAL

Case 1 has been used to create a MOSS tutorial, which contains step-by-step instructions and MOSS 2.0 screenshots to facilitate your use of the software as you complete Cases 2-10.

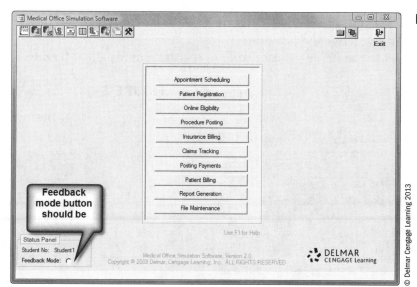

FIGURE 1

Case 1—Alice Jensen

Registration Information (Dr. Heath)

Patient Name	Alice Jensen
Social Security Number	987-22-5621
Marital Status	Single
Date of Birth/Gender	April 18, 1932/Female
Street Address	93 Sycamore Drive
City	Douglasville
State	NY
Zip Code	01234
Home Phone	123-528-9791
Occupation	Retired
Primary Insurance	Medicare-Statewide Corp.
Guarantor	Self
Insurance ID No.	999862554A
MD Participation	In-network; accepts assignment; signature on file

Visit Information

Physician	Dr. Heath
Date of Service	Admitted July 25, 2011, and discharged July 28, 2011
Location (Place of Service Code)	Inpatient Hospital (21)
Facility	Community General Hospital
Service/Procedure	Level I Initial Hospital Care (99221) (July 25) Level I Subsequent Hospital Care (99231) (July 26, July 27) Hospital Discharge Day Management, 30 minutes (99238) (July 28)
Diagnoses	Chest Pain and Pressure (786.59) Hypertension (401.9) Congestive Heart Failure (428.0)
Patient Reference No.	201

Ms. Alice Jensen was admitted to Community General Hospital by Dr. L.D. Heath on July 25, 2011, for chest pain and pressure, hypertension, and congestive heart failure (CHF), for which level 1 initial hospital care services were provided. The patient also received level 1 subsequent hospital care services on July 26 and July 27. Then, the patient was discharged from the hospital on July 28, and Dr. Heath provided the discharge services.

Mrs. Jensen was added to the practice registration system because Dr. Heath is covering for her primary care physician. Dr. Heath obtained a copy of the patient's registration information from the hospital admissions department and has provided it along with the information regarding services provided during the inpatient hospitalization.

Registering a Patient

1. At the Main Menu, click on *Patient Registration*.
2. At the bottom of the Search window, click on *Add* to register a new patient (Figure 2).

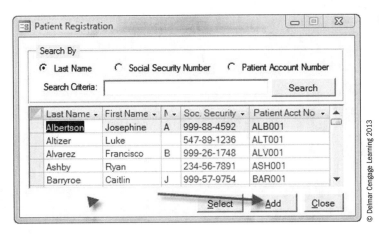

FIGURE 2

3. Verify that the name of the physician selected is **Dr. Heath** in the *Physician Name* field, located at the top of the *Patient Registration* window. To select a different physician, click on the drop-down arrow.
4. In Field 1, enter patient's last name (**Jensen**).
5. In Field 2, enter patient's first name (**Alice**).
6. In Field 4, enter the patient's social security number (**987-22-5621**).
7. In Field 5, click the *Gender* drop-down arrow, and select **Female**. With the cursor in Field 5, *Gender*, enter the letter *"f"* to display Female.
8. In Field 6, click the *Marital Status* drop-down arrow, and select **Single**.
9. In Field 7, enter the patient's date of birth (**April 18, 1932**) using the MMDDYYYY format. Do not enter backslashes. The cursor will automatically move to the next section of the field, where the patient's current age is calculated.
10. In Field 8, enter the patient's street address (**93 Sycamore Drive**).
11. In Field 9, enter the patient's city (**Douglasville**).
12. In Field 10, enter the patient's state (**NY**).
13. In Field 11, enter the patient's ZIP code (**01234**).
14. In Field 12, enter the patient's home telephone number as **1235289791**. MOSS will automatically enter the punctuation.
15. In Field 14, click on the *Employment Status* drop-down menu, and select **Retired**.
16. In Field 21, verify that a checkmark displays in the box located to the left of *Self* (Figure 3).

FIGURE 3

© Delmar, Cengage Learning 2013

17. Click *Save* at the bottom of the screen, and then click *OK* in the pop-up window.

18. Click on the *Primary Insurance* tab, located at the top of the *Patient Registration* window. Then, click on the magnifying glass, which is located to the right of Field 1.

19. In the *Search* field enter **Medi,** and click *Search*.

20. Click to the left of *Medicare-Statewide Corp.* and click on the *Select* tab, which is located at the bottom of the window.

21. In Field 2, click on the radio button located to the left of *Self*. Fields 3–7 will automatically populate.

22. In Field 8, enter the patient's Medicare ID number (**999862554A**).

23. In each of Fields 13–15, verify that checkmarks have been entered to the left of *Yes*.

24. Click *Save* at the bottom of the screen, and then click *OK* in the pop-up window (Figure 4).

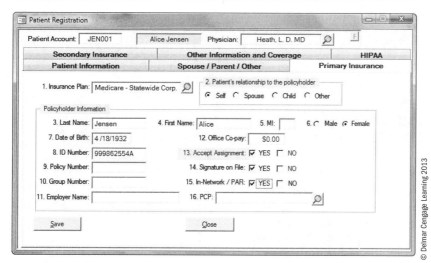

FIGURE 4

25. Click *Close* twice, and return to the *Main Menu*.

Posting Patient Charges

1. Open MOSS software and select *Procedure Posting* from the main menu (Figure 5).

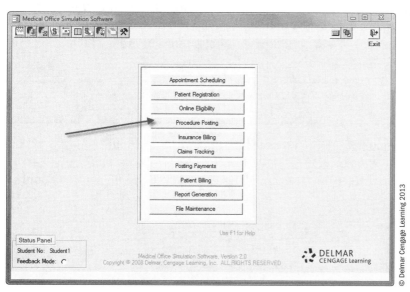

FIGURE 5

2. In the patient list *Search Criteria* box, enter **Jen** and click on *Search*. Patients whose last names begin with these letters will display (Figure 6).

FIGURE 6

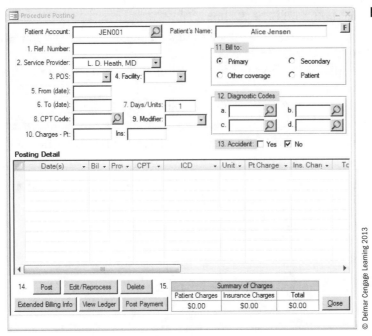

3. Click on the line that contains **Alice Jensen** to highlight the name, and select *Add* (because you will be adding procedures performed and/or services provided to her account). The *Procedure Posting* window will display.

4. In Field 1, enter 201 as the patient's *Reference Number*.

> **NOTE:** The reference number is created by each provider's office, and it is used to help locate accounts when posting procedures/services, payments, adjustments, and so on.

5. In Field 2, verify that the name of the physician selected is **Dr. Heath**. To select a different physician, click on the drop-down arrow.

6. In Field 3, select **Inpatient (21)** as the place of service.

7. In Field 4, click on the *Facility* drop-down arrow and select *Community General Hospital*.

8. In Field 5, enter **07/25/2011** as the date of service for the visit.

9. Leave Field 6 blank because it would be populated only to indicate that the same service had been provided on consecutive days.

> **NOTE:** Fields 5 and 6 are most commonly populated when the physician provides inpatient hospital and nursing facility evaluation and management services.

10. Field 7 will automatically populate based on the entries in Fields 5 and 6.

11. In Field 8, click on the magnifying glass. In the *Search Criteria* field, enter CPT code **99221** to report the level 1 initial hospital care service. Highlight the code, and click *Select* (Figure 7).

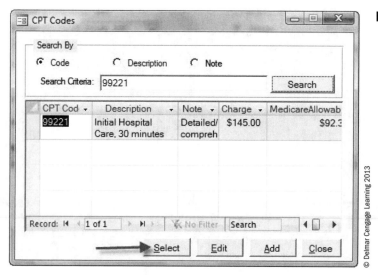

FIGURE 7

12. Field 10 will automatically populate based on the patient's payer and the fee schedules loaded into the MOSS database.

13. In Field 11, click on the radio button located to the left of *Primary*. This is the procedure billed to the patient's primary payer.

14. In Field 12a, click on the magnifying glass located to the right of the data entry box. In the *Diagnosis Code* window, verify that the radio button located to the left of *Description* is selected. In the *Search Criteria* box, enter **chest pain**, and click *Search*. Highlight *Chest Pain, Unspec (786.50)*, and click *Select* (Figure 8).

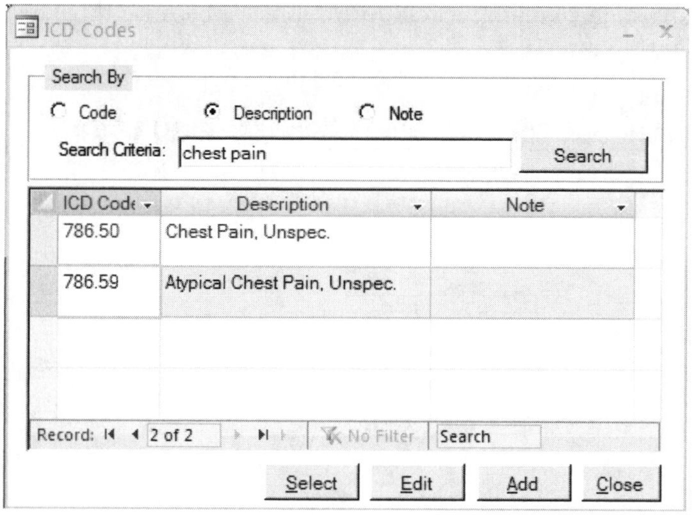

FIGURE 8

15. In Field 12b, click on the magnifying glass located to the right of the data entry box. In the *Diagnosis Code* window, verify that the radio button located to the left of *Code* is selected. In the *Search Criteria* box, enter code **401.9** for Hypertension, Unspec. Highlight code *401.9*, and click *Select* (Figure 9).

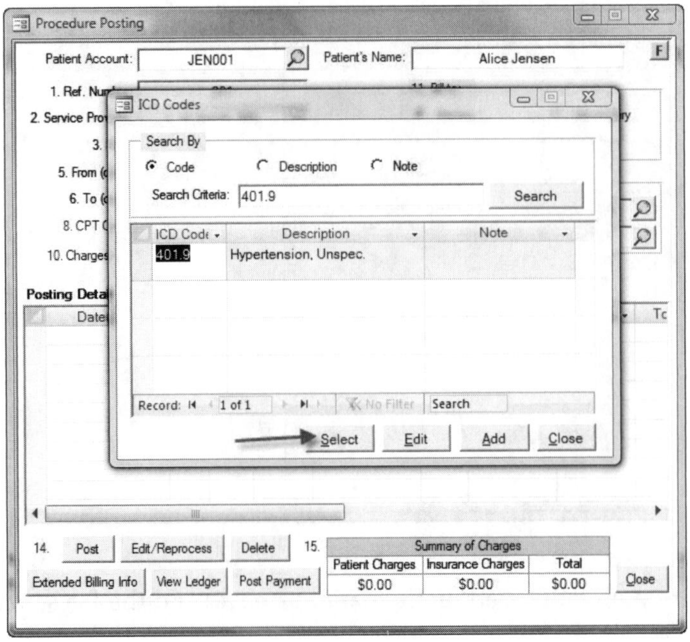

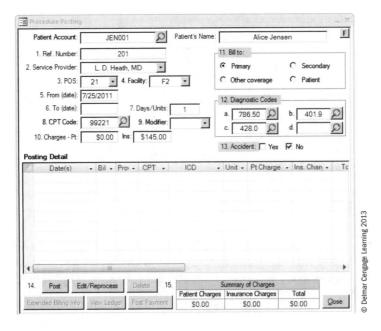

FIGURE 9

16. In Field 12c, click on the magnifying glass located to the right of the data entry box. Under *Description*, enter **congestive heart failure, unspecified** to search for the code (428.0).

17. Leave Field 12d blank.

> **NOTE:** Up to four diagnosis codes are reported on a CMS-1500 claim.

18. Verify that Field 13 displays a checkmark located in front of *No* because this encounter is not the result of an accident (Figure 10).

FIGURE 10

19. In Field 14, at the bottom of the *Procedure Posting* window, click *Post* (Figure 11).

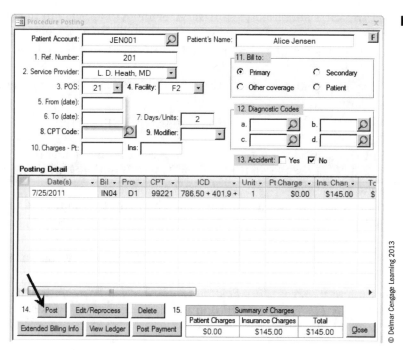

FIGURE 11

20. Return to Field 1, and enter **201** as the *Patient Reference Number*.

21. In Field 2, verify that the name of the physician selected is **Dr. Heath**. To select a different physician, click on the drop-down arrow.

22. Fields 3 and 4 will automatically populate with previous selections of *Inpatient (21)* and *Community General Hospital*.

23. In Field 5, enter **07/26/2011** as the *From* date.

24. In Field 6, enter **07/27/2011** as the *To* date (Figure 12).

> **NOTE:** Dates are entered in Fields 5 and 6 when the physician provides the same inpatient hospital and nursing facility evaluation and management services on consecutive dates. Field 7 automatically populates based on dates entered in Fields 5 and 6.

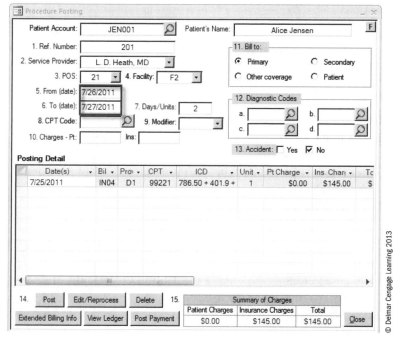

FIGURE 12

25. In Field 8, click on the magnifying glass located to the right of the data entry box. In the *Search Criteria* box, enter **99212** (Level I subsequent hospital care). Highlight the code, and click *Select*. Note that two days are billed for this service, and $79 appears in the charge field. The total charge of $158 for two days of service will be reflected when you post the charge.

26. Leave Field 9 blank. (Field 9 is populated with a CPT or HCPCS Level II modifier, if applicable to the case.)

27. Field 10 will automatically populate based on the patient's payer and the fee schedules loaded into the MOSS database.

28. In Field 11, click on the radio button to the left of *Primary*. This procedure is being billed to the patient's primary payer.

29. In Field 12a, click on the magnifying glass located to the right of the data entry box. In the *Diagnosis Code* window, enter **786.50** (Chest Pain, Unspec) in the *Search Criteria* box. Highlight this code, and click *Select*.

30. In Field 12b, enter code **401.9** (Hypertension, Unspec). Highlight this code, and click *Select*.

31. In Field 12c, enter code **428.0** (Congestive Heart Failure, Unspec). Highlight this code, and click *Select*.

32. In Field 13, verify that a checkmark is displayed in the box in front of *No* because this encounter was not the result of an accident.

33. In Field 14, at the bottom of the *Procedure Posting* window, click *Post*. Notice that two lines of information appear in the *Posting Detail* portion in the middle of the window, reflecting the two entries you posted (Figure 13).

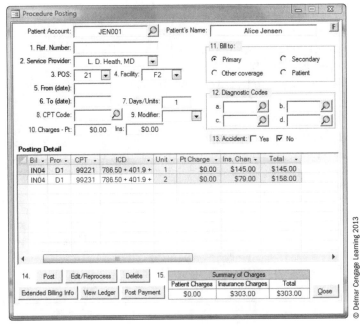

FIGURE 13

34. Return to Field 1, and enter **201** for the *Patient Reference Number*.

35. In Field 2, verify that the name of the physician selected is **Dr. Heath**. To select a different physician, click on the drop-down arrow.

36. Fields 3 and 4 will automatically populate with previous selections of *Inpatient (21)* and *Community General Hospital*.

37. In Field 5, enter **07/28/2011** as the *From* date.

38. Leave Field 6 blank.

39. Field 7 automatically populates based on dates entered in Field 5 (and Field 6, if applicable).

40. In Field 8, click on the magnifying glass located to the right of the data entry field. In the *Search Criteria* box, enter **99238** (Hospital discharge services). Highlight the code, and click *Select*.

41. Leave Field 9 blank.

42. Field 10 will automatically populate based on the patient's payer and the fee schedules loaded into the MOSS database.

43. In Field 11, click on the radio button to the left of *Primary*. This procedure is being billed to the patient's primary payer.

44. In Field 12a, click on the magnifying glass located to the right of the data entry box. In the *Diagnosis Code* window, enter **786.50** (Chest Pain, Unspec) in the *Search Criteria* box. Highlight this code, and click *Select*.

45. In Field 12b, enter code **401.9** (Hypertension, Unspec). Highlight this code, and click *Select*.

46. In Field 12c, enter code **428.0** (Congestive Heart Failure, Unspec). Highlight this code, and click *Select*.

47. In Field 13, verify that a checkmark displays in the box in front of *No* because this encounter was not the result of an accident.

48. In Field 14, at the bottom of the *Procedure Posting* window, click *Post*. Notice that three lines of information appear in the *Posting Detail* portion in the middle of the window, reflecting the two entries you posted (Figure 14).

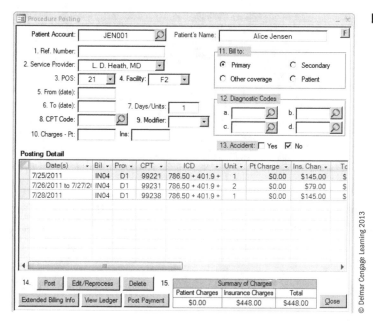

FIGURE 14

© Delmar Cengage Learning 2013

49. Click on the *Close*, located at the bottom right corner of the screen to close the patient listing window.

Submitting an Electronic Claim

1. From the MOSS main menu, click to select *Insurance Billing* (Figure 15).

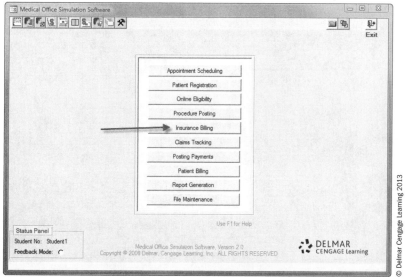

FIGURE 15

© Delmar Cengage Learning 2013

2. In Field 1, the *Claim Preparation* window, click on the drop-down arrow and select *Patient Name* as the sort order.

3. In Field 2, verify that the radio button located to the left of *Bill* is selected. Use the drop-down arrow in the *Provider* field to select **Dr. Heath**. Enter **07/25/2011** in the *From* field, and enter **07/28/2011** in the *Through* field. Use the drop-down arrows to select **Alice Jensen** and **JEN001** in the *Patient Name* and *Patient Number* fields located to the right of Patient Name, respectively.

4. In Field 3, verify that a checkmark displays in the box located to the left of *Electronic*.

5. In Field 4, verify that a checkmark displays in the box located to the left of *Primary*.

6. In Field 5, use the scroll bar in to locate and select *Medicare-Statewide Corp* (Figure 16).

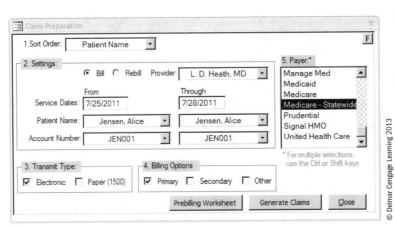

FIGURE 16

7. Click on the *Prebilling Worksheet* button, located at the bottom of the screen. This will create a report that can be used to verify the claims information before the claim is submitted (Figure 17).

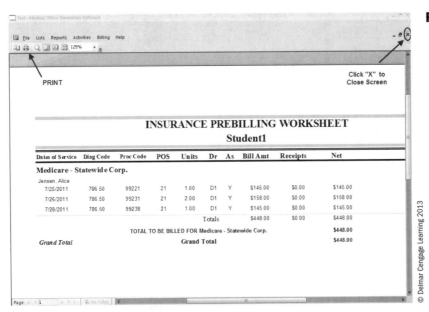

FIGURE 17

8. Review and verify the information located on the *Prebilling Worksheet*, and print a copy for your instructor. Then, click on the small "x" located in the right corner of the screen.
9. Upon returning to the *Claim Preparation* screen, click *Generate Claims*.
10. In the Preview Claims screen, a CMS-1500 claim will be visible (Figure 18). Review and verify the information located on the CMS-1500, and click *Transmit EMC*.

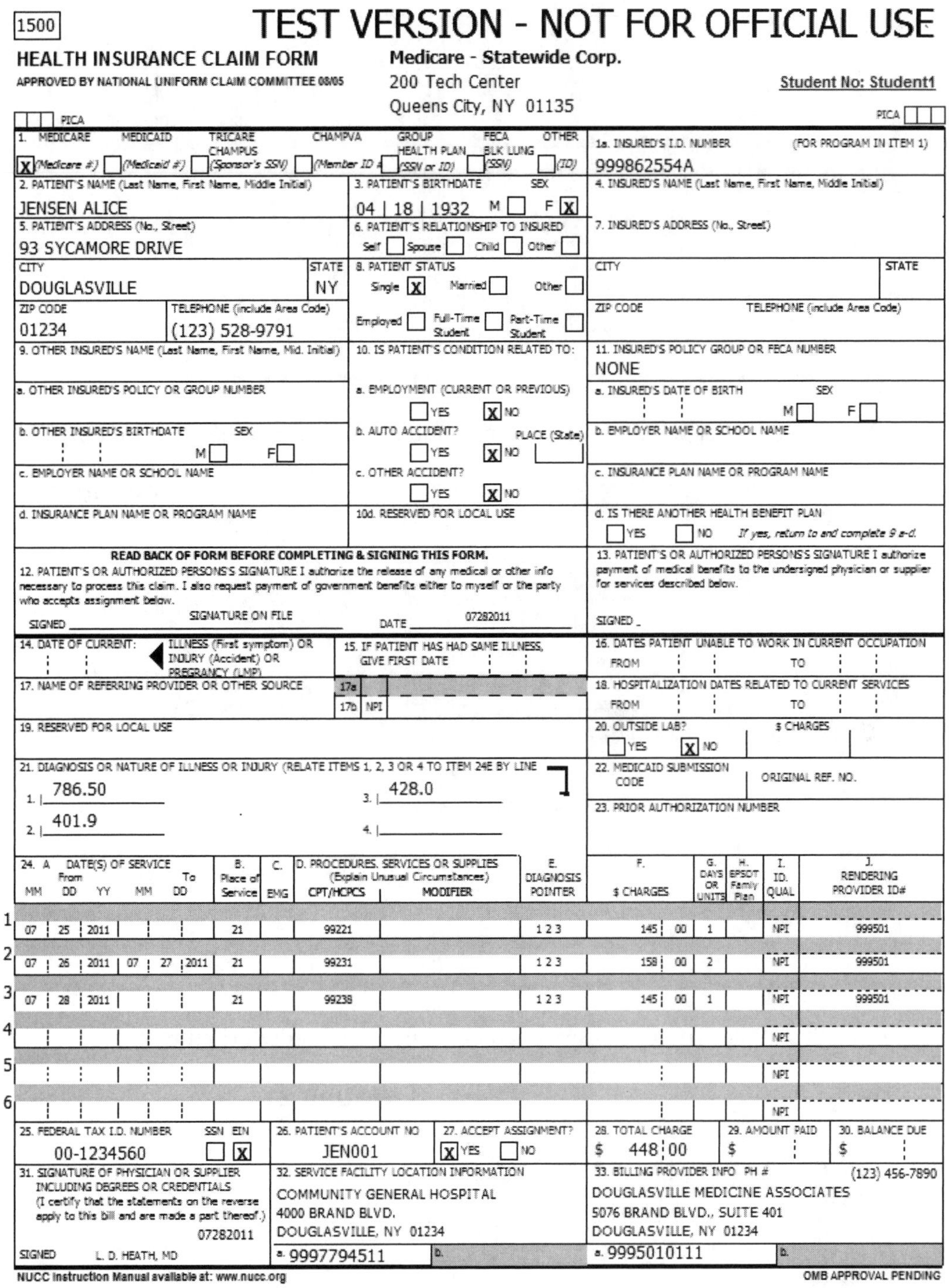

1500 TEST VERSION - NOT FOR OFFICIAL USE

HEALTH INSURANCE CLAIM FORM
APPROVED BY NATIONAL UNIFORM CLAIM COMMITTEE 08/05

Medicare - Statewide Corp.
200 Tech Center
Queens City, NY 01135

Student No: Student1

PICA PICA

1. MEDICARE [X] (Medicare #) MEDICAID (Medicaid #) TRICARE CHAMPUS (Sponsor's SSN) CHAMPVA (Member ID #) GROUP HEALTH PLAN (SSN or ID) FECA BLK LUNG (SSN) OTHER (ID)
1a. INSURED'S I.D. NUMBER (FOR PROGRAM IN ITEM 1): 999862554A
2. PATIENT'S NAME (Last Name, First Name, Middle Initial): JENSEN ALICE
3. PATIENT'S BIRTHDATE: 04 | 18 | 1932 SEX M [ ] F [X]
4. INSURED'S NAME (Last Name, First Name, Middle Initial)
5. PATIENT'S ADDRESS (No., Street): 93 SYCAMORE DRIVE
6. PATIENT'S RELATIONSHIP TO INSURED: Self Spouse Child Other
7. INSURED'S ADDRESS (No., Street)
CITY: DOUGLASVILLE STATE: NY
8. PATIENT STATUS: Single [X] Married [ ] Other [ ]; Employed [ ] Full-Time Student [ ] Part-Time Student [ ]
CITY STATE
ZIP CODE: 01234 TELEPHONE (include Area Code): (123) 528-9791
ZIP CODE TELEPHONE (include Area Code)
9. OTHER INSURED'S NAME (Last Name, First Name, Mid. Initial)
10. IS PATIENT'S CONDITION RELATED TO:
11. INSURED'S POLICY GROUP OR FECA NUMBER: NONE
a. OTHER INSURED'S POLICY OR GROUP NUMBER
a. EMPLOYMENT (CURRENT OR PREVIOUS) [ ] YES [X] NO
a. INSURED'S DATE OF BIRTH SEX M [ ] F [ ]
b. OTHER INSURED'S BIRTHDATE SEX M [ ] F [ ]
b. AUTO ACCIDENT? [ ] YES [X] NO PLACE (State)
b. EMPLOYER NAME OR SCHOOL NAME
c. EMPLOYER NAME OR SCHOOL NAME
c. OTHER ACCIDENT? [ ] YES [X] NO
c. INSURANCE PLAN NAME OR PROGRAM NAME
d. INSURANCE PLAN NAME OR PROGRAM NAME
10d. RESERVED FOR LOCAL USE
d. IS THERE ANOTHER HEALTH BENEFIT PLAN [ ] YES [ ] NO *If yes, return to and complete 9 a-d.*

READ BACK OF FORM BEFORE COMPLETING & SIGNING THIS FORM.
12. PATIENT'S OR AUTHORIZED PERSON'S SIGNATURE I authorize the release of any medical or other info necessary to process this claim. I also request payment of government benefits either to myself or the party who accepts assignment below.
SIGNED SIGNATURE ON FILE DATE 07282011
13. PATIENT'S OR AUTHORIZED PERSON'S SIGNATURE I authorize payment of medical benefits to the undersigned physician or supplier for services described below.
SIGNED

14. DATE OF CURRENT: ILLNESS (First symptom) OR INJURY (Accident) OR PREGNANCY (LMP)
15. IF PATIENT HAS HAD SAME ILLNESS, GIVE FIRST DATE
16. DATES PATIENT UNABLE TO WORK IN CURRENT OCCUPATION FROM TO
17. NAME OF REFERRING PROVIDER OR OTHER SOURCE 17a 17b NPI
18. HOSPITALIZATION DATES RELATED TO CURRENT SERVICES FROM TO
19. RESERVED FOR LOCAL USE
20. OUTSIDE LAB? [ ] YES [X] NO $ CHARGES
21. DIAGNOSIS OR NATURE OF ILLNESS OR INJURY (RELATE ITEMS 1, 2, 3 OR 4 TO ITEM 24E BY LINE)
1. 786.50 2. 401.9 3. 428.0 4.
22. MEDICAID SUBMISSION CODE ORIGINAL REF. NO.
23. PRIOR AUTHORIZATION NUMBER

	24. A DATE(S) OF SERVICE From MM DD YY	To MM DD YY	B. Place of Service	C. EMG	D. PROCEDURES, SERVICES OR SUPPLIES CPT/HCPCS	MODIFIER	E. DIAGNOSIS POINTER	F. $ CHARGES	G. DAYS OR UNITS	H. EPSDT Family Plan	I. ID. QUAL	J. RENDERING PROVIDER ID#
1	07 25 2011		21		99221		1 2 3	145 00	1		NPI	999501
2	07 26 2011	07 27 2011	21		99231		1 2 3	158 00	2		NPI	999501
3	07 28 2011		21		99238		1 2 3	145 00	1		NPI	999501
4											NPI	
5											NPI	
6											NPI	

25. FEDERAL TAX I.D. NUMBER: 00-1234560 SSN [ ] EIN [X]
26. PATIENT'S ACCOUNT NO: JEN001
27. ACCEPT ASSIGNMENT? [X] YES [ ] NO
28. TOTAL CHARGE: $ 448 00
29. AMOUNT PAID: $
30. BALANCE DUE: $
31. SIGNATURE OF PHYSICIAN OR SUPPLIER INCLUDING DEGREES OR CREDENTIALS (I certify that the statements on the reverse apply to this bill and are made a part thereof.) 07282011 SIGNED L. D. HEATH, MD
32. SERVICE FACILITY LOCATION INFORMATION: COMMUNITY GENERAL HOSPITAL, 4000 BRAND BLVD., DOUGLASVILLE, NY 01234; a. 9997794511 b.
33. BILLING PROVIDER INFO PH # (123) 456-7890: DOUGLASVILLE MEDICINE ASSOCIATES, 5076 BRAND BLVD., SUITE 401, DOUGLASVILLE, NY 01234; a. 9995010111 b.

NUCC Instruction Manual available at: www.nucc.org OMB APPROVAL PENDING

FIGURE 18

11. A Transmission Status screen will appear. When the process is complete, click on *Print* and this will generate a report of the claim submission indicating the success or failure of the transmission.
12. Click on *Close* to return to the Main Menu.

Claims Tracking

1. From the Main Menu, click on *Claims Tracking* (Figure 19).

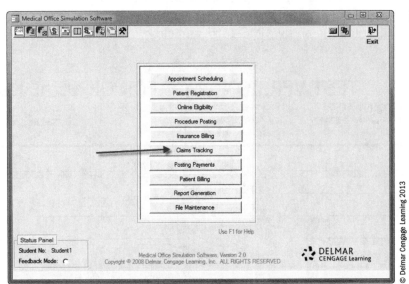

FIGURE 19

2. In the Select Payer window, scroll down and select *Medicare Statewide Corp* (Figure 20).

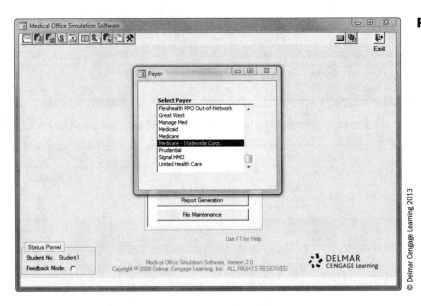

FIGURE 20

3. In the Start Date window, enter **07/25/2011** and click on *OK* (Figure 21).

FIGURE 21

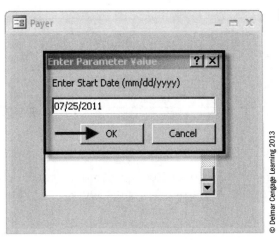

4. In the End Date window, enter **07/28/2011** and click on *OK* (Figure 22).

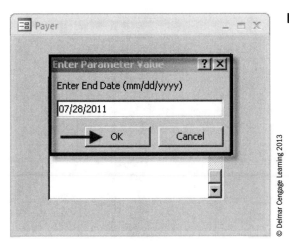

FIGURE 22

© Delmar Cengage Learning 2013

5. This will generate a Provider Payment Advice, and the patient's claim will appear on this report. Review and verify the Date of Service (DOS), Procedure Code, Patient Responsibility, and Paid to Provider columns (Figure 23).

FIGURE 23

PROVIDER PAYMENT ADVICE
Medicare - Statewide Corp.
Student1

Patient Name Alice Jensen (JEN001)

Claim ID	DOS	Procedure	Charges	Allowed Amount	Patient Responsibility	Rejected Amount	Paid to Provider	Remarks
1000328	7/28/2011	99238	$145.00	$73.16	$14.63	$0.00	$58.53	A
1000327	7/26/2011	99231	$158.00	$78.14	$15.63	$0.00	$62.51	A
1000326	7/25/2011	99221	$145.00	$92.33	$18.47	$0.00	$73.86	A
Patient Totals			$448.00	$243.63	$48.73	$0.00	$194.90	

© Delmar Cengage Learning 2013

6. Print the *Provider Payment Advice* report to use when posting payments by clicking on the *Print Icon* at the top left of the page under the drop-down menu (Figure 24).

FIGURE 24

© Delmar Cengage Learning 2013

7. Close the window by clicking on the small "x" located to the right of the screen. Then close the *Payer* window, returning to the main menu.

Posting Payments

1. From the Main Menu, click on *Posting Payments* (Figure 25).

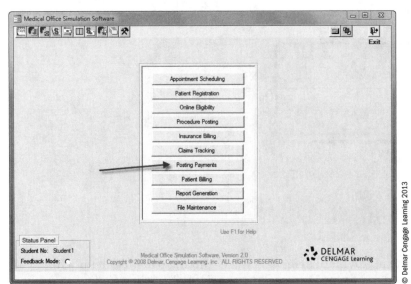

FIGURE 25

2. In the Posting Payments window, enter **Jensen** in the Search field and click on *Search*.
3. Highlight Alice Jensen's name, and click on *Apply Payment*. (Figure 26).

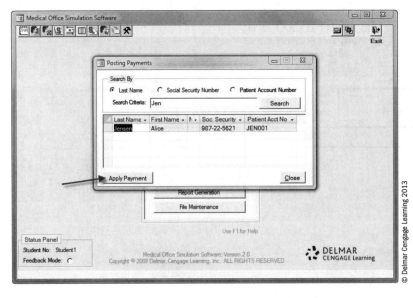

FIGURE 26

4. The Posting Payments screen will open with a view of the Procedure Charge History. Click on the line for the *07/25/2011* service and then click on *Select/Edit* at the bottom of the screen (Figure 27).

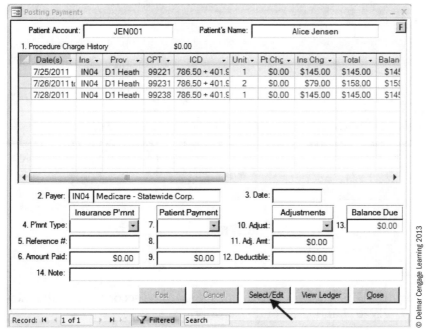

FIGURE 27

5. In Field 3, enter the payment date of **09/15/2011.**
6. Click on the drop-down arrow in Field 4 and click on *Payment Insurance.*
7. In Field 5, enter the *Claim ID* number from the *Provider Payment Advice*, **1000326.**

> **NOTE:** When students complete case studies using MOSS software, the claim ID number generated may differ from the claim ID number that appears on these MOSS tutorial screen shots.

8. Tab to Field 6 and enter the amount in the *Paid to Provider* column of the *Provider Payment Advice* for the 07/25/2011 date of service, **$73.86.**
9. In Field 10, click on the drop-down arrow and select *Adjustment Insurance.*
10. In Field 11, enter **$52.67,** which is the adjustment amount that is the difference between the charges billed by the practice and the allowed amount from the payer only if there is no secondary insurance. Be sure not to write off any amounts that are shown on the *Provider Payment Advice* as *patient responsibility*. Then, tab to Field 13.
11. The amount in Field 13 should be **$18.47** which is equal to the amount in the *Patient Responsibility* column of the *Provider Payment Advice*. If there is a discrepancy, check your posted amounts to be sure you posted the correct amounts.
12. Once you have verified that all amounts are correct, click on *Post* to record the payment (Figure 28).

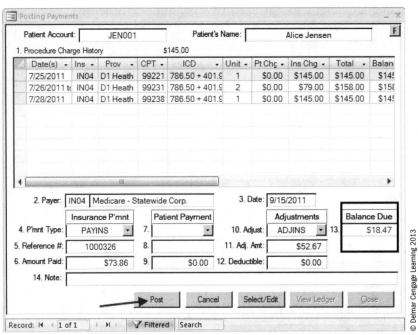

FIGURE 28

13. The *Posting Payment* window will remain open. Select the second line with dates of service *07/26/2011 to 07/27/2011* and click on *Select/Edit*.
14. In Field 3, enter **09/15/2011**.
15. Select *Payment Insurance* in Field 4.
16. In Field 5, enter **1000327**, the Claim ID from the *Provider Payment Advice*.
17. In Field 6, enter the *Paid to Provider* amount of **$62.51**.
18. In Field 10, click on the drop-down arrow and select *Adjustment Insurance*.
19. In Field 11, enter the adjustment amount of **$79.86**. Then, tab to Field 13.
20. The *Balance Due* amount should be **$15.63**, the same as the *Patient Responsibility* indicated on the *Provider Payment Advice*.
21. Verify posting and click on the *Post* button (Figure 29).

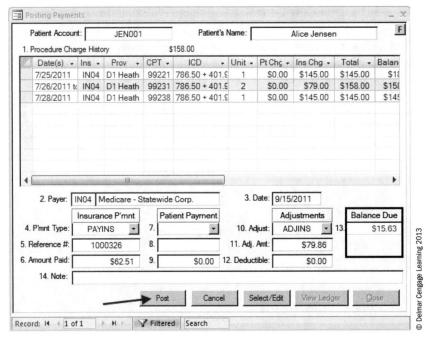

FIGURE 29

22. Click on the line with date of service 07/28/2011 and click on *Select/Edit.*

23. In Field 3, enter **09/15/2011.**

24. Select *Payment Insurance* in Field 4.

25. In Field 5, enter **1000327,** which is the Claim ID from the *Provider Payment Advice.*

26. In Field 6, enter the *Paid to Provider* amount of **$58.53.**

27. In Field 10, click on the drop-down arrow, and select *Adjustment Insurance.*

28. In Field 11, enter the adjustment amount of **$71.84.** Then, tab to Field 13.

29. The *Balance Due* amount should be **$14.63,** which is the same as the *Patient Responsibility* indicated on the *Provider Payment Advice.*

30. Verify posting and click on the *Post* button (Figure 30).

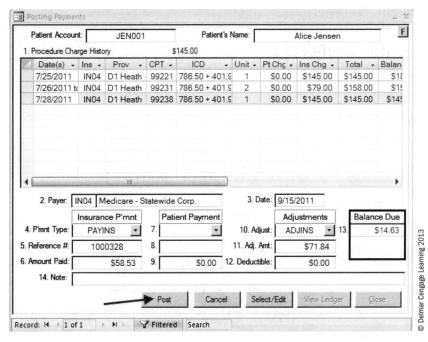

FIGURE 30

31. Return to the main menu by clicking on the *Close* buttons for any of screens that remain open.

CASES 2–10

The following information is to be used to complete Cases 2–10 using MOSS 2.0.

For case studies 2, 3, 4, 6, 8, and 9, begin with the posting procedure step as outlined in the MOSS Tutorial Case 1 Alice Jensen. Then, complete the remaining steps, as follows:

- Submitting an *Electronic CMS-1500 Claim*
- Printing the *Insurance Prebilling Worksheet* and the *Claims Submission Report*
- Processing a *Claims Tracking Report*, and printing the *Providers Payment Advice* report for each patient.

> **NOTE:** Enter September 15, 2011, as the date for posting payments for all cases.

For case studies 5, 7, and 10, begin by registering the new patients as described in MOSS Tutorial Case 1—Alice Jensen. Then, post the procedures and/or services, and continue by completing the remaining steps (as you did for case studies 2, 3, 4, 6, 8, and 9), as follows:

- Submitting an *Electronic CMS-1500 Claim*
- Printing the *Insurance Prebilling Worksheet* and the *Claims Submission Report*
- Processing a *Claims Tracking Report*, and printing the *Providers Payment Advice* report for each patient.

Case 2—Evan Lagasse (Flexihealth PPO Out-of-Network)

Physician	Dr. Heath
Date of Service	July 24, 2011
Location	Office (11)
Visit/Procedure	Level 4 Established Patient Office Visit (99214)
Diagnoses	Acute Sinusitis (461.9) Dehydration (276.51) Acute Pharyngitis (462)
Patient Reference No.	210

Case 3—Josephine Albertson (ConsumerOne HRA)

Physician	Dr. Heath
Date of Service	July 15, 2011
Location	Office (11)
Visit/Procedure	Level 3 Established Patient Office Visit (99213)
Diagnoses	Hypercholesterolemia (272.0) Gastroesophageal Reflux Disease (530.81)
Patient Reference No.	211

Case 4—Caitlin Barryroe (Flexihealth PPO In-Network)

Physician	Dr. Heath
Date of Service	July 18, 2011
Location	Emergency Room (23)
Facility	New York County Hospital
Visit/Procedure	Level 4 Emergency Room Visit (99284)
Diagnoses	Gastroenteritis (558.9) Dehydration (276.51) Weakness (780.79) Diarrhea (787.91)
Patient Reference No.	212

Case 5—Eric Robertson

Registration Information (Dr. Shwartz)

Patient Name	Eric Robertson
Social Security No.	999-26-8871
Marital Status	Single
Date of Birth/Gender	May 10, 1983/Male
Street Address	64 Cypress Garden Parkway

City	Douglasville
State	NY
Zip Code	01234
Home Phone	123-998-4682
Work Phone	123-555-6322 x2169
Employer	Back in Time
Employer Address	2193 Avery Street
Employer City	Preston
Employer State	NY
Employer Zip Code	01237
Primary Insurance	Signal HMO
Guarantor	Eric Robertson
Insurance ID No.	SSH21936245
Policy No.	BIT430
MD Participation	In network; accepts assignment; signature on file

Visit Information

Physician	Dr. Schwartz
Date of Service	July 12, 2011–July 16, 2011
Location	Inpatient (21)
Facility	Community General Hospital
Visit/Procedure	Level 1 Initial Hospital Care (99221)–7/12/2011 Level 1 Subsequent Hospital Care (99231)–7/13/2011 through 7/15/2011 Discharge (99238)–7/16/2011
Diagnoses	Infectious Mononucleosis (075) Urinary Tract Infection (599.0)
Patient Reference No.	213

Case 6—Donald Blair (Aetna)

Physician	Dr. Robyn Houser
Date of Service	July 17, 2011
Location	Office (11)
Visit/Procedure	Level 3 Established Patient Office Visit (99213) Urinalysis w/o Microscopy (81002)
Diagnoses	Diabetes Mellitus, Type II, Controlled (250.00) Hypertension, Unspecified (401.9)
Patient Reference No.	214

Case 7—Angelica L. Marzetti

> **NOTE:** When adding primary payer information, be sure to enter information in the **Spouse/Parent/Other Tab**, which will contain the spouses' complete information.

Registration Information (Dr. Schwartz)

Patient Name	Angelica L. Marzetti
Social Security No.	999-22-4467
Marital Status	Married
Date of Birth/Gender	April 22, 1976/Female
Street Address	1721 Fremont Avenue
City	Douglasville
State	NY
Zip Code	01234
Home Phone	123-645-9912
Occupation	Housewife
Spouse	Anthony S. Marzetti
Date of Birth	June 25, 1974
Social Security No.	999-21-8799
Work Phone	123-873-2165
Employer	Global Financing Corporation
Employer Address	865 West Juniper Boulevard
Employer City	Jenkins
Employer State	NY
Employer Zip Code	01239
Primary Insurance	United Health Care
Guarantor	Anthony
Insurance ID No.	986543220
Policy No.	GFC816
MD Participation	In network; accepts assignment; signature on file

Visit Information

Physician	Dr. Schwartz
Date of Service	July 20, 2011
Location	Office (11)
Visit/Procedure	Physical Exam for a New Patient (99385) Level 2 Established Patient Office Visit (99212) Urinalysis w/Microscopy (81000)
Diagnoses	Physical Exam (V70.0) Urinary Tract Infection (599.0)
Patient Reference No.	215

Case 8—John Conway (ConsumerOne HRA)

Physician	Dr. Heath
Date of Service	July 17, 2011–July 20, 2011
Location	Skilled Nursing Facility (31)
Facility	Retirement Inn Nursing Home
Visit/Procedure	Level 3 Subsequent Nursing Home Visit (99309)
Diagnoses	Hypercholesterolemia (272.0) Benign Hypertension (401.1)
Patient Reference No.	216

Case 9—Justin McNamara (Flexihealth PPO Out-of-Network)

Physician	Dr. Schwartz
Date of Service	July 24, 2011
Location	Office (11)
Visit/Procedure	Level 4 Established Patient Office Visit (99214)
Diagnoses	Acute Bronchitis (466.0) Otitis Media, Acute (382.9) Strep Throat (034.0)
Patient Reference No.	217

Case 10—Colin J. Travis

Registration Information (Dr. Heath)

Patient Name	Colin J. Travis
Social Security No.	999-86-1148
Marital Status	Single
Date of Birth/Gender	October 10, 1964/Male
Street Address	87 North Adams Road
City	Douglasville
State	NY
Zip Code	01234
Home Phone	123-456-9973
Work Phone	123-874-5691
Employer	Jamieson Woodworking (full-time)
Employer Address	436 Carigan Way
Employer City	Abbott
Employer State	NY
Employer Zip Code	01240
Primary Insurance	Signal HMO
Guarantor	Colin J. Travis

Insurance ID No.	973289012
Policy No.	JWW336
MD Participation	In network; accepts assignment; signature on file

Visit Information

Physician	Dr. Heath
Date of Service	July 29, 2011
Location	Emergency Room (23)
Facility	Community General Hospital
Visit/Procedure	Level 4 Emergency Room Visit (99284)
Diagnoses	Abdominal Pain (789.00) Nausea (787.02)
Patient Reference No.	218

IMPORTANT! READ CAREFULLY: This End User License Agreement ("Agreement") sets forth the conditions by which Cengage Learning will make electronic access to the Cengage Learning-owned licensed content and associated media, software, documentation, printed materials, and electronic documentation contained in this package and/or made available to you via this product (the "Licensed Content"), available to you (the "End User"). BY CLICKING THE "I ACCEPT" BUTTON AND/OR OPENING THIS PACKAGE, YOU ACKNOWLEDGE THAT YOU HAVE READ ALL OF THE TERMS AND CONDITIONS, AND THAT YOU AGREE TO BE BOUND BY ITS TERMS, CONDITIONS, AND ALL APPLICABLE LAWS AND REGULATIONS GOVERNING THE USE OF THE LICENSED CONTENT.

1.0 SCOPE OF LICENSE

1.1 <u>Licensed Content</u>. The Licensed Content may contain portions of modifiable content ("Modifiable Content") and content which may not be modified or otherwise altered by the End User ("Non-Modifiable Content"). For purposes of this Agreement, Modifiable Content and Non-Modifiable Content may be collectively referred to herein as the "Licensed Content." All Licensed Content shall be considered Non-Modifiable Content, unless such Licensed Content is presented to the End User in a modifiable format and it is clearly indicated that modification of the Licensed Content is permitted.

1.2 Subject to the End User's compliance with the terms and conditions of this Agreement, Cengage Learning hereby grants the End User, a nontransferable, nonexclusive, limited right to access and view a single copy of the Licensed Content on a single personal computer system for noncommercial, internal, personal use only. The End User shall not (i) reproduce, copy, modify (except in the case of Modifiable Content), distribute, display, transfer, sublicense, prepare derivative work(s) based on, sell, exchange, barter or transfer, rent, lease, loan, resell, or in any other manner exploit the Licensed Content; (ii) remove, obscure, or alter any notice of Cengage Learning's intellectual property rights present on or in the Licensed Content, including, but not limited to, copyright, trademark, and/or patent notices; or (iii) disassemble, decompile, translate, reverse engineer, or otherwise reduce the Licensed Content.

2.0 TERMINATION

2.1 Cengage Learning may at any time (without prejudice to its other rights or remedies) immediately terminate this Agreement and/or suspend access to some or all of the Licensed Content, in the event that the End User does not comply with any of the terms and conditions of this Agreement. In the event of such termination by Cengage Learning, the End User shall immediately return any and all copies of the Licensed Content to Cengage Learning.

3.0 PROPRIETARY RIGHTS

3.1 The End User acknowledges that Cengage Learning owns all rights, title and interest, including, but not limited to all copyright rights therein, in and to the Licensed Content, and that the End User shall not take any action inconsistent with such ownership. The Licensed Content is protected by U.S., Canadian and other applicable copyright laws and by international treaties, including the Berne Convention and the Universal Copyright Convention. Nothing contained in this Agreement shall be construed as granting the End User any ownership rights in or to the Licensed Content.

3.2 Cengage Learning reserves the right at any time to withdraw from the Licensed Content any item or part of an item for which it no longer retains the right to publish, or which it has reasonable grounds to believe infringes copyright or is defamatory, unlawful, or otherwise objectionable.

4.0 PROTECTION AND SECURITY

4.1 The End User shall use its best efforts and take all reasonable steps to safeguard its copy of the Licensed Content to ensure that no unauthorized reproduction, publication, disclosure, modification, or distribution of the Licensed Content, in whole or in part, is made. To the extent that the End User becomes aware of any such unauthorized use of the Licensed Content, the End User shall immediately notify Cengage Learning. Notification of such violations may be made by sending an e-mail to infringement@cengage.com.

5.0 MISUSE OF THE LICENSED PRODUCT

5.1 In the event that the End User uses the Licensed Content in violation of this Agreement, Cengage Learning shall have the option of electing liquidated damages, which shall include all profits generated by the End User's use of the Licensed Content plus interest computed at the maximum rate permitted by law and all legal fees and other expenses incurred by Cengage Learning in enforcing its rights, plus penalties.

6.0 FEDERAL GOVERNMENT CLIENTS

6.1 Except as expressly authorized by Cengage Learning, Federal Government clients obtain only the rights specified in this Agreement and no other rights. The Government acknowledges that (i) all software and related documentation incorporated in the Licensed Content is existing commercial computer software within the meaning of FAR 27.405(b)(2); and (2) all other data delivered in whatever form, is limited rights data within the meaning of FAR 27.401. The restrictions in this section are acceptable as consistent with the Government's need for software and other data under this Agreement.

7.0 DISCLAIMER OF WARRANTIES AND LIABILITIES

7.1 Although Cengage Learning believes the Licensed Content to be reliable, Cengage Learning does not guarantee or warrant (i) any information or materials contained in or produced by the Licensed Content, (ii) the accuracy, completeness, or reliability of the Licensed Content, or (iii) that the Licensed Content is free from errors or other material defects. THE LICENSED PRODUCT IS PROVIDED "AS IS," WITHOUT ANY WARRANTY OF ANY KIND AND CENGAGE LEARNING DISCLAIMS ANY AND ALL WARRANTIES, EXPRESSED OR IMPLIED, INCLUDING, WITHOUT LIMITATION, WARRANTIES OF MERCHANTABILITY OR FITNESS FOR A PARTICULAR PURPOSE. IN NO EVENT SHALL CENGAGE LEARNING BE LIABLE FOR: INDIRECT, SPECIAL, PUNITIVE OR CONSEQUENTIAL DAMAGES INCLUDING FOR LOST PROFITS, LOST DATA, OR OTHERWISE. IN NO EVENT SHALL CENGAGE LEARNING'S AGGREGATE LIABILITY HEREUNDER, WHETHER ARISING IN CONTRACT, TORT, STRICT LIABILITY OR OTHERWISE, EXCEED THE AMOUNT OF FEES PAID BY THE END USER HEREUNDER FOR THE LICENSE OF THE LICENSED CONTENT.

8.0 GENERAL

8.1 <u>Entire Agreement</u>. This Agreement shall constitute the entire Agreement between the Parties and supersedes all prior Agreements and understandings oral or written relating to the subject matter hereof.

8.2 <u>Enhancements/Modifications of Licensed Content</u>. From time to time, and in Cengage Learning's sole discretion, Cengage Learning may advise the End User of updates, upgrades, enhancements and/or improvements to the Licensed Content, and may permit the End User to access and use, subject to the terms and conditions of this Agreement, such modifications, upon payment of prices as may be established by Cengage Learning.

8.3 <u>No Export</u>. The End User shall use the Licensed Content solely in the United States and shall not transfer or export, directly or indirectly, the Licensed Content outside the United States.

8.4 <u>Severability</u>. If any provision of this Agreement is invalid, illegal, or unenforceable under any applicable statute or rule of law, the provision shall be deemed omitted to the extent that it is invalid, illegal, or unenforceable. In such a case, the remainder of the Agreement shall be construed in a manner as to give greatest effect to the original intention of the parties hereto.

8.5 <u>Waiver</u>. The waiver of any right or failure of either party to exercise in any respect any right provided in this Agreement in any instance shall not be deemed to be a waiver of such right in the future or a waiver of any other right under this Agreement.

8.6 <u>Choice of Law/Venue</u>. This Agreement shall be interpreted, construed, and governed by and in accordance with the laws of the State of New York, applicable to contracts executed and to be wholly preformed therein, without regard to its principles governing conflicts of law. Each party agrees that any proceeding arising out of or relating to this Agreement or the breach or threatened breach of this Agreement may be commenced and prosecuted in a court in the State and County of New York. Each party consents and submits to the nonexclusive personal jurisdiction of any court in the State and County of New York in respect of any such proceeding.

8.7 <u>Acknowledgment</u>. By opening this package and/or by accessing the Licensed Content on this Web site, THE END USER ACKNOWLEDGES THAT IT HAS READ THIS AGREEMENT, UNDERSTANDS IT, AND AGREES TO BE BOUND BY ITS TERMS AND CONDITIONS. IF YOU DO NOT ACCEPT THESE TERMS AND CONDITIONS, YOU MUST NOT ACCESS THE LICENSED CONTENT AND RETURN THE LICENSED PRODUCT TO CENGAGE LEARNING (WITHIN 30 CALENDAR DAYS OF THE END USER'S PURCHASE) WITH PROOF OF PAYMENT ACCEPTABLE TO CENGAGE LEARNING, FOR A CREDIT OR A REFUND. Should the End User have any questions/comments regarding this Agreement, please contact Cengage Learning at <u>Delmar.help@cengage.com</u>.

MOSS 2.0

System Requirements

- Processor: minimum required by operating system.
- Memory: minimum required by operating system
- Operating System: Microsoft Windows XP™ with Service Pack 2, Windows Vista™, Windows 7
- 75 MB free hard disk space
- 800 x 600 monitor display
- Recommended: MS Access 2007 (MS Access Runtime supplied on disk)

Set Up Instructions

1. Insert disc into CD-ROM drive. The CD installation program should start automatically. If it does not, go to step 2.
2. From My Computer, double click the icon for the CD drive.
3. Double click the "setup.exe" file to start the program.

Microsoft™, Windows™, Windows XP™, Windows Vista™, and Windows 7 are trademarks of the Microsoft Corporation.